A Country of Limitations: Canada and the World in 1939/

Un pays dans la gêne: le Canada et le Monde en 1939

Edited by
Sous la direction de

Norman Hillmer
Robert Bothwell
Roger Sarty
Claude Beauregard

Canadian Committee for the History of the Second World War
Comité canadien d'Histoire de la Deuxième Guerre mondiale
1996

TABLE OF CONTENTS
TABLE DES MATIÈRES

PAGE

PREFACE

At the Canadian Committee for the History of the Second World War's 1987 Annual General Meeting, held at McMaster University in Hamilton, Ontario, Professor Terry Copp recommended that we hold a series of anniversary conferences marking the major themes and events of the war from the distance of 50 years. Following this suggestion, the committee convened colloquia in Elora, Ontario (1989), Victoria, British Columbia (1991), Québec City (1992), Waterloo, Ontario (1993), Montreal and St. Jean, Québec (1994) and Winnipeg, Manitoba (1995).

The procession of historical anniversaries of the Second World War, the *New Yorker* has commented, "has kept reminding us that human beings inherit little History but many histories. The past bequeathes us a small nest egg of stable, undisputed facts and a thick portfolio of speculative issues — divergent, ever-changing interpretations — because presents and futures alter pasts." Presents and futures contain many dangers and temptations — history as interpretation or even speculation is easily transmogrified into history as mythology or instrument — but the passage of a half-century offers a welcome combination of fresh perspective and new evidence. Even "stable, undisputed facts" sometimes become open to question. Our 50-year conferences (and indeed the meeting of the International Committee for the History of the Second World War in Montreal on 4 September 1995), have demonstrated how vital the Second World War remains as a subject for research and debate, particularly among younger scholars, and how important it is to define the field in broader terms than diplomatic and military operational history, crucial though those issues continue to be.

This book, which has been a long time coming, collects the papers on the year 1939 given at the first of the committee's anniversary conferences, held in November 1989, in the pleasant surroundings of the Elora Mill in southwestern Ontario. We are grateful to the Social Sciences and Humanities Research Council of Canada and the Directorate of History, Department of National Defence, for their support of the conference and the publication of these proceedings, and to Serge Bernier, Hélène Desjardins and Brenda Donaldson for valuable assistance with the manuscript. Robert Bothwell, John English, J.L. Granatstein and Patricia Roy joined me on the conference's Programme Committee. Each of the papers was refereed, and we thank academics across the country and outside for their willingness to undertake this necessarily unpaid and anonymous work. The cover illustration, John A. Hall's "Interlude," appeared in the May 1939 edition of *Canadian Forum*, and is used with that publication's approval. *Ontario History* gave permission to reprint Terry Copp's article from its September 1994 issue.

The Canadian Second World War committee is a bilingual national component of the International Committee for the History of the Second World War. Our aim is to study the 1939-1945 war in all of its aspects, although there has been an increasing desire on the part of members to include the entire canvas of Canadian war and society in our mandate. The committee arranges regular conferences, publishes books and a regular newsletter, and gives the C.P. Stacey Prize for distinguished publications on the twentieth-century Canadian military experience. The secretary-treasurer is Greg Donaghy, and headquarters are located at 22 Downing Street, Ottawa K1S 2W1.

We dedicate this volume to Gloria McKeigan, who was for many years until her recent retirement the committee's indispensable administrator.

Norman Hillmer
President
Canadian Committee for the History
of the Second World War
24 November 1995

PRÉFACE

En 1987, au cours de l'assemblée annuelle du Comité canadien d'histoire de la Deuxième Guerre mondiale, tenue à l'Université McMaster, à Hamilton, Ontario, le Professeur Terry Copp a recommandé que soit mise sur pied une série de conférences qui souligneraient le cinquantième anniversaire des principaux thèmes et événements ayant marqué les années 1939-1945. Suite à cette suggestion, le Comité a organisé des colloques à Elora, Ontario (1989), Victoria, Colombie-Britannique (1991), Québec (1992), Waterloo, Ontario (1993), Montréal et Saint-Jean, Québec (1994) puis Winnipeg, Manitoba (1995).

Le *New Yorker* a commenté le cortège des anniversaires historiques de la Deuxième Guerre mondiale en écrivant qu'ils étaient là **"afin de nous rappeler que les êtres humains héritent de peu d'Histoire, mais de plusieurs histoires. Le passé nous a légué un petit nid de faits incontestables et un épais dossier de questions en suspens et d'interprétations changeantes – pour la simple raison que présent et avenir altèrent le passé"**. Présent et avenir contiennent plusieurs dangers et tentations et l'histoire, qui interprète et spécule parfois, peut facilement se métamorphoser en mythologie ou en un instrument politique. Les cinquante années qui nous séparent des événements troublants des années 1939-1945 nous offrent une heureuse combinaison de fraîches perspectives et de nouveaux faits. Même les «faits incontestables» peuvent être remis en question. Nos conférences du cinquantenaire (dont, bien entendu, la rencontre du comité international de l'histoire de la Deuxième Guerre mondiale de Montréal, du 2 septembre 1995) ont démontré que les sujets relatifs à la Deuxième Guerre mondiale restent d'une importance capitale en recherche. Cette période suscite des débats, plus spécifiquement parmi les jeunes universitaires, d'où la nécessité de définir le champ de recherche en termes larges plutôt que restreints aux affaires diplomatiques et aux opérations militaires, bien que ces questions soient capitales.

Ce livre, dont la parution s'est faite attendre, réunit les communications portant sur le Canada en 1939, qui avaient été présentées lors notre première conférence anniversaire, en novembre 1989, dans l'environnement charmant qu'est Elora Mill dans le sud-ouest de l'Ontario. Notre reconnaissance s'adresse au Conseil de recherches en sciences sociales et humaines du Canada et au Service historique du Ministère de la Défense nationale, pour leur appui en ce qui a trait à la conférence et à la publication de ces actes, ainsi qu'à Serge Bernier, Hélène Desjardins et Brenda Donaldson, pour leur précieuse collaboration concernant la préparation du manuscrit. Robert Bothwell, John English, J.L. Granatstein et Patricia Roy se sont joints à moi au sein du comité du programme de cette conférence. Comme chacune des communications était soumise à un jury qualifié, nous remercions ceux et celles, à l'intérieur comme à l'extérieur du pays, qui, grâce à leur volonté et à leur travail anonyme non rétribué, ont permis la réalisation de cet ouvrage. L'illustration de la couverture, "Interlude" de John A. Hall, apparaissait dans l'édition de mai 1939, de *Canadian Forum* et est utilisée avec l'approbation de cette revue. *Ontario History* nous a permis de republier l'article de Terry Copp qui était paru dans son numéro de septembre 1994.

Le Comité canadien d'histoire de la Deuxième Guerre mondiale est une composante bilingue du Comité international de l'histoire de la Deuxième Guerre mondiale. Notre but est d'étudier tous les aspects de la guerre de 1939-1945 même si, parmi les membres du Comité canadien, le désir se fait persistant d'inclure dans notre mandat ce qu'ont vécu le Canada et sa société au moment de la guerre. Le Comité convoque des conférences régulières, publie livres et bulletins et décerne le Prix C.P. Stacey aux auteurs d'ouvrages qui se sont distingués en relatant l'expérience militaire canadienne durant le 20e siècle. Le secrétaire-trésorier est Greg Donaghy et l'administration centrale est sise au 22 Downing Street, Ottawa, K1S 2W1.

Nous dédions ce volume à Gloria McKeigan, qui a été pendant de nombreuses années, jusqu'à son départ à la retraite, l'indispensable administratrice du Comité.

Norman Hillmer
Président
Comité canadien d'histoire
de la Deuxième Guerre mondiale
24 novembre 1995

INTRODUCTION

Nineteen thirty-nine was a junction, linking peace and war, domestic and foreign, an unhappy recent past with an uncertain future. The burden of Canadian history pointed to a country of limitations — one nation, as the distinguished historian J.M.S. Careless once put it, eminently divisible. Canadians, certainly, were unlikely to think of their country as a land of promise during the 1930s. A decade of economic depression exacerbated regional tensions and shook the established order to its roots. In international affairs, the memory of 1914-1918 seemed less a symbol of pride than an object lesson in the futility and cupidity of overseas adventuring. And yet, when there was war in Europe, it became Canada's war too.

Six years later, Canadians were united, confident in government, the economy and the future, and prepared to take on substantial international responsibilities. The experience of the Second World War suggests that limited policies and personalities, and limited identities, can be transformed, and their limitations transcended.

The transition was not sudden or complete, nor could it have been. The Liberal government of William Lyon Mackenzie King entered the war cautiously, wanting to fight on the basis of limited liability; that is, to keep both feet firmly planted on the home front through expedients such as the British Commonwealth Air Training Plan. As Doug Owram demonstrates in his groundbreaking study of the public service, Ottawa's officials were, with certain spectacular individual exceptions, aged and timid. The great Canadian bureaucratic revolution was yet to come. Those civil servants who had done the most strategic thinking, the military, were those accorded the least respect in Ottawa. In the sphere of economic planning, Paul Marsden laments, unimaginative politicians and officials cast their eyes backwards, rather than forward to the need for detailed attention to specific requirements.

The precision, indeed, with which this volume details Canada's unpreparedness — political, economic, military and psychological — raises the question why Canada went to war at all. The orthodox answer is because of blood and nostalgia; there was no option once the mother country had taken its decision. A number of the authors of this volume offer different perspectives, providing a great deal more textured portrait of the balance of sentiment and self-interest in Canada's response to the events of 1939 than the historiography has yet yielded. Terry Copp and Robert Young argue that Canadians were much more globally-minded than their isolationist reputation. Ian Drummond describes the vital trans-Atlantic trading connection. Roger Sarty emphasizes the role of indigenous military factors in propelling Canadians towards war. Angelika Sauer highlights self-interested ideology and economics.

The figure of Mackenzie King broods over the volume. Contemporary opinions of King — condemnation of his tepid support for Britain or celebration of his sensitivity to domestic restraints — were perpetuated in the postwar literature. Since the 1970s, however, writers with access to the prime minister's diary and other previously classified records have discovered the strength of King's conviction that Canada had a "self-evident national duty" to assist Britain in a major war. In this light, Canada's entry into the Second World War, aside from some new constitutional forms, differed little from the events of August 1914. First World War prime minister Robert Borden had also proclaimed that Canada was taking up arms as a self-assumed national mission to uphold the forces of good in the world. The present volume takes the discussion a step further by suggesting that the decision for participation in 1939 involved a calaculation of interests and public consciousness that had not featured in 1914.

Canada's armed forces were, as in 1914, structured to fit into larger British formations, but this was the result of something more than a colonial legacy. Canadian political and military leaders were convinced, not least by the statements of the US president, F.D. Roosevelt, and his service chiefs, that if Canada broke Commonwealth military ties, it would be nothing more than an American protectorate. This was a particular worry in the Pacific, where the US was predominant and Britain greatly weakened. As Roger Sarty and Gregory Johnson show, Canadian leaders were especially worried about an Anglo-American split over Far Eastern policy, with one or the other separately declaring war on Japan. In either case, Canada would be isolated in the US sphere. From this perspective, the outbreak of war in Europe first was something of a blessing. Within the Atlantic world Britain was still a dominant power, and in no small part for this reason the Anglo-US community of interests within which Canada had always defined itself still existed.

Canada's support for appeasement is well known. Less so is the fact that the King administration appreciated that appeasement rested upon a foundation of military power. King and O.D. Skelton, his most ardently anti-interventionist adviser, credited the partial British mobilization in September 1938 with persuading Hitler to accede to the Munich agreement. The government, having applauded British prime minister Neville Chamberlain's supremely-civilized bid for peace, also accepted that there would be "peace for our time" only so long as Hitler abided by the agreement. When, in March 1939, German forces occupied the rump of Czechoslovakia in defiance of Munich, the King administration was already doubling the defence budget. The alternative to force, questions of morality and sentiment aside, was an accelerated shift in the international order against the most vital political and economic interests of the democracies. There is evidence in the articles on the regions, most particularly Terry Copp's on Ontario, that significant portions of the population had similarly been persuaded, if not by Chamberlain's policies, then by the stark evidence of German aggression. Wesley Wark's paper indicates that a similar combination of fear and morality brought the British people to resist the Third Reich.

King's most careful calculations, of course, concerned the domestic situation. The government attached limits to Canadian participation. This was another distinction between Canada's entry into war in 1939 and 25 years earlier, and not surprisingly so because King had made a career out of capitalizing on the national divisions created by the Borden government's imposition of conscription for overseas service in 1917. On the complex question of limited liability, this collection offers fresh points of view and new information. There is evidence that King showed strong leadership in launching rearmament on however a modest scale in 1937, when increased defence spending was popular nowhere in the Depression-wracked country. Members of the government also spoke more frankly than has been appreciated about the unpreparedness of the country in the face of the large scale effort it might have to make overseas. Yet, as René Durocher argues, the government conveyed the quite different message in Québec that Canada would in no circumstances participate in any foreign war. By awaiting events after the outbreak of war to shape the Canadian overseas commitment, King left Québec isolated, for the third time in two generations, in the face of a wave of pro-British emotion.

For political reasons as well, the government stinted on the military programme in ways that created major problems on mobilization, and undermined the limited liability policy. King's deepest conviction was that the country should contribute with economic resources rather than with military personnel, but with the failure to prepare defence production in any significant way, people were virtually all Canada had to offer in September 1939.

Several of the regional papers suggest that, however bold in 1937, the government's preparations were in 1938 and certainly by 1939 lagging behind public opinion. René Durocher implies that even in Québec fuller, franker information about the exigencies of the world crisis would have been helpful to Québeckers and, in the long run, to the government. Part of the difficulty, as Professor Owram explains, was the absence in a civil service demoralized by draconian personnel policies during the Depression of the capacity for policy formulation and large scale planning. Angelika Sauer and Paul Marsden suggest that the very rationality and liberalism of the most talented bureaucrats made them reluctant — or in some cases, naïvely confident — in the face of the chaos that is the essence of war.

For Canadians, 1939 was punctuated by international crises and, on a lighter note, the Royal Tour, when George VI and his consort swept past with Mackenzie King in tow. One of the virtues of the regional papers, however, is that they demonstrate the degree to which daily life did not centre on such externals. Canadians in British Columbia, or on the prairies, or in Ontario and Quebec, or in the Maritimes — and their cousins in Newfoundland — had other things to worry about, pressing concerns that more directly affected their lives and their livelihood. King knew this, but also understood that the link between locality and Empire, or between Prince Edward Island and Poland, depended upon his political skill to manage. National unity, national history, Canadian economic and political survival, all depended on his making the right choice and, equally important, on his ability to explain his choice to the people. Once explained, once accepted, narrower priorities would have to give way, and for the indefinite future.

N.H.
R.B.
R.S.
C.B.

The International Framework
La structure internationale

THE WORLD ECONOMY IN 1939

Ian M. Drummond
University of Toronto

This chapter will survey economic conditions in the dominions of the British Commonwealth, each of the major powers — Germany, Britain, the United States, France, the Soviet Union, and Japan — and in India. For each country we emphasize the existing aspects of economic organization and management that would be pertinent to the operation of a wartime economy, and interdependency and dependency rising out of trading relationships, as well as extent and character of prior preparation for a major war; where relevant, we also note the main changes in circumstances since 1914.

◆◆◆

Forty years ago it was commonly said that Germany's Nazi regime had established a "fully mobilized war economy" in peacetime, so that in some sense or other the German economy was "ready for war" in 1939. These observations reflected several facts about German economic organization during the 1930s. First and most obviously, Hitler had inherited a system of foreign-exchange control from the dying Weimar regime, and under the guidance of the good Dr. Schacht this system had been endlessly elaborated. Secondly, by 1936 most German prices and wages were already controlled, while labour unions had been abolished. Thus the sorts of domestic and external controls which Britain and France had eschewed in peacetime and which they introduced only reluctantly, either at the outbreak of war or thereafter, as parts of their "war economies," were already well-established in Germany. Thirdly, under the Second Four-Year Plan, since 1936 Germany had been pursuing a policy of import-replacement, developing synthetic rubber and gasoline, finding ways to use low-quality domestic iron ore, producing ersatz coffee, and eating rhubarb instead of imported lemons. The government, in fact, had been driven to control imports because the German economy was booming while its export markets were not; nevertheless, and in addition, there was an obvious military side to the plans for iron ore, petrol, and rubber.

Fourthly, Germany was only too obviously establishing an economic hinterland in the Balkans — a group of countries, linked to the Reich through bilateral trade and payments agreements, that would supply food and raw materials in exchange for German manufactures or for blocked holdings of reichsmarks. The 1930s had seen a quite remarkable redirection of Balkan exports toward the Reich. Clearly, in case of war, the oil and the food of Romania and the foodstuffs of Hungary, Yugoslavia, and Bulgaria would be invaluable — and would be largely or wholly beyond allied interdiction. Already by 1939 Germany had become adept at extracting such supplies without having to pay out of current production: the Balkan lands were so anxious to sell that they would take reichsmarks in exchange, hoping that in due course the Reich would let them spend the marks on goods and services. To some extent, these bilateral arrangements provided a protected market for German exports, but in wartime their importance would be very different: in commodity terms, they would make an obvious and important contribution to the German war effort.

Finally, if one considers living standards, one finds a "wartime look" in the Germany of summer 1939. Admittedly, full employment had been restored in 1936. Indeed, by 1939 workers were hard to find. It is hardly surprising that wartime Germany imported forced labour, and made some efforts to recruit voluntary "guest workers" from the occupied lands. But German "full employment" did not mean high or rising real wages: at the outbreak of war, German workers seem to have been earning rather less, in real terms, than in 1929. That is what one would have expected of a "war economy": the burden of government spending, and of war-oriented investment, had tended to reduce civilian living standards, or at least to prevent them from rising with the return of full employment. Indeed, the authorities controlled money wages precisely for that reason — to regulate real consumption outlays.[1]

No one denies that the Nazi economy of 1939 did display these earmarks. But do they mean that the economy was "fully mobilized"? Or that it was a "war economy"? For 30 years or more there have been doubts. Relying chiefly upon data from the US Strategic Bombing Survey, Klein argued that in 1939 the German economy was still largely on a peace-time basis.[2] It was not yet able to produce really large quantities of most sorts of military hardware. Many civilian goods continued to gush from the factories. Few women had entered the work force, and much labour was still employed in unessential tasks — most obviously, in domestic service. Although imports were regulated, there was no functioning system for the overall planning and allocating of investment or of industrial inputs: the Nazi apparatus was largely a "front," partly because of industrial opposition and partly because of disputes among Nazi bigwigs. Klein's arguments were developed further by Milward, who maintained that the Nazi "Blitzkrieg" was in fact a conscious and rational reflection of the economic disarray. Lacking productive capacity "in depth," Milward maintained, Hitler had to fight short campaigns, pausing for breath between one and another, redirecting capacity from one form of materiel to another. It was only in 1943, with the looming prospect of defeat and with the advent of Albert Speer, that the deficient Nazi planning and regulating machinery was put in order.[3]

After 30 years, it was time for a new wave of revisionism, and indeed this was supplied by Overy, who argues that Klein and Milward have misread the evidence.[4] First of all, Overy finds no evidence that productive capacity was in fact redirected among military items: from tanks, say, to engines, or from planes to cruisers or submarines. He does not dispute the Blitzkrieg, or the internal disorganization of the Nazi economy at the outbreak of war. But he denies the element of conscious calculation. The Nazis, he says, were inept, and the Fuehrer uninterested in economic matters — indeed, irrational with respect to them. The problem for the war effort was that all-out war came unexpectedly soon — before the Four-Year Plan had reached full fruition, before various investment projects had come on stream.

The following conclusions appear to be reasonable. First of all, even though the German economy was "fully employed" in 1939, it still contained a great deal of "slack," with plenty of scope for increased military output. There was unused potential to mobilize and redirect labour, to cut back on the outputs of consumer goods, and to direct production in a more careful and purposeful way. Second, the main obstacle to this more effective mobilization seems to have been the Nazi Party itself. Thirdly, the "external side" of the German economy — the trade and financial links with other countries, especially in continental Europe — was comparatively well-organized, and in ways that could and would serve the German war effort in highly-effective ways, although the regulations had not been devised with an eye to wartime exigencies. Finally, the German economy had disengaged from dependence on Britain or on the overseas world. The financial links had been ruptured in 1931. In rubber, petrol, and textile fibres, ersatz production was on stream. Rare metals could be stockpiled, and apparently had been.

It seems to follow that Germany was better prepared for war in 1939 than in 1914, even for the much more "technological" warfare that was to come. Certainly in terms of economic administration she was better prepared than Britain and the other allied powers, or than the United States, where little or nothing had been done to create the administrative structure of a "war economy." Britain, indeed, avoided the imposition of exchange control until war had actually broken out, and in 1938-1939 London spent gold and dollar reserves to support the national currency on foreign-exchange markets. This was something the German authorities had not done since early summer 1931. Could the German economy support a long or complicated war? Allied opinion was far from certain, and with the benefit of hindsight we may detect a certain tendency to exaggerate the fragility of the allied economies, and the economic power of the Reich. This was the reverse of the 1914 situation, when the Allies exaggerated the extent — and the utility — of London's financial dominance. In 1939 it was common to emphasize Germany's military preparedness, such as the massive output of aircraft, the schemes to replace imported raw materials. Rather less was heard of the parallel, though less dramatic, efforts among the Allies.

By 1914 Britain had certainly lost its industrial pre-eminence to Germany and the United States. In 1913 the American economy was already twice as large as the British. But in international trade the United Kingdom remained competitive in all or almost all of its traditional lines. Its financial position, furthermore, appeared to be unchallengeable. Britain borrowed massively in the United States, but lent almost as massively to her dominions and to her continental allies. She was able to fight a war without significantly depleting her external assets; indeed, in most of the wartime years, she ran a surplus on current account.

The mythology of the interwar period emphasizes Britain's troubles. In fact, however, Britain had done rather better than many people think. In 1938 the British economy was larger, compared with the American, than it had been in 1913. This somewhat surprising fact reflected the events of the 1930s — Britain's comparatively healthy recovery from the slump, and America's dismal economic performance. In 1938 American GNP was still not as large as it had been in 1929; Britain's GDP was nearly 20 percent larger. During the 1920s and the 1930s, furthermore, the United Kingdom had modernized its economy, domesticating the industries whose goods characterized the "second industrial revolution" — cars, aircraft, oil refining, more sophisticated chemicals, telecommunications, electric and electronic items. These industries would be crucial in wartime. They had become important exporters, although their markets were largely in the sterling area. By 1938, Britain had displaced Canada as the world's second-largest exporter of motor cars. In several of these "new industries," furthermore, productive capacities had been deliberately expanded in the late 1930s under the government's "shadow factory" scheme, whereby private firms managed factories that could be quickly converted to war use. Meanwhile, in such "old industries" as shipbuilding and steelmaking, there was plenty of excess capacity, nor had the old skills been lost.[5]

The external position also appeared to be strong. In 1914, the national gold reserves were 35 million pounds; in 1937, 825 million. Although the pound had fallen sharply after Britain abandoned the gold standard in 1931, it quickly rebounded: from spring 1932 to summer 1938 the authorities struggled to prevent it from rising too far against the dollar. And throughout the 1930s, although overseas borrowing was regulated and often difficult, British firms continued to invest overseas, especially but not only in such empire lands as South Africa.[6]

Sad to say, the fundamentals were not as strong as they seemed. It appears that in 1939 the British government made its dispositions and commitments without assessing its financial weakness.[7] In the years of "appeasement" it never made such an assessment. If it had, the facts might well have given the government pause. For Britain was short of more than war materiel. Little of the interwar overseas investment had gone to the dollar area. Overseas assets, therefore, were less useful than they seemed — unless sterling assets could be sold to dollar-area buyers. True, the gold reserves were large. But as gold coin no longer circulated, there was now no "secondary reserve." Worse: the sterling balances were now 808 million pounds, so that net gold reserves were a mere 17 million pounds — not quite half the 1913 figure. Admittedly, there had been sterling balances before the First World War.[8] No one knows just how large they were. But in 1913 most sterling balances were needed for transactions, while some balances were the official monetary reserves of such countries as India and Japan. In 1937 there was still a transactions demand for sterling. But Britain's share of world trade had fallen: in 1913 she provided 30 percent of world exports of manufactures, and in 1938, 21 percent.

World trade, furthermore, had not grown in step with world production. The transactions demand, therefore, probably had diminished, though it had not vanished. The reserve demand, too, was still there;

indeed, because the sterling area had expanded and because many overseas lands no longer held monetary gold, that demand was in some sense larger than before the First World War. Empire countries, in particular, would be unlikely to move monetary balances out of sterling and into dollars. But not all holders of sterling would be so accommodating. The world had become much more sensitive about unpleasant possibilities: exchange control, devaluation, domestic inflation. Balances had flowed to London in the 1930s largely because the British exchequer was managed on conservative lines, because British politics were not upsetting, and because Britain was committed to the avoidance of exchange control in peacetime. Confidence was further supported by the fact that for five years the sterling-dollar exchange rate varied very little. But this confidence was fragile, and it did not survive the shocks of 1938. The pound depreciated, and the gold flowed out. By the end of 1938, the reserves had fallen to 615 million pounds, entirely because the sterling balances had fallen. Some money went back to France; some went to New York; some presumably went to Switzerland.

In 1939 the outflow continued, and if the Exchange Equalization Account had not spent lavishly to support sterling, the pound would have collapsed. In summer 1939, when support was withdrawn, the pound quickly fell from $4.68 to $4.03; a year before it had hovered around $5.00. By the end of 1939, even after the imposition of exchange control, reserves had shrunk to 545 million pounds. And in summer 1939, the Treasury knights told the Cabinet that, even without allowing for wartime procurement, in two years Britain would have neither gold nor dollars.[9]

This fragile position reflected the fact that Britain's interwar economy had developed in an asymmetrical way. Although less dependent on imported foodstuffs than in 1914, the country still could not feed itself, nor was it self-sufficient in such basic industrial materials as iron ore. It had no oil. The "new industries" depended heavily upon imported raw materials — copper, rubber, tin. And the "old industries" — textiles, coal, shipbuilding, iron and steel — were not thriving in export markets, nor could they be expected to do so while the world depression continued. Interest rates, furthermore, were at very low levels throughout the 1930s. Thus Britain's current-account earnings were depressed from several sides, and in spite of the encouragement that protectionism provided, her import spending was not depressed. The result, in the 1930s, was a chronic current-account deficit. Even in peacetime the country was living beyond its means. In wartime, she would export less, but her import needs would balloon. Fortunately, the sterling area could supply a large proportion of these needs. Also it could help feed the people. But most of the sterling area was a long way off.

In war-time, as it proved, Britain would have to borrow not only in the United States but from the sterling area itself. This was a new situation; in 1914-1918 Britain had lent massively to the overseas sterling area, and had even financed Canada to some extent. How would these new arrangements be managed? At the outbreak of war nothing had been devised, and it is not at all clear that either the Bank of England or the Treasury had worked out any contingency plans. But for Britain's war effort the overseas sterling area would be crucial — at least as important as the Anglo-American co-operation on which much attention has been focused.

Shortly before war broke out, the Treasury warned the Cabinet that there would be trouble ahead.[10] Without American aid, Britain's reserves would not support a major or a prolonged war. Some Cabinet members, it appears, were distressed, perplexed, and alarmed: "what had gone wrong?" they seemed to wonder. Their perplexity is understandable: for much of the 1930s, capital inflow had kept the pound healthy, while at the end of the decade the monetary authorities had spent reserves without telling anyone just what they were up to. Sad to say, soon enough the realities of Britain's position would be borne in on Britain's Cabinet.

In a war the contributions of Britain's dominions could well be crucial, and in Whitehall this fact was well-understood, although there was a noticeable tendency to believe that, though the Americans had to be kept sweet, the dominions would be sweet by nature. All the dominions had close economic ties with Britain, and only Canada had important economic links with anyone else. Eire, Australia and New Zealand traded almost exclusively with the United Kingdom. Indeed, America's protectionist measures had increased this dependence by diverting Antipodean wool and deflecting Antipodean lamb and dairy produce from the US market. The same had happened to Canada: the American slump was deeper and more prolonged than the British, while the American protectionist measures of 1930-1932 were only partially reversed in 1935-1938,[11] so that at the outbreak of war Britain was again, as she had been before 1914 and through most of the 1930s, Canada's largest export market. Conversely, for many years Canada had been buying far more from the United States than from Britain. She certainly was doing so in 1939. For the southern dominions and for Eire, there was no such sharp bilateral imbalance. Although all three southern dominions bought more in North America (largely in Canada) than they sold there, Britain dominated the pattern both of importation and exportation. Admittedly, for South Africa the situation is obscured because so much of the dominion's export trade consisted of gold and diamonds. Although these were shipped to Britain in the first instance, few of the diamonds remained there, and by 1938-1939 the same was true of the gold: the precious metal flew on to vaults in Paris, Zurich, and — especially — Fort Knox.

Although these intra-imperial trade flows were more complicated than is often thought, the inward flow consisted largely of temperate-zone foodstuffs and primary products, while the outward flow was still largely manufactures. Other parts of the world supplied Britain with other primary products — copper from Northern Rhodesia (Zambia), cocoa from Gold Coast (Ghana), palm oil from Nigeria, oil from Iran and Trinidad, tea from India and Ceylon, sisal from Tanganyika (Tanzania), sugar from the West Indies and Mauritius as well as Australia, and rubber and tin from Malaya. Thus Britain's deficiencies with respect to food and raw materials could be, and largely were, supplied from imperial sources. But extra-imperial trade mattered too. Softwood lumber came from the Baltic area, and from the Soviet Union. The Baltic states also sent dairy products and pig products. Argentina sent wheat and meat. So did Uruguay. And Ugandan cotton and Rhodesian tobacco merely supplemented the supplies from the United States, which also supplied massive amounts of temperate-zone foodstuffs.

All the British Empire countries except Canada were accustomed to bank in — and on — London. Their governments, their currency boards, or their banking systems regularly held "sterling balances" there, and only South Africa and Canada still maintained any domestic gold reserve. These arrangements reflected three facts. First of all, sterling was freely convertible into any other money, without any form of exchange control. Second, because trade and financial ties ran largely to and from London, most external financial transactions could most readily be cleared there, in sterling. Third, although access to the London new-issue market was regulated during the 1930s, the market generally remained open to new Empire borrowing, whether for refinancing or for the raising of "new money." Furthermore, the increasingly important British multinationals, in such industries as foodstuffs, cleaning products, and oil extraction and refining, naturally joined their head offices with their finances, especially in times when continental currencies were uncertain and when no one could be sure which way President Roosevelt was going to jump.

These pre-war arrangements were tailor-made for the automatic financing of Britain's wartime importations. No one had designed them for this purpose; indeed, no one had designed them at all. But most of the sterling area entered the war when Britain did. And with war came exchange control, while alternative markets in Europe were rapidly closing, and American markets were no more open than they had ever been. Goods and services, therefore, would flow to Britain, who would pay in commodities, services, or sterling balances, as suited her convenience and the pressures of her own war effort.

Because her economy was involved not only with the British economy but also with the American, Canada's situation was different. The central bank held gold and dollar balances, but not sterling, while the chartered (commercial) banks held most of their external assets in American dollars; sterling balances, though not zero, were comparatively small. Canada, therefore, had never been a member of the sterling area. Even in the 1930s the American market for Canadian goods was almost as important as the British, and to balance her peacetime international accounts Canada had to convert her net sterling earnings into American dollars, so as to pay for her net imports from the United States. Canada, therefore, would never be willing freely to accumulate inconvertible sterling balances in wartime; she would always want to manage such build-up, to limit it, and so far as possible to insist on payment in gold, American dollars, or both.

With respect to Canada's Commonwealth trade, the problem was identical. Canada had a large trade with certain Commonwealth countries, especially with India, Australia, New Zealand, South Africa, and Malaya; she sent cars and parts to the first four lands, and imported tea from the first and rubber and tin from the last as well as from Ceylon. In the late 1930s this Commonwealth trade earned Canada a surplus, which helped to cover the deficit on Canadian-American trade. But in wartime this surplus was almost certain to vanish: the Commonwealth would be likely to cut back on imports of American-style cars and trucks. Admittedly Canada, in all likelihood, would also import less tea and less rubber. Nevertheless, it would be reasonable to expect that the surplus would diminish. And it would certainly become inconvertible: the Commonwealth's earnings of American dollars would be pooled, and Canada would be left with inconvertible sterling which could not be spent automatically, or at all, in the United States.

In the 1930s, most Commonwealth currencies had been pegged to the money of the United Kingdom so that, in relation to the dollar, they went up and down with the pound sterling. I once described the result by pointing to Laputa, the Floating Island, in *Gulliver's Travels:*

> *The reader can hardly conceive my Astonishment, to behold an Island in the Air, inhabited by Men, who were able (as it would seem) to raise, or sink, or put into a Progressive Motion, as they pleased ... I ... chose to observe what course the Island would take, because it seemed for a while to stand still ... in the lowest gallery, I beheld some People fishing ... I called and shouted with the utmost strength of my voice ... I found by their pointing towards me and to each other, that they plainly discovered me, although they made no reply to my shouting.*[12]

Certainly that is the way in which Washington viewed the sterling area. The officials sometimes remembered that peacetime Britain had a large deficit in its trade with the United States. But they also noticed that the overseas sterling area had a large surplus: the Americans bought rubber, tin, cocoa, palm oil, and even some wool, and the United States also absorbed most of the Commonwealth's gold production, which, in turn, made up most of the world's output.

Did these facts influence President Roosevelt? Perhaps; there seems to be no documentary evidence. We know that he thought Britain could easily finance her war effort.[13] Did the facts influence Whitehall? Obviously, in wartime Britain could and would pay the sterling area in sterling, sequester the dollar proceeds in the "central pool," and use them to finance dollar imports. Again we do not yet know whether peacetime Whitehall had deliberately done the sums.

The Canadian situation was entirely different. The Bank of Canada held its external reserves partly in gold, and partly in American dollars; the chartered banks now held only transactions balances in any foreign currency, and these, in, turn, were held largely though not entirely in New York. Thus Canada was not a part of the emerging sterling area, and only a series of conscious decisions could ever make it so. In particular, the Canadian authorities would have to decide to accumulate sterling, and to hold sterling balances, as one way of financing Britain's war effort. But because Canada imported so much from the United States, any such decision would create severe problems for the senior dominion: only through stringent import-rationing and draconian foreign-exchange control might

Canada survive, or even mount a war effort herself. But in the southern dominions things would be a good deal easier, precisely because their industries did not depend in the same way, or to the same extent, upon American components and semi-fabricates.

Since 1914, the dominions had all gained greatly in financial sophistication and in industrial expertise. By 1939, Canada, South Africa, and New Zealand all possessed central banks, and the plentiful experience in domestic borrowing which had marked the First World War had not been forgotten. In all the dominions the industrial base had been greatly broadened, both in heavy industry and in consumer-durable industries. Once war had begun, these developments would be important. In the 1920s, Canada had been the world's second-largest exporter of motor vehicles and, although the plants had been under-utilized during the 1930s, capacity had remained almost intact. Australia had made considerable progress in motor-car assembly, and had acquired a modern steel industry, as had India. There was plenty of excess capacity in Canada's iron and steel industry, dependent though it was on American iron ore and coal. Electrical and radio industries had developed rapidly in the inter-war years, as had chemical production and oil-refining. Thanks to the rise in the gold price, South Africa had boomed during the 1930s; thanks to currency-depreciation, Australia had recovered quickly from the slump, and had managed a respectable amount of economic growth; thanks to the foreign-exchange control which was imposed in 1938, New Zealand had begun to move along the path of import-replacing industrialization.

All the dominions depended on foreign petroleum: Canada produced little, and the younger dominions produced none at all. Stringent rationing, therefore, could have been foreseen in 1939. Even in so far as the Antipodean dominions could buy Middle East oil with sterling, the problems of shipping would be severe. And American oil was "dollar oil," as was the oil of Mexico and Venezuela. Fortunately, Australia and South Africa had plenty of coal, and even Canada had a useful amount, although the coal mines were in awkward parts of the country.

In India and in the dependent African empire, economic structures had changed much less than in the dominions. Neither Africa nor India had any oil. But India now had a central bank, and virtually all the African colonies and protectorates operated the "currency board system" that pegged local currencies to the pound sterling, rigidly aligning exchange rates to the pound. Since 1914 the Indian economy had diversified somewhat. There was now a modern steel industry, and more manufactures were produced locally, in part because of direct investment from the United Kingdom. Thanks to these developments, in India the armed forces could largely be supplied from Indian factories and farms, against payment in sterling. In Africa there had been some development of infrastructure; also, primary products were exported in much larger quantities than before the war, and the array of such goods had considerably increased. Manufacturing, however, had made little progress, except in such locally-oriented consumer industries as brewing. The African colonies were not well-placed to begin import-replacing industrialization under war conditions. Africa's armies, therefore, would have to be provisioned from abroad.

The allied war effort would have to depend heavily on Middle East oil. Strictly speaking, none of the oil came from the British Empire. But Iraq was under British control, and soon the same could be said of southern Iran, where oil had already been produced by 1914. Iraq had come next, in the late 1920s, and in the 1930s there was successful exploration south of the Gulf. By 1939 there were large installations at Abadan, and pipelines from Iraq to the eastern Mediterranean. And most of the oil could be paid for in sterling: by 1939 the American companies still produced comparatively little crude. Furthermore, since 1914 Iran had acquired the rudiments of a railway system, over which the western powers could supply their Soviet ally. The cost would be political control over the recalcitrant Iranians.

At first sight, the French economy of 1939 could not be more different from the German. By pumping up government spending and investment, the Nazis had achieved a full economic recovery, and full employment; through political foolery and a regrettable exchange-rate policy, the French had achieved a stagnation that had lasted for a full decade. In 1939, national output was exactly what it had been in 1929; throughout the intervening years it had been lower. Although they had supported the franc by means of protective tariffs and quotas, both designed to reduce the value of imports, the French had eschewed foreign-exchange controls, and had tried to avoid the sorts of bilateral payments agreements in which Berlin's Dr. Schacht delighted: like Britain, France resorted to such agreements only when the exigencies of some other nation made them inevitable. Although France had tried to develop its own network of political allies in Eastern Europe, and although these lands had attracted some French direct and portfolio investment, as trading partners they were insignificant, nor could they supply France with foodstuffs or war materiel if war should break out. Indeed, for pre-war Poland the main export markets were in Britain and Germany, and for pre-war Czechoslovakia, in the Balkans and in the full range of industrialized states.

France had a large overseas empire, but, like her "Little Entente" partners, this too was not of central economical importance. Its currencies were pegged to the metropolitan franc, and it could supply cheap wine, sugar, rice, and groundnuts — hardly the sinews of modern war. There was no large oilfield in the French colonial empire. In peacetime, indeed, the empire had been of interest chiefly as a market for uncompetitive French manufactures — precisely the sorts of flows that would necessarily be curtailed in wartime. The situation was thus very different from that of Germany, with its Balkan sphere of tributaries, or of Britain, with its highly useful Empire-Commonwealth. It does not appear that this difference worried the French.

Indeed, Parisian publicists were loud in their praise of the "splendid equilibrium" of the French economy. By this statement they seemed to mean that the country could feed itself, that the non-agricultural population was not "excessively large," and that there was sufficient iron, coal, aluminum, and heavy industry to support a war effort. By 1939 nothing much had been done to ready this industrial base. Of course, much of it was underutilized, so that outputs could be raised in time of need. In addition, although measured unemployment had been low throughout the 1930s, extra labour could surely have been found for "priority tasks," if anyone had been willing to identify these or to channel resources toward them. This had not been done.

Nor had investment been planned or stimulated with an eye to security. France logically ought to have been developing a capacity in synthetic petrol. Her crude oil came mostly from the Middle East, and to a small extent from the United States. In wartime both would be vulnerable. She had no Romania to hand. Even Britain, where by 1939 there was some "oil-from-coal," had been more energetic. It is arguable that France should have been at work on synthetic rubber: submarine warfare might threaten supplies from the Far East. And with respect to such things as steel capacity and the coal mines, the France of 1939, like the France of 1914, was still very much the inferior of Germany. Not only was the French economy smaller; it was a great deal less urbanized and industrialized. The much-admired "equilibrium," whatever its social advantage, was a military handicap.

The French governments of the 1930s had certainly been economically activist, but not in a very helpful way. Much had been done, largely by import-management and price-support, to help the farmers. The high tariffs and other regulations had encouraged complacency among manufacturers, and by cutting off the French economy from world price-movements the governments' interventions had prevented France's manufactures from enjoying the sort of stimulus Britain's "new industries" had derived from the decline in world primary-product prices. French industrialists were said to be interested in market-management and a quiet life, not in competition and expansion. During the 1930s, there had been little new spending on plant and equipment. Machinery and methods, therefore, must often have been obsolescent. This ought to have been especially worrying in a country where population was stagnant and where labour was anything but plentiful. After French mobilization, who would work the machines?

Only in one respect — the gold reserves — had France been provident. After the great build-up of the period 1926-1931, and after the mighty fluctuations of 1931-1938, in the last year of peace the reserves had rebounded. The franc had been firmly pegged to the pound; the Daladier government exuded conservative confidence; the hot money flowed back to Paris from London — and perhaps from other places as well. The reserves increased splendidly. In midsummer 1939 they were larger than they had been in 1914. Admittedly, there was now no obvious "secondary reserve" of circulating gold coin — although there were large private hoards of coin and bullion. In 1914-1915, the French government had been able to double its gold holdings by calling coin out of circulation; in 1939 there was no such chance.

The "war chest" of gold was sizeable, and unlike the situation in 1914, it was all available for spending: there was now no link between the circulating currency and the gold reserves. Furthermore, unlike the gold reserves of the United Kingdom, the French reserves were not overhung by large external liabilities which might have to be paid, at short notice, in gold. On the other hand, precisely because Paris was not a centre of international banking, France could not conveniently borrow from the rest of the world. London could do this by letting the world accumulate "sterling balances." Nobody wanted to hold "franc balances" except for the French — and, as the 1930s had revealed, even the French were often not sure they wanted to. Admittedly within the French Empire, banks and colonial governments could and did hold balances in Paris. But, as we noticed above, the French Empire could not supply much to a warring France. Oil, rubber, metals, coal and temperate-zone foodstuffs — all came from outside the French Empire, and therefore from outside the Franc Zone. That Zone, therefore, would not help France very much.

On the domestic scene the productive potential was impressive, but far less so than that of Britain or Germany, not to mention the United States. The interwar years had seen some development of new industries, such as the motor car industry, and some modernization of old industries. But France was not really equipped industrially to fight a modern war: Germany had too great an edge in productive potential, and even in manpower. And although the Maginot Line was impressive, it did not cover the Franco-Belgian part of the northern frontier. Nor had there been any experience with exchange controls. In a long war France would have a good deal to learn; in the event, she did not have time to do so.

In 1939 Americans could look back on a decade of deepening economic isolationism. In 1929 the United States exported less than seven percent of her national output, and imported less than six percent of her needs. In 1939 the figures were 5.9 percent and 3.9 percent. No major economy was so nearly self-sufficient. Protectionism was partly to blame. By 1939 it was almost impossible to sell foreign manufactures in the United States, and American imports consisted chiefly of tropical primary products and of Canadian goods. During the 1920s American tariffs had risen, culminating in the Smoot-Hawley enactment of 1930. In 1930-1932, additional measures were taken to protect American producers against imports of wool, timber, and non-ferrous metals. The agricultural reconstruction of the New Deal involved new controls on the import of temperate-zone foodstuffs, and impeded the export of American cotton and tobacco, both of which were, in addition, suffering from third-country competition. Britain's new protective measures, and the elaboration of imperial preference, may also have hindered American exports. Washington's Reciprocal Trade Agreements Act had lowered many of the Smoot-Hawley tariffs, but as yet it had little impact on American trading patterns. Nor was it meant to do so: Cordell Hull's idea was to export more, but not to import.

More fundamental was the fact that the United States was a very large economy — much the largest in the world — and a very diverse one. Its array of resources was wide, and so was its climatic spread. Because of its own protectionist policies and those of other states, the competitiveness of its manufacturing industries is hard to assess. Yet no one doubts that capital-labour ratios were very high in the United States, or that mechanization had gone farther than anywhere else. In technological terms, though possibly not in cost-effectiveness, American manufacturing led the world. In all the basic raw materials including oil, and in primary foodstuffs, the country was self-sufficient. Indeed, except in years of crop-failure it was an exporter of temperate-zone foodstuffs, and it regularly exported oil.

American economic isolation extended to finance as well as to commerce. Throughout the interwar years American exports exceeded imports. The resultant current-account surplus could spell trouble for the rest of the world, and in the 1930s it had done so. During the 1920s, American capital exports kept the world supplied with dollars: although some of the current-account surplus was brought home as gold, most of it was lent abroad. In the 1930s the gold-inflow continued, but the capital-export did not. From 1930 to 1940, American private investments abroad fell from $17.2 billion to $12.2 billion. Both direct and portfolio investment was diminishing. Meanwhile, foreigners were moving money to the United States. Over the same period, foreign long-term investment in the United States rose from $5.7 billion to $8.1 billion, and their short-term holdings rose from $2.7 billion to $5.4 billion (both figures were very substantially lower in the early 1930s, but then rebounded at the end of the decade). These capital inflows, plus the continuing current-account surplus, could mean only one thing — an immense increase in the gold stock. At the end of 1929, the US Treasury held $4.0 billion in gold; at the end of 1938, it and the Exchange Stabilization Account held $14.6 billion, and at the end of 1939, $17.8 billion. There were small exports of gold in 1932 and 1933; in all other years the gold poured in, and the United States also retained all of its own domestic production. In 1940 the "gold cover" for short-term external liabilities – the dollar equivalent of sterling balances – was nearly 400 percent.

In a sense the nation's internal economic power matches its external strength. Undoubtedly the American economy had enormous productive potential, and in 1939 it was far from fully employed. There was plenty of spare capacity which could be mobilized. But the American authorities had done little to prepare for the possibility of war, which, indeed, they hoped to avoid. There had been nothing like the German Four-Year Plan. The New Dealers had constructed some public-utility projects, such as the series of dams in the Tennessee valley and in Washington. The enormous and under-employed automobile industry could be speedily converted. But the aircraft industry was still comparatively small, and so was the aluminum industry. Furthermore, for a decade there had been little non-residential investment — little spending on new industrial plant, machinery, and equipment. In 1929 non-residential fixed investment was $26.5 million; in 1932-1934 it collapsed, and even in 1937 it had risen only to $18.8 million, while in 1938-1939 it slipped again (data in constant 1958 prices). To a remarkable extent the American economy was relying on capital goods that dated from the 1920s, or even earlier. In this respect it resembled the French economy, but not the British, the German, or the Soviet. President Roosevelt's policies may have saved American capitalism; they had certainly not revived the economy.

Yet the New Deal had improved American's capacity to fight a major war. It had given unions a recognized place in society and in the economy. Most labour leaders were patriotic; the Wagner Act had ensured that they would co-operate with Washington. In the new environment it would be much easier for women to work with men, or instead of men, in blue-collar tasks. Unemployment insurance and old-age security meant fewer social tensions. And the masses were much more likely to think that the Roosevelt government was "our government" — especially because the bosses did not.

Certainly the governmental machine had been much developed during the New Deal years. The Washington of 1939 was not the provincial backwater of earlier decades. Now there were many more officials and agencies, doing a far wider range of things. Admittedly there was no co-ordinated economic policy-making, and nothing that one could call "planning." But the capital now possessed the statistics, the will, and many of the personnel with which a war effort could be managed. And their activities had become more weighty. In 1929 the federal government used less than 1.3 percent of American's national output. In 1939 the percentage was 5.5, and rising, even though defence still absorbed only 1.3 percent of the total.

With capacity has come hubris, especially in retrospect. An older generation of historians blamed the United States for so much interwar perplexity. If only she had joined the League! If only she had written off the inter-allied debts! If only Roosevelt had not torpedoed the London Conference of 1933! If only there had been no Smoot-Hawley! More recently, some scholars have blamed American monetary policy for deepening the nation's own depression, and, at least by implication, thereby exporting depression to the rest of the world. The problem, they tell us, was that the Federal Reserve System did not know what it ought to be doing, and so did the wrong things. Similarly, Charles P. Kindleberger has traced the Depression to a failure of American leadership — a failure, in fact, to accept a hegemonic role. The United States, Kindleberger says, should have provided leadership, a market for "distress goods," and a lavish flow of emergency credit. Nor should she have deliberately depreciated the American dollar. Had American policy been informed by the best economic advice, Kindleberger argues, the Great Depression would have been much more gentle, and much shorter.

An economic hegemon must have more than weight or bulk or gold or a strong current account. It must have the power to compel obedience, and the willingness to do so. If either is lacking, the best economic advice (which incidentally was not available at the time) will be otiose. It is also helpful, to say the least, if one has a unified control over one's own government, legislature, and policy — in fact, a parliamentary system with a strong majority, not a congressional system with division of powers and an independent central bank. It is, finally, important that other governments trust and respect the would-be hegemon.

It seems to me that the United States was congenitally ill-equipped for a peace-time hegemonic role. Neither policy nor psyche were well-suited, and American governments were disliked and distrusted abroad, as much for their self-righteousness as for their follies. Under wartime conditions, when the Allies would be desperate for dollar goods, things would be different. And here serendipity came to Washington's aid. During the 1930s, Congress had made it impossible for Americans to lend to any foreign government that had defaulted on its old war debts. The somewhat frantic devices of 1914-1917 would be unavailable; even trade credit was proscribed. The results are well-known — the exhaustion of Britain's gold and dollar holdings, the depletion of external investments, and the "consideration" in the Lend-Lease system. But in peacetime ... What weapons might the American government have deployed? And what weapons can we imagine them deploying? It is difficult to think of any, and even more difficult to believe the world of the 1930s would have welcomed American initiatives. Certainly the British government would not, and did not. When Washington tried to manage British tariff and exchange-rate policy, London's response was cool, not to say glacial. Washington got its way in 1936-1938 only because London realized that, given the condition of international politics, it was impolitic to antagonize Roosevelt and his Cabinet members, Morgenthau and Hull.

With respect to its external economic relations and internal arrangements, the Soviet Union of 1939 was somewhat closer to Nazi Germany than to France, although in some respects Soviet resemblances to Nazi practice may seem superficial.

The most striking similarities arose from the fact that both domestic economies operated under reigns of terror. In both countries these circumstances are thought to have worsened economic performance, although the evidence is clearer for Germany than for the Soviet Union. Could the Soviet Union have industrialized without terror? With respect to collectivization, scholars still debate the issue. With respect to central planning and the urban terror of the 1930s, there is really no debate. The planning did not require terror; the terror made the planning less effective and less fruitful. But the Communist Party wanted so rapid an advance that forceful government encouragement, if nothing more, was certainly required.

Another similarity was to be found in the management of international trade and payments. The Soviet authorities maintained a "monopoly of foreign trade," a control of foreign transactions that had become almost total with the advent of the Five-Year Plans in 1928. The Soviet authorities held a large gold reserve and some foreign-exchange assets, apparently as deposits in British banks and perhaps in French banks. These reserves could be freely spent, if only because their size was a state secret. They were augmented from domestic gold production and from export receipts, and drawn down in accordance with the priorities of the annual and quinquennial development plans, almost entirely to pay for imports of capital goods and essential raw materials, and, presumably, for espionage.

In relation to the size of the Soviet economy the trade flows, in turn, were small and growing smaller. The Soviet Union, like Nazi Germany, had been planning for import-replacement. The domestic dietary regime was appalling. Indeed, some millions had starved during the 1930s. Yet, as a matter of policy, the industrializing Soviet Union did not import breadstuffs, and in most years during the 1930s it was an exporter of grain, chiefly to pay for the capital goods that were required for industrialization. But this flow was diminishing. More capital goods, and more kinds of capital goods, were now produced within the country. In 1937 the official index of machine and metalworking production was 11 times the 1928 figure. The annual output of metal-cutting lathes had increased from 1,500 in 1913 to 55,300 in 1938.[14] In 1928 the Soviet Union produced 791 lorries and buses, and in 1939, 184,100, as well as 27,000 cars.[15] The output of radios increased from zero in 1928 to 203,200 in 1938.[16] For the several kinds of military hardware there are no published data, but it is relevant to note that between 1913 and 1939 the production of steel increased almost five-fold.[17] By 1939 Soviet steel output was 166 percent of Britain's, 221 percent of France's, and 74 percent of Germany's.[18] In the effort to dispense with inessential imports, the Soviet Union had also expanded its production of raw cotton and the rubber-substitute kok-sagyz. With respect to crude oil, whose production had more than tripled since 1913, the country was self-sufficient, and sometimes could export.[19]

Since 1913 the official index of national income had shown a five-fold increase,[20] while in 1938, the value of exports was barely one-fifth of the 1913 figure, and the value of imports, slightly more than one-quarter of 1913.[21] Indeed, both exports and imports had been substantially larger, both in value terms and in volume, during 1929-1931 — the start-up years of planned industrialization — than in 1938 or 1939. The United States and the United Kingdom provided 40 percent of Soviet imports and took 34 percent of Soviet exports; there was also significant trade with France, Germany, Belgium, and Holland. In Asia, 13 percent of total Soviet exports went to China, Mongolia, and Iran, which also provided 14 percent of Soviet imports. Four percent of Soviet imports came from Malaya and the Straits Settlements: presumably these goods consisted wholly of rubber and tin. It does not appear that the Soviet Union had learned how to produce synthetic rubber.

The Soviet Union thus stood in a rather special relation to the world economy. She had no role in the worldwide financial system. With respect to the circulation of goods, she had trading links both with Germany and with the future western allies, and also with some Asian countries, most of which lay on her borders. Her economy was very nearly self-sufficient, and increasingly so. Most imports were capital goods. If these were to be cut off, her industrialization drive might take a different course, prolong itself, or cost more, but by 1939 it would not be brought to a halt, so long as the country was neutral and the harvests were reasonably good. If critical inputs, such as rubber, were to be cut off, things might be more serious, but only until Soviet scientists had domesticated the technology of synthesis.

On the other hand, if war should engulf the Soviet Union, the country, in spite of its industrial efflorescence, would be very exposed. Its ports were few, and most were remote. Its populations and its resources were widely dispersed. Thus all of northern Russia-in-Europe was a food deficit area; grain came from the south, and so did oil and most of the nation's iron and coal, while machinery production was concentrated in the centre and the north. Cotton came from Central Asia, many thousands of miles away. The parts of this sprawling economy were connected by an efficient but under-capitalized railway system, and by riverine routes that could be used only part of each year. In 1914-1917 it had been distance, and the resultant disorganization, that had brought the Tsarist economy to the brink of collapse. Recognizing some of the risks to which the inherited locational pattern exposed the Soviet regime, Soviet planners had tried to develop a secondary centre of industry in the Urals and in Western Siberia. Their efforts had not been unsuccessful: by 1939 Magnitogorsk was in full production. But these projects, splendid though they were, could not change geography, nor could they affect the climate or the distribution of the Soviet population. Thus the risks remained.

Whatever the geographical risks, the Soviet Union had retained the great demographic advantage of 1914 — a large agrarian population. In 1914 there are thought to have been 106.2 million rural inhabitants within the Russian Empire. In January 1939, although the urban population had risen from 25 million to 56 million, there were still 114.5 million (at both dates, boundaries of pre-September-1939 territory).[22] Certainly the collectivized agrarian system did not put these millions to the best use. But precisely for that reason, many of the Soviet rural masses might be mobilized for war work, or for the army, without necessarily disrupting food production, unless the productive lands were actually occupied. Presumably it was countermarching armies, not loss of labour, that reduced food production by two-thirds between 1940 and 1942-1943.[23] For Soviet people, especially in unoccupied European Russia, the result would be disastrous: food importation was impossible, and there were no reserves. Hence much of the fall in the Soviet population: from 194 million in January 1940 to 178 million in 1950 (probably the present boundaries for 1940, and certainly for 1950).[24] Military action, of course, killed more millions. The terror, also, continued to wreak havoc. Nevertheless, a more completely-industrialized country, or one that had not already put so many urban women to work, would have found it far harder to field the sorts of army which the Soviet Union was able to mass.

The Soviet Union possessed nothing like the "overseas sterling area" from which Britain would be able to borrow, and nothing like the dependent Balkan fringe from which Germany would be able to do likewise. The ruble was not freely convertible, and the authorities had long practiced a mobilization of ruble earnings for the sake of the industrialization plans.

Under wartime conditions, the Soviet government might be able to arrange some short-time credits from western banks. But the prospects for doing so can never have been very bright. Government-to-Government credits, therefore, would play a large role in the Soviet war effort.

The Soviet authorities certainly recognized during the 1930s that war was a real possibility, and planned their industrialization, including the locations of many plants, with war in mind. At the same time they hoped to avoid attack, and arranged their relations with Hitler in the hope that a German attack could be averted. The industrialization of the 1930s had put the Soviet Union in a much better position with respect to war: compared with 1914, the country could now produce much larger quantities of military materiel, and of such necessary materials as steel and vehicles. The population, furthermore, had become used to rationing and to hardship: the industrialization drive had involved both, not only for peasants but for many city-dwellers as well. The authorities had become used to the operation of a centrally-planned economy, and knew how to mobilize resources for a major effort — in the 1930s, industrialization; after 1941, war. In this respect the situation was rather similar to that in Nazi Germany. And as we have learned to avoid assuming that the Germans ran a perfectly and meticulously planned economy, so we now suspect that Soviet "planning" was less successful than we had once thought. The point, however, is that by 1939 the necessary habits and institutions were already in place.

For Japan, war may be said to have begun with the Manchuria campaign in 1931, which created a client state little different from a colony, and with the resultant campaigns against China. Relying on expansionary fiscal and monetary policy and on a depreciating exchange rate, Japan had already recovered from the Depression when the China war broke out. Although the silk trade remained depressed, Japan's other textile industries had been largely transformed, and her capital goods industries had grown with especial speed; the Manchukuo economy had been developed with an emphasis on steel, coal, and capital goods, conveniently supplementing Japan's own economic structure. The government had begun to experiment with artificial petrol-production, and to widen the product-coverage of Japanese manufacturing, so that the national war economy was much more nearly self-contained. With an eye on the prospects of war, by 1937 the government had begun to accumulate the imports that war might make scarce. The zaibatsu, the great conglomerate firms of Japan, had preserved and enhanced their role in the tightly organized Japanese economy. Cartelisation had proceeded, encouraged by government; exchange control, of little account before 1937, then became increasingly rigorous. The Japanese economy, therefore, had come to resemble the "controlled" economy of Nazi Germany. And although there were still some embarrassing gaps in the range of industrial production, and although the country was still short of oil and of some other industrial raw materials, the nation was now well organized to mount a major war — much better organized than in 1904, when she had defeated Tsarist Russia, or in 1896, when she had routed the Chinese Empire.[25]

◆◆◆

In conclusion, we address some questions of global political economy. Did the British government clearly understand the United Kingdom's economic fragility when making the relevant diplomatic commitments? Did the governments of Canada, the United States, and France exaggerate Britain's economic power? To these questions, the answers, I believe, are "no" and "yes." Did the United States government believe that the United States occupied a hegemonic position in the world economy? It seems likely that, far from refusing to exercise hegemonic power, the United States government did not see the world economy in those terms. During the 1930s Washington had generally been unable to get its way when negotiating with other large powers. This experience, surely, would have made the "hegemonic model" unattractive in the United States. And certainly in economic matters, the New Deal government, though not uninterested in world recovery, was primarily oriented to the domestic scene. Even when it appeared to be looking outward, as in the Reciprocal Trade Agreements Act of 1934, Washington showed itself to be dominated by affairs at home. This was not the best orientation from which to begin a world war.

NOTES

1. The brief best account of Nazi economic policy is in R.J. Overy, *The Nazi Economic Recovery 1932-1938* (London, 1982). See also H. James, *The German Slump: Politics and Economics 1924-36* (Oxford, 1986), and K. Hardach, The Political Economy of Germany in the Twentieth Century (Berkeley, California, 1980). An indispensable source for information about Nazi Germany's financial position is Deutsche Bundesbank, *Währung und Wirtschaft in Deutschland 1876-1975* (Frankfurt, 1976), 283-366, and the accompanying statistical volume, *Deutsches Geld und Bankwesen in Zahlen 1876-1975* (Frankfurt, 1976).

2. B.H. Klein, *Germany's Economic Preparations for War* (Cambridge, Mass., 1959).

3. Alan Milward, *The German Economy at War* (London, 1965).

4. R.J. Overy, "Hitler's War and the German Economy: A Re-interpretation," *Economic History Review*, New Series, XXXV-2, 272-91.

5. For a summary of the literature, see B.W.E. Alford, *Depression or Recovery? British Economic Growth 1918-1939* (London, 1972). The accumulating weight of scholarly re-interpretation requires us to think much more positively about the state of the British economy during the Depression years.

6. On all monetary topics, the basic reference must be R.S. Sayers, *The Bank of England 1891-1944* (Cambridge, 1976), including the statistical and other matter in the volume of appendices, where we find, among other things, careful re-estimations of the interwar British balance of payments.

7. See Ian Drummond and Norman Hillmer, *Negotiating Freer Trade: The United Kingdom, the United States, Canada, and the Trade Agreements of 1938* (Waterloo, Ontario, 1989), 151-67.

8. Details on the movement of Britain's gold reserves and on the external position are to be found in Sayers.

9. Drummond and Hillmer, 159.

10. Public Record Office, Kew, England, Cabinet Papers, CAB 23/100, Cabinet Conclusions, 5 July 1939.

11. Drummond and Hillmer, 137-68.

12. Jonathan Swift, *Gulliver's Travels* (1726), pt. 3, ch. 1.

13. Drummond and Hillmer, 159-60.

14. Roger A. Clarke, *Soviet Economic Facts 1917-1970* (London, 1972), Tables 32, 33.

15. *Ibid.*, Table 25.

16. *Ibid.*, Table 49.

17. *Ibid.*, Table 23.

18. Brian Mitchell, *European Historical Statistics 1750-1970* (London, 1975), Table E 9, 400-1.

19. Clarke, Table 18.

20. *Ibid.*, Table 3.

21. *Ibid.*, Table 16.

22. *Ibid.*, Table 1.

23. *Ibid.*, Table 5.

24. *Ibid.*, Table 1.

25. The matter of this paragraph relies chiefly upon G.C. Allen, *A Short Economic History of Modern Japan* (London, 1981), part 1, chs. 9-11 and Appendix B, as well as the sources cited therein.

Editors' Note:

It is with sadness that we report the death of Professor Drummond in the fall of 1994. We remember him with respect and affection.

DIPLOMATIC REVOLUTION IN THE WEST: 1939, THE END OF APPEASEMENT AND THE ORIGINS OF THE SECOND WORLD WAR

Wesley K. Wark
University of Toronto

The image of appeasement, as practised in Europe in the 1930s, has proven a potent rhetorical weapon in postwar debates over the conduct of foreign policy. The use of appeasement — and, equally important, the refusal to use it — is closely linked to conceptions of international morality and proper conduct among states. This point was first made by E.H. Carr in the very midst of appeasement's final crisis, when he talked of the nature of morality in international politics as a heavy burden carried inevitably by the major status quo powers, who must be prepared to enforce their understanding of tolerable behaviour between states. Carr also argued that the moral imperative must be balanced by careful calculation of political realities and national interests.[1]

Despite Carr's plea for an understanding of power and morality as intertwined forces, some subsequent interpretations have attempted to sunder realism and idealism as elements in the outbreak of the Second World War, with profound consequences for our understanding of appeasement. Studs Terkel, for example, has helped popularise the notion of the Second World War as a "good war." At the opposite extreme, Paul Fussell, in his recent book *Wartime*, has argued that the war and its causes were without moral force. In both readings, appeasement 1930s-style is condemned as morally bankrupt. The appeasement analogy, the effort to draw and apply lessons from the 1930s, typically carries with it a strong moral argument; calculations of power and reflections on the nature of foreign-policy decision-making in the period are thereby obscured.[2]

The appeasement analogy has regularly resurfaced since 1939: at the outset of the Cold War, during Vietnam, and most recently during the Persian Gulf crisis of 1990-1991. It is an analogy based on a tempting, but misleading, vision of how appeasement brought catastrophe in the 1930s; as such, it helps define the limits of action in the contemporary world.[3]

Each time appeasement is used in this way it seems natural that historians should think again about myth and reality in the popular notion of appeasement.

The repetitious use of an historical analogy about appeasement as a powerful political weapon in post-1945 international crises, and the indictment of the Second World War, born from the failure of appeasement, as a moral nullity, both rest on an interpretation of British foreign policy in the 1930s that is long overdue for revision. Central to this interpretation is an understanding of appeasement as an essentially static diplomatic process, which the British government, under Neville Chamberlain especially, persisted in right down to the outbreak of war. Persistence in appeasement, against all the evidence of the ambitions and evils of the Nazi regime, is taken as proof of the amorality of the British approach to European political problems in the 1930s. The "guilty man" school of thought about appeasement, derived from these ideas, is the oldest and most tenacious interpretation to influence the historiography of the 1930s.[4]

The appeasement analogy becomes a very different issue if it can be shown that the policy had been largely abandoned, under pressure of events and profound shifts in thinking, well before 3 September 1939. However appropriate the traditional and popular critique of appeasement might be to the policy's earlier days, it is arguably incapable of dealing with a "revolutionised" British foreign policy operating in the crucial period on the eve of the outbreak of the Second World War. In this interpretation, appeasement came to an end in the tumultuous months between September 1938 and September 1939, as a result of revolutionary changes in European politics and in British foreign policy. These changes worked, by stages, to erode the structural foundations of British policy and to shift the major thrust of British diplomacy in Europe from an emphasis on negotiations and peaceful resolution of disputes with the Third Reich, to efforts at deterring Hitler via the construction of encircling diplomatic alliances and vague military threats. In sum, the end of appeasement was evolutionary in its unfolding, revolutionary in its import. Geopolitically, it was centred in Britain, although appeasement was far from being a uniquely British policy.

I. High Hopes at Munich

The place to seek the earliest roots of the collapse of appeasement are at the policy's apogee during the Munich Crisis of 1938. The crisis was one of the most long drawn-out affairs in modern European diplomacy, lasting some seven months, from Hitler's annexation of Austria in March 1938 down to the end of September. As the crisis accelerated, the British government faced, for the first time since 1918, the prospect of being engaged in a major war in Europe. As diplomatic expedients were tried and failed, nerves were stretched to breaking point and beyond. In London, trenches were dug in Hyde Park and gas masks distributed to the populace. The leading proponent of resistance to Germany within the Foreign Office, Sir Robert Vansittart, kept suicide pills and burnt his private papers, as did one of Winston Churchill's confidants, Major Desmond Morton, head of the clandestine Industrial Intelligence Centre.[5] Virginia and Leonard Woolf kept a can of gasoline in their garage, for a suicide pact in the event of a German attack.[6] Baffy Dugdale, a prominent figure in the Zionist campaign and an intimate of many British Cabinet ministers, recorded in her diary her sense of physical nausea and shame throughout the Munich Crisis.[7] The atmosphere was one of increasing war hysteria.[8]

The denouement, when it came, was startlingly swift and unexpected. On 28 September 1938, after Hitler's inflexibility had driven the British as a last resort to mobilization of the Royal Navy in preparation for war, Neville Chamberlain learned that the German Chancellor had agreed to a four-power conference to settle the Sudetenland issue. The arrival of this news produced a moment of tremendous catharsis. The scene in the House of Commons when Hitler's message arrived was described by one back-bench member of parliament, Harold Nicolson, in his diary:

> *"Herr Hitler," he [Chamberlain] said, "has just agreed to postpone his mobilization for twenty-four hours and to meet me in conference with Signor Mussolini and Monsieur Daladier at Munich."*
>
> *That, I think, was one of the most dramatic moments which I have ever witnessed. For a second, the House was hushed in absolute silence. And then the whole House burst into a roar of cheering, since they knew that this might mean peace. That was the end of the Prime Minister's speech, and when he sat down the whole House rose as a man to pay tribute to his achievement.*[9]

As A.J.P. Taylor has delighted in reminding his readers, the Munich Crisis of September 1938 represented the high point of British appeasement.[10] The reason, according to Taylor, is that the Munich settlement stood for all that was best and brightest in British life. It brought blessed peace; it was testimony to rational negotiation of conflict in international relations; it helped wipe away the stain of Versailles Treaty guilt from the collective British soul. Yet Taylor's explanation can be extended far beyond the portrait of Munich as moral fulfilment for the British. The settlement was the apogee of appeasement for two further reasons. Munich was among the most dramatic and emotional moments in European history in the interwar years. Its very drama compelled exaggerated notions of the significance of what had occurred and what might be in store for the future. Secondly, the resolution of the German-Czech dispute seemed to satisfy all the structural components on which the pursuit of appeasement was founded. From the moment that Hitler had come to power, appeasement in its Anglo-German dimension had functioned as a combination of traditional foreign policy pursuits (concern for European stability, the maintenance of peace, and a balance of power) and some unique 1930s considerations (the rise of Fascism, the erosion of the Versailles peace settlement, and the Depression).[11] We can see, in retrospect, a visible architecture for appeasement. The now infamous policy can be understood to have had five building blocks:

1. concern for domestic political consensus and harmony in Britain;
2. maintenance of British national and imperial security;
3. the pursuit of economic prosperity, at home and abroad;
4. a reading of Hitler and Nazism;
5. (unspoken) assumptions about the nature of the international system.

What made the Munich settlement seem so complete a triumph for the British in September 1938 was not simply the wave of emotional relief that swept the country at the avoidance of war, but the fact that Munich seemed to satisfy every one of Britain's fundamental foreign policy needs. Domestic political harmony was secured. The "fearful gamble" of a continental war occurring at a time when British rearmament was far from complete and, coincidentally, when British perceptions of German military power were considerably exaggerated, was successfully avoided. Economic prosperity might finally be achieved, and the Great Depression conquered, if the burden of the arms race could at last be eased. Hitler had emerged as a rational man: a political leader who understood the need to avoid war and solve disputes between states by diplomacy rather than force. Perhaps Hitler had identified with the "moderate" camp in the Nazi state. Perhaps, as with British ambassador Sir Nevile Henderson's portrait, the schizophrenia of the man had been resolved. Finally, the Munich settlement, characterised as it was by a nineteenth-century style of forceful British mediation, showed that a European concert of nations, sharing some fundamental rules about the aims and conduct of international relations, still survived. Ideological blocs, the fear of high Tory statesmen, did not yet divide and set Europe upon itself. Neville Chamberlain dreamed of himself as Disraeli incarnate, returned from the Congress of Berlin to bring "peace with honour." Overcome by the drama of events, he told a crowd in Downing Street that "I believe it is peace for our time."[12]

What Munich was supposed to have satisfied in particular was contained in the document that Chamberlain brought back from Germany at the end of his shuttle diplomacy. This "scrap of paper," often treated as a risible product of Chamberlain's capacity for self-delusion in his dealings with Adolf Hitler, deserves a second look. It contained three short clauses, all drawn up by Chamberlain, and attested by the German Chancellor. The first read "that the question of Anglo-German relations is of the first importance for the two countries and for Europe." The second clause stated that "we regard the agreement signed last night and the Anglo-German Naval Convention [of 1935] as symbolic of the desire of our two peoples never to go to war again." The final clause contained the following expression: "We are resolved that the method of consultation shall be the method adopted to deal with any other questions that may concern our two countries, and we are determined to continue our efforts to remove possible sources of differences and thus contribute to assure the peace of Europe."[13] In summary, Chamberlain's notorious piece of paper attempted to define both the aim and the methods of future Anglo-German diplomacy. The aim was bilateral peace, founded on a recognition of the primacy of importance of Anglo-German relations. The methods to be used to reach this goal were to involve a continuation of summit-level diplomacy on the Munich model. What this piece of paper did, in effect, was to define British diplomatic expectations for the future. The legacy of Munich was the hope that a turning point had been reached in Europe; that brinkmanship need not be employed again and that future crises could be defused by timely applications of diplomatic will. Appeasement looked for smoother sailing ahead.

The Chamberlain document also, it might be argued, gave expression to a moral code of conduct for future Anglo-German relations. This was part of the high expectations that surrounded the future after Munich. It affirmed the like-mindedness of the British and German peoples, stressed peace as the greatest good, and implicitly defined all action outside the sphere of normal diplomacy as inappropriate behaviour.

II. Post-Munich Blues

In the post-Munich period, these expectations, both general and specific, political and moral, quickly proved hollow. None of the anticipated benefits of appeasement emerged. The rules of the game that Chamberlain had attempted to codify with his charter with Hitler were quickly cast into doubt. The British moral code was challenged.

Post-mortems conducted after September 1938 within the service departments and the Foreign Office on the future of British military and political strategy stressed the unacceptable vulnerability of Britain to further German exercises in machtpolitik, the dangers ahead, and the need to rearm at top speed. Donald Lammers comments on the internal Foreign Office review, that "most of these papers ... were punctuated by a powerful sense of indignation at having undergone a humiliating experience and by a strong wish to avoid any repetition of it."[14]

In parallel with the Munich post-mortem, a singular debate continued within the Foreign Office over the respective dangers posed to Britain by the ideological systems of Fascism and Communism. Although characterised by an unwillingness to believe that a state might subordinate national interests to ideological proclivities, this debate nevertheless gave rise to some remarkable sentiments. While a Rome embassy official, Paul Grey, plumped for Communism as the graver ideological menace, Sir Laurence Collier, of the Northern Department, labelled the ideology of Fascism as the true threat. Collier argued that the combination of the Fascist vision of perpetual struggle in world politics, the regimentation of domestic politics necessary to prepare for war, and greater efficiency made states such as Nazi Germany and Italy the main preoccupation of British policy. These Foreign Office reflections never entered the mainstream of Cabinet discussions of British foreign policy, but show yet another way in which the fundamental outlook of appeasement, and in particular its moral code, was being called into question soon after Munich.[15]

Inside the military, similar anxious and questioning sentiments were being expressed. General Pownall, the director of military operations and intelligence at the War Office, wrote in his diary on 3 October 1938: "There is a remarkable degree of agreement throughout the country that we cannot take Hitler's assurances as guaranteeing 'peace in our time.' ... If Hitler's next demand is for Colonies at our expense we must not cave in miserably as Austria and Czechoslovakia had to do for lack of strength to resist."[16] Another assiduous diary keeper, General Ironside, penned a remarkable statement of his anxieties from his post as governor of Gibraltar. On 2 November, Ironside wrote:

> *A most unsatisfactory statement by the Prime Minister as regards his Foreign Policy and Defence. He made it clear that our rearmament was not against Germany. No compulsion and no Ministry of Supply ... What I dislike is the unctuous speeches of men like Halifax trying to explain away our humiliation. They ought to tell the truth ... This ramshackle state [Czechoslovakia] has been dismembered by force. We avoided war, but at the expense of handing over the Czechs to the Germans ...*[17]

The first stage in the unwinding of appeasement was marked not only by internal unease spawned by reflections on the Munich Crisis, but also by troubling foreign developments. The cumulative trend of German policy after Munich quickly tarnished some of the bright hopes expressed in the Chamberlain-Hitler peace pledge. A German press campaign, launched early in October, which openly attacked leading British statesmen as war-mongers and depicted the British as the enemy of the German people, was one such disappointment. The November Vienna award, which led to further territorial diminution of Czechoslovakia, was stage-managed by Germany without any consultation with Britain. The *Kristallnacht* may have alarmed and disgusted the upright Chamberlain. His biographer, Keith Feiling, tells us that Chamberlain wrote private letters denouncing this "barbarity."[18] And in a symbolic action, he declined the honour of being named president of the "Deutsche-Shakespeare-Genossenschaft" because that organization had expelled its Jewish members.[19]

Further, there is the mysterious business of the intercepted German diplomatic communications. In the autumn of 1938 signals intelligence, probably obtained from MI5 wiretaps on the German Embassy in London, apparently contained extremely disobliging remarks about British statecraft and about Chamberlain himself.[20] This material came into the hands of the British Cabinet sometime after Munich. The analogous case of Lord Curzon's emotional response to the contents of signals intelligence depicting perfidy on the part of the French and Soviets in the 1920s suggests the visceral impact that such political decrypts might have had.[21]

If the Fuehrer was in an unaccountably black mood after Munich, and behaving badly, neither was appeasement paying its dividends in terms of a release from the expected pressures of the arms race. Inside the Third Reich, Goering's Luftwaffe was ordered to embark on a five-fold expansion, while the German navy got the go-ahead for its ambitious Z-Plan battlefleet, designed to allow it to challenge the Royal Navy for supremacy of the seas.[22] Signs of armaments acceleration in Germany did not go unnoticed in London and the government braced itself for increased arms spending and a deeper economic commitment to guns instead of butter.[23] As spending on armaments was considered the primary obstacle to the betterment of normal economic relations between Nazi Germany, Europe and Great Britain, hopes for economic appeasement were thus undermined.

The only positive sign on the political horizon after September 1938 was that Hitler did not seem to be pursuing any aggressive intentions in Western Europe. Instead, German aims were rather over-confidently assumed to be centred on Ukraine, owing to the less than clandestine activities of the SS in fomenting troubles in the Carpatho-Ukraine.[24] Confidence in the eastward orientation of German aggression was soon, however, to come to an abrupt end.

By mid-November 1938, the first stage in the slow and painful unwinding of appeasement was essentially complete. Munich post-mortems, intelligence reporting and the force of events all combined to convince the makers of British foreign policy that the high expectations of the Munich settlement were premature, to say the least, and that an alternative policy would need to be formulated. The first manifestations of this new policy, adopted in a meeting of the Cabinet Foreign Policy Committee on 14 November, were scarcely revolutionary.[25] The decision to shift the diplomatic effort to Italy represented merely an adaptation of appeasement, not its abandonment. The same, of course, held true for the agreed-upon measures of faster rearmament and initiation of a covert British propaganda campaign, to counter German vilification of Britain. What was potentially revolutionary about the situation as it was perceived in mid-November 1938 was that the moral code of the Chamberlain-Hitler declaration had apparently been dishonoured by Hitler, who was showing too little interest in Anglo-German friendship, peace, and consultation. Hitler was not acting within the spirit of the declaration. But he had yet to act directly against that spirit with any finality. So long as this remained true, hopes for appeasement's legitimacy remained alive.

III. A Winter of War Scares

In the winter of 1938-1939, Anglo-German relations and the conduct of appeasement entered a new phase, dominated by a series of war scares. These had the effect of further unsettling British foreign policy, accelerating the unwinding of appeasement, and adding a larger burden of questions about the true intent of Hitler. What was most disobliging about the war scares was that they quickly shifted from the anticipated sphere of German interest in the East to rumours of direct action in the West. Christopher Andrew tells us that at least 20 warnings reached Whitehall from secret sources reporting imminent Axis aggression in the period from December 1938 to mid-April 1939.[26] Some were reminiscent of the "bolt from the blue" invasion scares that so affected Britain in the period before 1914. This time, there was no William le Queux stoking the fires of jingoism and alarm; instead it seems likely that at least some of the warnings were stimulated by circles in the Abwehr around Admiral Canaris, who were seeking ways to give Britain a good fright in order to provide a foreign brake on Hitler's adventurous policy.[27] Whatever their true origins, these war scares did indeed give British statesmen a fright. One of the more alarming of the reports came in mid-December 1938 to Ivone Kirkpatrick, on the staff of the British embassy in Berlin. Kirkpatrick trusted his source and brought the report personally, posthaste, to London. It concerned the prospect of a surprise Luftwaffe assault, without any prior declaration of war, on London. The Cabinet responded by stationing anti-aircraft guns in full view of the German Embassy in London, and ordering an investigation of methods for ensuring the air defence of major British centres in peacetime.[28]

The war scare that had the most decided impact on the course of British foreign policy concerned not a direct attack on Britain, but stories of an imminent German descent on Holland. The idea of a German assault on Holland touched strategic nerves. It brought into play the long tradition of British interest in and defence of the Low Countries. It seemed to confirm a pre-conception that Germany would, in any war in the West, inevitably concentrate her forces on a knock-out blow against Britain. Holland was, in this scenario, a form of aircraft carrier for the Luftwaffe, and a harbour mouth for German naval forces. The Holland war scare came at a fertile psychological moment, when exhaustion created by the uncertainties of the post-Munich situation was setting in. A German attack on Holland was not so fantastic that it could be ignored; and British intelligence possessed no other yardstick than plausibility for judging the information that came into its possession about Hitler's plans and intentions. All of these factors help explain why the British authorities were prepared to accept the Dutch war scare. But they are merely the immediate background to the tale of the British response.[29]

Stimulated in large measure by the war scares, a new perception of Adolf Hitler began to take shape in British decision-making circles, one significantly at odds with the old picture of the potentially-moderate statesman conceived within the appeasement framework. During January 1939, Foreign Office, Secret Service and military intelligence sources attained a rare moment of unanimity in their characterisation of a violent Hitler. The SIS viewed Hitler as "scarcely sane" and told the Cabinet so; military intelligence reported Hitler as a "visionary, fanatic and megalamaniac; a being of violent complexes," who was nevertheless capable of choosing the right moment to act, and who held the power to concentrate all the available resources of the totalitarian state once a decision had been reached.[30] Taken literally, the portrait was of a statesman whom appeasement policies could not reach.

Reception of the war scares and intelligence appreciations in Cabinet helped inaugurate the first of two revolutions in British foreign policy that occurred during 1939. Appeasement had lost its bearings. In an effort to anchor a new policy in national security concerns, Britain moved, in late January and early February 1939, away from its traditional "limited liability" stance towards Europe to embrace the first of a series of continental commitments.[31] At the end of January, in a symbolic move in response to the war scare over Holland, the Cabinet agreed that any German aggression against that country would have to be treated as a direct challenge to the security of Britain.[32] In early February, responding to French fears about Italian designs in Spain and on the Pyrenees frontier, the British government pledged itself firmly to the defence of France.[33]

IV. From Appeasement to Deterrence

But the war scares were not yet over, and the re-jigging of British grand strategy had only begun. The next phase in the development of British policy, which lasted between February and April 1939, saw further revolutionary change come over British policy in Europe. Calculations of national security and a quickening moral outrage were to blend together in a new policy of deterrence directed against Germany.

The immediate stimulus behind the adoption of a policy of deterrence was provided by the German occupation of Prague on the wintry morning of 15 March 1939. German action came as an undoubted shock to the British, especially so to British public opinion, which had not been privy to the alarming intelligence available to the government. The force of the shock felt in government circles needs to be carefully delineated. It was not that the government lacked short- or long-term warnings of the likelihood of German action. On this occasion, various branches of British intelligence were able to provide up to four days' advance notice of the German "Einmarsch" against Czechoslovakia.[34] Longer-term warnings of likely German aggression in Eastern Europe, as we have seen, were available in abundance. Nor was the government taken by surprise by the German use of force to achieve its goals. The evidence does not show any surviving preconception in British minds that Germany would restrict itself to a programme of expansion based on the fulfilment of Versailles and German nationalist claims.

The quality of shock inflicted on senior British policy-makers resided, instead, in two features of the situation in March 1939. One was that German action came immediately after a month of relative calm in February — described as "the lull" — which had led more optimistic spirits in the Cabinet to hope that the Third Reich's programme for aggression had been delayed.[35] More importantly, the nature of the German action against Czechoslovakia was a stark and unwelcome confirmation of the warnings contained in political intelligence reports after Munich. The shock was, simply, a product of the fact that unwelcome intelligence had come true with such lightning speed and finality. The inevitable gap between acceptance of intelligence warnings and complete belief was closed by Hitler's action in March.

Lord Halifax expressed the nature of the British government's final conversion in a bitter communication to the German ambassador in London on the day of the German invasion of Czechoslovakia. "I could well understand Herr Hitler's taste for bloodless victories," Halifax remarked, "but one of these days he would find himself up against something that was not bloodless ... The conclusion which everybody in this country and far outside it would draw must be that [the German government] had no great desire to establish good relations with this country, that they were prepared to disregard world opinion and were seeking to establish a position in which they could by force dominate Europe and if possible the world."[36]

The character of Britain's revolutionised grand strategy was shaped by events that followed immediately upon the Prague coup and which left little time for coherent thought or planning. In the wake of the confused military situation that developed as German military forces poured into Czechoslovakia, war scares were soon spawned, featuring rumours of further German assaults on first Roumania, then Poland. The history of these war scares has been treated at length in the existing literature and need not be revisited here.[37] The principal result was that Britain decided to move immediately to attempt to construct an Eastern front of allied states, as a block to further German aggression, even though intelligence assessments gave little support to the notion of imminent German moves. Guarantees were given to Poland on 31 March and, following French pressure, to Roumania on 13 April 1939.

Two principal influences exerted themselves on British foreign policy, as appeasement was finally abandoned and deterrence adopted as the main thrust of British policy. One influence stemmed from the new calculus of the balance of power in Europe described by the chiefs of staff (COS) and the military authorities. The combination of increases in British arms production, especially in aircraft output, and wilful attention paid to potential weaknesses in the German war machine, allowed the military authorities to indulge in cautious expressions of strategic confidence about the ability of Britain and her allies to withstand an initial German attack and prevail in a long war. The most prominent expression given to this new vision of the strategic balance was contained in the COS "European Appreciation" for 1939-40, circulated in late February 1939 and thus available to the government well in advance of decisions reached in March and April.[38]

The COS survey, the most complete accounting of the military balance prepared for the government in 1939, was of such importance because its statement of strategic confidence was in marked contrast to earlier papers that it had prepared in the same series, and because the timing of its appearance was propitious. Greater military confidence opened the way for a revolution in foreign policy by allowing calculations of deterrence to come to the fore and by making expressions of moral outrage and resistance to Nazi Germany appear something other than foolhardy or suicidal.

Political intelligence that had, since Munich, characterised Hitler as a force for evil now, in the spring of 1939, broke through the surface to take its place in both private and official formulations of the right course for

British foreign policy. The impact of this moralistic strain should not be under-estimated. It was at its most powerful in the days immediately after the Prague coup, as a sampling of British political diaries helps reveal. On the 13th of March, General Pownall noted:

> *The next few days are indeed to be critical. This country is thoroughly sick of Hitler and his ways and deeply sympathetic with Chamberlain, who saved the peace in September, at the slap in the face that Hitler has given him and therefore all of us ... This deliberate flaunting of an agreement not six months old and the ruthless power politics of the man are not to be borne. It is a pretty rotten world.*[39]

One week later, the permanent under-secretary at the Foreign Office, Sir Alexander Cadogan, wrote in his diary that the time had come for the prime minister to call a halt to German aggression. "We must have a moral position," Cadogan wrote, "and we shall lose it if we don't do something now."[40] The Foreign Office view of what was to be done coalesced within the last week of March. Cadogan referred to it as "Building a dam in the East." He was far from optimistic about the chances for success of the policy, but was willing to argue its merits on moral grounds. The Eastern front might, Cadogan thought, "act as a deterrent to avert war, though I confess I think the chances of that are rather slight. But on the whole, it is probably the right thing to do."[41] Despite the tribulations that were to come for British policy in the summer of 1939, Cadogan never retreated from this view of the moral soundness of the deterrent/Eastern front strategy.

The British grand strategy that emerged from the shock of March 1939, and the final denunciation through action of the Chamberlain-Hitler pledge of September 1938, were thus rooted in detectable trends in political intelligence reporting and strategic thinking, as well as in the more intangible sense of moral outrage against Hitler and Nazism that had simmered since September 1938 and erupted after the "rape of Prague." The events of March and April 1939 were not altogether, as A.J.P. Taylor wrote, "an underground explosion" of the kind that the historian "cannot trace in precise terms."[42] In fact, we probably owe this strongly-entrenched historiographical wisdom in the first place to Winston Churchill's talent for journalism. In a widely-syndicated column published on 24 March 1939, Churchill wrote an article that he titled "The Crunch." It spoke of the change that had come over British attitudes in the aftermath of Prague:

A veritable revolution in feeling and opinion has occurred in Britain, and reverberates through all the self-governing Dominions ... It was not an explosion, but the kindling of a fire which rose steadily, hour by hour, to an intense furnace heat of inward conviction ... All are united in a resolve to meet the awful danger which threatens the civilisation of the world."[43]

The failure of the Eastern front strategy that Britain adopted in March 1939 has been analysed on many occasions. Historians have noted the weakness of its strategic logic and the unwillingness of the British government to give it any military teeth, especially in the form of economic and military support to the principal unit of the "Eastern dam" — Poland. Equally, attention has been called to the political illogic of the Eastern front strategy. It served to rob British foreign policy of a large degree of independence, by tying London to decisions reached in Warsaw and Berlin. It operated, in effect, as a guarantee of the Soviet Union without any prior negotiation over the Soviet role. Even after the necessity of Soviet participation was recognized, British diplomacy was dilatory and suspicious in its approaches to the Soviet Union. Britain suffered a major intelligence failure in the inability to predict the Nazi-Soviet Pact, and a concurrent security disaster of major proportions in its failure to protect Foreign Office secrets from the activities of freelance traitor Captain King.[44] Perhaps most important, the Eastern front strategy never addressed the issue directly of whether and how Hitler might be deterred from war. Altogether, the Eastern front was, as a recent historian has puzzled out, a psychological "gesture."[45]

But it was a gesture rooted in the necessity of counter-action (stimulated greatly by moral censure) and in the promise of strategic survival. What is most important about the Eastern front was not its failure, which was widely predicted within Whitehall, but its enduring legacy of British military commitment to Europe and moral certainty. Even Neville Chamberlain, who could be optimistic about the chances of deterrence in 1939 and who continued to believe that it was possible to convince Hitler that war was untenable, is proof of this. For what the adoption of the Eastern front did for British grand strategy was to provide an intermediate stage of revolution, between the western continental commitment of January-February 1939, and the declaration of a moral crusade, in September 1939.

V. The Moral Crusade

The very last stage in the unwinding of appeasement thus came with the British justification of war in moral terms in September. For appeasement had been founded on assumptions about the nature of the Nazi regime and the international system that stressed the existence of a concert of nations and the possibilities of rational and peaceful discourse between them that cut across ideological divides. Moral outrage filled the gap left by the destruction of such assumptions. Neville Chamberlain gave heartfelt expression to the new moral crusade in his public broadcast on 3 September announcing the declaration of war: "For it is evil things that we shall be fighting against, brute force, bad faith, injustice, oppression and persecution. And against them I am certain that the right will prevail."[46]

No new political intelligence shaped the moral crusade of September 1939. Rather the previously-digested portraits of Hitler and Nazism, supplied in the fall and winter of 1938-1939, were sustained by their public expression in the media after March 1939. Secret intelligence and public opinion merged in the "war of nerves" of 1939. The British press was one barometer of change. In January 1939, only the irrepressible H.G. Wells, writing for the *News Chronicle*, was moved to call Adolf Hitler a "certifiable lunatic" and to suggest that it would be a "patriotic act" for the Germans to put him away.[47] Mainstream opinion was more nearly expressed by the *Times*, in a leader for the 2nd of January:

> *The total conception of race and state has had certain repercussions, such as the wholesale expulsion of the Jews, which not only affect the interests of other countries, but challenge the general conscience of humanity; and in other ways too, the theories of Fuehrer and Duce, whether intended for export or not, cannot possibly leave foreign countries indifferent, either politically or morally. Yet the instinct is sound that there is in these differences of political creed alone no sane cause for armed conflict.*[48]

But this was to change with the German occupation of Prague on 15 March, and was to change across the entire spectrum of the British press. The *Daily Telegraph* proclaimed, on 16 March that Munich was dead and buried "for who can hope to appease a boa-constrictor." The *Times* was now prepared to bring moral judgement to bear. National Socialism, it commented on 20 March 1939, "has come to mean the expansion of political tyranny, cruel police methods and a new kind of paganism."

Perhaps more ambiguous, but still touching moral sentiment among British readers, J.L. Garvin in the *Observer* likened Hitler to Macbeth.[49]

Neville Chamberlain's famous speech delivered at Birmingham on 17 March 1939, often described as a climacteric, takes on a different shade of meaning in the context of the available secret intelligence and the developing state of public and media opinion. Chamberlain asked whether the occupation of Prague denoted "the end of an old adventure, or the beginning of a new?" Was Hitler's policy, he wondered, "a first step in the direction of an attempt to dominate the world by force?"[50] In terms of the inner development of British foreign policy, the question of the limits of Hitlerian ambitions was a purely rhetorical one. Political intelligence had already supplied the answer, and the government had already acted on such intelligence by, for example, abandoning its policy of limited liability in January. But the public was not apprised of the intelligence on which the government had acted, and Chamberlain's speech, with its air of honest and agonising reappraisal, was designed as part of an effort to educate the public into political realities already long accepted by the government.

Between March and September 1939, while the government's image of the German menace remained relatively stable, the British public's change of heart caught up with, and perhaps surpassed, official policy.[51] Each sustained the other. Publicly-expressed fears that the government might attempt a second "Munich" exasperated the Chamberlain administration and restricted its limits of manoeuvre with respect to European affairs and Anglo-German relations. At the same time, the administration took comfort in the fact that a solid consensus existed in support of British resistance to the Third Reich. Chamberlain himself wrote of "that consensus of moral right, which is impossible for the Germans to feel." He considered that it must be "a tremendous force on our side."[52] Harold Nicolson, in a perceptive pamphlet written shortly after the outbreak of war, argued that fear and morality combined had propelled the country into war. He was aware, he said, that the assertion that the British were fighting both for self-preservation and to "save humanity" would bring a scream of rage to the Fuehrer's lips. But he was certain that world opinion would support the notion that "the Anglo-Saxon Ideal does in fact represent for mankind something higher than the ideals of the rubber truncheon and the concentration camp."[53]

By the time the Poland campaign opened, appeasement was long dead and could not be resurrected, either in response to Hitler's peace feelers in the fall of 1939 or even in the desperate plight in which Britain later found itself in June 1940.[54] A new foreign policy and grand strategy based on, first, hopes for deterrence, and finally on acceptance of the inevitability of war, were now supported by a public feeling of moral rectitude, a sense that Britain had been given a lofty role to play in the defence of civilisation and the purging of Nazism.

Between September 1938 and September 1939 the basic structural foundations of appeasement policy had been destroyed and a new set of concepts, often born in crisis, had replaced them. In part, the scale of the revolution in British foreign policy that ensued during these months can be measured by the distance between old and new thinking. Let us reconsider appeasement's "building blocks," mentioned earlier in this paper, in this light. Concern for domestic political harmony in Britain, especially the fear that Britain might find itself at war without popular support and faced by a pacifist and divided public, was overturned by a new mood of popular belligerence towards the Third Reich. From feeling constrained in their diplomatic options towards Germany by an uncertain and isolationist public before Munich, the government was eventually to feel itself, in some ways, the prisoner of strong expectations that Britain would stand up to Hitler in 1939.

Calculations of national and imperial security before and during the Munich Crisis had uniformly stressed the unreadiness of Britain's peacetime forces for a major conflict with any combination of such potential enemies as Germany, Italy and Japan. However, the new calculus of the balance of power, arrived at in the early months of 1939, changed the picture by substituting strategic optimism for the previous gloom of worst-case assessments. Part of this effect was achieved by the mutual reassurance that was engaged in by Britain and France after February 1939, as each partner in the emerging anti-Hitler Western bloc found itself needing to take comfort from the supposed military strengths of the other. Thus the British came to believe in the capabilities of the Maginot Line and the French army; while the military command of France looked to the imponderables of British naval and air power and the hoped-for revival of Kitchener-sized armies.[55]

With respect to the economic calculations that had underpinned appeasement, these were simply given up for lost in the period after Munich. The notions that the arms race could be slowed down by diplomatic triumphs and that the Third Reich could be reintegrated, to the benefit of all, in a normalised European economic structure, were abandoned. In their place, no new economic doctrine emerged. In fact, British authorities remained divided on the economic implications of the new diplomacy of 1939. The Treasury argued that Britain was coming close to financial collapse in its spending on arms; but the government, led by the previously parsimonious Neville Chamberlain, simply affirmed the need to keep on spending at unprecedented levels.[56]

The portrait of Hitler that had legitimised appeasement until September 1938, a portrait that had stressed his role as a potential moderate balanced between competing wings of the Nazi Party was, as we have seen, completely repainted.[57] Instead Hitler emerged as the monster, the extremist, the wild man of the Nazi party. His newly-revealed character made appeasement literally impossible, while casting uncomfortable doubt on the likely success of alternative policies. Finally, and most intangibly, the reigning ideas held in Britain about the nature of the international system were revolutionised after September 1938. Gone was the notion that the European system of states was a functional entity in which mutual toleration of survival and rights would provide the framework for political revision and peaceful settlement. Instead, a new understanding took hold that the system contained a pariah state, one whose leadership, at the very least, would have to be removed by force, before peace and tranquillity could be assured.[58]

If the concept of a revolution in British foreign policy during 1938-1939 is accepted, the old static model of appeasement as a persistent force in British diplomacy down to the bitter end on 3 September 1939, and perhaps beyond, must be dispensed with. What are the consequences for the use of appeasement as an historical analogy? Everything becomes more slippery and complex. But this was noted long ago, by one of appeasement's most prescient critics, E.H. Carr.[59] Carr argued, as early as 1939, that British foreign policy between Versailles and the attack on Poland never remotely achieved the necessary balance of idealist and realist calculations. The tragedy would appear to be that British policy was indeed groping its way towards just such a balance in the period 1938-1939. But this progress was rendered futile by its timing, by the nature of the enemies that Britain confronted, by lack of hard thinking about just what deterrence required, and above all by the unfortunate dislocation of British (or Anglo-French) and Soviet responses to Hitler. In the end it was no use having a diplomatic revolution in the West underway in 1939, when

Soviet foreign policy proceeded to revolutionise itself in the opposite direction by abandoning collective security just as the West embraced it, and choosing for appeasement, ultimately signalled by the Ribbentrop-Molotov Pact of 23 August 1939, just as Britain abandoned its efforts in this direction.

If appeasement and its contribution to the origins of the Second World War must be used as an historical analogy, and it probably must, this paper suggests that the more illuminating links between the 1930s and the present conduct of international relations are to be found in the difficulties of managing the balance between idealism and realism in foreign policy, the complexities of controlling revolutionary changes in a state's diplomacy, and the importance of accurate perceptions of the nature and aims of foreign states. None of this is nearly as satisfying as the old bogey of appeasement, but it may be closer to the truth. The 1939 analogy rests ultimately on recognition of the difficulties of confronting strong revisionist powers rather than on the old tale of a diplomacy of resistance never tried.

NOTES

1. E.H. Carr, *The Twenty Years Crisis, 1919-1939* (London, 1939).
2. Paul Fussell, *Wartime: Understanding and Behaviour in the Second World War* (New York, 1989).
3. Ernest May discusses the uses of this, and other historical analogies, in *Lessons of the Past: The Use and Misuse of History in American Foreign Policy* (New York, 1973).
4. For accounts of the historiographical development of appeasement studies, see D.C. Watt, "Appeasement: The Rise of a Revisionist School?" *Political Quarterly*, 36 (1965), 191-213; and his "The Historiography of Appeasement," in Alan Sked and Chris Cook, eds., *Crisis and Controversy: Essays in Honour of A.J.P. Taylor* (London, 1976). For a reconsideration of the "guilty man" approach, see the essay by Sidney Aster, "'Guilty Men': The Case of Neville Chamberlain," in Robert Boyce and Esmonde M. Robertson, eds., *Paths to War: New Essays on the Origins of the Second World War* (London, 1989).
5. For Vansittart, see Norman Rose, *Vansittart: Study of a Diplomat* (London, 1978); for Morton, see R.W. Thompson, *Churchill and Morton* (London, 1976). The Morton story was confirmed for me by Morton's heir.
6. Quentin Bell, *Virginia Woolf: A Biography* (London, 1972), 216.
7. Norman Rose, ed., *"Baffy": The Diaries of Blanche Dugdale, 1936-1947* (London, 1973).

8. See Robert Kee, *Munich: The 11th Hour* (London, 1988) for a portrait of this time drawn from many sources; also the interesting essay on Munich by David Clay Large, *Between Two Fires: Europe's Path in the 1930s* (New York, 1990).

9. Nigel Nicolson, ed., *Harold Nicolson: Diaries and Letters, 1930-1939* (London, 1966), entry for 28 September 1938.

10. A.J.P. Taylor, *The Origins of the Second World War*, 2nd ed. (London, 1963).

11. The best summary account of appeasement policy is contained in Paul Kennedy, *The Realities behind Diplomacy: Background Influences on British External Policy 1865-1980* (London, 1981); see also the argument in Kennedy, "The Tradition of Appeasement in British Foreign Policy, 1865-1939," *British Journal of International Studies*, 2 (1976), 195-215. D.C. Watt, *How War Came: The Immediate Origins of the Second World War, 1938-1939* (London, 1989) is now the premier study of the outbreak of the Second World War.

12. Quoted in Keith Feiling, *The Life of Neville Chamberlain* (London, 1946), 381.

13. *Ibid.*

14. Donald Lammers, "From Whitehall after Munich: The Foreign Office and the Future Course of British Policy," *The Historical Journal*, XVI, 4 (1973), 850.

15. Donald Lammers, "Fascism, Communism and the Foreign Office, 1937-39," *Journal of Contemporary History*, 6 (1971), 66-86.

16. Brian Bond, ed., *Chief of Staff: The Diaries of Lieutenant-General Sir Henry Pownall*, Vol. 1: *1933-1940* (London, 1972), 164.

17. Colonel R. Macleod and Denis Kelly, eds., *The Ironside Diaries 1937-1940* (London, 1962), 70.

18. Feiling, 390.

19. *Ibid.*

20. The evidence is referred to in "Notes on Conversations with Sir Alexander Cadogan and Lord Halifax, Nov-Dec 1951," Templewood XIX/5, Templewood Papers (Sir Samuel Hoare), Cambridge University Library. The case is discussed by D.C. Watt, "British Intelligence and the Coming of the Second World War in Europe," in Ernest May, ed., *Knowing One's Enemies: Intelligence Assessment before the Two World Wars* (Princeton, 1984), 247.

21. For Curzon and secret intelligence, see Christopher Andrew, *Secret Service: The Making of the British Intelligence Community* (London, 1985), and the essay on Curzon as foreign secretary by Keith Jeffery and Alan Sharp in Andrew and Noakes, eds., *Intelligence and International Relations* (London, 1987).

22. German rearmament programmes are discussed in the excellent work by Wilhelm Deist, *The Wehrmacht and German Rearmament* (London, 1981). For details on the Z-Plan fleet, see Charles S. Thomas, *The German Navy in the Nazi Era* (London, 1990).

23. See N.H. Gibbs, *Grand Strategy,* Vol. 1: *Rearmament Policy* (London, 1976) for details of British rearmament policy after September 1938. The Air Ministry responded to evidence of accelerated Luftwaffe growth by submitting its "Plan M," significant for its concentration on production for fighter defences, C[abinet] P[aper] 218(38), 25 Oct. 1938, Public Record Office, Kew, England (hereafter PRO), Cabinet Records (hereafter CAB) 24/279.

24. On political developments in the troubled region of the Carpatho-Ukraine in late 1938, see Watt, *How War Came,* 59-61.

25. FP(36) 32nd mtg., 14 November 1938, CAB 27/624.

26. Christopher Andrew, *Secret Service: The Making of the British Intelligence Community* (London, 1985), 414.

27. Professor Watt makes this case in his essay in May, *Knowing One's Enemies,* 248.

28. Ivone Kirkpatrick, *The Inner Circle* (London, 1959), 139.

29. For the development of the Holland war scare, see Wesley K. Wark, *The Ultimate Enemy: British Intelligence and Nazi Germany 1933-1939* (Ithaca, 1985), 113-4; and Sidney Aster, *1939: The Making of the Second World War* (London, 1973).

30. Secret Service and Foreign Office images of Hitler were summarized in an influential paper for the Cabinet, FP(36) 74, 19 January 1939, CAB 27/627. Similar War Office views are found in "Note on Germany's Present Position and Future Aims," 17 January 1939, PRO, War Office Records (hereafter WO) 190/745.

31. This development is accorded excellent treatment by Michael Howard, *The Continental Commitment: The Dilemma of British Defence Policy in the Era of Two World Wars* (London, 1972) and Brian Bond, *British Military Policy between the Two World Wars* (Oxford, 1980), ch. 10.

32. FP(36) 36 mtg., 26 January 1939, CAB 27/624.

33. Great Britain, House of Commons, *Debates,* 6 February 1939; D. Dilks, ed., *The Diaries of Sir Alexander Cadogan* (London, 1971), entry for 6 February 1939.

34. Cadogan mentions warnings supplied by both MI6 and MI5. Kell, chief of MI5, provided the first alarm on 11 March, beating out the SIS by a few hours. See *ibid.,* entries for 11, 12 and 14 March 1939.

35. Wark, 218-9.

36. *Documents on British Foreign Policy,* ser. III, vol. VII, 270-2.

37. See Aster, *1939*; Simon Newman, *March 1939: The British Guarantee to Poland* (Oxford, 1976); Wark, 116-9.

38. COS 843, "European Appreciation 1939-40," 20 February 1939, CAB 53/45; its genesis is discussed at length in Wark, 211-24.

39. *Pownall Diaries,* 193.

40. *Cadogan Diaries,* entry for 20 March 1939.

41. *Ibid.*, entry for 26 March 1939.

42. Taylor, 251.

43. Reprinted in Winston Churchill, *Step by Step 1936-1939* (London, 1939), 328.

44. The Foreign Office's post-mortem on the failure to predict the Nazi-Soviet pact is in a memorandum by Laurence Collier, 26 August 1939, N4146, PRO, Foreign Office Records (hereafter FO) 371/23686. On King, see the article by D.C. Watt, "Captain Herbert King and the Foreign Office," *Intelligence and National Security*, 3 (October 1988).

45. Anita Prazmowska, *Britain, Poland and the Eastern Front, 1939* (Cambridge, 1987).

46. Quoted in Feiling, 416.

47. For this account of newspaper coverage of Germany in 1939, I am indebted to the work of Franklin Gannon, *The British Press and Germany 1936-1939 (Oxford, 1971); News Chronicle*, 2 and 3 January 1939; the articles sparked a vigorous protest from the German ambassador, see *Documents on German Foreign Policy*, ser. D, vol. IV, doc. 290.

48. *The Times*, 2 January 1939.

49. Garvin, *The Observer*, 27 August 1939, 10.

50. Quoted in Feiling, 400.

51. For all that has been written on appeasement, we still lack a thorough study of British public opinion in 1938-1939.

52. Feiling, 418.

53. Harold Nicolson, *Why Britain is at War* (London, 1939), 137.

54. For the debate over the survival of appeasement in certain British circles after September 1939, see David Reynolds, "Churchill and the British Decision to Fight on in 1940: Right Policy, Wrong Reasons," in Richard Langhorne, ed., *Diplomacy and Intelligence during the Second World War: Essays in Honour of F.H. Hinsley* (Cambridge, 1985), 147-67; and Peter W. Ludlow, "The Unwinding of Appeasement," in Lothar Kettenacker, ed., *Das 'Andere Deutschland' im Zweiten Weltkrieg: Emigration und Widerstand in Internationaler Perspective* (Stuttgart, 1977).

55. See Martin S. Alexander, "The Fall of France, 1940," *The Journal of Strategic Studies*, 13 (March 1990), 10-44, for a review of the literature and evidence.

56. For the economic debate in 1939, see George Peden, *British Rearmament and the Treasury, 1932-1939* (Edinburgh, 1979); R.A.C. Parker, "Economics, Rearmament and Foreign Policy: The United Kingdom before 1939," *Journal of Contemporary History*, 10 (October 1975), 637-47; and Paul Shay, *British Rearmament in the Thirties: Politics and Profits* (Princeton, 1977).

57. For the best short account of this image of Hitler as moderate, see C.A. MacDonald, "Economic Appeasement and the German Moderates, 1937-1939," *Past and Present*, 56 (1972), 105-35.

58. D.C. Watt, "The European Civil War," in Wolfgang J. Mommsen and Lothar Kettenacker, eds., *The Fascist Challenge and the Policy of Appeasement* (London,1983) discusses the problems posed for Britain by the Third Reich's "national solipsism."

59. See Carr's *Twenty Years Crisis.*

THE NAZI-SOVIET PACT: A REVOLUTION IN THE EAST?

George Urbaniak
Wilfrid Laurier University

Half a century of scholarship has produced an impressive body of literature on the Nazi-Soviet Pact of 23 August 1939. Many important observations about the significance of the pact have emerged. For both Nazi Germany and the Soviet Union, the pact removed the threat of total encirclement and two-front war. It made nonsense of Poland's policy of maintaining "equidistance" between its more powerful neighbours. It obliterated the balance of power and placed the Baltic States at the mercy of aggressors. It pulled the rug from under the Western democracies because it ruined their plans for a multi-tiered alliance system in Eastern Europe. The pact annulled the Franco-Soviet Mutual Assistance Pact, the Polish Soviet Non-Aggression Pact, and the anti-Comintern Pact. It undermined the British policy of blockade and shattered the American policy of separating the two European territorial giants. In short, it freed the jackboots of both Nazi Germany and the Soviet Union to trample Eastern Europe and world peace. Not unnaturally, the diplomatic revolution symbolized by the Nazi-Soviet agreement has widely been excoriated as a "devil's pact" and an "unholy alliance."[1]

Two aspects of the Nazi-Soviet Pact have engendered considerable controversy: first, the motivations of the two contracting parties in signing the pact; and second, the reaction of the first apparent victim, Poland. A fresh evaluation to clarify persistent misunderstandings about the pact can be attempted on the basis of newly-released Soviet and other untapped archival sources.[2] These sources permit a more refined interpretation that better accommodates the complexities of the past. The new evidence shows that the path from assumed causes to purported effects twists more tortuously than previously imagined. It suggests that many arguments used to explain the significance of the Nazi-Soviet Pact rest on a *post hoc ergo propter hoc* fallacy.

Nazi Germany and Soviet Russia had contradictory aims in signing the Nazi-Soviet Pact. The Nazis used it primarily to intimidate the Allies and to isolate their quarry, Poland. The Soviets had in mind a general European war between the Nazis and the West, with themselves on the sidelines reaping the benefits. These divergent aims prompted the two signatories to work at cross-purposes in the days immediately following the announcement of the pact. The partners enjoyed no honeymoon.[3] Early misunderstanding caused diplomatic tiffs which created confusion among international observers. These events show that the Nazi-Soviet Pact did not, in itself, contain a clearcut program for future German-Soviet cooperation. Instead, it was the interreaction of events and institutions after the signing which determined the course of Nazi-Soviet relations.

Historians have been particularly diligent in uncovering the roots of the pact.[4] They appear to have found the basic factors which initiated the rapprochement. The Soviet Union had surreptitiously wooed Germany throughout the mid-1930s even when the former ostensibly supported collective security and had a Jew, Maxim Litvinov, as its foreign commissar. The evidence clearly shows that the Russians had made periodic overtures to the Germans for serious talks.[5] The memoirs of Walter G. Krivitsky, a Soviet spy who defected to the West in 1939, link these low-level contacts with Stalin's own personal ambitions.[6]

Two signals directly from Stalin in the spring of 1939 made a particular impression in Germany. On 10 March, Stalin made a speech to the Eighteenth Congress of the Communist Party. He denounced *inter alia* the Western powers for attempting to provoke a war between the Soviet Union and Germany. In a famous declaration, Stalin declined to be the monkey "to pull the chestnuts out of the fire for the Western powers."[7] Even more significantly, on 4 May he dismissed Maxim Litvinov, and replaced him with Viacheslav Molotov, later described by Winston Churchill as the perfect modern robot.[8] Molotov, when accepting his new office, accused Litvinov of "anti-fascist agitation."[9]

The Germans readily received these signals. Count Friedrich Werner von der Schulenburg, the russophile German ambassador in Moscow, actively supported the idea of a Russo-German entente. As early as 1938, Schulenburg had stated that he personally favoured a rapprochement, but feared that any open suggestions would receive a reprimand from the Fuehrer.[10] However, his pro-Soviet reports struck a responsive chord with Joachim von Ribbentrop, the Nazi foreign minister, who pointed out the benefits of a Soviet alliance to a skeptical Hitler.[11] Robert Coulondre, the French ambassador at Berlin in 1939, corroborated Ribbentrop's testimony to this effect at his Nuremberg trial, claiming that Ribbentrop had personally been instrumental in reorienting German policy towards the Soviet

Union.[12] Wolfgang Michalka, a German historian, has argued that the Nazi-Soviet Pact marked the ultimate testimony to Ribbentrop's anti-British bias.[13]

The ultimate decision for the pact rested with Adolf Hitler. Hitler rebuffed the approaches of the Soviets until March 1939 when the Poles once and for all rejected Germany's overtures for an alliance against the Soviet Union.[14] The British government, after Hitler's *coup* in Prague, appeared to endorse Poland's obstinate policy with the Polish guarantee of 31 March 1939. These developments left Hitler little choice but to re-evaluate his options in the East and view the Soviet Union in a different light.[15]

In his letter to Stalin on 20 August, three days before the signing of the pact, he suggested that the tension between Poland and Germany had become unbearable and that the Reich would begin to look after its own interests with all the means at its disposal. Poland's "insolence" invited German cooperation with the Soviets so that Hitler could launch his scheduled invasion of Poland in relative security.[16] "I have knocked the weapon out of the hands of this gentry [England and France] and manoeuvred Poland into a position where our military victory is assured," Hitler boasted to his generals on the morning of 22 August 1939.[17] Communicating with Mussolini a few days after the signing of the pact, Hitler added the Japanese refusal of a general alliance against England as a primary cause.[18] Finally, in a speech on 22 June 1941, the day of the Nazi attack on the Soviet Union, Hitler explained to the party faithful that he had tactically reversed his ideological anti-Bolshevik direction to rupture the British encirclement of Germany.[19]

Hitler's decision had a grander ideological purpose. He evidently saw the Soviet pact as a step in his grandiose programme of "world domination."[20] German scholars have collected Hitler's pronouncements on "world domination" and attempted to show that they form not mere propaganda but a cohesive foreign policy program. Andreas Hillgruber and Klaus Hildebrand most clearly apply this method to the Nazi-Soviet Pact.[21] Critics point to the vagueness of the notion of "world dominion" and argue that the looser concept of "expansion without object" better suits the ethos of Nazism.[22] But Hitler does provide grist for the "world domination" view. When he heard that Stalin had agreed to Ribbentrop's visit to Moscow, he exclaimed: "I have the world in my pocket."[23] On hearing that the pact had actually been signed, he hammered his fists against a wall and shouted: "Now Europe is mine. The others can have Asia."[24]

Soviet motives cannot be ascertained so easily in the absence of copious documentation. In the popular mind, Molotov is sometimes seen as the real force behind the accord with the Germans. On the evening that Ribbentrop signed the Nazi-Soviet Pact, a popular legend in Russia recounts that Stalin invited a certain Khrapchenko, president of the Arts Committee, to accompany Stalin, Molotov, and Ribbentrop to the Bolshoi theatre. Stalin allegedly told Khrapchenko privately that he had just signed an alliance with the Germans. Khrapchenko appeared dumbstruck. Stalin added, "Like you, Comrade Khrapchenko, I am against an alliance with Hitler but he (pointing to Molotov) forced me into it."[25] The anecdote is no doubt apocryphal because Ribbentrop had no time during his brief stay in Moscow for a night at the opera. Nevertheless, the recently-released evidence reveals Molotov as adept in manipulating Soviet-German discussions.[26] But both Lavrenti Beria, the head of the secret police *(OGPU)* and Klimenti Voroshilov, the defence commissar, probably played more significant roles in convincing Stalin of the merits of the pact.[27]

Historians have attributed both "offensive" and "defensive" motivations to Stalin. George Kennan ranks as the major exponent of the "offensive" school. In his *Memoirs* he wrote, "the men in the Kremlin have never abandoned their faith in the program of territorial and political expansion which had once commended itself so strongly to Tsarist diplomats, and which underlay the German Russian Nonaggression Pact of 1939."[28] The "defensive" view has been well articulated by Lord Beloff in his essay on Soviet appeasement. "The Ribbentrop-Molotov pact of August 1939 with its secret protocols was thus fully in line with Soviet policy at the time when the army purges of the past two years made it more than ever unthinkable for the Soviet Union willingly to accept the idea of war against a major power."[29] Such interpretations are rarely incompatible and often complementary. Stalin wished to avoid war with major powers and yet profit at the expense of lesser neighbours.

Stalin's own explanations might provide some clues about his motives for signing the Nazi-Soviet Pact. On 3 July 1941, after surviving an attempted *coup* in the aftermath of the Nazi attack, Stalin tried to justify his signing of the agreement with "cannibals" like Hitler and Ribbentrop. Stalin claimed that the pact permitted the Soviet Union a breathing space of one-and-a-half years to prepare its defenses.[30] Yet, on the faulty advice of his sycophantic commanders, he did little to breathe life into his armed forces.[31] In August 1942, Stalin told Churchill that he had signed the Nazi-Soviet Pact because he did not believe that the peace front of Britain,

France and the Soviet Union could restrain Hitler.[32] He evidently meant that he could not be sure that the British and French would stick by their Polish allies. He apparently knew that Hitler had determined to destroy Poland well in advance of the pact. In August 1939, Stalin suspected that the West might sacrifice Poland in a "second Munich."[33]

Stalin's explanations, however, appear to be at odds with the evidence from August 1939. In particular, two documents leaked from the politburo in August 1939 suggest a bolder interpretation. Late on 19 August, a special session of the Politburo and the leading members of the Russian section of the Comintern took place. Stalin argued that the Nazi-Soviet Pact would lead to a European war and that it did not matter whether the Allies or Germany won. If the Allies won, and Stalin believed that they had sufficient strength to prevail, they would occupy Berlin and destroy Germany without cost to the Red Army. In the process, Stalin argued, the Allies would be completely debilitated. France, in particular, would be completely undermined by attrition and would succumb to Soviet revolution. If Germany won, then it would be enfeebled to a degree that would make an attack on the Soviet Union impossible for a decade. Stalin concluded:

> *I repeat that it is of interest for war to break out between the Reich and the Anglo-French bloc. It is essential for us that this war lasts as long as possible, so that the two parties weaken. It is for this reason that we should accept the pact proposed by the Germans and work so that ... we will be prepared for the moment when the war ends.*

The audience listened reverently to Stalin's speech and accepted his reasoning without discussion.[34]

At a meeting of the Politburo the following night, discussion revolved about the possible reactions in the Soviet Union to the announcement of the Nazi-Soviet Pact. The Politburo approved Molotov's speech to the fourth session of the Supreme Soviet, which would be published to satisfy the masses. The Western Allies, the speech argued, wished to provoke a war between Nazi Germany and the Soviet Union while Germany asked only for the USSR's neutrality. The Politburo feared that such a simple explanation might not satisfy the doctrinaire communists who would view the agreement with Germany as a deviation from the established party line. The Politburo therefore approved the urgent preparation of an explanatory text in the form of a dialogue.

A copy of this revolutionary catechism fell into the hands of the Lithuanian legation in Moscow, which leaked it to the United States military attaché. He in turn slipped this important document to his British counterpart in Riga on the condition that no one outside his legation could see it. The contents of the document soon became widely known. The Polish military attaché in Kaunas, and numerous other diplomats, verified the sources.[35] As a result, the authenticity of the document appears to be well established.

The document deserves quotation because it presents the clearest rationale for the USSR's decision to sign the Pact:

> *Have the basic aims of the Comintern changed? No, as formerly the purpose of the work of the Comintern is to bring about world revolution. Is a world revolution possible now? No, all efforts to activate a revolution have been unsuccessful ... What are the natural conditions for revolution? A prolonged war ... Is the war in the interests of the Comintern? Yes! ... Would the pact between the USSR and England and France hasten the outbreak of war? No, since a union of the allies with the U.S.S.R. would cause Germany to refrain from military adventure. Would a pact between the U.S.S.R. and Germany hasten the outbreak of war? Yes, with the U.S.S.R. in the position of a neutral, Germany would be able to carry through its plans. What would happen if the U.S.S.R. would conclude a pact with neither side? Until the U.S.S.R. says what it is going to do, a peaceful solution to the conflict is always possible. What must therefore be the position of the U.S.S.R. to hasten world revolution? Assist Germany enough so that she will begin war, and have Moscow take measures to assure that this war will drag on.*[36]

Stalin justified the Nazi-Soviet Pact because it would recreate the preconditions that led to the Bolshevik Revolution of 1917. Ultimately, his decision rested on the Leninist doctrine that conflict between capitalist states should be exploited for the benefit of socialism.[37]

The Hitler-Stalin pact differed in two ways from the usual non-aggression pacts that the Soviet Union had signed. Unlike previous settlements, this agreement would come into effect from the moment of signature, and not upon ratification. Hitler happily traded space for time: when the Soviets asked for the two small Baltic ports of Libau and Windau to be included in their sphere of influence, Hitler quickly agreed.[38] Also unlike previous settlements, the August agreement permitted an attack on a third party without annulling the pact. The Soviets conveniently defended themselves from their critics by indicating that the Polish-German non-aggression pact of 1934 and the Anglo-German non-aggression pact of 1939 had similar provisions. The world did not miss the significance of these terms.[39]

From the shadows of the secret negotiations, sufficient information leaked abroad about the clauses of the treaty to prompt observers to pose some probing questions. Did the Nazi-Soviet Pact fundamentally change the foreign policies of the two signatories? Would it entail the partition of Eastern Europe? Did the agreement actually constitute a pact of aggression, and would the Soviet Union automatically join a military alliance with Nazi Germany once war erupted? The available evidence suggests that not even the signatories had clear answers to these questions.

Newspaper reaction varied. In Germany, the captive press described the Nazi-Soviet "Non-Aggression and Consultation Pact" as a great diplomatic achievement. Germans awoke on 23 August 1939 to learn that a new European order had been born. The newspapers heralded the pact as a return to the Bismarckian traditions of friendship with Russia for mutual profit and the rout of the encircling powers.[40] The Nazi Propaganda Ministry and the Foreign Office claimed, for their part, that the agreement entailed much more than a non-aggression pact. These institutions apprised Western dignitaries that the agreement prepared the way for the demise of Poland, with the return of some disputed regions to Germany and Russia.[41] The Germans clearly intended these declarations to intimidate Poland's allies into abandoning that country by exaggerating the significance of the pact. Hitler preferred to wage a localized war against an isolated Poland, but he would risk a European war if necessary.

In the Soviet Union, the state-controlled press adopted a more cautious approach. Soviet newspapers initially refrained from direct comment on the Nazi-Soviet Pact, instead reproducing articles from the foreign press depicting the agreement as a triumph for Soviet diplomacy.[42] Yet Soviet diplomats unanimously claimed that the pact entailed no change in Soviet policy. The Soviet leadership carefully guarded its freedom of action.[43] Molotov himself told the French ambassador in Moscow that the Nazi-Soviet Pact did not annul the Soviet-French Pact because the latter did not constitute an alliance.[44] Voroshilov insisted that Western delegates in Moscow could influence the future course of Nazi-Soviet relations by continuing the military conversations.[45] As a symbol of the low priority the

Soviets assigned to the pact, they placed its ratification at the bottom of the daily agenda on 30 August.

The different German and Soviet perceptions of the agreement can be explained in terms of their interpretations of the secret protocol attached to the pact. Ostensibly, it divided Eastern Europe into "spheres of influence," which have frequently been understood simply as a euphemism for "partitions."[46] Dr. Papirnik, a Czech journalist with well-placed connections in the Soviet Politburo, argued on the basis of information from Nikita Khrushchev that the Soviet Union had every intention of annexing Eastern Poland.[47] Yet in the actual negotiations the Soviets left themselves an escape hatch. According to American sources in Moscow, who were being fed information by Hans "Johnny" Herwarth (the second secretary in the German Embassy in Moscow), Soviet negotiators did distinguish between "spheres of influence" and territorial partition.[48] In fact, the Soviets argued that they could not be certain of actual frontiers because of the uncertainty of future developments. Both sides agreed to further consultation and to the principle of full compensation for any territorial rearrangement. Even during the September campaign, Hitler stated that the territorial shape of Poland depended on its behaviour during the war.[49] In effect, both signatories agreed to postpone any discussions of partition until the situation became clearer.

The same reason led the signatories to postpone any detailed discussion of alliance. For one thing, it remained uncertain whether a military alliance would be necessary. Hitler thought poorly of the Red Army and did not allow it to influence his calculations. Nor did the haste of negotiations allow for the formation of an explicit military alliance. Shortly after the announcement of the pact, a Russian official in Berlin insisted that in the event of a flagrant attack on Poland, Russia might align itself against Germany.[50] Not until after the outbreak of war with Poland did a Soviet military mission arrive in Berlin to coordinate strategy. When German sources imputed that the mission intended to negotiate a German-Russian alliance, the Russian delegation displayed considerable resentment and issued a denial.[51]

It is not surprising, given the Soviet Union's restrained behaviour, that Molotov complained about "the wiseacres who construe from the pact more than is written."[52] Soviet diplomats abroad were kept in the dark during the negotiation of the pact, but it does not appear, as David Dallin has written, that "Moscow completely misjudged European events."[53] Caution more than perfidy motivated the Soviet Union in late August 1939.[54] In playing for high stakes it tried to hedge its bets. Soviet leaders not only held back from total commitment to Germany but they also kept open the lines of communication to the West. Perhaps they genuinely feared a backlash from the Soviet people, who had eagerly supported an alliance with the West. As a result, they refrained from actions which would discourage the West from confronting Germany over Poland. In that way, they hoped to incite world revolution. The Soviets proffered the mirage of help to the West only to entrap them in a war with Germany.

In the week after the signing of the Nazi-Soviet Pact, the Soviet Union gave Poland two assurances. First of all, the Soviet ambassador in Warsaw, Nikolai Sharanov, used the pretext of a minor frontier incident to assure the Polish foreign minister, Jozef Beck, that the non-aggression agreement would not alter Moscow's relations with Warsaw.[55] Second, Marshal Voroshilov promised to give Poland economic assistance in the event of a Polish-German war.[56] What was behind these promises? In one scenario, the illusion of aid from the Soviet Union might buttress Poland's resolve to resist Germany. Poland's intransigence would then activate the Anglo-French guarantees to Poland and start the European war that Stalin desired. In an alternate scenario, the West might renege on its obligations to Poland. Such a development might possibly make the offers of economic aid genuine. In the event of a localized German war against Poland, the Soviets would not want German forces sweeping through Poland and standing virtually undiminished on their border. They would surely become Hitler's next victims. Their interests might best be served by aiding Poland materially to prolong the conflict. The Soviet Union could not afford to burn its bridges to Poland entirely.

Jozef Beck had intimate knowledge of both German and Soviet intentions *vis-à-vis* Poland through his intelligence network and remained unperturbed by news of the agreement. He never counted on Soviet help and therefore the Nazi-Soviet Pact made no difference to him. He thought that the pact had been poorly timed by the Soviets because they could not lay the blame for the collapse of military talks with the West at Poland's doorstep. He even joked that Ribbentrop would soon discover the measure of his patience in dealing with the Soviets.[57] Beck stated openly that he believed Nazi-Soviet collusion against Poland would be limited because the Soviet Union would not wish to be an immediate neighbour of the Reich.[58] Nevertheless, Beck understood the real significance of the Nazi-Soviet Pact. He wrote to Count Edward Raczynski, his London ambassador: "It is evidence of the Soviet double game not to commit itself to either of the groupings of bourgeois states but instead to look favourably on the outbreak of a European war."[59]

Beck's ambassadors kept him well informed of developments. Waclaw Grzybowski in Moscow had the clearest understanding of the deal. The ambassador wrote on 29 August that he had become convinced of the "ambivalence of the pact and its purely tactical advantages." He continued: "It also appears that the pact does not prejudge the actions of the Soviets in the event of conflict and it is only the starting point for further maneuver." Grzybowski discounted reports in the Italian Press (based on German sources) that Poland would have an Eastern front.[60] Rzczynski wrote in his memoirs that he viewed the Ribbentrop-Molotov Pact from the outset as a prelude to the fourth partition of Poland and expected the worst at any moment.[61] If he did, he kept it *in pectoris*, because he failed to report it back to Poland. The Poles generally did not believe that the Soviet Union would wage war against them. They realized, however, that if both Germany and the Soviet Union attacked, Poland could only tremble and collapse.

The Soviet Union changed its policy towards Poland only after Britain and France declared war on Germany. On 1 September, after the German invasion, the Soviet ambassador visited Beck and stated that Moscow considered it extraordinary that Poland had not responded to Voroshilov's offer of economic assistance. Beck decided to send his ambassador to explore the offer at the Commissariat for Foreign Affairs in Moscow.[62] When Grzybowski inquired about economic aid on 5 September, Molotov informed him that the statements of Marshal Voroshilov had been delivered when the war in question had involved only Germany and Poland. With the outbreak of a general European conflict, his offer no longer applied. By virtue of Molotov's promise to the Germans not to aid Britain, the Soviet Union could no longer furnish Poland, as Britain's ally, with military supplies.[63]

On 6 September, the Soviet Union began to mobilize three million troops. It also initiated a press campaign against Poland and sent agents across the border to stir up the minorities in Poland. On 17 September, the Soviet Union, after lengthy military discussions with the *Wehrmacht*, invaded Poland.[64] On the one hand, Stalin had obtained what he wanted from the pact: a major war between Nazi Germany and the West with the Soviet Union in the position of *tertius gaudens*. On the other hand, Hitler succeeded only partially in his aims. He waged his war against Poland with minimal outside involvement but failed to keep the West out of the war.

The Nazi-Soviet Pact, when examined in detail, cannot in itself be viewed as a diplomatic revolution. Rather, it should be seen as an incompatible marriage of megalomanias. Far from making an end to ideology, the pact reaffirmed the ultimate aims of both sides. Hitler impatiently strove for "world domination." Stalin patiently awaited the conditions that would permit "world revolution." Events leading to the Second World War marked the triumph of Hitler's wilfulness. Soviet policy, like that of the West, embodied the triumph of the "wait and see."[65] The marriage of the two dictators could not be consummated until after the outbreak of a general European war. To most Eastern Europeans, the union appeared to be a marriage of spiders — not unnatural but repulsive. They waited patiently for the more vicious partner to devour the other.

NOTES

1. Walter Laqueur appears to have popularized the term "devil's alliance" [*Teufelspakt*] in his book *Russia and Germany: A Century of Conflict* (London, 1965). Hitler himself referred to the pact as a "devil's brew" [Teufelstrank]. Gerald Freund used the term "unholy alliance" as the title of his book (New York, 1957) dealing with German-Russian relations between 1918 and 1926. The term has been adopted recently by Geoffrey Roberts, *The Unholy Alliance: Stalin's Pact with Hitler* (Bloomington, Illinois, 1989).

2. See "Vokrug pakta o Nenapadnenii," *Mezhdunarodnaia Zhizn*, September 1989; the English version is entitled, "Around the Non-Aggression Pact," (Documents of Soviet-German Relations in 1939), *International Affairs* (Moscow), 87-116. Two major collections of Soviet documents appeared after this article was writen: Ministerstvo innistrannykh del SSSR, *God krizisa 1938-1939: Dokumenty I material'y* Moscow: Izdatel'stvo politicheskoi literatury, 1990; Ministerstvo inostrannykh del Rossiiskoi Federatsii, *Dokumenty vneshnei politiki, 1939 g.* Moscow: Mezhdunarodnoye otnosheniia, 1992. Records of the German Foreign Office Received by the Department of State, United States National Archives (hereafter USNA), Washington, microfilm T120, rolls 18-19; Records of the Department of State (hereafter DS), USNA, microfilm T1247, roll 3. In addition, there is much British material scattered through numerous files in the Public Record Office, Kew, England (hereafter PRO) and Polish sources can be found in the Hoover Archives at Stanford, California, and the Sikorski Institute Archives in London, England.

3. Coulondre to Connet, 22 August 1939, *Documents Diplomatiques francais* (hereafter *DDF*), 2me serie, vol. XVIII (Paris, 1985), 295. Louis Fischer misunderstands the situation after the pact when he writes: "Immediately after the marriage, the two partners were touchingly considerate, indeed naturally forgiving and helpful." See his *Russia's Road from Peace to War: Soviet Foreign Relations, 1917-1941* (New York, 1969), 368.

4. The most thorough analysis remains Reinhold W. Weber, *Die Entstehungsgeschichte des Hitler-Stalin-Paktes, 1939* (Frankfurt-am-Main, 1980).

5. See Jonathan Haslam, *The Soviet Union and the Struggle for Collective Security in Europe, 1933-1939* (New York, 1984), 82; Jiri Hochman, *The Soviet Union and the Failure of Collective Security, 1934-1938* (Ithaca, 1984), 105-15, 173. On the disagreement over the relative importance of the Soviet overtures, see Robert C. Tucker, "The Emergence of Stalin's Foreign Policy," *Slavic Review*, XXXVI (December 1977), 563-8 and 604-7; and Teddy J. Uldricks, "Stalin and Nazi Germany," *ibid.*, 599-603.

6. Walter G. Krivitsky, *In Stalin's Secret Service: An Exposé of Russia's Secret Policies by the Former Chief of the Soviet Intelligence in Western Europe* (New York, 1939), 3.

7. Augusto Rossi, the Italian ambassador in Moscow in 1939, concluded on the basis of Nuremberg evidence and German documentation that Stalin's speech was critical. See his *The Russo-German Alliance* (Boston, 1951), 8.

8. Winston S. Churchill, *The Gathering Storm* (Boston, 1948), 368.

9. Haslam, 201.

10. Major Kirkman's secret memorandum of 10 July 1939, "The Possibilities of a Soviet-German Rapprochement," PRO, Foreign Office Records (hereafter FO) 371/23686, 149; C.E. Schorske, "Two German Ambassadors: Dirksen and Schulenburg," in G. Craig and M. Gilbert, *The Diplomats, 1919-1939, Vol. II: The Thirties* (New York, 1972), 489.

11. International Military Tribunal, *Trial of the Major War Criminals* (Nuremberg, 1947), X, 267.

12. Coulondre to Bonnet, 22 August 1939, *DDF*, 2me serie, vol. XVIII, 293. Robert Coulondre, *De Staline à Hitler; Souvenirs de deux ambassades* (Paris, 1950), 274.

13. *Ribbentrop und die deutsche Weltpolitik: Aussenpolitische Konzeptionen und Entscheidungsprozesse im Dritten Reich* (Munich, 1980), 278.

14. D. C. Watt, "The Initiation of the Negotiations Leading to the Nazi Soviet Pact," in C. Abramsky, ed., *Essays in Honour of E.H. Carr* (Hamden, Conn., 1974), 165.

15. Adam Ulam, *Expansion and Coexistence: Soviet Foreign Policy, 1917-73* (New York, 1974), 267.

16. Raymond J. Sontag and James Stuart Beddie, eds., *Nazi-Soviet Relations, 1939-1941: Documents from the Archives of the German Foreign Office [hereafter NSR]* (Westport, Conn., 1948), 67.

17. Charles Burdick and Hans-Adolf Jacobsen, eds., *The Halder War Diary, 1939-1942* (Novato, Calif., 1988), 31.

18. 25 August 1939, *Documents on German Foreign Policy* [hereafter *DGFP*], Ser. D, vol. VII, 281.

19. Max Domarus, *Hitler Reden und Proklamationen, 1932-1945*, vol. II(2) (Munich, 1965), 1727.

20. See the discussion and bibliography in Gerhard Schreiber, *Hitler Interpretationen, 1923-1983* (Darmstadt, 1984), 364-6.

21. Andreas Hillgruber/Klaus Hildebrand, *Kalkuel zwischen Macht und Ideologie; Der Hitler-Stalin Pakt: Parallelen bis heute?* (Zurich, 1980).

22. Dietrich Aigner, "Hitler's Ultimate Aims — A Programme of World Domination" in H.W. Koch, ed., *Aspects of the Third Reich* (London, 1985), 251-66; Ian Kershaw, *The Nazi Dictatorship: Problems and Perspectives of Interpretation* (London, 1989), 129.

23. Walther Hewel Diaries, quoted in Anthony Read and David Fisher, *The Deadly Embrace: Hitler, Stalin and the Nazi-Soviet Pact, 1939-1941* (New York, 1988), 225.

24. D. C. Watt, *How War Came* (London, 1989), 462.

25. Jurij Boriew, *Prywatne zycie Stalina* (Warsaw, 1989), 113. (The Polish translation of this work has appeared before the Russian original.) For evidence supporting the apocryphal nature of the anecdote, see Joachim von Ribbentrop, *The Ribbentrop Memoirs* (London, 1954); Peter Kleist, *European Tragedy* (translation of *Zwischen Moskau und Berlin* [Bonn, 1950]); Heinrich Hoffmann, *Hitler Was My Friend* (London, 1962) and Paul Schmidt, *Hitler's Interpreter* (London, 1951).

26. "Vokrug pakta o Nenapadnenii," *Mezhdunaradnaia Zhizn*, September 1989, 98; for the English version: "Around the Non-Aggression Pact," *International Affairs* (Moscow), September 1989, 89.

27. Gladwyn Jebb's Memorandum, 24 August 1939, PRO, FO 371/23697, 157. See also Christopher Andrew and Oleg Gordievsky, *KGB: The Inside Story of its Foreign Operations from Lenin to Gorbachev* (London, 1990), 197.

28. *Memoirs, 1925-1950* (Toronto, 1967), 519; see also Isaac Deutscher, *Stalin: A Political Biography* (New York, 1949), 438.

29. "Was There a Soviet Appeasement Policy?" in Wolfgang J. Mommsen and Lothar Kettenacker, eds., *The Fascist Challenge and the Policy of Appeasement* (London, 1983), 285.

30. S. Axel, ed., *Der Hitler-Stalin-Pakt von 1939* (Cologne, 1979), document nr.7, 124.

31. Nikolai Tolstoy, *Stalin's Secret War*, (London, 1981), 115.

32. Churchill, *The Gathering Storm*, 305.

33. Kirk (Berlin) to Hull (reporting a conversation with Soviet official), 22 August 1939, USNA, DS, microfilm T1247, 761.6211/67.

34. This interesting document was eventually leaked to the Havas Press Agency. It was published with the title "Pourquoi l'U.R.S.S. aurait signé son accord avec le Reich?" *Revue de droit international* (Geneva), September 1939, 249. I owe this to Pawel Zaremba in his *Historia dwudziestolecia* (Paris, 1981), 392. A similar interpretation is put forward in Coulondre to Bonnet, 22 August 1939, *DDF*, 2me serie, XVIII, 299.

35. "I do not overlook the possibility that with world revolution in the back of his mind, Stalin seized the psychological moment to encourage Hitler in fresh adventures by neutralizing Russia's imponderable force with a view to eliminating in Hitler's mind what might otherwise have been a deterrent force." Biddle to Hull 22 August 1939, USNA, DS, microfilm T1247, 761.6211/65; Orde (Riga) to minister Riga, 7 September 1939, PRO, FO 371/153147, Minute no. 1, 177.

36. Orde (Riga) to minister (Riga), 7 September 1939, PRO, FO 371/153147, 179. Kirk, the US ambassador at Berlin, also suspected that "the real intent of the Kremlin is to reserve itself for a conspicuous role in a Europe weakened by war." See Kirk to Hull, 22 August 1939, USNA, DS, microfilm T1247, 761.6211/64.

37. A discussion of the concept of World Revolution in Soviet policy in 1939 is provided by Erwin Steinhauer, "Zum Hitler-Stalin-Pakt: Weltrevolutionaere Strategie und nationalstaatliche Interessen," in S. Axel, ed., *Das Hitler-Stalin Pakt von 1939* (Cologne, 1979), 5-19. See also Mikhail Heller and Aleksandr M. Nekrich, *Utopia in Power* (New York, 1986), 350.

38. *NSR*, 71-72; Esmonde M. Robertson, "German Mobilization Preparations and the Treaties Between Germany and the Soviet Union of August and September 1939," in his *Paths to War: New Essays on the Origins of the Second World War* (Basingstoke, 1989), 341.

39. Gerhard Weinberg, *The Foreign Policy of Hitler's Germany, Vol. II: Starting World War II* (Chicago, 1980), 609; Marilyn Hitchens, *Germany, Russia and the Balkans: Prelude to the Nazi-Soviet Pact* (Boulder, Colorado, 1983), 220.

40. Kirk to Hull, 22 August 1939, USNA, DS, microfilm T1247, 761.6211/64 and 66; Kirk to Hull, 23 August 1939, *ibid.*, 761.6211/75.

41. Kirk to Hull, 23 August 1939, *ibid.*, 761.6211/83.

42. Steinhardt to Hull, 25 August 1939, *ibid.*, 761.6211/112.

43. Rosso to Ciano, 22 August 1939, *Documenti diplomatici italiani*, series VIII, vol. XIII, 107.

44. Jozef Zaranski, ed., *Diariusz i teki Jana Szembeka*, vol. IV, (London, 1972), 771.

45. Coulondre to Bonnet, 22 August 1939, *DDF*, XVIII, 273; Naggiar to Bonnet, 23 August 1939, ibid., vol. XVIII, 328; Steinhardt to Hull, 25 August 1939, USNA, DS, microfilm T1247, 761.6211/125 and 133.

46. Roberts, *Unholy Alliance*, 158.

47. "Memorandum by Mr. Jebb," 24 August 1939, PRO, FO 371/23697, 156-157.

48. *Foreign Relations of the United States* [hereafter *FRUS*] 1939, vol. 1 (Washington, 1955), 342; Charles Bohlen, *Witness to History, 1929-1969* (New York, 1973), 83.

49. Hitler, in *Halder's War Diary*, 51.

50. Kirk to Hull, 22 August 1939, USNA, DS, microfilm T1247, 761.6211/67, 1-2.

51. Kirk to Hull, 1 September 1939, *ibid.*, 761.6211/64; Kirk to Hull, 9 September 1939, *ibid.*, 761.6211/182; Aleksander Bregman, *Najlepszy Sojuznik Hitlera* (London, 1958), 56.

52. Molotov's statement of 31 August 1939, USNA, DS, microfilm T1247, 760.6211/192, 10; also quoted in David J. Dallin, *Soviet Russia's Foreign Policy, 1939-1942* (translated by Leon Dennan) (New Haven, 1942), 56.

53. Dallin, 66.

54. Ulam, 277-78.

55. Biddle to Roosevelt and Hull, 25 August 1939, USNA, DS, microfilm T1247, 761.6211/121, 1-2.

56. Republic of Poland, Ministry of Foreign Affairs, *Official Documents Concerning Polish-German and Polish Soviet Relations, 1933-1939* (London, 1939), 187; Steinhardt to Hull, 28 August 1939, USNA, DS, microfilm T1247, 761.6211/142; FRUS, 1939 I, 343.

57. Noël to Bonnet, 22 August 1939, *DDF*, XVIII, 263.

58. Noël to Bonnet, 22 August 1939, *ibid.*, 217-8.

59. Beck to E. Raczynski, 23 August 1939, London ciphered telegrams, Sikorski Institute Archives (London), A 12.53/25, nr. 229.

60. Zaranski, *Diariusz*, vol. IV, 771.

61. Edward Raczynski, *In Allied London* (London, 1962), 22.

62. Beck to Raczynski, 2 September 1939, *Official Documents*, 187; Bullitt to Hull, 2 September 1939, USNA, DS, microfilm T1247, 761.6211/170.

63. Grzybowski to Beck, 8 September 1939, *Official Documents*, 188; Seeds to Halifax, 6 September 1939, PRO, FO 371/24658 C13097/15/18, 1. A Soviet account which generally supports this view and outlines the long process by which the Soviet Union decided to invade Eastern Poland can be found in V.K. Volkov *et al.*, *1939 god; uroki istorii* (The Year 1939; Lessons of History) (Moscow, 1990), 348-9.

64. Noël to Bonnet, 11 September 1939, Ministère des affaires étrangères de la France, série Z, 619/16; Jerzy Lojek, *Agresia 17 wrzesnia 1939* [The Aggression of 17 September 1939] (Warsaw, 1990), 185. Originally published in 1979 under the pseudonym Leopold Jerzewski.

65. François Bédarida's phrase, quoted in Heinrich Bartel, *Frankreich und die Sowjetunion* (Stuttgart, 1986), 278.

The Regions
Les régions

BRITISH COLUMBIA IN 1939

Patricia E. Roy
University of Victoria

In the spring of 1939 a Vancouver *Province* cartoon suggested some of the "great things" expected of the coming summer: "T.C.A.'s First Season," "Better Business," and, of course, the "Royal Visit."[1] These happy events all occurred, but at year's end few of the approximately 774,000 British Columbians would have questioned the assertion of the Prince Rupert *Daily News* that "The outstanding event of 1939 was the entry of Canada into the war in defence of the Empire and of small defenceless nations."[2]

For people long familiar with the antics of Hitler and Mussolini and the horrors of the Sino-Japanese War, the outbreak of war relieved tension. Moreover, British preparations for war and the war itself increased demand for many of British Columbia's primary products. The total value of production in forestry, the province's most important industry, rose a dramatic 31 percent over 1938. The other major industries, mining and agriculture, were up slightly and the five percent decline in the fisheries was largely the result of normal cycles. Most important, total employment was up three percent and the average weekly industrial wage had risen to $28.60, the highest level since 1930.[3]

Yet there were reminders of the Depression.[4] The lumber industry offers the best examples. Drastic price cutting by Russia and the Baltic states forced the Canadian Western Lumber Company, the largest mill in the province, to cut wages by ten percent in March; by June, British orders meant the restoration of wages, the introduction of double shifts, and the setting of an all-time record for waterborne shipments.[5] Demand continued high; a shipping shortage at the outbreak of the war caused only brief and isolated panic. After the premier, T. Dufferin Pattullo, said he would make the railway freight issue "urgent government business," the federal government, the railways, and the lumber companies worked out an arrangement to export BC lumber via Atlantic ports.[6]

War, and anticipation of war, also helped the mining industry. Although coal mining on Vancouver Island was declining, production in the Crow's Nest Pass was rising and there was a real growth in metals.

Early in the year, falling prices for lead and zinc led the giant Consolidated Mining and Smelting Company to curtail exploration activities and lay off 500 employees. By summer, rising metal prices revived optimism; in November, when the British government announced it would purchase all the lead and zinc Canada could produce, the prosperity of the Kootenay seemed assured.[7]

Moreover, the major forestry and mining firms had few concerns about organized labour. Such traditional craft organizations as the Vancouver Trades and Labour Council seemed as concerned about parking meters and Daylight Saving Time as about wages and working conditions.[8] Unions affiliated with the Congress of Industrial Organizations (CIO), however, had little success in taking advantage of the collective bargaining provisions of the provincial Industrial Conciliation and Arbitration Act, 1937, to organize workers in the lumber and mining industries. The new International Woodworkers of America-CIO had had only a few hundred members, mostly loggers around Lake Cowichan on Vancouver Island. In the mining industry, A.H. 'Slim' Evans, an organizer for the militant Mine Mill and Smelter Workers Union-CIO, overcame adversity, including the mysterious burning of his car, to sign up about a quarter of the approximately 4,000 smelter workers at Trail and to draw as many as 2,000 people to a mass rally. Unfortunately for Evans, a short time later he was sentenced to seven days in jail for drunkenness. That crime destroyed "his usefulness" to the union. Mine Mill chartered local 480 in August 1939, but had too few members to gain certification.[9]

While Mine Mill invited itself to Trail, gold miners at the Pioneer Mine in the Bridge River Valley asked Mine Mill to organize them. When the Pioneer miners struck in September 1939, the key issues quickly became collective bargaining and the Industrial Conciliation and Arbitration Act. As the strike dragged on, the provincial government prosecuted officers of Local 308. A dramatic sit-in at the mine brought matters to a head. The Provincial Police persuaded Mine Mill members to withdraw peacefully by promising they would not be prosecuted. On 6 March 1940, after 134 working days, the strike ended with "No change in wages and working conditions. No concessions to C.I.O."[10] The advance of the CIO in British Columbia had apparently been checked.

While forestry and mining were the most significant primary industries, agriculture and the fisheries gained new importance with the outbreak of the war. Okanagan fruit growers enjoyed good crops, a reviving prairie market and a new central selling scheme for domestic sales.[11] After briefly fearing that shipping shortages and possible import restrictions might reduce British sales, fruit growers were relieved when the devaluation of the British pound reduced American competition and the depreciated Canadian dollar protected domestic markets.[12] The war also brought optimism to Peace River farmers, who expected good prices for wheat and an increased British demand for bacon.[13]

For fishermen, catches were at best mediocre and, in some cases, failures. Shipping shortages, higher insurance rates, and exchange problems added to their woes.[14] So too did the action of the Department of National Defence in commandeering three large halibut boats for coast defence work. Premier Pattullo, however, urged the federal government to replace them with ten to twelve smaller boats built at the government drydock in Prince Rupert, his home constituency.[15]

Pattullo's complaint about the halibut boats did not mean a lack of concern about defence. Far from it. British Columbians used "military necessity" to argue for public works, including the Alaska and Hope-Princeton Highways;[16] some communities sought federal aid for airports.[17]

In January, Department of National Defence officials, while indicating that coastal defences would be increased against possible raids designed to disrupt commerce, had assured Vancouver *Sun* reporter Bruce Hutchison that "no armada will descend upon Victoria and Vancouver."[18] Indeed, believing they were in "one of the safest spots in the country," British Columbians thought they were ideally located to manufacture munitions of all kinds.[19] In pressing for the appointment of a British Columbian to the National Defence Purchasing Board, however, the Vancouver Board of Trade complained that British Columbia was at a disadvantage with eastern manufacturers and producers who "because of their geographical situation, are constantly in touch with our Capital City."[20] The Vancouver *Sun's* exaggerated assertion that the naming of W.C. Woodward, a Vancouver department store owner, to the War Supply Board was "probably the most important [appointment] in Canada for the last decade," reflected the satisfaction of British Columbians that they would not be discriminated against in the placing of war orders.[21] By the end of 1939, British Columbia firms had orders for military uniforms and boots.[22]

The beginning of war-related industries and increased demand for provincial resources helped create jobs. Yet, while employment reached its highest level in the decade in November 1939, the number of heads of families on relief rose slightly.[23] The number of single men on relief, however, fell about 17 percent.[24] For the authorities, who vividly remembered the On-To-Ottawa Trek of 1935 and the Sit-Downers' Strike of 1938, this was good news. Relief camp workers were confining their protests to petitions and, although some went to Vancouver for the spring Royal Visit, they waited until ten minutes after the King and Queen left the city to begin "tin-canning."[25] Further evidence of the decline of unemployment was the "disappointing" response of young men to accept training in government-sponsored forestry and mining camps.[26]

While government hoped training would solve economic problems and the CIO looked to organization, other British Columbians turned to different panaceas. A popular one was Technocracy, Inc., the invention of Howard Scott, an American engineer, who proposed to establish a North American technate in which engineers would govern. To overcome the problem of poverty in the midst of the plenty created by modern technology, they proposed, for example, that only people between the ages of 25 and 45 should work for a living and only four hours a day, four days a week. The rest of the population would receive a stipend that had to be spent each month.[27] At places as diverse as Comox and Kimberley, Vancouver and Princeton, Scott and his disciples spoke to large crowds and attracted new members.

Technocracy might not have drawn any official attention but, within days of the outbreak of the war, Technocrats publicly opposed the conscription of Canadian manpower for service outside North America.[28] In Duncan, vandals ransacked the Technocracy office and left a note — in Latin — to the effect that "the dart defends the crown." In Trail, where the Technocracy movement was especially active, a Technocracy sign was thrown in the Columbia River, but authorities would not cancel a speech by Scott even though S.G. Blaylock, the general manager of Consolidated Mining & Smelting, warned most of the three to four hundred Technocrats in the area had "a screw loose [and] it might make a nasty mess".[29] The meeting went ahead without incident before an overflow crowd. Though all speakers saluted and wore Nazi-like uniforms, the chief complaint of the Trail *Daily Times* was Scott's use of such words as "hell" and "damn." In succeeding days, Scott spoke to 3,000 people in Vancouver, to a "packed" hall in Nanaimo, and to 1,200 people in Victoria but he wisely refused to allow questions about the war. When the federal government banned the import of Technocracy magazines, the Vancouver Sun, which had once championed Technocracy, criticized the censorship because few people who had read *Technocracy* would want to have anything to do with the movement![30]

A more realistic, more popular, and more successful economic reform was the formation of co-operatives and credit unions with the blessing of the provincial government. In 1938, the provincial government had recognized that credit unions had no legal protection. Drawing on Nova Scotia legislation, it devised a Credit Union Act which, Attorney-General Gordon Wismer asserted, would allow people "to practice thrift and raise funds without having to go to loan sharks." Spokesmen for both the Conservatives and the Co-operative Commonwealth Federation (CCF) agreed; the legislation passed easily. When experts in the co-operative movement, such as Nova Scotians Rev. Dr. J.D. Nelson MacDonald of St. Francis Xavier University and Ambrose Forgeron, toured British Columbia, they drew interested audiences that included prominent citizens.[31] In the spring of 1939, the government named an inspector of credit unions and during the summer sent a civil servant around the province to explain the new law. In many places, people organized new credit unions; members of existing credit unions formed the British Columbia Credit Union Association.[32]

The passage of the credit union legislation could be perceived as a social reform of the Pattullo government, although the impetus came from the CCF, principally Dorothy Steeves, MLA for Vancouver North. According to his biographer, Robin Fisher, Pattullo's reformism had been "starved to death by the tightfisted leader of the Liberal Party [Mackenzie King]."[33] Certainly that is what Pattullo thought, and with reason.

In a sense, federal-provincial financial policies were on "hold" pending publication of the "Rowell Report" on Dominion-Provincial Relations. British Columbia still wanted Ottawa to assist with unemployment relief and debt payments. Pattullo, however, had the same embarrassment as many of his predecessors: pleading poverty, boasting of prosperity, and expecting sympathy. In seeking a loan to help pay the provincial share of unemployment relief, Pattullo warned that the province might have to default on maturing obligations, but vigorously denied that BC was in the same weak economic position as the prairie provinces.[34] Pattullo's wanted to "find ways and means of financing desirable and necessary public undertakings"; the real problem, he repeatedly proclaimed, was Ottawa's invasion of the income tax field.[35]

Pattullo also thought it a "queer thing" that "eastern financial houses" were unwilling to loan the province some three million dollars to meet maturing debts.[36] Indeed, Toronto and Montreal financiers knew British Columbia was a good risk, but considered the province's terms commercially unattractive. Moreover, as the federal finance minister, C.A. Dunning, chastised John Hart, his provincial counterpart, "as long as you continue to borrow from the Dominion, private investors will be inclined to class you with that of the Prairie provinces."[37]

If Pattullo and Hart thought a crusade against Ottawa or Bay and St. James Streets would win votes at home, they misconstrued the evidence. Even before the outbreak of the war, many British Columbians had little regard for Pattullo's plea of unfair treatment in the East. Several editors suggested the provincial government should practice retrenchment rather than beg for help from Ottawa.[38] A good test of public opinion was the Vancouver Centre by-election in May. At the Liberal nominating meeting, Pattullo recalled how his government was elected on a Better Terms platform, that the Rowell Commission would soon be reporting, and his government needed evidence to show Eastern Canadians that British Columbians were "still behind their government." Pattullo's message drew little sympathy. Although Vancouver Centre had been represented by a Liberal, the voters turned to the CCF. The Nanaimo *Free Press* sensibly observed that people were no longer satisfied with the old-line parties, with unemployment, and continuous federal-provincial bickering.[39]

A somewhat chastened Pattullo set out on a planned pilgrimage to Ottawa and Toronto. As he left, he stressed that British Columbia "had no quarrel with the Dominion" and denied that he had ever "asked Ottawa or anyone else to pay a single dollar of B.C. obligations."[40] Rebuffed in Ottawa, the province turned to New York where, by raising a loan, it demonstrated it could maintain its own credit.[41]

When war came, Pattullo briefly put aside his grievances against Ottawa. On 8 September, he assured Mackenzie King "that our Provincial Government will co-operate with you to the fullest extent in war which is being thrust upon us." At home, Pattullo already enjoyed political peace as R.L Maitland, the Conservative leader, publicly declared his party would co-operate with Pattullo in any way during the emergency and the Union of BC Municipalities promised not to embarrass the senior governments.[42] Similarly, even though Ottawa deferred action on his request for a million-dollar loan against the provincial share of unemployment relief expenditures, Hart promised the province would "not raise any issue of provincial rights during the war." British Columbians, who increasingly realized the need to pay for past profligacy and the indefensibility of going deeper into debt in wartime, welcomed this patriotic action. Hart, who proudly contrasted his approach with that of the Québec premier, Maurice Duplessis, sent favourable clippings to Ottawa.[43]

The harmony was short-lived. Hart persisted in seeking the million-dollar loan even though his mid-November budget revealed the highest revenues ever and an apparent surplus of over a million dollars.[44] A disappointed finance minister, J.L. Ralston, eventually approved the loan.[45] In thanking Ralston, an ungracious Pattullo complained the province was advancing the federal share of unemployment relief payments while paying three percent interest to Ottawa on the loan which allegedly financed them.[46] Pattullo had been fighting Ottawa too long to recognize the opportunity to make a graceful retreat.

In more than financial matters, British Columbians were keen to promote national unity. They promoted the idea of a national flag,[47] enthusiastically greeted the introduction of Trans-Canada Airlines service which made it possible to go to Ottawa in less than a day[48] and demonstrated their interest in national affairs by complaining about the inability of CBC transmitters to cope with mountainous terrain!

The Canadian Broadcasting Corporation (CBC) also created controversy through censorship. Early in January, Dr. G.M. Weir, the minister of education, launched a war on social diseases after Dr. Donald H. Williams, the provincial director of VD control, reported 3,054 new cases in 1938 and observed that VD, a major health problem, resulted mainly from prostitution.[49] Over 2,500 people attended the Vancouver meeting opening the province-wide crusade. Because of what Weir described as "false modesty," the CBC refused to broadcast it. This was good publicity; when Dr. Williams went elsewhere, his lecture was advertised as the talk the CBC would not broadcast. Indeed, the campaign had some success; 441 fewer new cases of VD were reported in 1939 than in 1938[50] and the government closed 51 bawdy houses in the province.[51]

In the campaign against prostitution, Williams and Weir antagonized hotel owners by describing "mixed beer parlors" as "an unmitigated curse." Nevertheless, New Westminster voters overwhelmingly approved the sale of beer by the glass. In Victoria, however, even a plea of "Let's Be British" did not convince voters to accept such sales.[52]

The Britishness of British Columbia had been brought to the fore by the Royal Visit in May. Naturally, the excitement was greatest where the

King and Queen visited but enthusiasm appeared everywhere. As the Prince Rupert *Daily News* explained, "British Columbia is the only province in which the word 'British' is used. It has remained from the first more British than the others ... We feel sure that the King and Queen will like Victoria and Vancouver and we wish they were coming here."[53]

British Columbia in 1939 was overwhelmingly composed of people of British racial origin[54] who wanted to remain so. Although children of "Foreign Parentage" accounted for only 20 percent of the school population, the *Colonist* warned of future racial problems if non-British immigrants outnumbered British immigrants and more young men went to Britain to join the Royal Air Force or to seek skilled work in British shipyards.[55] Yet, when some editors and politicians welcomed the Hornby and Page Croft British immigration schemes as a means of getting good settlers to open up empty lands and create new markets,[56] other British Columbians wondered how inexperienced farmers could survive.[57]

There was also some sympathy for refugees from Hitler. When Jewish refugees en route to Australia passed through Vancouver, the *Province* commented that, if they were a sample of the quality of people seeking refuge, by "giving them asylum [Canada] ... could discharge a debt to humanity and benefit herself at the same time." Nevertheless, when local representatives of the Canadian National Refugee Committee requested assistance in settling victims of Nazi and Fascist oppression, the provincial government reserved its decision.[58] Thus, with the exception of several hundred Sudetenlanders, who, with capital provided by the British and French governments, were settled by the Canadian Pacific Railway on uncultivated land in the Peace River district, the only refugees to find their way to British Columbia were a few well-to-do persons such as the Koerner Brothers from Czechoslovakia, who developed new aspects of the forest industry.[59]

While British Columbians sympathized with Hitler's victims, they could not be proud of their own treatment of minorities, particularly native Indians, Doukhobors, and Asians. For most British Columbians, native Indians, who formed about four percent of the population, were a federal responsibility: if they were not already invisible, they should be far removed from "the corrupting influences of the white." Such paternalism was not always altruistic. In Kamloops, the City Council asked Ottawa to move the reserve because the Indians insisted on compensation if their hay meadow was drained for mosquito control purposes. A resident of the

Reserve complained, "A new Hitler has risen among us to crush the timid, the poor and faltering Indian." She asked, "must we starve and die, so that an odd mosquito might not worry or trouble the white community across the river?"[60]

British Columbians did make humanitarian noises about improving the situation of the Indian. After a murder trial brought the overcrowding and poverty of the No. 1 Indian Reserve at the South end of Nanaimo to public attention, the Nanaimo *Free Press* proclaimed this "terrible state of affairs ... should not be permitted in a civilized country." In commenting on a speech in which Andrew Paull told the North Vancouver Kiwanis Club of the social and economic system under which his people had once lived, the *Sun* remarked on how the Squamish people had had a system of justice, had known nothing of many diseases, lived to an old age, shared their wealth through the potlatch, and preserved wild life and the forests.[61]

Yet it is evident that British Columbians believed the Indians should be "civilized" according to white men's ideas. For example, in praising the performance of a fife and drum band from the Kamloops Indian Residential School at a basketball game between an Indian and a city team, the *Sentinel* referred to "the responsibility of the white man to a race that he conquered and demoralized, and whose land he usurped. The undertaking is the task ... of re-establishing the Indian, and educating him in useful arts so that he may become a worthwhile part of Canada."[62] The Indians, of course, already regarded themselves as Canadians. In November, at the annual convention of the Native Brotherhood at Bella Bella, Andrew Reid told them, in English, Chinook and Tsimshian that "it is our duty as patriotic citizens to put aside our personal claims or the claims of our brotherhood and aid our country in this time of stress."[63]

British Columbians hoped that education might solve problems with another ethnic minority, the Sons of Freedom, residents of the West Kootenay and Boundary districts who were notorious for arson, bombings and nude parades protesting government actions or reflecting internal unrest. Although only some Doukhobors belonged to the Sons of Freedom sect, all Doukhobors suffered from the illegal acts of the dissidents.[64]

When the Doukhobors sought permission to bring Peter Verigin III from Russia to replace the deceased Peter Verigin II as their leader, opposition appeared even where there were few, if any, Doukhobors. One problem of the Doukhobors, especially the Sons of Freedom, was their belief in the communal ownership of property. When their Christian Community of Universal Brotherhood (CCUB) could not meet its mortgage because of the poor stewardship of Peter Verigin II, the destruction by arson of several CCUB industries such as sawmills, and the economic ravages of the Depression, the Sun Life Assurance Company and the National Trust Company foreclosed. Sons of Freedom tried to prevent members from buying individual holdings in the expectation that the provincial government would not allow the dispossession of the entire community. Over the weekend of 23-24 April arsonists completely destroyed one school and a pile of 3,000 fence posts and set several minor fires. Provincial police expected more trouble; the Grand Forks Gazette warned that "trust company and government officials must get together on some rational policy for Doukhobor lands or firebug protests will probably continue forever."[65]

The protests were effective. Acting on advice from the attorney-general, the sheriff of Nelson, M.E. Harper, refused further assistance in carrying out eviction orders. The Sun Life Company was willing to sell individual parcels of land, but since the government was denying "necessary policy protection," the company would not guarantee "peaceable possession." To force the government's hand, Sun Life sued the sheriff for contempt and suggested the government take over the lands itself.[66] Fearing "wholesale acts of destruction, sabotage, and possibly more serious breaches of the law," the government bought out the Sun Life's interests. The attorney-general admitted that the only alternative, dispossession, "was certain to lead to riots and bloodshed." The Grand Forks *Gazette* accused the Pattullo government of giving the Doukhobors a present "in recognition for the nuisance they have been hereabouts".[67] In the short run, however, the government's action maintained calm within the Doukhobor community.

The most visible ethnic groups were the Chinese and Japanese. Yet, with limited exceptions, British Columbians no longer lumped them into one all encompassing "oriental" or "Asiatic" group. In fact, ever since the Chinese Immigration Act, 1923, stopped Chinese immigration, tolerance for the Chinese had been increasing. By 1939, continued reports of Japanese attacks on civilians, including Canadian missionaries, in China had aroused considerable sympathy for the Chinese cause. In all parts of the province, Caucasians joined their Chinese neighbours in raising funds for Chinese War Relief, in listening to speakers from China such as Miss Loh Tsei, the Chinese "Joan of Arc," in watching Chinese war films, and in calling for an embargo on exports, particularly of war materials, to Japan and a boycott of Japanese-made products.

Mounting hostility did not help the Japanese settlers in British Columbia or their *Nisei* children. Observations such as that of the Vernon *News* that "condemnation of Japan at war with China is one thing. Our attitude to the Japanese in Canada is another" were rare. The Canadian prime minister, however, persuaded Pattullo that Japanese exclusionary legislation would embarrass Britain diplomatically. Privately, Pattullo continued to urge the repatriation of the Japanese; publicly he was silent. Other British Columbia politicians — federal, provincial and municipal — were unrestrained and reiterated old cries for a halt to Japanese immigration and economic competition.[68] The Canadian Japanese, aware of their unpopularity, kept a low profile except when demonstrating their loyalty to Canada by greeting the King and Queen, by trying to enlist for Home Defence and the Canadian armed forces, by donating money to Canada's war effort, and by passing resolutions endorsing Canada's war policies.[69]

In 1939, of course, the enemy was Germany or, to be precise, Hitler and the Nazis, not all Germans.[70] As the Victoria *Times* asserted in mid-September, "Canada is not at war with the German people ... She is at war with the system of which Adolph Hitler is the living exponent." Earlier in the year, some editors had told Nazis to "go back to Naziland" and criticized the German consul in Vancouver for attempting to raise money from German-Canadians. Rumours circulated about the presence of Nazi groups in the Creston, Fraser, and Kootenay valleys.[71] Concrete evidence of organized Nazi sympathizers appeared on 1 May when the Oliver and Osoyoos Labour Front celebrated May Day. The meeting opened with the singing of "O Canada" — in German. After a supper, Dr. Ernest Wiese, an Austrian engineer, who drove a German-made car with German license plates and gave Nazi salutes, showed films of the Sudetenlanders' relief at being liberated from Czech rule and of Mussolini's work in Ethiopia. Dr. Wiese planned to show his films in Kelowna but when local veterans became agitated, provincial police seized the films and advised him to cancel his speech. Later reports of a naturalized Canadian leading a Nazi bund at Summerland reinforced arguments that "people of foreign birth who abuse their citizenship by taking part in objectionable propaganda" should have their citizenship cancelled and be deported.[72]

When war came, apprehension about the loyalty of Germans increased.[73] The Anglican bishop of the Cariboo, for example, told his Kamloops congregation, "there should be no bitterness and hatred against members of enemy nations who have made their homes in this city and district — but they should be watched. Germans are very loyal to their

Fatherland and do not easily change their flag." Meanwhile, German-Canadian organizations and congregations, including Fraser Valley Mennonites, pledged their loyalty to Canada. In the first week of September, a few Germans in the Okanagan Valley were taken into custody.[74]

British Columbians, in fact, had been thinking of war for months. While no one really liked the increase in the national defence budget announced in April, it was generally accepted as being "more than justified by the growth of the aggressive spirit among nations and the vulnerability of our shores."[75]

By the last week of August, militia units were appealing for recruits and sending men to guard local fortifications, where they existed, armouries, and public utilities. When local resources were insufficient, units were brought in from elsewhere. For example, the Irish Fusiliers of Vancouver relieved Prince Rupert men from guard duty on railway bridges. Civilian volunteers were keen to protect local utilities, but the province claimed that neither it nor the municipalities could pay.[76]

Canada was not legally at war until 10 September, but British Columbians seemed unaware of the political and constitutional niceties of letting Parliament decide. Though normal events continued, the Labour Day weekend was not the "traditional jubilant farewell to summer holidays." A few people stayed up all night to listen to their radios and took portable radios to picnic and camp grounds. An unusually large number attended church services where special prayers were said. Britain's declaration of war brought "a general feeling of relief," but "no outward demonstrations, no cheers, no parades." Those, such as Torchy Anderson of the *Province*, who remembered 1914 commented how "the fever" of that time was "lacking entirely" as "Canadians took their position with a seriousness engendered of more knowledge ... It was a spirit of determined resignation."[77]

There was no "rush to the colours" as in 1914, but only within the CCF was there public opposition to the war effort.[78] In the Legislature, after party leader Harold Winch pointed out that the CCF "accepted the war as a fight for liberty, freedom and democracy," Dorothy Steeves blamed the Allies' policies after the last war and economic conditions for creating Hitler and declared, "What a farce it is to accuse Germany of broken promises when the road of international dealings is just strewn with broken promises. Can you trust these governments that handed Manchuria to Japan and smashed democracy in Spain." Her speech set off "a conflagration."

Pattullo warned that if she spoke again along such lines, he would report her to Ottawa for possible action under the War Measures Act.[79] Editorial comment was unanimously critical. The Vancouver *Province*, for example, suggested that the CCF members had "set forth deliberately, maliciously and, one might almost say, reasonably to sabotage Canada's war effort."[80] Some CCF members feared Mrs. Steeves' outburst would lose them support.[81]

Conscription was not an issue. Most recruiting was deferred at the end of September. The militia withdrew from some duties protecting civilian property and relaxed the intensity of its guard around military installations. For soldiers, guard duty was "a pretty dull war."[82]

Except possibly in Prince Rupert, where the *Daily News* felt obliged to reassure readers that German submarines would not torpedo anything as small as the *Prince John*, or fishing craft because "the cost of sinking them would be too great," few British Columbians seriously expected a German attack. Though the press thought test blackouts unwarranted, it admitted the wisdom of preparing for possible civil disasters.[83]

By October and November, some regular soldiers were leaving to "unknown destinations," which turned out to be guard duty in Prince Rupert or training elsewhere in Canada. Although their departures were supposedly secret, crowds gathered to see them off but, except in the Kootenays, there were few cheers. "Perhaps we did not cheer so light-heartedly yesterday as we did when the boys went off to that other war," remarked the *Times*, "for through experience we know, what we did not fully realize then, that war is a grim business and not a glorious excursion."[84]

As in the rest of Canada, in small towns as well as large, civilians organized for the war effort, gave new life to established Red Cross branches, and established new ones to raise money, to sew and knit, and to make bandages for the expected wounded. The Imperial Order Daughters of the Empire began collecting warm clothing for child evacuees in England. Nevertheless, despite exhortations from the press, women seemed reluctant to sign up for the national "voluntary registration of women who are ready and willing to undertake war work of any kind." The decision not to register was an individual one, but Doris Milligan, author of a daily Vancouver *Sun* column on "Women's War Work," suggested that many women thought registration committed them to war work, that many were already involved with other organizations, and that some simply "didn't get around" to it.[85] In fact, earlier in the year, women in Victoria, Vancouver and several other cities had eagerly joined a Women's Service Corps modelled on a similar organization in Britain. Women who were accepted learned first aid, stretcher bearing, auto mechanics, map reading and other skills that might "relieve a man for war." Women's enthusiasm was high, but the Department of National Defence did not formally recognize the Corps and this may have discouraged some women for volunteering for other war service.[86]

During the first two weeks of the war, some people panicked at the grocery store. Prices of flour, butter, and meat rose sharply; the hoarding of flour and sugar was common. In anticipation of new war taxes, consumers stocked up on tea, coffee and tobacco, but the new taxes on alcoholic beverages drew the most attention. Then, when some British Columbians practiced rigid personal economy, the press warned that retrenchment would contribute to depression and not help the war effort. By late November, retail trade was returning to normal and many merchants reported one of the best Christmas seasons in recent memory.[87] "Knowing that our cause is right though the way to a just victory and a just peace may be long and dreary, we felt much better about these definite matters than we did about the pall of uncertainty which had begun to settle on us last Christmas," observed the Victoria *Times* in a Christmas Eve message.[88]

Although there was sadness in the homes of those British Columbians whose sons, serving in the Royal Navy, the Royal Air Force or the Merchant Marine, had already been casualties, for most British Columbians, 1939 had been a good year. It was also a year of transition. Unemployment still plagued some British Columbians, but war-related demands for the province's natural resources created new jobs and raised wages. Premier Pattullo still fought for lower freight rates, federally-funded public works and financial assistance from Ottawa or eastern financiers, but many British Columbians had forsaken such limited interests and welcomed national agencies such as the CBC and TCA. For them, it was easy to recognize that war required a national effort.

NOTES

1. Vancouver *Province*, 28 March 1939.
2. Prince Rupert *Daily News*, 30 December 1939.
3. British Columbia, Department of Labour, *Annual Report*, 1939 in British Columbia, *Sessional Papers*, (hereafter *BCSP*), 1940, G8 and G11.

4. Department of Trade and Industry, *Annual Report*, 1939, in *BCSP*, 1940, 012-014.
5. *New Westminster British Columbian*, 4 January and 22 February 1939; Powell River *Town Crier*, 12 January 1939; Vancouver *Sun*, 10 and 17 March and 14 June 1939; *B.C. Lumber Workers Union Bulletin*, 11 June 1939.
6. Victoria *Daily Times*, 26 December 1939 (hereafter *Times*); *Sun*, 1 August and 30 December 1939; *Province*, 6 January and 29 December 1939; E.G.Perrault, *Wood & Water: The Story of Seaboard Lumber and Shipping* (Vancouver, 1985), 128. The war-time demand for lumber accentuated a long-recognized problem — the need for forest conservation. In December 1939, the Legislature passed laws for the better protection of forests and parks without providing the necessary funds. In any case, the provincial Forest Service was already losing employees to the armed forces.
7. Minister of Mines, *Annual Report*, 1939, *BCSP*, 1940, A5; C.W. Guillaume to W.J. Asseltine, 30 August 1939, British Columbia Archives (hereafter BCARS), GR202, Department of Mines, Mineralogical Division, Chief Mining Engineer, box 1, file 5; Trail *Daily Times*, 25 July 1939; Nelson *Daily News*, 26 July and 10 November 1939; Kimberley *Courier*, 9 November 1939; *Province*, 9 August 1939. It was also good news for provincial finances. Consolidated Mining and Smelting was such a significant contributor to the provincial treasury that when two years of its income taxes were received in the same fiscal year, the provincial comptroller had to explain the aberration in provincial revenues to Ottawa. (Comptroller to W.C. Clark, 28 August 1939, National Archives of Canada (hereafter NA), Department of Finance Records, (hereafter Finance), vol. 682.
8. Vancouver and New Westminster and District Trades and Labour Council, Minute Book, *passim*, University of British Columbia, Special Collections, (hereafter UBCSC).
9. On Trail generally, see Elsie G. Turnbull, *Trail Between Two Wars* (Victoria, 1980), 72. On Evans' work see Stanton, *Never Say Die!*, 30-37 and Jean Evans Sheils and Ben Swankey, *"Work and Wages!": Semi-Documentary Account of the Life and Times of Arthur H. (Slim) Evans* (Vancouver, 1977), ch. XXIV.
10. Mrs. E.F. Chatham to Pattullo, 10 January 1940, GR1222, box 29, file 7; *Sun*, 1 March 1940; *Province*, 2 March 1940; "Notice of Termination of Strike," NA, Department of Labour, Strikes and Lockout File, vol. 402, Strike 111.
11. British Columbia, Department of Agriculture, *Annual Report*, 1939, *BCSP*, 1940, B27, B30-B31.
12. Vernon *News*, 28 September and 2 November 1939; Penticton *Herald*, 28 September 1939.
13. Department of Agriculture, *Annual Report*, 1939, *BCSP*, 1940, B15.
14. *Pacific Coast News*, 9 November 1939 and 4 January 1940.
15. Pattullo to J.E. Michaud, 29 September 1939, GR1222, box 157, file 6; G. Omori to King, 2 October 1939, NA, King Papers, #227227; Pattullo to N. McL. Rogers, 2 November 1939, BCARS, Pattullo Papers, box 69, file 2.

16. E.g., *Columbian,* 24 February 1939. For a comprehensive account of Pattullo and the highway, see Robin Fisher, "T.D. Pattullo and the British Columbia to Alaska Highway", in Kenneth Coates, ed., *The Alaska Highway: Papers of the 40th Anniversary Symposium* (Vancouver, 1985), 9-24; Penticton *Herald,* 5 October 1939.

17. Kamloops *Sentinel,* 20 January and 4 April 1939; Prince Rupert *Daily News,* 25 March 1939; F.C. Rodgers, Creston Board of Trade to W.K. Esling, 18 March 1939, NA, H.H. Stevens Papers, vol. 157; Chilliwack *Progress,* 1 November 1939.

18. *Sun,* 19 January 1939.

19. *Colonist,* 5 April 1939; *Sun,* 16 January 1939. See also J.F. Keen and J.E. Buerk, Building and Construction Industries Exchanges of B.C. to King, 18 September 1939, King Papers, #228640-2.

20. Brief Prepared by the Vancouver Board of Trade Advocating Representation from British Columbia on the War Supply Board of Canada, 14 November 1939, GR1222, box 158, file 8. The Vancouver, New Westminster and District Trades and Labour Council had similar concerns.

21. *Sun,* 8 December 1939; *Province,* 8 and 23 December 1939; *Times,* 9 December 1939.

22. *Times,* 29 December 1939.

23. Henry A. Hill to King, 19 December 1939, King Papers, #228074.

24. *Province,* 6 December 1939.

25. Copies of the petition, a form letter from the Project workers to Pattullo and George S. Pearson, may be found in GR1222, box 157, file 15; *The Federationist,* 1 June 1939; *Sun,* 1 June 1939.

26. Laura Hardy to King, 20 April 1939, King Papers, #227828; Cranbrook *Courier,* 27 July 1939; Nanaimo *Free Press,* 18 May 1939; *Province,* 29 August 1939; *Times,* 7 June 1939; *Province,* 7 June 1939; Minister of Mines to C.B. Browning, 16 October 1939 and P.B. Ireland to Dr. J.F. Walker, 3 April 1940, GR202, Department of Mines, Mineralogical Division, Chief Mining Engineer, box 1, file 5; Griffith to E.C. Manning, 9 September 1939, GR1222, box 158, file 8.

27. *Times,* 17 February 1939. A useful introduction to Technocracy is William E. Akin, *Technocracy and the American Dream: The Technocrat Movement, 1900-1941* (Berkeley, 1977).

28. E.g., M. Slingsby and C. Wigen to H.H. Stevens, 11 September 1939, Stevens Papers, vol. 158; *Columbian,* 11 September 1939; Vernon *News,* 14 September 1939.

29. *Cowichan Leader,* 5 October 1939; S.G. Blaylock to N. Rogers, 13 October 1939, Pattullo Papers, box 72, file 14; other information is from "W.A. Curran's Memo re Technocracy Incorporated," in the same file.

30. Trail *Daily Times,* 30 and 31 October 1939; *Sun,* 7 and 25 November 1939; Nanaimo *Free Press,* 9 November 1939; *Colonist,* 13 November 1939.

31. E.g., *Province,* 28 January 1939; Powell River *Town Crier,* 30 January 1939; Chilliwack *Progress,* 15 November 1939. A good introduction to the history of

co-operatives may be found in Ian MacPherson, *Each For All: A History of the Co-operative Movement in English Canada, 1900-1945* (Toronto, 1979), passim and on credit unions, Ian MacPherson, "From the Secretary's Desk to Main Street: Change and Transition in the British Columbia Credit Union Movement 1936-1950," Canadian Historical Association, *Historical Papers*, 1987, 212-29.

32. *Times*, 6 December 1938; *Province*, 20 April and 11 May 1939; Grand Forks *Gazette*, 20 and 27 July 1939; Vernon *News*, 27 July 1939; Powell River *Town Crier*, 15 June 1939.

33. Robin Fisher, "The Decline of Reform: British Columbia Politics in the 1930s," Paper Presented to the B.C. Studies Conference, November 1986.

34. Pattullo to Leo Derman, 21 November 1939, BCARC, Premiers' Papers, GR1222, box 32, file 8; Pattullo to King, 26 April, Pattullo Papers, box 70, file 3 and King Papers, #233293. See also Hart to Dunning, 23 February 1939, Finance, vol. 683.

35. Pattullo to King, 6 January 1939, King Papers, #233372-3; Pattullo to King, 28 January 1939, Pattullo Papers, box 70, file 3 and King Papers, #233282-4; Prince Rupert *Daily News*, 28 February 1939; *Sun*, 22 April 1939; *Times*, 4 May 1939; Powell River *Town Crier*, 24 April 1939.

36. *Colonist*, 7 May 1939; Pattullo to King, 26 April 1939, Pattullo Papers, box 70, file 3 and King Papers, #233293.

37. Memorandum from deputy minister of finance to Dunning, 8 May 1939, Finance, vol. 3986; Clark to Dunning, 11 April 1939 and Dunning to Hart, 5 May 1939, Finance, vol. 683.

38. E.g., *Colonist*, 8 January and 5 February 1939; *Sun*, 13 March and 16 May 1939.

39. *Sun*, 18 April 1939; *Province*, 25 and 28 April 1939; Nanaimo *Free Press*, 2 May 1939.

40. *Colonist*, 7 May 1939; *Times*, 4 May 1939.

41. *Times*, 10 May 1939; *Sun*, 5 and 11 June 1939; *Columbian*, 30 June 1939; Hart to Ilsley, 5 August 1939 and comptroller of Treasury to W.C. Clark, 28 August 1939, Finance, vol. 682.

42. Pattullo to King, 4 September 1939, GR1222, box 157, file 6; Prince Rupert *Daily News*, 1 September 1939; *Times*, 23 October 1939.

43. Ralston to Hart, 2 October 1939, Finance, vol. 682; *Times*, 4 and 7 October 1939; *Sun*, 7 October 1939; Hart to King, 12 October 1939, King Papers, #227848.

44. *Times*, 13 November 1939.

45. Ralston to Hart, 8 December 1939, Finance, vol. 681.

46. Pattullo to Ralston, 21 December 1939, GR1222, box 94, file 8.

47. E.g., Cowichan *Leader*, 19 and 26 January 1939; *Times*, 3 February 1939; *Colonist*, 15 February 1939.

48. *Colonist*, 1 March 1939.

49. *Province*, 11 January 1939; *Sun*, 14 January and 2 February 1939.

50. The Cranbrook *Courier* cynically remarked, "Shakeups in Vancouver's police force and collapses in the French government seem to vie with each other for honours in frequency of appearance in the day's news" as it warned interior police to prepare for an influx of "prostitutes, pimps, and tinhorns." (Cranbrook *Courier*, 14 January 1939). *Province*, 13 January 1939; *Sun*, 31 January 1939; Nelson *Daily News*, 19 April 1939; Board of Health, *Annual Report*, 1939, *BCSP*, 1940, CC27.

51. Dr. D.H. Williams to Vancouver Medical Association, 5 December 1935 in Vancouver Medical Association, *Bulletin*, c. February 1940.

52. D.H. Williams, Report on Soliciting and Prostitution in Beer Parlours and Hotels, Vancouver, 18 January 1939, copy in GR1222, vol. 32, file 4; *Province*, 13 January 1939; *Columbian*, 11 May 1939; *Colonist*, 22 and 25 August 1939.

53. *Sun*, 1 June 1939; Prince Rupert *Daily News*, 29 May 1939; Colonist, 22 November 1939.

54. According to the 1941 census, 85 percent of British Columbians were of British origin. This figure, of course, included individuals whose ancestors had come to Canada from the British Isles some generations earlier but 23 percent of British Columbians were actually born in Britain or its possessions. (See tables in Jean Barman, *Growing Up British in British Columbia: Boys in Private School* (Vancouver, 1984), 176.)

55. *Colonist*, 24 January 1939.

56. Prince George *Citizen*, 10 May and 19 October 1939; *Province*, 29 November 1939.

57. *The Federationist*, 5 January 1939; Kelowna *Courier*, 19 January 1939; Peace River Block *News*, 2 February 1939.

58. *Province*, 17 February 1939. The Victoria City Council tabled a motion to make tax and other concessions for some Jewish refugees who proposed to establish industrial undertakings. *Times*, 17 and 28 February 1939.

59. *Sun*, 13 October and 13 November 1939; *Times*, 13 June 1939; Pattullo to C.R. Bull, 17 May 1939, GR1222, box 153, file 2; Peace River Block *News*, 16 March and 27 April 1939; Nanaimo *Free Press*, 4 March 1939; Trail *Daily Times*, 30 August 1939; Kamloops *Sentinel*, 7 March 1939; *Province*, 8 March 1939; *Sun*, 18 April 1939. For details on the background of the Sudetenlanders' settlement, see J.F. Wagner, "British Columbia's Anti-Nazi Germans: The Tupper Creek Refugees," *BC Studies*, 39 (Autumn 1978), 3-19.

60. Kamloops *Sentinel*, 21 February, 9 and 16 June 1939; Penticton *Herald*, 12 October and 2 November 1939.

61. *Province*, 28 February 1939; *Sun*, 5 June and 18 August 1939; Nanaimo *Free Press*, 14 and 15 November 1939.

62. *Sentinel*, 7 February 1939.

63. *Colonist*, 30 November 1939.

64. Nelson *Daily News*, 3 June 1939; *Province*, 13 July 1939.

65. B.C. Provincial Police, Memorandum for Pattullo, 5 May 1939 and E.C. Henniger to G. Wismer, 1 May 1939, GR1222, vol. 25, file 8; Grand Forks *Gazette*, 27 April 1939; *Nelson Daily News*, 7 and 8 July 1939.

66. Arthur Wood to Pattullo, 27 June 1939, Pattullo Papers, box 66; Nelson *Daily News*, 1-7 August 1939, *passim.*

67. Wismer to Wood, 30 August 1939, Pattullo to Sun Life, 17 November 1939 and W.M. Moore to Pattullo, 18 November 1939, Pattullo Papers, box 66, file 3; *Times*, 28 November 1939; Kenneth Wallace to Pattullo, 30 November 1939, GR1222, box 25, file 8; Grand Forks *Gazette*, 7 December 1939.

68. Vernon *News*, 6 July 1939; King Diary, 10 January 1939; Pattullo to King, 20 October 1939, Pattullo Papers, box 69, file 1; *News-Herald*, 25 April 1939.

69. *Columbian*, 1 June 1939; *Province*, 4 September, 23 October and 13 November 1939; *News-Herald*, 13 April 1939.

70. One exception was the Nanaimo *Free Press*, 23 October 1939.

71. Prince George *Citizen*, 19 January 1939; Nanaimo *Free Press*, 27 February 1939; Chilliwack *Progress*, 22 February 1939; Jas. Cook to E. Lapointe, 3 February 1939, H.H. Stevens Papers, vol. 157; Nelson *Daily News*, 7 April 1939.

72. Penticton *Herald*, 4, 18 and 25 May, 1 June and 20 July 1939; Vernon *News*, 11 May 1939; Prince Rupert *Daily News*, 1 June 1939. See also *Sun*, 29 June 1939; Cranbrook *Courier*, 27 July 1939.

73. *Province*, 12 September 1939; Kelowna *Courier*, 7 September 1939; Kimberley *Courier*, 7 September 1939; *Sentinel*, 8 September 1939; Nanaimo *Free Press*, 16 September 1939; Prince George *Citizen*, 12 October 1939.

74. *Sentinel*, 12 September 1939; Penticton *Herald*, 7 September 1939; T.P. O'Kelly to Pattullo, 14 September 1939, GR1222, box 155, file 12; *Province*, 4 September 1939; *Sun*, 11 September 1939; Cowichan *Leader*, 14 September 1939; Kelowna *Courier*, 7 September 1939; Chilliwack *Progress*, 27 September 1939.

75. Prince Rupert *Daily News*, 11 January 1939; *Province*, 30 January and 11 April 1939; *Times*, 21 March and 14 April 1939; Bridge River-Lillooet *News*, 20 April 1939; Prince George *Citizen*, 2 March, 4 May, 13 July and *passim*; Cowichan *Leader*, 30 March 1939; T.W.S. Parsons, Confidential Memo, 1 May 1939; Cranbrook *Courier*, 30 March 1939.

76. *Times*, 26, 28 and 31 August 1939; Cowichan *Leader*, 31 August 1939; Trail *Daily Times*, 29 August 1939; Kelowna *Courier*, 31 August 1939; Nelson *Daily News*, 4 September 1939; *Columbian*, 5 September 1939; Prince Rupert *Daily News*, 31 August 1939; Pattullo to King, 8 September 1939, GR1222, box 157, file 6.

77. *Times*, 5 September 1939; Trail *Daily Times*, 3 September 1939; Kelowna *Courier*, 7 September 1939; *Province*, 1 September 1939; *Colonist*, 5 September 1939; *Columbian*, 15 September 1939.

78. Provincial Executive Meeting, 18 September 1939 and Regular Monthly Meeting of Provincial Council, 30 September 1939, both in UBCSC, CCF, Provincial Party, Minute Book.

79. *Sun*, 4 November 1939; *Times*, 4 November 1939. Pattullo did not carry out his threat but Arthur Beauchesne, the clerk of the House of Commons, voluntarily advised him that Mrs. Steeves had violated her oath of office and could be suspended. Her "immunity as a member of the Legislative Assembly," he explained, "does not protect her against seditious speeches. She is free to criticize the conduct of the war, but if in doing so, she encourages the enemy, she commits a disloyal act." (Arthur Beauchesne to Pattullo, 7 November 1939, Pattullo Papers, box 72, file 3).

80. *Province*, 7 November 1939. See also *Sun*, 8 November 1939; Penticton *Herald*, 9 November 1939; Vernon *News*, 9 November 1939; West Coast *Advocate*, 9 November 1939; Prince George *Citizen*, 16 November 1939; Nanaimo *Free Press*, 4 November 1939.

81. Provincial Council Meeting, 16 December 1939, UBCSC, CCF, Provincial Party, Minute Book; Grace MacInnis to David Lewis, 19 December 1939, quoted in Susan Walsh, "The Peacock and the Guinea Hen: Political Profiles of Dorothy Gretchen Steeves and Grace MacInnis," in Barbara Latham and Roberta Pazdro, eds., *Not Just Pin Money: Selected Essays on The History of Women's Work in British Columbia* (Victoria, 1984), 370.

82. Vernon *News*, 14 September 1939; *Colonist*, 28 September 1939; Cowichan *Leader*, 5 and 19 October 1939; Prince George *Citizen*, 19 October 1939; Peter Stursberg in the *Province*, 23 October 1939.

83. Prince Rupert *Daily News*, 23 September 1939; *Sun*, 7 September 1939; *Province*, 30 September 1939; *Times*, 4 October 1939; Nanaimo *Free Press*, 27 September 1939.

84. *Times*, 15 November 1939; Cranbrook *Courier*, 26 October 1939. See also Nanaimo *Free Press*, 3 October 1939; *Sun*, 8 November 1939.

85. *Sun*, 6 November 1939.

86. *Sun*, 28 April and 6 May 1939; Cowichan *Leader*, 14 September 1939. For a fuller account of the Corps see Ruth Roach Pierson, *"They're Still Women After All": The Second World War and Canadian Womanhood* (Toronto, 1986), 97-101 and, especially, Susan Wade, "Joan Kennedy and the British Columbia Women's Service Corps", in Latham and Pazdro, 407-28.

87. Prince George *Citizen*, 7 September and 28 December 1939; Nanaimo *Free Press*, 8 and 24 September 1939; *Colonist*, 9 and 13 September and 22 December 1939; *Columbian*, 13 September 1939; Trail *Daily Times*, 15 September 1939; West Coast *Advocate*, 26 October 1939; *Province*, 13 September and 16 December 1939; Penticton *Herald*, 5 October and 23 November 1939; Powell River *Town Crier*, 23 November 1939; Prince Rupert *Daily News*, 4 December 1939.

88. *Times*, 23 December 1939.

A PERIOD OF WAITING OVER: THE PRAIRIES IN 1939

David E. Smith
University of Saskatchewan

On the prairies the two dominant news events of 1939 were the Royal visit and the outbreak of war. In terms of immediate impact on the region's residents, preparations for the Royal visit surpassed those associated with mobilization for war. Local and provincial bodies in each of the three provinces spent months planning ceremonies and routes as well as organizing mass transportation for tens of thousands of loyal subjects, young and old, to the principal cities to be visited by the Royal couple. By way of contrast, war with Germany assumed a fatal inevitability after the Nazi occupation of Czechoslovakia in March, while the organized response to this deteriorating situation rested almost exclusively with the federal government. And except for expressions of concern after 1 September about the impact of hostilities on the grain trade (which had yet to become manifest by year's end), the immediate effect of the war on the prairies remained minimal. In October a hint of the magnitude of change to come appeared with the proposed of the British Commonwealth Air Training Plan which, as columnist Grant Dexter presciently noted, would have particular implications for the region, because "only on the prairies can scores of airdromes be created overnight."[1]

Although far from the scene of trouble, prairie residents were not immune to international developments. In February 1939, 4000 Winnipeggers turned out to greet members of the Mackenzie-Papineau battalion returning from Spain, 79 of whom were Westerners, 18 from Winnipeg. Manitoba's political gadfly, L. St. George Stubbs (Independent MLA), captured the spirit of the occasion and of the year, when he linked that event to the much bigger celebration planned for May: "The humblest of these boys is more entitled to a royal welcome than the King and Queen, because of what they have done individually for humanity."[2] A month later, a more subdued welcome awaited the first of one thousand Sudeten-German refugees, who arrived in the Peace River district and northern Saskatchewan that spring and summer to begin life anew as western farmers, the first substantial number of immigrants to the region in a decade. The Canadian National Railway's colonization department settled the

Saskatchewan contingent, comprising nearly half of the total number, on land in the St. Walburg district, 150 miles northwest of Saskatoon. Initially, the refugees were housed in railroad boxcars, but by late summer the CNR's agents had "purchased one hundred and forty-three quarter sections and one farm of seven quarter sections," and had constructed, where buildings did not exist, a "standard size" house of 18-feet by 20-feet.[3]

While most of the war-talk emanated from Europe, Japan's military expansion in China had led the United States to open discussions with Canada in January on the feasibility of building a highway to Alaska. Albertans immediately promoted a route east of the mountains, although an article in the *Edmonton Journal* warned about the consequences associated with such a mammoth project, including the possibility that Canada might become bound to the United States though a military treaty which would make the highway a target for enemy attack.[4]

Great events in distant lands helped explain the results that winter of an *Edmonton Journal* poll of University of Alberta students. In answer to the question "who is the greatest man in the world today," Neville Chamberlain, the British prime minister, won hands down, while Franklin Roosevelt, the US president, came second and Anthony Eden, formerly Chamberlain's foreign secretary, and William Aberhart, Alberta's premier, tied for third place. On the distaff side, the winner was Madame Chiang, wife of the Chinese nationalist leader, with Mrs. Roosevelt and the Queen (now, Elizabeth the Queen Mother) as runners up. Sixty-two percent of the same students favoured Canada's entry in a war that involved England, a strong endorsement when compared to University of Saskatchewan students who narrowly supported the same proposition: 330 to 324.[5]

Throughout 1939 only one other story consistently shared the front page of prairie newspapers with the Royal visit and the war — grain prospects. The drought and the Depression which had begun ten years before were at an end. As early as January, the director of rehabilitation of the Prairie Farm Rehabilitation Administration (PFRA) had predicted that "the Dust Bowl" no longer exists," and the harvest ten months later — the largest since 1928 — bore out his optimism. In 1939 cash income from grain in Saskatchewan alone exceeded the previous year's total by $40 million.[6] The per-acre yield of wheat in Saskatchewan shot from 2.6 bushels in 1937 (the worst year of the drought) to 19.1 bushels two years later. In April, when Italy invaded Albania and one Regina *Leader-Post* headline screamed “Europe!,” another parallel headline announced “Aid to Small Farms” and reported the introduction in the House of Commons of the Prairie Farm Assistance Act (PFAA). In June, when the same paper featured a story on the King and Queen's departure from Canada, the reassuring headline read “Southwest Soakers Banish Drought Fear.”[7] After years of repeated disappointment, reports in May that “the new wheat is holding” despite high winds was news indeed.

As welcome as a good crop was, the harvest of 1939 in itself did not signal an end to the endemic instability of prairie incomes. Fundamental change did occur, however, with the introduction of the PFAA by the federal minister of agriculture, J.G. Gardiner. The year before, with the support of the prime minister, Mackenzie King, Gardiner had pressed his cabinet colleagues into agreeing to include a bonus, or cash subsidy, as part of the Canadian Wheat Board's initial payment to western farmers. This was the first time a federal agricultural transfer (as opposed to relief payments) had been made on the basis of need. In 1939 Gardiner increased the pressure, this time arguing for a programme that would provide special payments to farmers whose crop yields were abnormally low. Again, and against great opposition, he carried the legislation through Parliament. The achievement of PFAA (*Statutes of Canada*, 3 George VI, c.50) lay less in the immediate aid it rendered disadvantaged farmers than in the principle it embraced: the use of the public treasury to alleviate regional economic disparity. As a result of PFAA, the national government acknowledged responsibility for maintaining the integrity of Western agriculture, an obligation it continued to accept, if sometimes uneasily, for several decades after the war. As Gardiner made explicit to the House, Ottawa's commitment to the farmers now extended much further than an assurance of orderly marketing:

> *Between 1935 and now we have had a continuation of crop failures which has necessitated government assistance. It is now evident that marketing legislation alone will not solve the problems of the wheat growing areas. It is evident that an area which produced the wealth of the period from 1922 to 1928 must be utilized to the fullest possible extent in the effort to develop a nation of home builders ...*
>
> *The objective of this government has been and will continue to be to set up as many homes as can possibly be maintained on farms in the prairie section of western Canada. We believe that to do so will assist in solving our labour problem, our railway problem and every other national problem ...*[8]

In 1939 the fulcrum of prairie life was still the wheat economy, a truth documented that year in a book of the same title by G.E. Britnell, "one of our younger members," wrote the president of the University of Saskatchewan in his annual report for 1938-1939. In the same report, Walter Murray acknowledged two other works of "outstanding merit" published by faculty members: A.S. Morton, *A History of the Canadian West to 1870* and Gerhard Herzberg, *Molecular Spectra and Molecular Structure* (this latter work was cited in 1971, when Herzberg won the Nobel Prize for Chemistry). Next door, in Manitoba, Chester Martin had chartered the historical development of western land ownership in his *"Dominion Lands" Policy*, which appeared in 1938, but was reviewed by R.O. MacFarlane in the *Winnipeg Free Press* the first week of 1939.[9]

Perennial hopes for diversifying the prairie economy flickered briefly in January as a result of an oil strike at Lloydminster on the Alberta-Saskatchewan boundary, and this led in May to the first shipment of crude in a tank car "bedecked with banners and ribbons." But like the Turner Valley discovery 25 years before, no sustained development of the industry followed. Indeed, despite the improved fortunes of wheat evident in the fall, the economic outlook for most of that year on the prairies remained sombre.

Saskatchewan, the province most dependent on grain, sought diversity where it could find it. In 1939 that meant promoting a fence-post industry using Saskatchewan trees and provincially-mined lignite for creosote.[10] Alberta began the year by reducing (for the fifth time since 1936) interest paid on provincial government bonds and then followed that item of Social Credit faith by another — the issue of Treasury Board vouchers to civil servants to cover one-quarter of their wages.[11] Manitoba, the province with the broadest economic base, showed the most improvement, increasing provincial expenditures by $680,000 and using nearly a third of the amount partially to restore the salaries of public servants cut earlier in the Depression. But a major investigation, by Carl Goldenberg, into Winnipeg's local government structures and finances had revealed an ominous finding: the population of the city had declined for the first time in its history, by an estimated 9,000 persons between 1938 and 1939.[12] The contraction of Winnipeg as the regional metropolis (hinted at in the Goldenberg findings) and the federal assumption of responsibility for the welfare of the grain industry (evident in PFRA and PFAA) were harbingers of a structural change in the prairie economy which the bountiful harvest of 1939 temporarily disguised.

At the end of 1939, the reformation of the prairie economy still lay in the future. The determinative event occurred in the spring of 1940, with the fall of France and the closing of European markets. Great Britain, the sole remaining major purchaser of Canadian agricultural products, increased its demand for meat and dairy products but reduced its imports of wheat. For the West, whose herds had been depleted by drought and feed shortages during the 1930s, this was bad news. For the federal government, now committed to maintaining some stability in prairie farm incomes, the challenges of this dramatic reversal in export demand were formidable. In an attempt to wean Canadian wheat farmers from their traditional crop, the government for the first time paid them to plant something other than wheat or, better yet, nothing at all. In the same year delivery quotas were introduced in an attempt to ration elevator space. Within two years, these and other drastic interventions had caused acreage sown in wheat to decline by 42 percent over 1940, while that in feed grains (oats and barley) increased by 72 percent.[13] By 1943, for the first time in the West's history, more coarse grains were sown than wheat. Beginning with the bacon agreement in 1939, a series of food contracts, negotiated with the British government, had replaced the prewar open market in agricultural goods. The security the contracts provided — in price, quantities and delivery dates — helped the prairie economy adjust to the rapid changes confronting it. But despite the success in new production, the disruption caused to the region's principal industry proved politically damaging to the governing Liberals. The damage lay in the emergency's undermining of traditional government-industry relations, which had rested ultimately on Gardiner's personal and political skills of advocacy.

Within two weeks of war's declaration, the minister of agriculture was cautioning Mackenzie King to leave wartime agricultural policies and regulations to his department. Agriculture might be an industry but farms were unlike factories, Gardiner said, "where you can turn on the electricity and start production."[14] Agricultural production was determined by hundreds of thousands of farmers, whose calculations were based on "the relationship which the return for one product ... has upon the return from another." These decisions could not be made by some central authority ignorant of climate and growing seasons, and he instructed the non-agrarian prime minister that "there is a time for seeding crops and well defined times for breeding livestock." Two weeks later, when no decision had yet been reached on how to proceed for the next year's crops, Gardiner admitted to a western confidant that he had "become very restless." It was "hard to get [these] idea[s] over here."[15]

By the end of 1939, the outline of wartime agriculture's administration was far from clear. In the event, Gardiner and his department did play the commanding role he had envisioned, but not without repeated challenges from the new bureaucracy that mushroomed after the outbreak of war. The Wartime Prices and Trade Board was his *bête noire*, although he was disdainful of all such bodies for their determination to do their job without regard for the responsibilities and concerns of others. By this he meant their imperviousness to political considerations. A large part of the problem as far as the West was concerned lay in the wartime appointment process; as early as December 1939, Gardiner was complaining to Ernest Lapointe, federal minister of justice and Mackenzie King's French lieutenant, that "as far as I know, they pay no attention to the central prairie section of Canada at all in choosing their staff for any of these boards."[16] Such inattention to personnel, and therefore party, matters confounded the principles of the Liberal organization Gardiner had bequeathed to his successor in Saskatchewan, W.J. Patterson, and the organization he had resurrected in Alberta after 1935; in this last instance, Gardiner had assumed responsibility for party affairs while King embarked on a search for an Alberta minister that ended in January 1939 with the appointment of J.A. MacKinnon.[17]

By the spring of 1940, the same lack of concern for party — this time in the award of contracts for the building of prairie air bases under the Commonwealth Air Training Plan — had begun to alarm those responsible for overseeing the Liberal organization in Saskatchewan. Failure to consult Gardiner or those close to him in these matters threatened the organization's structure, which was built on intricate but time-consuming exchanges of information. "I still do not know," wrote a key man from Regina, "how we are going to run a political organization with as little information as is available at the present time."[18] Gardiner justified these unusual practices on the grounds that "speed was urgent," but from the first year of war he too recognized that he was constrained in what he might do to limit the dislocations caused by the emergency.

The pattern of prairie life was also being challenged in other ways, most particularly as a result of new developments in communication. After a decade of inactivity, road construction and improvement recommenced in each province, with hard surface highways scheduled for completion between Calgary and Edmonton and Edmonton and Jasper, while in Saskatchewan and Manitoba roads to the north to exploit resources and encourage tourism were actively investigated and promoted.[19] The large and dispersed farm population of the prairie began to move; in Saskatchewan vehicle registration grew by 8.4 percent between 1938 and 1939, a nearly three-fold increase over the previous year.[20] In response to the heavier traffic, Saskatchewan imposed a night-time speed limit of 45 m.p.h.; Manitoba debated a similar proposal, while Alberta (along with Nova Scotia, Québec and Prince Edward Island) kept its maximum limit of 30 m.p.h.[21] The isolation of remote sections of the region was breached in other ways when, for example, it was announced that the Peace River district, which already had an internal phone service, would be linked "to Edmonton and the outside world by radio-telephone."[22]

Communication between the region and the rest of the country vastly improved as a result of three innovations in the spring and summer of 1939. Early in March overnight air mail service began, as mail planes left Montreal, Toronto and Vancouver each evening with scheduled stops in the principal prairie cities. The first day's flights from the East and West brought 13,000 letters to Regina, along with shipments of cut flowers ordered by Saskatchewan florists, some of which were then flown by waiting aircraft north to Saskatoon and Prince Albert.[23] At the end of the month Trans-Canada Airlines inaugurated transcontinental passenger service, with an advertised return fare between Regina and Ottawa of $158.20. In July, national broadcasting arrived in Saskatchewan with the construction of a 50-kw transmitter bearing the callsign CBK, at Watrous. CBK was the third high-powered transmitter built by the Canadian Broadcasting Corporation (CBC)(the first two were at Toronto and Montreal) and the only one erected on the prairie before the Second World War. Located on salt flats and occupying the most effective frequency on the radio band (540 kcs), CBK's signal covered the whole of the prairie region. A full range of national programmes (some in French) thus became available to prairie listeners, although the absence of CBC production facilities in the region until 1948 meant that regional programmes continued to emanate from affiliated stations.

National radio ended forever the isolation of the prairie as a region and of its rural residents in particular. According to the Census of 1931, 68 percent of Saskatchewan's population was rural, while in Alberta and Manitoba the figures were 62 and 55 percent respectively. The same Census showed that while 50.9 percent of Canadians lived in cities, towns and villages of 1000 or more people, in the prairie provinces, beginning in Manitoba and moving west, only 41.21 and 31 percent of the respective populations lived in communities of this minimum size.[24] Significantly, external migration from the region during the 1930s and internal migration within the prairie provinces, from the drought-ravaged southern plains to the more hospitable northern parkland, meant fewer people lived in most of the region's urban areas at the outbreak of war than ten years before. The quinquennial Census for the prairie provinces in 1936 revealed that in the five years since 1931, the urban population of Manitoba and Saskatchewan had declined by 1.60 and 3.65 percent respectively, while in Alberta it had grown by 2.85 percent. In the first two provinces, the decline in the urban male population approached the precipitous: 6.12 percent in Saskatchewan and 3.65 percent in Manitoba.[25]

Roads were poor and impassable for long stretches of the winter and spring. Rural electrification was almost unknown except for those farms close to urban areas or which generated their own power (those farmers who had radios commonly used battery sets — W.R. Motherwell, a former minister of agriculture in both the Saskatchewan and federal governments, and not poor by community standards, being one of them). Rural subscribers to daily newspapers were few, and fewer in 1939 than in 1931 after "mixed" train service used to deliver the papers had been cut because of reduced crops.[26] The effects of depression and isolation lasted long after the conditions that caused them had disappeared. As late as 1956, J.G. Gardiner explained his role in securing the passage of Prairie Farm Assistance Act to a correspondent, who noted that "since we had no radio [in the 1930s] many important facts escaped us, for we were too tired usually to read and in fact could not afford to subscribe to newspapers."[27]

Private radio stations had been operating on the prairie since the early 1920s. While some were owned by newspapers — Saskatchewan's first station, CKCK in Regina, was owned by the *Leader-Post* — their overriding purpose was to entertain listeners. So much was this the case that for the first ten years of its life, CKCK did not carry commercials for fear of depriving its newspaper parent of advertising revenue. The result was, in the words of one Gardiner correspondent, that "we out here have to pretty well take our information from the newspapers and their interpretation."[28] In view of the fact that daily newspapers in Saskatchewan in 1939 were paid for by one in sixteen persons (even in 1948, only one in six rural homes received a daily newspaper), while in Manitoba and Alberta the figures were one in six and seven respectively, the need for greater communication was evident.[29]

At the outbreak of war, one group for whom it was thought radio might be used to good advantage was the prairie provinces' large non-English/non-French population. The 1931 Census revealed that 40 percent of Saskatchewan's population and 37 and 34 percent of the population of Manitoba and Alberta was comprised of persons whose mother tongue was neither English nor French.[30] The problem about "the complex and mixed nationalities," wrote the indefatigable T.H. Wood to Gardiner, was that "some way [must] be devised whereby they can feel that this is their country — not necessarily British, but Canadian."[31] Although there is no evidence that the broadcasts he urged, of "citizenship-type" appeals to "young Canadians, born of parents from other countries," ever took place, Gardiner was alive to the nature of the problem the ethnically-heterogeneous prairies presented. Even if he had not been personally aware of the region's multicultural traditions, as a result of his earlier career as a teacher and principal in ethnically-distinct communities, more recent developments underlined the volatile potential of the ethnic mix. On the one hand, the Co-operative Commonwealth Federation (CCF) had made significant inroads among "people who come from outside the British Empire," a truth underlined in the general election of 1940, when the CCF vote in his own seat of Melville tripled and his margin of victory shrank from 5000 votes in 1935 to 1,100.[32]

On the other hand, the provincial Liberals responded to the crisis in ways that could only alienate the province's large ethnic vote. Reflecting in part widespread unease throughout the province at the activities of the Deutscher Bund, which had entered the prairies in 1934, the Patterson Government in 1940 pushed Ottawa for easier internment of alleged Nazi sympathizers and for prohibition of Communist organizations.[33] In June 1940, by order-in-council, the Saskatchewan Veterans Civil Security Corps was formed to combat subversion.[34] At about the same time, Patterson personally warned Gardiner against appointing any Germans to the public service. Gardiner himself was appalled at these suggestions, recalling similar hysteria at the beginning of the First World War, and predicted that "many people will be more or less ashamed of their actions when the war is over." While he was always circumspect when it came to making personal comments in his own correspondence, he did not dispute T.H. Wood's description of the situation that "every member of the Government is going goofy right now."[35]

Gardiner's own approach was to stimulate, and capitalize upon, evidence of support by ethnic individuals and groups for the war effort. To this end he welcomed enlistment of the non-English and non-French in the military services. To a serviceman who had gone overseas in 1939, he wrote that "the fact ... you were taken over early in the war, will be heartening to all young men born in this country of European parentage." It constituted proof that "everyone who has lived under our Institutions ... appreciate[s] the freedom which can be enjoyed under them."[36] To George Simpson, a member of the History Department at the University of Saskatchewan and the "Anglo" academic who had done a great deal to make the history of the Slavic peoples known to his compatriots, he offered continued encouragement in "uniting the Ukrainian population behind the war effort."[37] (Simpson had given a talk over CBC Radio which defended the Ukrainian nationalists, who to the general public often appeared as extremists.)[38]

The war created uncertainty for the heterogeneous cultures of the prairies in the same way that it created uncertainty for the wheat economy. The four months of the "Phoney War" in 1939 (and the first half of 1940) did little else but create unease. At the end of the year, Wood told Gardiner that "in so far as the West is concerned, one would hardly know that there was a war,"[39] but the crisis was no less real nor the potential disruption to accepted practices any less great for that. The illiberal response of the province to the outbreak of hostilities contrasted sharply with the sense of evolving purpose behind federal wartime initiatives. In the preceding passages, a great deal has been said about Gardiner and, necessarily, about Saskatchewan. That prominence is justified in light of agriculture's central importance to all of the prairies. In 1940-1941, Gardiner was also minister of national war services, a responsibility which brought wartime ethnic questions to his immediate attention and which as a result enhanced his importance in western eyes.[40]

Even when the focus of discussion is limited to 1939, it is clear that wartime politics, along with the technological changes in communication already mentioned, were set to accentuate the decline of the prairie's regional identity. Although some years still in the future, the change would eventually be translated into a contraction of the region's political influence: under the redistribution in effect in 1939, however, Saskatchewan and Manitoba had the largest number of seats in the House of Commons that either of them would ever possess. For now, they had influence.

Events in 1939 permanently altered some of the conditions that had given the West its distinctiveness. There was one exception, however. The feature of prairie life most frequently cited as setting the region apart from others in Canada — its provincial politics — was little in evidence in 1939. In Alberta the Social Credit government had recently passed through a period of great internal dissent, in part because of the contemporaneous conflict with the federal government over constitutional and jurisdictional matters. A provincial election was expected in 1940, but in the meantime Alberta politics were as quiescent as they could be with a mesmeric premier like William Aberhart. One Alberta political event, remarkable only for its peculiarity in a system of parliamentary government, occurred when after four years the premier made his maiden speech in the legislature. When chided by the opposition for his unusual timidity, Aberhart cited a Chinese proverb that "crowing hens never lay eggs," and then spoke for an hour-and-a- half in defence of Social Credit principles.[41]

The most recent Saskatchewan election, in 1938, had seen the strength of the CCF double in the legislature (from five to ten seats), while a concerted effort by Alberta's Social Credit forces to carry their revolution eastward had produced only two victories. The reigning but tired Liberals now grudgingly accepted the possibility that the CCF had become a permanent political force in the province, a conclusion the socialists cheerfully acknowledged. Most significantly, by 1939 it was clear that Saskatchewan would continue as a two-party system, as it had since the province's beginning in 1905, although it was equally undeniable that a new party, the CCF, had replaced the now-vanished Conservatives. The situation in Manitoba differed from either of the other two provinces. Here, there was neither a single dominant party, like Social Credit in Alberta, or two-party competition, as in Saskatchewan, but rather an emerging fusion of political forces. The year 1939 marked the half-way point between provincial elections: at the last the Liberals and Progressives had coalesced, at the next an unabashed non-party coalition would take control. Thus, local political factors, coupled with the approaching visit of the monarch, the possibility of war and a widespread assumption early in the year that a federal election would be called in the autumn, kept the normally colourful parade of prairie politics at a canter.

At year's end it seemed just possible that this political quiescence might actually last for the duration. To hold off proposals for a union or a national government, Mackenzie King had declared in the first week of the war his government's determination to set partisan differences aside during the emergency. This pronouncement had a differential impact on prairie political parties. In Manitoba where, with the exception of the CCF, partisanship was already so muted as to be virtually imperceptible, the consequences of this national development hardly mattered. In Alberta, Liberals and Conservatives were already united in their opposition to Aberhart, but the premier found himself restrained now by other wartime measures, such as the CBC ruling that Aberhart must excise references to politics from his weekly religious broadcasts.[42] Because of these restraints and attracted by its programme of the structural reform of Canada's economic and political systems, Aberhart began to flirt with W.D. Herridge's New Democracy movement. Common cause among unorthodox politicians led Liberals and Conservatives in Saskatchewan to commiserate about the future. For instance, on the eve of war, T.C. Davis informed Gardiner that M.A. MacPherson, one of the province's most respected public figures and a former Conservative attorney-general in the government of J.T.M. Anderson (1929-34), believed it would be "disastrous" for the "two-party system" and "the Conservative party" if the latter "became merely a sectional Party, representing Eastern Canada, and some crack-pot organization, like Social Credit, C.C.F., New Democracy, or National Reform became the Western Party."[43]

The West's kaleidoscope of third parties and King's pledge of a moratorium on partisanship alarmed so inveterate a partisan as Gardiner. Nor could he look to Saskatchewan Liberals for reassurance, since they — tired from the struggles of governing during the Depression and worried about the rise of the CCF — looked on the wartime party truce with a sense of relief. Because he and his informants in Saskatchewan did not expect the CCF to "recognize the truce," Gardiner therefore publicly echoed his leader's pledge but privately counselled his confidants to act "circumspectly" and not to break up the old political organization.[44]

In the last month of 1939, the Liberals witnessed a chilling demonstration of what would happen to those who forgot the importance of organization. The death of the sitting Liberal member necessitated a federal by-election in Saskatoon City in December. Local Liberals dithered about whether they should invite a candidate like Colonel J.L. Ralston, a Nova Scotian and former minister, whom the prime minister had brought into Cabinet in September and who was in need of a seat. In the event, an open convention led to the selection of a weak candidate, who suffered ignominious defeat before the only United (sometimes called National) Reform candidate ever to be elected to the House of Commons. The United Reform Group comprised an amalgam of Social Credit and Herridge supporters. As fate would have it, the victor, a Presbyterian minister from Saskatoon, was unable to take his seat in January 1940 because of Parliament's sudden dissolution; he was re-elected at the general election in March 1940, but died before the new Parliament met, thus achieving immortality as the only person twice elected to Parliament but never to take a seat. In the subsequent six-candidate by-election, in the summer of 1940, the Liberal vote collapsed even further than in 1939, because in addition to an official Liberal candidate, two others of Liberal origin ran. This time the Conservative candidate won, marginally defeating the new United Reform candidate, Agnes MacPhail. So disreputable a performance on the part of Saskatchewan Liberals, traditionally the best-organized of prairie parties, hinted at a period of political uncertainty which would accompany the war. With few other political surprises on the prairies in 1939, however, the Saskatoon upset could be interpreted as an aberration only. Aberration or not, the by-election results added one more disturbing note to the sombre close of the decade.

After nine years of unrelieved economic gloom, the events of 1939 had offered a break from the tedium of the Depression. Whatever the future held for prairie Canadians, it could hardly be more perilous than the dislocations that they had suffered because of the Depression and drought. And it had this great advantage — it was unknown. As so often on the prairies, the promise of "next year" would signal the real direction of the change that had begun in 1939. More than anything else, it can be said that for prairie residents the first half of 1939 constituted a period of waiting — for the King and Queen, the war, and evidence that the worst drought in living memory was over. By September, with the monarch departed, war declared and the second largest harvest in history underway, the region thankfully turned its back on a period everyone wished to but none could forget. The *Leader-Post* got the region's sentiments and their priorities about right the day the King arrived in Regina, when in bold type it trumpeted: "It's a Great Country: It Really Does Rain and Royalty to Make History."[45]

NOTES

1. Regina *Leader-Post*, 18 October 1939. Some indication of the consequences of the plan, which began to become evident in 1940, can be found in Brereton Greenhous and Norman Hillmer, "The Impact of the British Commonwealth Air Training Plan on Western Canada: Some Saskatchewan Case Studies," *Journal of Canadian Studies*, 16, 3 and 4 (Fall-Winter, 1981), 133-44.

2. *Winnipeg Free Press*, 6 February 1939, 1.

3. Jonathan Wagner, "Saskatchewan's Sudetendeutsche: The Anti-Nazi Germans of St. Walburg," *Saskatchewan History*, XXXIII 3 (Autumn, 1980), 90-101, at 92.

4. *Edmonton Journal*, 21 January 1939, 23; see also *ibid.*, 4 February 1939, 1 and 3.

5. *Ibid.*, 8 February 1939, 9, and Regina *Leader-Post*, 27 March 1939, 5.

6. Regina *Leader-Post*, 14 October 1939, 1. The most concise discussion of wheat matters in this period is G.E. Britnell and V.C. Fowke, *Canadian Agriculture in War and Peace, 1935-50* (Stanford, 1962), 196-205.

7. Regina *Leader-Post*, 6 April 1939, 1 and 16 June 1939, 1.

8. Canada, House of Commons, *Debates*, 16 February 1939, 1036-37.

9. G.E. Britnell, *The Wheat Economy* (Toronto, 1939); A.S. Morton, *A History of the Canadian West to 1870* (Toronto, 1939); Gerhard Herzberg, *Molecular Spectra and Molecular Structure* (New York, 1939); and Arthur S. Morton and Chester Martin, *History of Prairie Settlement and "Dominion Lands" Policy* (Toronto, 1938).

10. Regina *Leader-Post*, 4 January 1939, 3.

11. *Edmonton Journal*, 3 January 1939, 4, and *Winnipeg Free Press*, 13 February 1939, 1.

12. *Winnipeg Free Press*, 22 March 1939, 3.

13. Britnell and Fowke, 210.

14. Saskatchewan Archives Board (SAB), Papers of James G. Gardiner, 43493-5, Gardiner to King, 26 September 1939.

15. *Ibid.*, 43709-10, Gardiner to D.A. McNiven, 7 October 1939.

16. *Ibid.*, 43547-8, Gardiner to Lapointe, 9 December 1939.

17. See Norman Ward, "Hon. James Gardiner and the Liberal Party of Alberta, 1935-40," *Canadian Historical Review*, LVI, 3 (September 1975), 303-22.

18. SAB, Gardiner Papers, 45162-3, T.H. Wood To Gardiner, 4 June 1940.

19. *Edmonton Journal*, 27 March 1939, 4 and *Winnipeg Free Press*, 11 February 1939, 3.

20. *Canada Year Book, 1941* (Ottawa, 1941), 572. In Alberta between the same years, motor-vehicle registration increased by 5.7 percent.

21. Regina *Leader-Post*, 14 May 1939, 3 and Winnipeg Free Press, 2 March 1939, 5.

22. *Edmonton Journal*, 27 January 1939, 1.

23. Regina *Leader-Post*, 2 March 1939, 3.

24. Jack C. Stabler, *Prairie Regional Development and Prospects* (Supporting Study No.1, prepared for the Royal Commission on Consumer Problems and Inflation; Regina, 1968), 16.

25. *Census of the Prairie Provinces, 1936* (Ottawa, 1936), Table I for each province, 4 (Manitoba), 359 (Saskatchewan), and 832 (Alberta).

26. Bill NcNeil and Morris Wolfe, *Signing On: The Birth of Radio in Canada* (Toronto, 1982), 125 (interview, Andy McDermott).

27. Gardiner Papers, 25189-92, Ellen (Mrs. V.) Hadley to Gardiner, 9 April 1956.

28. *Ibid.*, 45031-2, T.H. Wood to Gardiner, 31 March 1939.

29. *Canada Year Book, 1941* (Ottawa, 1941), 648 (Table 2).

30. *Canada Year Book, 1934-35* (Ottawa, 1935), 146 (Table 36); SAB, Papers of T.C. Douglas, file 757, "A Study of Radio Listening Habits in the Province of Saskatchewan," August 1948 (Toronto, 1948), unpaginated.

31. Gardiner Papers, 45029, T.H. Wood to Gardiner, 17 March 1939.

32. *Ibid.*, 52592-3, Gardiner to J.A. Watson, 20 April 1940, and *Directory of Members of Parliament and Federal Elections for the North-West Territories and Saskatchewan, 1887-1966* (Regina and Saskatoon, 1967), 37.

33. See Jonathan F. Wagner, "The Deutscher Bund Canada in Saskatchewan," *Saskatchewan History*, XXXI, 2 (Spring 1978), 41-50; Gardiner Papers, 37595-6, W.J. Patterson to Gardiner, 25 May 1940.

34. See Robert J. MacDonald, "The Silent Column: Civil Security in Saskatchewan During World War II," *Saskatchewan History*, XXXIX, 2 (Spring 1986), 41-61.

35. Gardiner Papers, 37595-6, Patterson to Gardiner, 25 May 1940; 37597-8, Gardiner to Patterson, 1 June 1940; and 45171, Wood to Gardiner, 5 June 1940.

36. *Ibid.*, 43759-66, Gardiner to Capt. J.J. Mildenburger, 29 January 1940.

37. Thomas M. Prymak, "George Simpson, the Ukrainian Canadians, and the 'Pre-History' of Slavic Studies in Canada," *Saskatchewan History*, XLI, 2 (Spring 1988), 53-66, at 57.

38. *Ibid.*, 55.

39. SAB, Gardiner Papers, 45106-9, Wood to Gardiner, 28 December 1939.

40. For more on the Department of National War Services, see N.F. Dreisziger, "The Rise of a Bureaucracy for Multiculturalism: The Origins of the Nationalities Branch, 1939-1941," in Norman Hillmer *et al.*, *On Guard for Thee: War, Ethnicity, and the Canadian State, 1939-1945* (Ottawa, 1988), 1-29; see too Leslie A. Pal, "Identity, Citizenship, and Mobilization: The Nationalities Branch and World War Two," *Canadian Public Administration*, 32, 3 (Fall, 1989), 407-26.

41. *Winnipeg Free Press*, 18 February 1939, 3.

42. David R. Elliot and Iris Miller, *Bible Bill: A Biography of William Aberhart* (Edmonton, 1987), 290-1.

43. SAB, Gardiner Papers, 41490-1, 19 June 1939.

44. *Ibid.*, 45086-7, Gardiner to Wood, 16 October 1939; see also Thomas Miller to Gardiner, 43908-9, 18 June 1940, and reply, 43910, 22 June 1940.

45. Regina *Leader-Post*, 22 May 1939, 1.

ONTARIO 1939: THE DECISION FOR WAR

Terry Copp
Wilfrid Laurier University

Canadian historians have long assumed that they know most of what there is to learn about English-Canadian and Ontario attitudes towards the outbreak of war in 1939. The leading historian in the field, J.L. Granatstein, is definite. The country, he writes, went to war "because Britain went to war. Not for democracy, not to stop Hitler, not to save Poland." For Granatstein, Canada's decision was based on "sentiment and ties of blood and culture."[1] Other specialists have offered similar views. Robert Bothwell and Norman Hillmer describe Canada's decision in 1939 as an "irrational, incoherent, and to most intellectuals, unintelligent flow of opinion," stemming from their commitment to fighting "from time to time in the interests of English-speaking safety and solidarity."[2] Michiel Horn, when explaining F.R. Scott's advocacy of neutrality, declares that the "main argument in favour of belligerency was that Canada had a duty to join the mother country."[3] John Thompson's summary of the issue in *Decades of Discord* begins with the statement: "It was for imperial solidarity that they [English Canadians] went to war."[4]

This scholarly consensus seems to be derived from the study of the views of a number of intellectuals who opposed Canadian participation. Frank Scott, O.D. Skelton, and other critics of Canadian policy in 1939 had slight respect for the views of the vast majority of English Canadians and tended to dismiss their opinions as immature, ignorant, or simply colonial. This essay will attempt to demonstrate that, in the province of Ontario, broad public support for Canada's entry into a European war developed after the signing of the Munich Agreement and crystallized in March of 1939. The consensus was based upon a belief that Hitler presented a threat to world peace and to the fundamental values of western civilization. Canada would not have gone to war if Britain had not done so — for obvious reasons — but the people of Ontario supported a declaration of war out of their informed convictions that fundamental issues were at stake.

The population of Ontario in 1939 was approximately 3.8 million, just less than one-third of the Canadian total. The 1930s had seen a ten percent growth but almost all of it was due to natural increase and migration from other provinces. Fewer than 10,000 overseas immigrants were added during the decade. Fully 80 percent of the provincial population were born in Canada, while another 12 percent were British-born. According to the 1941 Census, the "racial origin" of the citizenry was 72 percent British, ten percent French, 6.3 percent Germanic (a strange category encompassing Germans, Belgians and Dutch) and 4.1 percent Slavic. "Native Indians and half breeds" at 2.8 percent formed the next largest group, followed by Jews and Italians at 1.6 percent each.[5]

If, as Norman Hillmer argues, "Canada in the Second World War was already a multi-cultural country,"[6] Ontario was not. In 30 of Ontario's 48 counties more than 80 percent of the population was "British." Eleven "mixed" counties had sufficient numbers of French Canadians to reduce the British percentage to below 80. In only eight counties, six of them in Northern Ontario, were there large enough groups of "ethnics" to constitute a fifth to a quarter of the population.

The children of these small minority groups registered in one of two educational systems which schooled the entire population of the province in a common set of values. No doubt the new educational historians will eventually get around to showing us that the insistence on literacy, self-discipline, personal cleanliness, ambition, fair play and a patriotism which included Canada's British heritage was part of a bourgeois conspiracy to exercise social control. But for our purposes it is sufficient to note that the educational systems were designed to transmit a set of highly-regarded majoritarian values, not to challenge them with notions of moral or cultural relativism. The schools of Ontario, with their Union Jacks, *Empire Songsters* and portraits of the King on every classroom wall, were among the many institutions which tied Ontarians to Britain and the Empire-Commonwealth. The British connection was a central fact of Ontario life in the 1930s. It was therefore impossible for most people to think of themselves as isolated from events in Europe.

Most citizens of Ontario also attended church, another institution which often linked Canadians with Britain. United, Anglican, Presbyterian and Baptist congregations together accounted for 56 percent of the total, while 22.5 percent were Roman Catholic. Lutherans at 2.7 percent and Jews at just under two percent formed the next largest groups.[7] However, the churches of the 1930s, or at least individual churchmen, were not always content with their role as transmitters of agreed values. The clergy provided much of the opposition to Canadian participation in a new European war. Pacifism, or at least a strong distaste for war, had become an issue of some importance in church circles during the early 1930s. The United Church's Council declared that "armed warfare between nations was contrary to the spirit and teachings of Christ"[8] in late 1932; this theme was repeated at conferences through to 1938. *The New Outlook*, the official journal of the church, actively promoted peace causes by endorsing the League of Nations and suggesting that it was capitalism, Versailles and original sin — not Hitler, Mussolini and Japanese militarism — that threatened the peace of the world. *The New Outlook* gave much publicity to the Oxford Conference of Churches held in Britain in 1937, which had denounced war as "a particular demonstration of the power of sin in the world."[9] By the spring of 1938, there was less certainty. An editorial titled "Wake Up Canada" began: "Fascism means war. It has meant war and conquest in every land in which it has so far reared its ugly head. And our awakening to this state readily cannot come a moment too soon."[10]

By the end of 1938, Ontario was fully awake. Public euphoria over the resolution of the Munich crisis had given way to doubts as the details of German actions in the Sudetenland became known. Then, on 9 November, the *Reichskristallnacht*, or night of broken glass, shattered more illusions about the nature of the Nazi state. The Toronto *Globe's* reaction was typical. The events of *Kristallnacht* demonstrated that Hitler and Nazi Germany "could not be trusted." "The world," the *Globe* stated, "was shocked by the horrible vengeance wrought on the Jewish race ... It has seen, perhaps not too late, the viciousness and uncompromising spirit of Nazi philosophy."[11]

The public response to *Kristallnacht* forced many in the Christian churches to re-examine their commitment to rhetorical pacificism. When the Canadian Jewish Congress organized a rally to express sympathy and solidarity with German Jews, Maple Leaf Gardens was filled to capacity and overflow meetings were held at other locations. The Reverend Peter Bryce, a past moderator of the United Church, as well as a number of other prominent religious leaders, spoke at the rally condemning "the Nazi gospel of hate."[12] Throughout 1938 and 1939, the United Church journal provided a steady stream of articles on events in Europe, all of which seemed to point to the need for Christians to reassess their role. J.S. Woodsworth, leader of the Co-operative Commonwealth Federation (CCF), watched this retreat from pacifist rhetoric with growing unease. In a letter which appeared in February 1939,[13] he pointed out the vagueness of the church's pronouncements and asked for a clear statement of what the church would do if England were attacked. Woodsworth's letter touched off a debate which dominated the magazine, now renamed the *Observer*, throughout 1939. A small minority of anti-war ministers and laymen continued to press the case against Canadian participation, but it is evident that they were aware it was a lost cause. Increasingly, the pacifist minority was treated with contempt. As one reader put it, "Cannot you and other pacifists distinguish between the moral significance of different wars ... war with all its horror is a less dreadful alternative than that which Hitler would force upon the world."[14]

In October 1939, 68 United Church ministers, most from Ontario, signed a "Witness Against War" letter in the *Observer*.[15] Few in the congregations or among their colleagues, however, offered support and many were simply outraged. The debate in the United Church had centered on the challenge posed to the Christian conscience by the threat of war. Two positions, both articulated in terms of morality, had been put forward, but there was never really any doubt about the views of the majority. As the Oshawa Presbytery put it, "We deplore war, and while we recognize the sincerity of the pacifist, we must insist that Christian principles, upon which our democracy is based, must be upheld today even at the risk of life itself."[16] When the time came to change the official church stand on war, the General Council declared, "The United Church of Canada reaffirms the entire and perfect love and loyalty of the people of the United Church to His Majesty, the King and its unfailing adherence to the cause for which he stands; it pledges the unfaltering support to the King in his struggle against the evil forces which seek to dominate the souls of man ..."[17] The debate within the other churches was far less intense and less public, but it was equally focused on the Christian response to the threat posed by fascism and the prospect of war.

For many in Ontario, the question of war or peace did not become urgent until the occupation of Prague in March 1939. You may recall A.J.P. Taylor's statement about the impact of that event in Britain. Taylor wrote "There followed an underground explosion of public opinion such as the historian cannot trace in precise terms."[18] While Taylor could not trace it in the narrow range of diplomatic source material he chose to examine, it is not difficult to find details of the transformation of public opinion in the newspapers, British or Canadian.

Ontario in the 1930s possessed a rich and diverse free press. Many daily newspapers, now defunct or brain-dead under chain control, waged fierce competition for readers. Weekly newspapers, not yet fully rationalized as advertising bulletins, provided yet more opportunities for vigorous debate. And debate there was. Partisan politics accounts for much of it, but partisanship and competition can provide a healthy basis for the exchange of ideas. The prospect of war had long divided the Ontario press, at least in terms of the rhetoric employed. Newspapers like the Toronto *Globe* and *Ottawa Evening Journal* were much more prone to use terms like "loyalty" and "British Empire" than were the *Toronto Star* and *London Free Press*. But the most careful researcher will find difficulty in making much of this division after March of 1939.[19]

What is particularly striking in the Ontario newspapers is the evidence of the "explosion of public opinion" after the Nazi occupation of Prague on 14 March and before Neville Chamberlain's reversal of British foreign policy in his Birmingham speech of 17 March. The *Globe*, that most loyal of journals, echoed Chamberlain's initial dismissal of the fall of Czechoslovakia in an editorial published on the morning of 15 March. The next day the newspaper was full of stories, with headlines proclaiming: "Hitler Enters Prague as Veil is Dropped from Imperial Aims," "Czech Coup Opens Nazi Expansion Drive," "Smashing of Czech State is Preliminary for German Action Against Soviet Russia."[20] The *Globe* would not formally abandon its editorial support for appeasement until Chamberlain did, but it was certainly ready for the new policy before it was announced.

The news in the *Globe*, as in other Ontario newspapers, came largely from the American Press or Canadian Press wires, but each newspaper had its own way of packaging the news with headlines and leaders. The *Brantford Expositor* ignored Chamberlain's attempt to downplay the crisis. The large headline on 14 March cried "Czech Torn Asunder," and the editorial praised the French government for a statement the *Expositor* editor chose to interpret as a sign that "bluster and threats" would no longer serve to advance the cause of the dictators. By the 16th, the *Expositor* headline, "Danzig, Memel, Ukraine, Next for Nazis?" coincided with an editorial criticizing Chamberlain's failure to act and noting that some members of the British cabinet felt otherwise. The editorial then concluded: "If the members of the British government are shocked by Hitler's aggressive seizure of this ancient country and subjugation of a people who are not Germans by race or language it shows they have come to understand his ambitious, ruthless and aggressive policy. Is anything more needed to reveal the true character of Hitler?"[21] The *Expositor* also carried an account of a speech by the leader of the opposition in Ontario, Colonel George Drew. On the 16th, he delivered a "fifty minute talk dealing in bitter language with Germany's recent seizure of Bohemia and Moravia. [Drew] was enthusiastically received throughout." Chamberlain's Birmingham speech, reported on the 18th, was welcomed by the newspaper with an editorial which described Chamberlain as having "echoed the sentiments of the Empire and the world democracies."[22]

The *Kitchener-Waterloo Record* offered a much more restrained version of events, but an editorial on the 15th did remind readers that: "It will be recalled that Hitler said Sudetenland was his last territorial ambition in Europe ... His promises cannot be relied upon."[23] The next day, the *Record* headline read, "Fear Hitler May Strike Quickly for Danzig and Memel," and a feature story on "Alleged Nazi Timetable of Domination Published"[24] was given prominence. The *Record*, an evening paper, reported Chamberlain's Birmingham speech on the 17th and endorsed the logic of his new position.

The *Ottawa Evening Journal* vied with the *Globe* in the intensity of its admiration for Chamberlain. Throughout the three crucial days before the British cabinet reversed its policy, the *Journal* was on the defensive against "those who say that England is betraying her own interests [and] betraying freedom and democracy." The editor demanded to know why it was that Britain had to be democracy's policeman. "What of the United States? What of Canada?" the *Journal* demanded.[25] Chamberlain's Birmingham speech caught the *Journal* by surprise. The newspaper headlines and stories conveyed the same atmosphere of crisis that marked the reporting of other newspapers, but the *Journal's* editor insisted that "he still held to his faith that there will be no prospect of war this year and no prospect of war with Germany in the near future." Finally, on the 18th, the *Journal* accepted the inevitable and proclaimed that "People and Politicians Rally as Premier Ends Appeasement Policy."[26]

That consensus may be described as a belief in the probability of war in response to further German aggression and the certainty that Canada would participate. The *Toronto Star* expressed it on 12 March: "As international developments in Europe move tragically towards a culmination — the nations of good will, free and law abiding, under the compulsion of the instinct for self preservation, seek the support of one another's strength and comradeship."[27]

Opinion was much the same in smaller centres. The Sarnia *Canadian Observer* editorialist, who had welcomed the Munich agreement and insisted that Czechoslovakia must "not provide a frivolous excuse for endangering its benefactors,"[28] changed his views within days of the occupation of Prague. On 15 March, he wrote, "the events of this week serve warning that sooner than later we will have to stop Germany and the only way this can be done is war." When Canada declared war on 10 September 1939, the *Observer* offered this statement of explanation:

> *Canada is now at war. This country has taken the step expected of it by its own people first of all and by other sister nations within the Empire. That we are at war with Germany is the will of the Canadian people, the most peace-loving people on earth, but also the most honourable. Canada is a democracy that is not afraid to fight for democracy. We have now committed ourselves to do the utmost that lies in our power to wage war until Hitlerism and all that it means is destroyed.*

A similar view developed in the provincial universities.[29] For example, shortly after the annexation of Austria, the McMaster *Silhouette* held a plebiscite in which 57 out of 77 students voted to oppose military intervention in support of Czechoslovakia.[30] After the occupation of Prague, however, a national student plebiscite which asked "Do you support military action to check the expansion of the totalitarian states?" revealed that 54 percent of McMaster students favoured such action, while 64 percent would go to war if England became involved. Students at the University of Western Ontario recorded a 70 percent pro-intervention majority, 71 percent if war involved England.[31]

The members of the Ontario legislature were under no illusions about the meaning of Prague. Hitler had told Chamberlain that the Sudetenland was his last territorial ambition in Europe and now he had broken that pledge. On 23 March, a full week before Chamberlain's guarantee to Poland, all 78 MLAs passed a resolution which declared:

> *That in the opinion of this House the Government of Ontario should take cognizance of the fact that the present international crisis in Europe calls for immediate action on the part of the component parts of the British Empire in support of any action which it may be necessary for the Imperial Government to take.*
>
> *And that this Legislative Assembly of Ontario hereby petitions the Federal parliament of Canada to immediately pass legislation providing that, in the event of a war emergency, the wealth and manpower of Canada should be mobilized by proclamation ... for the duration of the war.*[32]

Two days before, the federal parliament had debated what the prime minister called "the wanton and unjustified seizure of Czechoslovakia." In the course of his speech, Mackenzie King delivered his oft-cited view of the galvanizing impact that "bombers raining death on London" would have on Canadian public opinion. King clearly hoped that Chamberlain would continue to pursue a peace at any price policy, but he was equally aware of the political significance of the explosion of public opinion in Ontario and the rest of English-speaking Canada. Indeed, he shared many of the same values and assumptions. The two debates took place in the week of Hitler's occupation of Memel and new reports of pressure on Iceland to grant air bases to Germany.[33] No one who reads the newspapers of the period or analyzes the debate in the Ontario legislature could fail to recognize that English-speaking Canadians believed that war was now inevitable and that they would have to play a part in resisting the forces of evil.

The Polish guarantee was accepted as a necessary drawing of the line and for a brief period war news receded from the front pages. The visit of the King and Queen, so often interpreted as part of a necessary campaign to win Canadian support for Britain in the event of war, provided Ontarians with a marvellous spectacle, but there was no need to convince the province about Hitler. Throughout August, as the crisis over Poland deepened, there was no sign that either public opinion leaders or the public had reverted to appeasement. The views of the handful of intellectuals and civil servants who advocated Canadian neutrality were ignored. The internal battle in the CCF, which resulted in a position favouring full economic assistance to Britain but no expeditionary force, simply illustrated the marginality of a party which would not win a single seat in Ontario in the federal election of 1940.

J.S. Woodsworth's dissenting statement on the declaration of war in the House of Commons has attracted much attention. Historians have tended to follow Kenneth McNaught's version of this speech and its reception. McNaught describes the respectful silence that greeted the "Prophet" and notes there was "a single interruption when the Conservative Mr. Tustin cried 'shame.'"[34] In fact, Tustin's interjection was only one of eight recorded for posterity by the *Hansard* reporter. Woodsworth's speech was not well received. It was another version of his left-book club views of capitalism, and phrases such as war is "the inevitable outcome of the present economic and international system with its injustices, exploitations and class interests"[35] were no longer in fashion.

Woodsworth, however much he has fascinated Canadian historians, spoke only for a tiny minority in 1939. The mover of the address on the Speech from the Throne, an obscure Liberal backbencher from Algoma West, spoke for the people of Ontario. H.S. Hamilton declared:

> *It would be idle for me to take up the time of the house in any effort to review the events that have been taking place in Europe or their significance in Canada. He who has eyes has seen or read, he who has ears has heard, and he who has understanding must realize their deep significance in this dominion. I suggest that never in all history have the democratic or liberty-loving countries engaged in a greater and more necessary effort to see to it that government of the people, by the people and for the people shall not perish from the earth.*
>
> *We are confronted with a philosophy that knows nothing of the individual man but his obligation to obey; that knows nothing of the value of human individuality and human liberty, whose instruments are ruthless and unscrupulous force and violence, an utter negation of all the things we have been taught to value, of the philosophy, to which we hold, that has regard for human personality and human liberty, within and by which philosophy we shall yet achieve the splendid destiny that lies ahead of the Canadian people.*
>
> *Believing this, Mr. Speaker, to me this war is Canada's war. To me the defeat of Britain is the defeat of Canada; the defeat of France is the defeat of Canada. To me the death of every British, French or Polish soldier, sailor or aviator in resisting German force and violence at this time is a life given in the service of Canada.*
>
> *To my mind the effective defence of Canada consists in the utilization of the organized and united power and strength of this dominion however, whatever, and whenever it can best be used to defeat Germany's armed forces and to destroy the philosophy on which they are based. If the method of doing it involves primarily the utilization of our industrial and productive resources, then I am for that. If it involves partly the use of such forces and also the use of armed forces, expeditionary or otherwise, I am for that. If a certain type of assistance would be most advantageous now, changing to a different type of assistance later, then I am for that. And if the assistance which can effect that which I believe to be so vital can best be given on the Atlantic, on the North Sea, on the fields of Europe, I am also for that.*[36]

Hamilton sat down to thunderous applause. Ontario was at war.

NOTES

1. J.L. Granatstein, *Canada's War* (Toronto, 1975), 19.
2. Robert Bothwell and Norman Hillmer, eds., *The In-Between Time: Canadian External Policy in the 1930s* (Toronto, 1975), 17.
3. Michiel Horn, *A New Endeavour* (Toronto, 1986), xxiv.
4. John Thompson and Alan Seager, *Canada 1922-1939: Decades of Discord* (Toronto, 1985), 328.
5. Canada, *Eighth Census of Canada 1941* (Ottawa, 1950), vol. I, 653, 671, 686.
6. Norman Hillmer *et al.*, eds., *On Guard For Thee: War, Ethnicity, and the Canadian State, 1939-1945* (Ottawa, 1988), xii.
7. *Census 1941*, vol. I.
8. Quoted in R. Ritchie, "When Loyalties Divide: Pacifism in the United Church of Canada, 1936-40," BA Thesis, Wilfrid Laurier University, 1984. See Tom Socknat, *Witness Against War* (Toronto, 1988), for a description of these events from a different point of view.
9. The text of the Oxford Declaration is in *The Record of Proceedings* of the 6th, 7th and 8th General Council of the United Church (Toronto, 1937, 1938, 1939).
10. *New Outlook*, 22 April 1938.
11. Toronto *Globe*, 12 November 1938.
12. *Ibid.*, 21 November 1938, On *Kristallnacht*, see I. Abella and H. Troper, *None Is Too Many* (Toronto, 1983), 40-41.
13. *The United Church Observer*, 17 February 1939.
14. *Ibid.*, 1 October 1939.
15. *Ibid.*, 15 October 1939. See David R. Rothwell, "United Church Pacificism – October 1939," *The Bulletin*, 22 (1975).
16. *Ibid.*
17. *Proceedings*, 9th General Council (Toronto, 1940), 32.
18. A.J.P. Taylor, *The Origins of the Second World War* (London, 1961), 97.
19. The following newspapers were surveyed for this paper: Toronto *Globe*, *Toronto Star*, *Ottawa Evening Journal*, *London Free Press*, Windsor *Star*, *Kitchener-Waterloo Record*, *Brantford Expositor*, Sarnia *Canadian Observer*.
20. Toronto *Globe*, 16-18 March 1939.
21. *Brantford Expositor*, 16 March 1939.
22. *Ibid.*, 17-18 March 1939, Author's emphasis.
23. *Kitchener-Waterloo Record*, 15 March 1939.

24. *Ibid.*, 16 March 1939.

25. *Ottawa Evening Journal*, 15 March 1939.

26. *Ibid.*, 18 March 1939.

27. Editorial, "Where Canada Stands," *Toronto Star*, 21 March 1939.

28. Sarnia *Canadian Observer*, 30 September 1938, cited in Alan Oman, "The Sarnia *Observer* and the Events of 1938-39," seminar paper, Wilfrid Laurier University, 1990. The next two quotations are from the *Observer*, 15 March and 11 September.

29. Daniel Byers, "The Canadian Students Press and the Second World War: 1938-1942," seminar paper, Wilfrid Laurier University, 1990.

30. *Silhouette*, 24 March 1939, 1.

31. Six newspapers agreed to the proposal for a national student plebiscite instigated by the University of Saskatchewan *Sheaf*. Students at the Universities of British Columbia, Alberta and Saskatchewan voted 66 percent in favour of intervention, while 70 percent of the votes cast at the University of New Brunswick were affirmative. I thank Dan Byers for this information.

32. Toronto *Globe*, 24 March 1939.

33. References to German demands for bases in Iceland featured prominently in newspaper reports of the events of March-April 1939.

34. K. McNaught, *A Prophet in Politics* (Toronto, 1959), 310-11.

35. Canada, House of Commons, *Debates*, 8 September 1939, 45.

36. *Ibid.*, 7. It has been suggested that Hamilton's speech was written by J.W. Pickersgill and was thus a calculated government position. In response to my inquiry, the Rt. Hon. J.W. Pickersgill wrote: "The speeches on the address in reply to the Speech from the Throne were almost invariably seen by me from 1939-1948. Mackenzie King told the MPs he would like to have them discuss their speeches with me. I looked at the drafts and occasionally recommended changes in specific phrases which I feared might offend MK or injure the government. In September 1939, my first experience, I was very sparing. Both speakers were veterans of the First World War and I felt they should be encouraged to express their own sentiments which I recollect both did. Hamilton, I felt, was expressing a Tory attitude in Ontario, which incidentally I did not share. My own attitude to Canada's basic interest was very like Skelton's. I did not feel Canada had a realistic reason for participating until after the fall of France, but I did not believe the government or the P.M. shared that position." Letter from J.W. Pickersgill to Terry Copp, 6 January 1994.

Editors' Note:

We are grateful to the editors and publisher of *Ontario History* for their permission to reprint this article, which originally appeared in that journal (LXXXVI, 3 (September 1994), 269-78).

MITCH HEPBURN AND WILLIE KING'S WAR

John T. Saywell
York University

Just hours before the Luftwaffe and the Wehrmacht struck into Poland, on 31 August 1939, Mackenzie King was depressed by the news that Hitler was becoming exasperated by the Poles' delay in accepting his ultimatum and "feared that knowing Britain and France were at their side the Poles might, with their war-like natures, prefer to fight."[1]

King had no public engagements that day, said nothing memorable to the newspapers, and kept his own counsel. That was not true of his Ontario counterpart, Mitch Hepburn. Mitch was at Magnetawan that day, speaking at a nomination convention. "Two million men were on the march," he dramatically told the Parry Sound Liberals, and a war that could destroy western civilization seemed inevitable. Canada must support Britain, Mitch said to resounding cheers, and "when Parliament meets, as apparently it must in a few days, I hope Canada's voice will be heard in no uncertain way."[2]

Parliament did meet on 7 September, and three days later Canada was at war. The most moving speech of the debate was made by justice minister Ernest Lapointe, who denounced the thought of neutrality and prayed that "God give Canadians the light which will indicate to them where their duty lies in this hour of trial ..." From Toronto, Mitch wired: "You were absolutely magnificent and you are still my Sir Ernest." Sixteen months later, Mitch Hepburn's condemnation of the war effort gave Mackenzie King the pretext he needed to call a sudden election before more widespread criticism dealt a fatal blow to his hold on power.[3]

Mackenzie King's view of those four or five months, from August 1939 to January 1940, has been recorded and re-recorded over the years. King wrote in his private diary, and kept voluminous records. Mitch Hepburn by contrast spoke to the newspapers, achieved great public effect, but his words, recorded by others, have perished. This paper aims to restore the balance, for balance there was.

Mitch did not always disagree with Mackenzie King on foreign policy. As a federal member of parliament and then as Ontario premier from 1934, he generally followed the party position, praising autonomy and damning Downing Street. By the beginning of 1938, his position on defence was changing. Early in the year he referred again to "the almost maniacal armament race among the major powers of Europe" and argued that Canada should strengthen its own defences and co-operate with the United States in continental defence "so other countries will consider it advisable to leave us alone." Mitch sounded a new note when he praised Neville Chamberlain's trip to Munich as the work of a man who "makes us all proud that we are British, all part of the British Commonwealth of Nations and obligated in loyalty to one King and one cause." But Canada could not "hide under the paw of the British lion or the wing of the American eagle," he told Wiarton Liberals a few days later, and had to rearm. "When I was a member of the House of Commons I was one of those who strenuously opposed any major armament policy in Canada," he admitted. "Today, through force of circumstances I have changed my mind."[4]

Mitch visited Australia in January 1939. On board the SS *Mariposa* when it left San Francisco was S.M. Bruce, the Australian high commissioner in London who had been called home for foreign policy discussions (and unlike the Canadian high commissioner, Vincent Massey, was encouraged to keep in close touch with the Foreign Office and War Office). Bruce gave Mitch a bleak picture of the prospects for peace in Europe and the Pacific. During his two weeks of talks with leading politicians and officials, Mitch found that, while Australians still hoped for peace in the days after Munich, they realized that time was not on their side and were strenuously preparing for a war that could even involve an attack on Australia. On his arrival Mitch told reporters that Canada was a country without national leadership and on his departure said that he was determined "to force the issue of proper defence in Canada." His discussions in Australia had convinced him that Canada was burying its head in the sand, living in an atmosphere of false security, while events in Europe and Asia revealed that the "law of the jungle" governed international relations.[5]

The session at Queen's Park opened two weeks after Mitch returned from Australia. With the royal visit scheduled for May, the time was opportune to demonstrate that Ontario, at least, stood "Ready, Aye, Ready" to answer the call of the empire when it came. Mitch introduced a resolution on the second day praising the imperial connection as the backbone of civilization. Liberals and Tories followed Conservative leader George Drew in endorsing the resolution, and W.J. Stewart, prominent Tory Orangeman and sometime mayor of Toronto, drew applause from both sides of the house when he declared that University of Toronto professor Frank Underhill should be fired for his subversive remarks about the shrinking Union Jack. The much-decorated Colonel F.F. Hunter (Indian Army, retired) denounced those responsible for the Statute of Westminster and the destruction of the unity of the empire, while J.J. Glass said that as a Jew he applauded the British spirit of fair play. Only J.A. Habel cautioned that such hyperbolic flag-waving was not the essence of patriotism.[6]

Much more was needed than resolutions of loyalty and attacks on left-wing professors. Hitler's occupation of Prague on 14 March ended the illusion of appeasement, and even Chamberlain agreed that the game was over. Mackenzie King, who continued to prefer "Chamberlain the appeaser to Chamberlain the avenger," also knew the time for evasion was over and agonized for days over a statement of Canadian policy. Soon after the Commons met on 20 March, King solemnly confessed that the latest "disturbance" had come as a surprise. Whatever the circumstances, Parliament would decide on Canada's course, and while he did not feel that Canada should be involved in some conflict over trade or prestige "in some far corner of the world," if "there were a prospect of an aggressor launching an attack on Britain, with bombers raining death on London, I have no doubt what the decision of the Canadian people and Parliament would be. We would regard it as an act of aggression, menacing freedom in all parts of the British Commonwealth."[7]

Coincidentally, that same afternoon the legislature of Ontario was staking out its position in a debate on a motion by Colonel Hunter and Ian Strachan that the international situation called "for immediate action on the part of the component parts of the British Empire in support of any action which it may be necessary for the Imperial Government to take. And this House hereby requests the Government to introduce a Bill at the earliest possible moment for the purpose of conscripting the property and civil rights of every individual in Ontario to the defence of our free institutions." Drew and Mitch concurred at once with the sentiments, but Mitch suggested that it was not advisable to embarrass Ottawa in any way at "this inopportune time." If King refused to take a stand, he promised, the debate would be resumed. And if war came, he added, "I believe we should have equality of sacrifice in this country."[8]

Like much of English Canada — and probably most of Ontario where a key member of Senator Lambert's Ontario Committee had resigned because of King's equivocation — Mitch did not find King's statement sufficiently forthright. It did not deter Hitler, who sent his troops into Memel and made aggressive demands on Danzig a day later. On 23 March, Mitch resumed the debate on foreign policy. With Germany determined to master Europe, Italy to dominate the Mediterranean, and Japan certain to move into Southeast Asia once China had been devoured, Canada itself was endangered. There was no question, he continued, "that a national emergency exists. I have said we should await a definite pronouncement from the Federal Government, and I don't want to be particularly critical of the Federal Government at this particularly critical time, because I realize that this Dominion is a most difficult country to govern, with its various factions and schools of thought." But if Ottawa could not make a definitive statement, the province of Ontario could. And in a tight, clipped voice, he substituted for the last sentence in the Hunter-Strachan motion an amendment that read that the Assembly "hereby petitions the Federal Parliament of Canada now in session to immediately pass Legislation providing that in event of a War emergency the wealth and manpower of Canada shall be mobilized by proclamation of the Governor-in-Council for the duration of the war, in defence of our free institutions."

Grits and Tories leaped to their feet to applaud. Cheers resounded from the galleries. Drew endorsed it all and more. The loudest cheers were for Aurelien Bélanger, whose ancestors he liked to say had come with Champlain. Bélanger found the resolution a little too sweeping but promised that the descendants of those who had fought in 1775 and at Chateauguay to keep Canada free and British would be loyal to the last man. "Ontario struck for the Empire yesterday, and for all the Empire stands for in this hour of crisis," ran the *Globe and Mail* headline story. "In dignified but determined terms — with a forcefulness of action that brooked no interference — with unity of purpose before which racial passion and political prejudice and parochial pride crumbled like moths in a candleflame," Ontario without a dissenting voice had taken its stand.[9]

By the spring of 1939 Mitch had long since ceased to be a Mackenzie King Liberal, and in federal politics it was not clear whether he was a Liberal at all. By 1938-1939 King saw Mitch as a key player in a move to get rid of him. The prime minister had hinted or even demanded from time to time that the party excommunicate Hepburn. But the Ontario ministers were afraid to take the war to Queen's Park, and the caucus preferred soft declarations of loyalty to King to an open denunciation of Mitch.[10]

Mitch's likely opposition, and the threat of a Hepburn alliance with Québec premier Duplessis, were key factors as King and the Liberals considered a fall 1939 election. Mitch insisted there was no alliance. Personally, he would put "country before party" but would take no part in the election; individual members and ministers could do as they pleased. The consensus in the Cabinet, King concluded, was that they "should go ahead, regardless of the attitude of the Ontario government; that the people were really with us and would show that, and Hepburn would learn his lesson as to where he stood when his own campaign came." Late in July King decided to go to the country on 23 October, the twentieth anniversary of the day he took his seat as leader of the opposition, with dissolution in September. As he noted in his diary, "by 11th of September we should know if war is probable in Europe – & wd. be justified in going to people if not probable – if war comes before, would be wise in not having made this move earlier."[11]

A giant rally in Toronto to commemorate 20 years of his leadership was to start the adrenaline flowing and show the country that the party was united behind King. But the rally, held on 8 August, was a disaster. Neither Mitch nor his cabinet showed up, and only 14 backbenchers dared to come. Three weeks later, Hitler marched into Poland and the election was forgotten.[12]

As early as April Mitch had attempted to persuade Ottawa to take over the defence of Hydro installations. He repeated the request at a meeting with defence minister Ian Mackenzie and federal officials on 29 August. Ottawa unwilling, a council of war at Queen's Park on 1 September had called up additional Ontario Provincial Police (OPP) constables; created the Veterans Guard within the OPP; mobilized the 1937 "Hepburn Hussars"; instructed Hydro commissioner Hogg to protect the Niagara installations with barbed wire, armed guards, and river nets to intercept floating bombs; created a special committee to deal with Fascist organizations, already under the eye of the Criminal Investigations Bureau through what became the Special Branch of Anti-Sabotage Squad to deal with subversives; and laid the foundations for Cabinet committees to deal with production facilities and security. At another meeting on 5 September, Mitch informed Ottawa that buildings were available for defence purposes, the provincial air service, already transferred from the north to Toronto Island, was ready for wartime service, and the physical and human resources of the province were awaiting the call.[13]

At a short September session the province was put on a war footing. Although Mitch said that until an hour before the session opened he had intended to speak about the critical situation in which Canada found herself, "I decided to refrain, as my remarks might have been construed as criticism of the administration charged with the pursuit of the war." His restraint was short-lived, as he went on to say that Canada was "entering the war less prepared than any other country in the world. There is no use in disguising the obvious fact." The non-partisan nature of the session was underlined by the creation of the Organization of Resources Committee composed of the lieutenant-governor, Drew and Mitch. A few days later, Mitch announced that the Committee had asked to meet King and his colleagues. They would go to Ottawa, Mitch told reporters, to pledge Ontario's assistance to the rapid and efficient mobilization of the nation's resources. "We will go down there and find everything that is required. We will base everything on that information." The committee would be expanded to include representatives of labour, agriculture and industry to stimulate production, ensure an adequate labour supply, and assist in the recruitment of men for the Canadian Expeditionary Force with "the least possible disturbance to agriculture or industry."[14]

The war had inevitably raised the spectre of the "National Government," much talked of during the Depression, and King was obsessed by the prospect of a movement that he thought not only would divide the country and the party but, in the process, might remove his crown. Even Toronto *Globe and Mail* proprietor George McCullagh's repeated assurance during two long meetings with King that he and his newspaper were in his corner and that a National Government was, for the moment at least, out of the question did not allay King's fears that Mitch was the political spearhead of a union government movement. And when Mitch wired for an appointment for the War Resources Committee, King saw it at once as "part of the foundations of a scheme to further Union government later on from Ontario." With Duplessis already attacking Ottawa on one front from Québec, King concluded that "Hepburn and his crowd will try to make the fight one against our Government; that we are not imperialistic enough, and a lukewarm Liberal party not throwing enough energy into the war effort. My own opinion is that they will be badly fooled in the end by the strong position which the Government will get, if our people defeat Duplessis. That would mean that no other government than the one of which Lapointe and I are members, would be thought of until this war is over."[15]

King had planned to hold a brief strategy session with his colleagues before the meeting with Mitch and Drew on 3 October, but arrived to find them already talking outside his office.[16] Mitch admitted at once that he had been openly critical of King's tardy and indecisive preparation for war, although he did not suggest as he had to a member of the Press Gallery that King should be impeached. Canada was now at war, however, and he had come to pledge his total support to the war effort.

Mitch reiterated many of the proposals and offers that he and his ministers had made concerning buildings, use of interned aliens on road work and freeing up prisons by allowing short-term prisoners to enlist. He criticized the delay in securing adequate uniforms and supplies for the recruits, and, although the formation of a division for possible despatch overseas had been announced two weeks before, Mitch bluntly stated that the feeling in Ontario was that "the government was not taking quick enough steps for getting expeditionary force under way, etc." As the industrial heartland of Canada, the protection and expansion of power resources were essential. He could not adequately guard Niagara with civilians, Mitch claimed, and if King would supply the militia, Ontario would pay the cost. And finally, if he and US president Roosevelt would agree to the northern diversions at once, Mitch agreed to accept Roosevelt's St. Lawrence Seaway proposal completely, but for the moment wanted his agreement kept secret. However, he needed a quick decision, for without the northern diversion or other additional sources Ontario would face a power shortage. King suggested that Hydro's Hogg discuss the matter with federal officials and Mitch agreed that King could inform Roosevelt.

Drew concurred with Mitch that the war would be a long one, and that even with the defeat of Germany the struggle with the USSR would go on for years. The Colonel was even more disturbed by the lack of military protection of Hydro plants and other critical war industries, and also urged greater use of the radio to stimulate the war effort in Canada and propagandize in the United States. Drew and King differed as to whether Canada was any further ahead than in the First World War, with Drew suggesting King should check behind the word of his officials. King replied that the issue was not simply an expeditionary force, but a navy, air force, defences on two coasts, and cooperation in the defence of Newfoundland and the West Indies. Moreover, he argued, accomplishing the almost miraculous feat of bringing a united Canada into the war had involved "restraint in some directions."

King made it clear that the government was concerned about the enormous cost of war, not only for the military but also for the financial credits Britain was expected to request, and was attempting "to visualize the picture as a whole, allotting to the different demands what we felt the country could afford." He then asked Colonel Ralston, who had joined the Cabinet as minister of finance on 6 September, to run over the dimensions and problems of financing the war. Ralston discussed the estimated billion for the first two years of the air training program, the enormous credits being asked by Britain, and the necessity of ensuring that Canada would have the economic strength to fight a long war. However, said Ralston, he was doing everything he could to cut through the "red tape" and secure the funds to get the essential requirements underway. After the meeting, by agreement, King told the press it had been most useful. Mitch agreed.

King had been generally non-committal during the meeting, but that afternoon in Cabinet said that the meeting "had really been helpful" and that he was "prepared to start anew all relations with the Ontario government and to make no reference to the past." He asked Lapointe to consider the question of work camps for aliens and the enlistment of prisoners, and secured the general agreement of Cabinet that a good case could be made for military protection of "bridges and power plants along the US border, including, possibly, interprovincial bridges as well." Transport minister Howe was instructed to take up the power business and Cabinet, including Lapointe, agreed that the St. Lawrence should go ahead to keep "the good will of the United States." King bowed to the request to take to the airwaves, but only if someone would help prepare the material.[17]

After they left the meeting with King, Drew and Mitch compared notes. Neither was impressed. Drew's "most vivid impression was of a group of extremely tired and befuddled old men, with the exception of Ralston and [newly-appointed defence minister Norman] Rogers. Ralston appeared anything but befuddled, tired and insignificant." Although Drew felt that Ralston's firm statement was welcome, he remained unconvinced that "there was any real driving power behind the war effort" or any purpose "in the mind of the man who is driving the machine." Mitch generally agreed, but he told Drew that because of Ralston he had "reason for confidence," a statement, Drew concluded, that revealed "that what was really on his mind was that on looking over the situation Ralston's statement had given some reason to believe that he could still safely be a Liberal, because in my own mind nothing was said even including Ralston's statement that gave any assurance that there is any real driving power behind the war effort."

Mitch unburdened himself in a long off-the-record talk with Jack Hambleton of the *Star*. Only with great difficulty had they been able to hold their temper, he said, for they could get no definite answers on any of the matters proposed, except the acceptance of some Stinson aircraft offered a month before. "The only man in the cabinet who seems to know anything is Ralston," said Mitch, and "he is about to quit in disgust." Mitch assured Hambleton that he went to Ottawa with the "best intentions" and the determination to submerge any personal feelings. "But honestly, it would make you sick to see how confused and distraught everything and everyone is in Ottawa. I wanted to break the story and tell the country just what is going on, but I realize my personal feelings towards King would neutralize any effort I made. Surely, some newspaper will sooner or later open up. It would be a great national service because we are unprepared." A copy of the interview was on King's desk a day later. King read the document to Cabinet on 10 October, describing it as a "thoroughly deceitful and lying report" and the next day stated that Mitch's outburst "ended everything."[17]

Mitch remained silent for weeks and even assured critics of the King government that he had confidence in Ralston and had "received his positive assurance that Canada will prosecute the war — not in the manner of the past or the present but with every possible effort put forward." Mitch was not alone in his private view of King and his faith in Ralston. Wallace R. Campbell, the Ford president, called to Ottawa to head the War Supply Board, explained to Floyd Chalmers of the *Financial Post* that his chief difficulty was that the "government has no war programme; has not made up its mind whether it wants to plan for a war of one month or one or three years. It shows no disposition to plan ahead. Cabinet is simply not strong enough to prosecute a war effort vigorously or efficiently. Only man showing any vigour at all is Ralston." And the army could "parade up the street with their Great War rifles on their shoulder but they could not fight in a war."[18]

That was precisely the point Mitch made when be broke his long silence late in November. His informal talk to a group of local farmers and businessmen at the Grand Central Hotel in St. Thomas was an earnest appeal to everyone to pitch in, but the press was quick to emphasize his critical comments. "I don't think that the war is being prosecuted the way that Canadians want it to be prosecuted," he said. "A modernly mechanized force of 2,000 men could lick the whole Canadian Army, today, gentlemen, and I don't mean anything disparaging to the Canadian forces when I say that ... But they are not getting a break and are not getting the training and equipment they must have." The next night at Aylmer, he urged Ottawa to "shake off its lethargy and get on with the war." The failure to go all out, he argued, was because of the "now clearly defined policy at Ottawa of putting the dollar in the driver's seat." Mitch also attacked King for not agreeing to the British Commonwealth Air Training Program two years earlier and, with it still not operational, asked "Are they still fiddling at Ottawa while Rome burns?" Both charges King described as "direct lies." But both had an element of the truth. Ralston replied indirectly to Mitch in a radio address, which King thought "would astonish the country when he lets them see how far we have committed the country financially," when he observed that if "our efforts of the last 10 weeks can be called inactivity, then heaven help us if we ever get down to work." Only on 17 December could King announce an agreement on the air training program after a long and drawn-out battle which led the British to wonder whether King's priorities lay in furthering the common cause or determining "what the common cause can be made to do to help Canada."[19]

Other than the two mild criticisms of King's war effort, Mitch lived up to his promise of total support. Mitch told Rogers he could have any government buildings he wanted for training schools. Ottawa refused to enlist short-term prisoners or to let Ontario establish work camps for interned enemy aliens, so Mitch decided to relieve the congestion by sending the short-term prisoners to work camps on the Trans-Canada highway. The Royal Canadian Mounted Police (RCMP) did take over responsibility for security in the Niagara-Welland region on 1 November, but attorney-general Gordon Conant was so dissatisfied with the discipline and quality of the force of the special RCMP constables that he peremptorily removed them three weeks later. Although the federal surtax in the 13 September budget trimmed $350,000 to $400,000 from the provincial income tax and the increased tax on booze cut sales $244,000 in October, Mitch told King he was quite prepared to forgo a balanced budget and would not raise taxes or liquor prices to recover the lost income. He nevertheless warned King that the increased price was already being reflected in more bootlegging and smuggling, and he wanted some assurance that there would be no further increases. The federal government assured Mitch that, while no firm promises could be made, further increases in liquor taxes were not contemplated at the moment. When Ralston asked him to sit on the National War Loan Committee for the first war loan scheduled for the spring, Mitch was delighted.[20]

Mitch was particularly anxious to see the St. Lawrence agreement move ahead, but again there was delay. It was not until 21 December that King officially informed the Americans that Canada was ready to re-open negotiations. King saw the St. Lawrence as "another great progressive stroke" of his administration, and one which, as a bonus, might avoid a troublesome dispute with Mitch in the next election.[21]

The 1940 session of the Ontario legislature opened on 10 January with little pomp and ceremony, but a long throne speech, much of which praised the government's war effort on the economic and financial front and its cooperation with Ottawa. Mitch paid tribute to the patriotism of Private David Croll, who took his seat in the kilt of the Essex Scottish, and his colleague, Lieutenant Colin Campbell, who was absent due to illness. The occasion prompted Mitch to observe that Canadians did not seem to be taking the war very seriously, while Drew, agreeing that it would be a long war, insisted that Canadians must "awaken to the imminence of the danger" and realise that the true path of patriotism was not "to remain silent in the face of incompetence." The war was not of Britain's making, said Mitch, for it had a peace-loving prime minister, while in Canada the prime minister was so peaceful that even "I have not been able to provoke him into an open quarrel, although I have tried with great dexterity on frequent occasions." The press chose to view these comments as an attack on King.[22]

There was no doubt that King was under attack when Drew and Mitch spoke on Leaders' Day. With one-third of the population and one-half of the country's industrial production, Drew said that Ontario had the right and the duty to speak out. "In this legislature we can sound a clear trumpet call to action, or we can utter pious and ineffective platitudes about our faith in democracy," said the former colonel, leaving no doubt that his impassioned attack on Ottawa's failure to prepare for war and to mobilize the resources once it began was designed to be the trumpet call to action.[23]

Mitch did not have a speech on the war effort prepared. Indeed, by the sound of it, it was difficult to tell if he had anything prepared. Rather than see the first Toronto showing of "Gone With the Wind," he had worked until four in the morning preparing a defence of his administration, only to find that, with Drew choosing another front, his efforts, too, had "gone with the wind." Assuring the house that he and Drew agreed on "matters which are basic," Mitch then embarked on a long rambling account of men without uniforms contracting tuberculosis; of his close friend Coly Campbell falling sick because he had no greatcoat; of the six days it took to evacuate the 1400 inmates of the St. Thomas asylum because Rogers needed it urgently for the air force, only to see it sit empty for months; of the prospect of half-trained men with antiquated equipment being sent into battle. "And the men responsible for sending those men over are the men who are going to some day answer to the Canadian people for the lack of preparation, regardless of the radio speeches." Mitch warned: "No one is listening to that kind of "bunk" because there are so many soldiers around who are telling the truth about the matter." Mitch agreed with Drew that the time had arrived "to speak our minds, because national security, to me, is much greater than any political affiliation." After the cheers subsided, Mitch promised to study Drew's address in detail, "after which time, I can tell him, the Government will be in a position to make its own position clear."[24]

Before the Orders of the Day were called on 18 January, Mitch denounced the *Star* and the *Globe and Mail* for criticizing him and Drew for their attacks on King two days earlier. When a Liberal member, Morgan Baker, approvingly cited extracts from a King speech, Mitch snapped "Why should we be subject to that kind of twaddle?" And when Baker went on to say that Drew's "vitriolic attacks" do "more harm and cause more confusion than all the German bombs and tanks and poison gas," Mitch leaped to his feet and whirled to confront his fellow-Liberal. "I ask to be associated with Colonel Drew in his attack on the King government to which you refer," he shouted, and when Baker tried to joke that Mitch's statement was not quite as vitriolic, Mitch replied "Well, if it wasn't, it was not because I didn't mean it to be."

The donnybrook went on until, after many appeals from the Liberal side of the house, the speaker finally called the orders of the day. But Mitch challenged the decision, and no member voted to suspend the debate on the war. As the mêlée continued, Mitch moved restlessly around in his seat until he suddenly jumped up, waved down a Liberal backbencher trying to get the speaker's attention and, with a yellow piece of paper in his hand on which something was scrawled, announced that he was going to test the opinion of the legislature. After a bitter review of his relations with King, Mitch declared that the issue now was not personal, nor was it political; it was a question of national security. Then came the astonishing ultimatum:

I don't care if I am defeated — and you must construe the resolution I am about to read out as a Government measure — I shall have done what I consider to be the right thing. Of course, if I am defeated, there is only one course open to me — to resign. If I am wrong, if in the opinion of this House we are not reflecting the overwhelming opinion of the people of Canada this moment, then I shall bow to the decision. I am ready to take my political future in my hands. I am not going to take it on the chin as Federal Cabinet Ministers have and go down without fighting.

Let me say again than I stand firm in my statements that Mackenzie King has not done his duty to his country — never had and never will.

Holding the yellow paper before him, Mitch began to read the scrawled resolution:

That this House had heard with interest the reports made by the Prime Minister and the Leader of the Opposition of the result of their visit to Ottawa to discuss war measures with the National Government and this House hereby endorses the statements made by the two members in question and joins with them in regretting that the Federal Government at Ottawa has made so little effort to prosecute Canada's duty in the war in the vigorous manner the people of Canada desire to see.

A few minutes earlier, Mitch had handed the resolution to provincial secretary Harry Nixon and asked him to second it. Nixon whispered: "Oh Mitch, it is very foolish, I do not think it is at all wise to do it. However, I have stuck with you this long and if you insist I will, but it is a —- —— mistake." Mitch grabbed it back and turned to Thomas McQuesten: "here you are the President of the Liberal Association, second this."

Everyone was taken by surprise, and even Drew seemed to have no advance warning of Mitch's intention. At a Liberal caucus there had been a general feeling that the government should continue to offer its help, rather than criticize King, and members of the Cabinet were dumbfounded when Mitch produced his resolution. They and the backbenchers had minutes to reach a decision. Would defeat mean Mitch's resignation and a new Liberal leader? Or a dissolution? If an election, where would Mitch be? With Drew? With them? Each member was left on his own. As Thomas Blakelock, who voted Aye, explained to his constituents. "An emergency arose in the House and we had only two or three minutes to decide how to vote. At least I didn't get down on my knees and sneak out. I have voted for the Hepburn government when I thought it was right and I've voted for the Hepburn government when I knew DAMN well it was wrong." As the resolution was being read again and while some members tried to have it ruled out of order or have a vote delayed, there were many Liberals who got down on their knees and snuck out. When the vote was taken, the resolution passed 44-10. All 18 Tories and every member of the Cabinet supported Mitch. The Liberal backbenchers split: ten dared his wrath and voted Nay, and 12 supported him. The estimates of those who fled the House ranged from a dozen to over 20.[25]

The news reached King as he was on his way to the theatre to see himself in a war loan movie. When he returned to Laurier House later to write a statement for the press, he had concluded that it was "the most important night since the war began. It was of such importance, that on tonight's decision depends pretty much the whole future of the Government." Indeed, King had concluded at once that Mitch had given him the excuse he had been waiting for to call an election before the war turned nasty in the spring when Hitler was expected to move against western Europe. "At any rate, Hepburn had made an appeal absolutely necessary, and has made the issue that of the Government's conduct of the war." In drafting a statement for the press, King began with the promise that "The fullest opportunity to discuss Canada's war effort will be afforded when Parliament re-assembles," but he then struck out the passage, "having in mind that I might announce an immediate dissolution, and not give any pledge in advance of discussions in Parliament."[26]

King's strategy was so secretive that only the privileged few in the War Cabinet knew his real intentions, and even there Ralston believed that the proper course was to allow Parliament the right to debate before a dissolution. But King persisted, arguing that the end of the "Phoney War" might hurt the chances of re-election. "I pointed out, too, the danger of Hepburn dissolving the Ontario Legislature and making an issue in Ontario on war effort, and also attempts to form union government, but, above all, pointed out that once we went on with the session, and men were free to discuss things, knowing that elections were coming soon, we should have even some of our men voting in the directions that they think might best serve their own ends politically, regardless of the well-being of the party as well as of the country in time of war." The answer to the charge that they were "running away from criticisms," lectured King, was that "we were running into the arms of those who were our masters, not away from them."[27]

At the full Cabinet later that day, King kept his intentions secret, but found that, while most of his colleagues believed there should be an election during the year, few of them felt that an issue should be made of the Ontario Resolution and that Mitch and Drew had hurt themselves and could be ignored. "I think I left the entire Cabinet feeling that I had made up my mind for an early appeal," King noted. "Those that were not in the secret, believing it might come some time, perhaps immediately after the session or after the debate of the Address. I doubt if those not of the War Cabinet realized the announcement could possibly come before Monday at the earliest."[28]

Despite the views of his colleagues and the near unanimity of the press that an election was unnecessary and even irresponsible as the clouds darkened over Europe, King was determined to go ahead. The backbenchers would be dismayed to be sent home at once, he realized. "On the other hand, to have the Opposition, in this case oppositions, begin to shout like wild men, denouncing myself as a coward, running away from judgement, seeking to conceal misdoings, etc., there is only one thing that could be worse, and that is to have Parliament continue on, attempt to carry on the war with men criticizing day in and day out every word that is being said, misconstructing and misrepresenting, and the enemy deriving what comfort it might therefrom. The People will like and appreciate the bold course." King wanted the election over before the war really began and he was faced with the demand for a union government and conscription. As he told Cabinet, "the sooner we got this whole question over, if we were to continue in office, got safely in the saddle for the purpose of government, the better." His decision reached, King got Cabinet to agree to a second overseas army division to bolster the government's image but still kept his decision to himself. He did include a paragraph in the throne speech declaring that the government had decided on "an immediate appeal to the country," but how immediate no one knew.[29]

The session began on 25 January. In the morning, King decided that he would dissolve Parliament that same night, pre-empting all but the briefest discussion. The prime minister had Lapointe, a somewhat reluctant accomplice, inform a shocked Cabinet just two hours before the governor general read the speech from the throne. In the House of Commons that afternoon, King attempted to justify breaking his promise that there would be another session before an election by insisting that Mitch's resolution had made an appeal to the people essential. The Commons recessed at six, the members expecting to return after dinner. But King was already on his way to Rideau Hall, and at 7:07 came the news that Parliament had been dissolved.

King began his campaign in caucus the next morning. Mitch Hepburn was responsible for the election, King insisted, and to back away from the Ontario premier's vote of censure would have deserved the charge of "cowardice." And if Mitch was the cause, he was also in part the issue. King demanded one hundred percent loyalty to himself and the government: "There could be no other than Mackenzie King Liberals as candidates," and anyone who had any doubt about his loyalty should leave at once. Nor could any King Liberal countenance the thought of a National Government, the first step toward dictatorship and the denial of the British freedom of debate and discussion in which, as he had just demonstrated, he so passionately believed.[30]

Hepburn had refused any comment until after the weekend, and the galleries in the Assembly were crowded on Monday. Drew was immediately on his feet to deny that he had seconded the resolution, knew it was to be introduced, or had called for an immediate election, as King had charged. Both Drew and Mitch mocked King's argument that the resolution necessitated an election. Like the commander of the *Graf Spee*, who scuttled his pocket battleship rather than face three British cruisers, exclaimed Mitch, King had scuttled the ship of state rather than face the criticism of the Conservative Party leader and his 39 followers. Outside the House, Mitch quipped that there were now three famous coats in history: Joseph's, Sir Walter Raleigh's and Colin Campbell's. With the election over, and King firmly in the saddle, Campbell wrote Hepburn from his base in England, recalling Mitch's tirade about inadequate clothing for the troops which had begun it all: "I suppose it will be called "The Coat that put Mackenzie King back in Power." It had certainly helped.[31]

NOTES

1. National Archives of Canada (hereafter NA), King Diary, 31 August 1939. This paper was largely drawn from a manuscript which has now been published, *"Just Call Me Mitch": The Life of Mitchell F. Hepburn*, University of Toronto Press, 1991. The editors and author decided to publish this version in the interests of historians with little interest in the broader life of Mitchell Hepburn.

2. *Globe and Mail* (Toronto), 1 September 1939;

3. Archives of Ontario (hereafter AO), Hepburn Papers, Hepburn to Lapointe, 11 September 1939.

4. Toronto *Daily Star*, *Globe and Mail*, 19 January 1938; *Globe and Mail*, 29 September, 27, 29 October 1938.

5. Sydney *Morning Herald*, 24 January 1939; *Globe and Mail*, 4, 21 February 1939; London *Free Press*, 24 February 1939.

6. *Globe and Mail*, 10, 11 March 1939.

7. James Eayrs, *In Defence of Canada: Appeasement and Rearmament* (Toronto, 1965), 74; King Diary, 20 March 1939; Canada, House of Commons, *Debates*, 20 March 1939, 2943.

8. *Journals of the Legislative Assembly of Ontario*, 20 March 1939, 34; *Globe and Mail*, 31 March 1939.

9. *Journals of the Legislative Assembly of Ontario*, 23 March 1939; *Globe and Mail*, Toronto *Daily Star*, 24 March 1939.

10. See Reginald Whitaker, *The Government Party: Organizing and Financing the Liberal Party of Canada 1930-1958* (Toronto, 1977).

11. *Globe and Mail*, 11, 12 July 1939; *Windsor Star*, 11 July 1939; Toronto *Daily Star*, 20 July 1939; King Papers, Crerar to King, 25 July 1939; King Diary, 20, 26 July, 11 August 1939.

12. King Diary, 26 July, 8 August 1939; Queens University Archives, Lambert Papers, Diary, 8 August 1939.

13. This brief account is based on a large amount of correspondence in the Hepburn and King Papers between April and September 1939. See also Hepburn Papers, Addresses and Speeches, "A Report on the War Activities of the Departments of the Hepburn Government," 27 October 1942. The fear of a torpedo attack on the Niagara power plants had been aroused by the discovery in a Chicago restaurant of a drawing of a torpedo with floats and a Hydro installation with instructions as to how it could be used to destroy the plant. King Papers, Colonel K. Stuart, "Record of Conversation with the Premier and Attorney General of Ontario Regarding Subject of Civil Security," 20 April 1939.

14. *Globe and Mail*, Toronto *Daily Star*, 20-23 September 1939.

15. King Diary, 13, 15, 20 September 1939.

16. Three accounts of the meeting differ less in substance than in emphasis: King's (King Diary, 3 October 1939); Mitch's (Lambert Papers, [Jack Hambleton] to Mr. Brown (Toronto *Daily Star*), "Confidential," 5 October 1939, enc. in H.C. Hindmarch to Lambert, 6 October 1939); and Drew's (NA, Drew Papers, Memorandum, "Extremely Confidential," Toronto, 4 October 1939).

17. Drew, Memorandum, 4 October 1939; [Hambleton], 5 October 1939; King Diary, 10 October 1939; Lambert Diary, 11 October 1939.

18. Hepburn Papers, Hepburn to Aemelious Jarvis, 19 October 1939; Chalmers Papers, Private Collection, Memorandum, Conversation with Wallace R. Campbell, 26 October 1939.

19. *Globe and Mail*, 23, 24, 25 November 1939; King Diary, 24 November 1939; British high commissioner to London, 19 December 1939, cited in J. Granatstein, *Canada's War: The Politics of the Mackenzie King Government 1939-1945* (Toronto, 1975), 57.

20. Hepburn Papers, Rogers to Hepburn, 14 October, 4 December 1939; Hepburn to Rogers, 18 October, 5 December 1939; Lapointe to McQuesten, 17 October 1939; *Globe and Mail*, 24 October 1939; RCMP Commissioner S.T. Wood, "Memorandum for the ... Minister of Justice," 20, 22 November 1939; AO, RG 6, series II-2, box 73, C. Fraser Elliott to C. Walters, 13 September 1939; King Papers, Hepburn to King, 1 December 1939; Hepburn Papers, Ralston to Hepburn, 7, 20 December 1939; King to Hepburn, 17 October, 15 November 1939; Hepburn to King, 28 October, 4 December 1939.

21. King Diary, 21 December 1939.

22. *Globe and Mail*, 11 January 1940.

23. NA, Manion Papers, Drew to Manion, 15 January 1940; Manion to Drew, 16 January 1940; Globe and Mail, 17 January 1940.

24. *Globe and Mail*, 17 January 1940.

25. *Journal of the Legislative Assembly of Ontario*, 18 January 1940; *Globe and Mail*, 19 January 1940; Toronto *Daily Star*, 19 January, 12 February 1940; King Diary, 16 January 1940; King Papers, W. Ross Macdonald to King, 6 February 1940.

26. King Diary, 18 January 1940.

27. *Ibid.*, 22 January 1940.

28. *Ibid.*

29. *Ibid.*, 22-23 January 1940.

30. *Ibid.*, 24-26 January 1940.

31. *Globe and Mail*, *Ottawa Citizen*, 30 January 1940; Hepburn Papers, Campbell to Hepburn, 7 April 1940.

LE QUÉBEC EN 1939

René Durocher
Université de Montréal

Au lieu de faire une revue chronologique des événements en 1939 au Québec, j'ai choisi de centrer mon exposé sur l'aspect le plus fondamental à propos des Canadiens français et de la Deuxième Guerre mondiale en cette année 1939, à savoir ce qu'on pourrait appeler le **pacte** élaboré par les libéraux fédéraux pour contrer la résistance des Canadiens français qui refusaient de participer à la guerre. En effet, au début de la guerre, la position des libéraux peut se résumer en trois mots: **participation sans conscription.** Cette politique servira de base pour pacifier le Québec et obtenir sa collaboration à l'effort de guerre.

Pourquoi a-t-il fallu élaborer un tel pacte? Pourquoi a-t-il été accepté? A-t-il été respecté? Comment ce pacte nous aide-t-il à mieux comprendre l'attitude et le comportement du Québec pendant la Deuxième Guerre mondiale?

À l'occasion du 50e anniversaire de l'entrée en guerre du Canada, Paul-André Comeau a publié dans *Le Devoir* un article intéressant sur le Québec et la guerre où il écrit: **Personne n'a osé reconnaître l'erreur d'aiguillage qui a lancé tout un peuple dans une aventure isolée, triste.**[1]

Lorsqu'on regarde la Deuxième Guerre mondiale avec toutes les horreurs qu'elle a entraînées (50 millions de morts, Hiroshima, l'Holocauste, etc.) et qu'on voit l'attitude des Canadiens français qui majoritairement résistent à la participation à cette guerre et qui mènent une bataille contre la conscription pour service outre-mer, on se dit qu'effectivement on a lancé un peuple dans une aventure triste et qu'il y a eu une erreur d'aiguillage.

Mais avant d'aller plus loin, il faut bien noter que même si on oppose Canadiens-français et Canadiens-anglais ou le Québec et le reste du Canada, ni dans un cas ni dans l'autre, il ne s'agit de blocs monolithiques. Ainsi, par exemple, des milliers de Canadiens français se sont enrôlés volontairement, tandis que des milliers de Canadiens anglais se sont opposés à la conscription.

Globalement toutefois, il est certain que proportionnellement aux Canadiens anglais, les enrôlés volontaires Canadiens français ont été beaucoup moins nombreux et ceux qui, passivement ou activement, rejetaient la conscription étaient plus nombreux au Québec français qu'ailleurs. En 1939, des milliers de jeunes Canadiens français espéraient qu'ils n'auraient pas à participer à cette guerre, tandis que d'autres, jeunes et moins jeunes, étaient décidés à résister et ils scandaient dans des assemblées publiques de protestation: NOUS NE PARTIRONS PAS.

Il ne fait pas de doute que le Québec français a réagi différemment du Canada anglais face à la guerre. Plusieurs ans après l'événement, on peut parler d'erreur d'aiguillage, mais si on ne veut pas faire un anachronisme historique, il faut retourner en arrière et essayer de comprendre pourquoi les Canadiens français ont réagi ainsi et dans quel contexte se situait leur réaction.

Les Canadiens français du Québec qui s'opposaient à la participation du Canada à la guerre manifestaient le même réflexe isolationniste que la majorité des Nords-Américains. En 1939, comme en 1914, c'est le Canada anglais qui a une réaction différente du reste de tous les peuples des deux Amériques. Ainsi, par exemple, lors de la Première Guerre mondiale, il a fallu attendre 1917 pour que les Américains entrent en guerre, et lors de la Deuxième Guerre, ils ne l'ont fait qu'après le choc de Pearl Harbor, en décembre 1941.

Au-delà de l'isolationnisme typiquement américain des Canadiens français, une des raisons majeures de leur opposition à la participation à la guerre est certainement le nationalisme qui s'est développé chez ce peuple au cours des siècles. Le nationalisme canadien-français, presque par définition, a été un nationalisme où il y avait une composante anti-anglaise importante. Il pouvait en être difficilement autrement chez un peuple conquis par l'Angleterre. Le peuple canadien-français a toujours du se définir par rapport à l'Anglais et le rapport a souvent été conflictuel. Cela a été particulièrement vrai lorsqu'il a été question de participer à une guerre qui, ne l'oublions pas, est tout de même la contribution ultime qu'on puisse demander à un citoyen.

Le problème s'est posé avec acuité à trois reprises au cours du 20e siècle. En 1899-1901 avec la Guerre des Boers en Afrique du Sud, avec la Guerre de 1914-1918 et en 1939-1945. Il est très difficile de comprendre l'attitude du Québec sans la situer dans cette plus longue durée de la première moitié du 20e siècle.

Lorsqu'en 1899 l'Angleterre déclenche en Afrique du Sud une guerre purement coloniale contre les Boers, c'est bien l'intention du Premier ministre du Canada, Wilfrid Laurier, de refuser toute participation à cette guerre. Mais il sera obligé d'accepter une participation limitée du Canada, à cause des sentiments d'attachement très profonds d'une partie des Anglo-canadiens à l'égard de la Grande-Bretagne. Cela aura pour effet de développer au Canada français une idéologie anti-impérialiste de plus en plus forte au Québec.

Lorsqu'éclate la Première Guerre mondiale, en 1914, le Canada français, comme le reste du Canada, ressent une très vive émotion et une forte sympathie pour la France et la Belgique mais aucune hostilité à l'égard de la Grande-Bretagne. Il existe, à cause d'une conjoncture assez particulière chez les nationalistes, un large consensus en faveur de la participation du Canada à la guerre.[2] Le gouvernement canadien, appuyé par l'opposition, n'hésite pas à tout mettre en oeuvre pour engager le pays dans l'effort de guerre. Les gouvernements provinciaux, y compris celui du Québec, appuient cette politique. Mais à mesure que se prolonge la guerre, que l'effort se fait extrêmement intense et que la conscription devient de plus en plus inéluctable, la tension monte au Québec et l'opposition des nationalistes se fait plus impitoyable.

Lorsque le Premier ministre Robert Borden présente un projet de loi rendant le service militaire obligatoire, la réaction au Québec est véhémente, des émeutes éclatent à Montréal. Mgr Bruchési, l'archevêque de Montréal, qui a fait preuve d'une indéfectible loyauté à propos de la participation, écrit à Borden, le 31 août 1917:

> *Le peuple est ameuté. Il peut se porter à tous les excès. Les bagarres se succèdent. Des tueries sont à craindre dans nos ville. Les gens des campagnes ne se rendront pas. Ils semblent décidés à tout, et il n'y a personne capable de les calmer. La vie de tous ceux qui ont favorisé ou voté cette loi [la conscription] est en danger.*[3]

Malgré tout, la Conscription sera imposée et elle provoquera une véritable cassure entre Canadiens français et Canadiens anglais, de même qu'elle confirmera l'échec du type de nationalisme canadien bi-ethnique reposant sur la dualité culturelle, linguistique et religieuse proposée par le leader nationaliste, Henri Bourassa. Ses disciples s'orienteront de plus en plus vers un nationalisme purement québécois et trouveront un nouveau leader en la personne d'un jeune prêtre historien, l'abbé Lionel Groulx.

Comme l'a écrit l'historien Desmond Morton: "If war was one of those shared experiences which transform a people into a nation, Canada, indeed became a country of two nations."[4]

Après la Première Guerre mondiale, les Canadiens français étaient très isolés politiquement. En 1921, le Québec vote massivement pour les libéraux (65 sièges sur 65) dirigés par Mackenzie King qui était resté fidèle à Laurier qui s'était opposé à la conscription. King va s'identifier, ou être identifié, à une politique autonomiste, voire même à une politique presque isolationniste sur la scène internationale.

Pendant tout l'entre-deux-guerres, les libéraux jouiront d'un appui massif des Québécois. à chacune des élections fédérales – en 1921, 1925, 1926, 1930 et 1935 – ils répètent, non sans démagogie, que les conservateurs sont les suppôts de l'impérialisme et qu'ils ont été responsables de la conscription de 1917. À l'inverse, évidemment, les libéraux sont les héritiers de Laurier, les défenseurs de l'autonomie du Canada et, avec eux, les Canadiens ne seront plus jamais conscrits pour défendre l'Empire. Cette tactique des libéraux a été très rentable politiquement pour leur parti, mais elle a singulièrement contribué à enfoncer les Canadiens français dans leur isolationnisme.

Lorsque les libéraux reviennent au pouvoir, en 1935, même s'ils sont bien placés pour saisir la réalité d'un système international en décomposition avec la montée du fascisme et du nazisme, ils continuent, jusqu'en 1939, à raconter aux Québécois que le Canada ne participera pas à une guerre extérieure.

À compter de 1937 cependant les libéraux augmentent le budget de la défense, mais ils affirment solennellement que c'est uniquement pour pourvoir à la défense du Canada. L'année suivante, à l'occasion d'une élection partielle où se présente Camilien Houde contre un candidat libéral, le ministre des Travaux publics, Arthur Cardin, dit: "Voilà dix fois que je le déclare, le Canada ne va pas participer aux guerres extérieures, voilà dix fois que monsieur Rinfret, le Secrétaire d'état le déclare, voilà dix fois que Mackenzie King le dit au Parlement canadien, le Canada ne sera pour rien dans les guerres au dehors du territoire canadien."[5]

Même en janvier 1939, Ernest Lapointe, le lieutenant de King, le porte-parole francophone le plus autorisé du Cabinet, déclare à une délégation de la Confédération des Travailleurs Catholiques du Canada, qui lui a présenté un mémoire: "Je remarque cette phrase dans votre mémoire. La CTCC est opposée à la participation du Canada à toute guerre extérieure. Je partage votre opinion."[6]

Pendant ce temps, sur la scène politique provinciale, le crise économique se fait sentir de façon aiguë. Le régime libéral, qui est au pouvoir à Québec sans interruption depuis près de 40 ans, s'effondre. Il y eut dans les années 1930 au Québec une grande effervescence idéologique qui allait de l'extrême gauche communiste à l'extrême droite fasciste. Mais la réaction était d'abord une réaction nationaliste et c'est un nouveau parti, l'Action libérale nationale, qui se fera le véhicule de cette réaction nationaliste. L'Action libérale nationale doit s'unir aux conservateurs dans une coalition d'union nationale dirigée par Maurice Duplessis pour prendre le pouvoir en 1936.

Maurice Duplessis prend le contrôle du nouveau parti de l'Union nationale et élimine les éléments les plus radicaux de l'Action libérale nationale. De 1936 à 1939, Duplessis, qui se fait le défenseur de l'autonomie provinciale, refuse de s'impliquer dans le débat sur la participation à la guerre. Lorsque des députés nationalistes veulent présenter une motion à propos de la guerre, comme on l'avait fait en Ontario, Duplessis refuse qu'on en discute à l'Assemblée législative du Québec, alléguant que cette question relève d'Ottawa. Et c'est vers la capitale fédérale que se tournent les nationalistes et les Québécois en général, lorsqu'il s'agit de politique de guerre ou de politique extérieure.

Lorsque King ou d'autres parlementaires en 1939 rappellent le mot de Laurier qui disait que lorsque l'Angleterre est en guerre, le Canada est en guerre, des nationalistes, inspirés par Lionel-Groulx, veulent opposer à cette doctrine le statut de Westminster. Celui-ci qui était passé presque inaperçu, en décembre 1931, lorsqu'il a été sanctionné à Londres, redevient d'actualité en 1939. Un député francophone demande à la Chambre des Communes d'instituer une fête nationale, le 11 décembre, anniversaire du Statut de Westminster, qui érige le Canada au rang de nation souveraine. Ernest Lapointe, le ministre de la Justice, qui est un juriste compétent, réplique sèchement que le Canada n'est pas un pays souverain que l'on ne pourra le considérer comme tel, en droit international, tant qu'il devra s'adresser au Parlement d'un autre pays pour faire modifier sa constitution.[7]

En 1939, le débat sur la participation à la guerre devient de plus en plus important. Ainsi Léopold Richer du *Devoir* écrit en janvier: "Le problème de la neutralité du Canada, dans le cas d'une guerre de l'Angleterre, dépasse tous les autres, qu'ils soient d'ordre constitutionnel, social ou économique."[8]

Lapointe et ses collègues libéraux canadiens-français qui s'étaient montrés fort téméraires en promettant à maintes reprises que le Canada ne participerait pas à une guerre extérieure deviennent beaucoup plus prudents. Mieux encore, ils réussissent à faire dévier le débat de l'opposition à la participation à une opposition à la conscription. C'est ainsi qu'en mars 1939, King et Lapointe, après avoir exclu l'hypothèse de la neutralité du Canada, déclarent solennellement que jamais ils n'imposeront la conscription pour service outre-mer, si évidemment le Parlement décide que le Canada doit participer à la guerre.

Durant l'été, il y a une période d'accalmie. Les Québécois, toujours ambivalents dans leurs sentiments vis-à-vis l'Angleterre, font un accueil chaleureux au Roi et à la Reine, tant à Québec qu'à Montréal. La situation internationale est si confuse qu'après tout il est possible, pensent plusieurs observateurs, qu'on échappe à la guerre. Ainsi, le Cardinal Villeneuve, qui rentre d'un voyage en France, déclare, le 16 juillet: "À moins d'événements fortuits imprévus, il n'y aura pas de guerre en Europe. L'heure de la guerre est passée, de l'avis des militaires bien renseignés."[9]

Début septembre pourtant, l'orage éclate. Le Canada réagit très rapidement. On voit des assemblées anti-participationnistes à Montréal, à Québec, à Sherbrooke, à Jonquière et tous les porte-paroles nationalistes, les Gouin, Bouchard, Laurendeau, etc., y sont présents. Dans ces assemblées, on demande que le Canada proclame sa neutralité et qu'il ne participe pas à la guerre. De nombreux députés, qui ont été convoqués à une session d'urgence où le Parlement doit se prononcer sur une déclaration de guerre à l'Allemagne, réunissent leurs électeurs et s'engagent à voter contre la participation. Il y a une agitation, un mouvement, mais pas de violence.

Lors de la session d'urgence, Ernest Lapointe prononce un grand discours à la Chambre des Communes le 9 septembre où il explique pourquoi le Canada ne peut rester neutre. Mais ajoute-t-il en contrepartie: "Je suis autorisé par mes collègues de la province de Québec dans le Cabinet à déclarer que nous ne consentirons jamais à la conscription, que nous ne serons jamais membres d'un gouvernement qui essaiera d'appliquer la conscription, et que nous n'appuierons jamais un tel gouvernement."[10]

Cette déclaration solennelle maintes fois répétée et cautionnée par King, sera perçue par les Canadiens français du Québec comme un pacte entre Canadiens français et Canadiens anglais. André Laurendeau, dans son livre remarquable sur *La Crise de la conscription* s'interroge sur ce **pacte** aussi flou que celui de 1867 et se demande qui il engage véritablement?

> *King, sans doute, et de là viendra la nécessité morale du plébiscite [de 1942]. Mais l'ensemble du Canada anglais? Il ratifie silencieusement le compromis, parce que les souvenirs de 1917 restent puissants et que Lapointe est seul à pouvoir écarter le péril de la désunion; aussi parce que la guerre commence à peine, que personne n'en prévoit la durée, l'intensité ni les exigences. Mais il ne se sent pas engagé. Le ministre de la justice compte assurément sur son prestige personnel pour exiger l'exécution du pacte: mais il entre désarmé dans le compromis, ayant tout de suite versé sa part. D'ailleurs quand il sera temps d'exiger que les autres consentent la leur, Lapointe sera mort.*[11]

Malgré l'agitation de quelques députés libéraux, la déclaration de guerre est entérinée massivement. Il y a quelques assemblées de protestation au Québec, mais aucun remous significatif.

Dès septembre, le gouvernement fédéral crée une Commission de contrôle des changes étrangers. Les provinces ne peuvent emprunter à l'étranger sans l'autorisation de cette Commission. Celle-ci refuse au gouvernement Duplessis l'autorisation d'emprunter 40 millions de dollars. Le gouvernement québécois est aux abois, il doit même puiser dans la caisse de la Commission des accidents de travail pour payer les fonctionnaires. Le 24 septembre, prenant tout le monde par surprise, Duplessis qui est au pouvoir depuis à peine trois ans, annonce des élections qui auront lieu le 25 octobre. Il fait remettre aux journalistes une déclaration expliquant les motifs qui l'obligent à déclencher l'élection. Il accuse Ottawa de menacer l'autonomie de la province "dans le but de ne former qu'un seul gouvernement dirigé par Ottawa." En s'appuyant sur la loi des mesures de guerre, Ottawa mène une campagne intolérable de centralisation et d'assimilation. Ottawa centralise toute la finance des particuliers, des municipalités, des provinces et du pays. Cette longue et obscure déclaration[12] devait être à peu près incompréhensible pour l'immense majorité de la population et à noter qu'il ne prend pas position sur la participation à la guerre.

La première réaction des libéraux provinciaux est d'accuser Duplessis de profiter de la guerre pour faire appel aux préjugés de la population et tenter par la même occasion de camoufler l'état délabré des finances provinciales. Bref, ils entendent faire l'élection sur les vrais problèmes de l'administration provinciale, et non sur les questions de compétence fédérale.

À Ottawa cependant on rejette cette stratégie et Lapointe accuse Duplessis de porter la lutte sur le terrain fédéral. En somme, dit Lapointe, c'est la question même de la participation du Canada à la guerre qui est en jeu. "Cette élection du 25 octobre, Monsieur Duplessis a voulu en faire un débat sur la politique de guerre du gouvernement King, ses voeux seront exaucés."[13]

Lapointe avertit la population qu'elle doit choisir entre lui et Duplessis. Si l'électorat choisit l'Union Nationale, lui et ses collègues se soumettront, c'est-à-dire qu'ils démissionneront du cabinet fédéral laissant ainsi la porte ouverte à un gouvernement d'union qui inévitablement imposera la Conscription. Si en revanche la population rejette Duplessis, il s'engage à faire respecter le **pacte** conclu avec le Canada anglais, c'est-à-dire qu'il y aura participation à la guerre, mais sans conscription. Et Lapointe ajoutait: "Entre la conscription et vous, nous sommes la barrière, nous sommes le rempart ..."[14]

Adélard Godbout reprend le message de ses confrères libéraux et y ajoute son engagement personnel dans un discours radiodiffusé:

> *Je m'engage sur l'honneur, en pesant chacun de ces mots, à quitter mon parti et même à le combattre, si un seul Canadien français, d'ici la fin des hostilités en Europe, est mobilisé contre son gré sous un régime libéral, ou même un régime provisoire auquel participeraient nos ministres actuels dans le cabinet de M. King.*[15]

Duplessis ouvre sa campagne tardivement et n'utilise pas la radio car il refuse de soumettre ses textes à un censeur fédéral. Dans son premier grand discours à Trois-Rivières, il se déclare opposé à la conscription et même à la participation, mais sans développer sa pensée. Seule *The Gazette* rapportera ce fait qu'il s'oppose à la participation, ce qui lui vaudra encore plus l'hostilité des anglophones, si bien qu'un de ses ministres et un député anglophone démissionnent du parti. Quant aux nationalistes, ils sont partagés et certains militent contre Duplessis qui a trahi les espoirs nationalistes de 1936. Pour comble, à cause de la propagande libérale et de la menace de Lapointe et de ses collègues canadiens-français de démissionner du cabinet, on en vient en plusieurs milieux à croire, comme l'écrit le journal libéral *le Canada*: Un vote pour Duplessis, c'est un vote pour la conscription.[16]

Les Canadiens français sont tellement opposés à la conscription, ils ont tellement été traumatisés par 1917 qu'ils ne voient pas d'autres possibilités que de céder au chantage des libéraux qui obtiennent 70 sièges avec 55 pourcent des voix et ne laissent à l'Union nationale que 14 sièges avec 36 pourcent du suffrage.

Mais contrairement à ce que King déclare au lendemain de l'élection, les Québécois francophones n'ont pas voté pour la participation. Ils s'y sont résignés pour éviter que le Canada anglais ne leur impose la conscription. Pourtant ils seront conscrits d'abord pour service au Canada, en 1940, puis pour service outre-mer, en 1944.

On peut peut-être penser aujourd'hui qu'il y eut une erreur d'aiguillage comme le dit Paul-André Comeau, mais il faut bien replacer cette erreur dans son contexte. Comme l'a remarqué André Laurendeau: "Rétrospectivement, nous pensons la guerre de 1939-1945 comme un conflit mondial: elle l'est devenue. En 1939, elle était européenne." Et si le Canada en 1939 est en guerre contrairement à tous les autres pays de deux Amériques, c'est, dit Laurendeau, "Parce que l'Angleterre était en guerre, et uniquement pur cela."[17]

Au Québec, chose certaine, plusieurs sont convaincus que si le Canada est en guerre, c'est pour défendre l'Empire, on leur a dit et répété cela depuis 40 ans. Quoi qu'il en soit, il est vrai, comme l'a écrit Paul-André Comeau, qu'avec cette guerre un peuple a été lancé dans une aventure isolée, triste.

NOTES

1. Paul-André Comeau, "Le Deuxième conflit mondial, il y a 50 ans," Le Québec et la guerre, *Le Devoir*, 2 septembre 1989.

2. René Durocher, "Henri Bourassa, les évêques et la guerre de 1914-1918," La Société historique du Canada, *Communications historiques* (1971), 248-75.

3. Paul Bruchesi, cité dans Jean Bruchesi, *Témoignages* (Montréal, 1961), 273.

4. Desmond Morton, "French Canada and War, 1868-1917: The Military Background to the Conscription Crisis of 1917," in J.L. Granatstein and R.D. Cuff, eds., *War and Society in North America* (Toronto, 1971), 85.

5. Arthur Cardin, cité par Robert Rumilly, *Histoire de la Province de Québec*, vol. XXXVI (Montréal, 1966), 240.

6. André Laurendeau, *La Crise de la conscription* (Montréal, 1962), 21.

7. Rumilly, XXXVII, 189.

8. *Ibid.*, 170.

9. *Ibid.*, 248.

10. Canada, *Débats de la Chambre des Communes*, 9 septembre 1939, 71-72.

11. Laurendeau, 32.

12. Rumilly, XXXVIII, 35-6.

13. *Le Canada*, 30 septembre 1939.

14. Laurendeau, 45.

15. *Ibid.*, 47.

16. Rumilly, *XXXVIII*, 51.

17. Laurendeau, 36-7.

MARITIMERS RISE TO WAR

R.A. Young
University of Western Ontario

By 1939, the dragging Depression had reinforced the deep localism which had long characterized the Maritime provinces. The region's inhabitants were bound together by the common preoccupation of coping with the economic problems afflicting each of the diverse local economies. The small provincial governments and the various regional elites were pinched and worn from their struggle to maintain material decency and social integration in the face of enduring hardship and, in some cases, despair.

Yet these immediate burdens had not isolated the Maritimes. Large segments of the population shared national, continental and global interests, all of which were sharpened in 1939 as Nazi adventurism drove the consolidation of Europe into tight, feverishly-arming alliances. Maritimers watched these developments with sentiments ranging from bravado through to confidence, trepidation, and disgust. War was not theirs to declare; nevertheless, over the course of the year a consensus emerged about what stance was imperative should war erupt, a collective view assembled by the region's leaders and cemented first by the Royal Tour and then by Germany's ceaseless aggression.

The people of the Maritimes, along with Canada and the empire, were willing to fight Hitler. Many preferred to meet the enemy in a "limited-liability war," by producing goods at full capacity, and indeed it was evident by the autumn of 1939 that the long slump was over for the duration. Prosperity was no motive for war, however: Maritimers made huge sacrifices in the Second World War, and they did so ultimately because in the great common cause could be identified those shared values which each regional community had struggled to sustain through the bitter Depression years.

The 1930s were hard and roughening for Maritimers, as incomes dropped throughout the region. The proportional declines in personal incomes between 1929 and 1933, and the recoveries between 1933 and 1938, mirrored the national figures, but absolute incomes consistently were only two-thirds of the Canadian average.[1] Economic conditions and prospects varied widely within the region, where it was true, as the

Rowell-Sirois Commission said of the whole country, that the "economy was like a huge bonded corporation in which the export producers held the equity interest."[2]

This meant that in some manufacturing and service sectors, workers still employed had real wages rise, as lower prices for food, fuel, clothing and rent more than offset pay cuts, if not making up for longer hours and fearful uncertainty.[3] The same could not be said of any primary sector. In agriculture, falling produce prices reinforced subsistence life. Decapitalization and massive waste occurred in specialties like potato farming, where prices fell 80 percent and much of the crop was dumped. Among Annapolis Valley apple producers, when crops were good, finding markets was a constant struggle — in 1939, one promising new market was Germany. In long-established, mixed-farming areas, including much of Prince Edward Island, the Depression simply tightened the bonds of a familiar frugality. But for those with large families, those with few chances for cash sales in the towns, and those with no land or new land, life in the country became tougher and sometimes brutal. Supplying produce and labour for the lumber and pulp and paper industries kept some money flowing in the rural areas, especially in New Brunswick, though in 1939 it was possible to cut wood in camp for three months and take home only $7.60.[4] Men were forced into the fishery, where, despite lower prices and variable catches, the number trying to make a living rose from 29,593 in 1930 to 34,797 in 1939.[5] New technology had also entered the industry off Nova Scotia, in the form of trawlers bitterly resisted by the "hook and line" fishermen. As in other primary sectors, market conditions had improved somewhat in 1937, but receipts slid in 1938 despite a higher catch, and in 1939, as prices continued to soften, hundreds of southern Nova Scotia fishermen had been left without gear by fierce winter storms.[6]

In the coal and steel industry, prospects were mixed. On the strength of the armaments race, steel was reviving: the Sydney mill of the Dominion Steel and Coal Corporation (Dosco) ran at 82 percent of capacity throughout 1938, and hit 100 percent by May 1939.[7] But coal was in trouble. Rising American imports were likely to jump as tariff protection declined under the 1938 Canada-U.S. trade agreement. With high production costs, Dosco sought more subventions from Ottawa while meeting miners' pressure for wage increases with the full range of divisive and oppressive techniques available to management. As 1939 opened, 1,200 men had just lost jobs when a Dosco subsidiary, bled white by its parent, closed the Thorburn mine at Stellarton; more than 10,000 Dosco miners were working under an expired contract at 1937 wages; and ceaseless wildcat strikes and lockouts were causing real hardship in the coalfields.[8] In the Minto coal area of New Brunswick, where wages were about 70 percent of Nova Scotia rates and miners often hacked at shallow seams on their knees and elbows, the situation was still more grim.

In these bleak and worsening economic times, Maritimers had shifted their federal votes from the Conservatives to the Liberals in 1935.[9] As well, each Maritime province was governed by Liberal administrations — and successfully, too, if the criterion of success is winning elections. Angus L. Macdonald gained power in Nova Scotia in 1933, taking 22 seats of 30, and increased his standing to 25 seats in 1937. In P.E.I., Thane Campbell took over as premier from W.M. Lea, who had swept the province entirely in 1935. Campbell held on easily in the election of 18 May 1939, losing only three seats. Under Allison Dysart, the New Brunswick Liberals routed the Tories in 1935, and in the election of 20 November 1939, their popular vote was 55 percent, a decline of only three percent. Each administration made much of its efforts to achieve economic progress, in 1939 as before, but provincial governments in the Maritimes could not solve the region's problems, and voters did not really expect them to do so. Politicians blasted Ottawa's neglect, applauded any welcome news, accommodated efforts by primary producers and businessmen to create growth, and mitigated the worst effects of the Depression on the poor. In the end, their impact was necessarily marginal.

The sheer weight of these governments was small by modern standards. In New Brunswick, the gross value of production in 1939 was about $139 million, while total provincial government spending on current account was $9.4 million. Moreover, state activities were squeezed between debt and the tax base. By the late 1930s, capital spending by each provincial government had produced swelling debt loads, large drains from ordinary revenues to meet interest obligations, and heavy pressure for restraint from provincial creditors.[10] At the same time, provincial and municipal tax bases shrank, and collection was difficult. There was strong resistance to tax increases on the part of businessmen and primary producers who lacked the cash to maintain existing equipment, let alone invest in new assets. The political influence of these groups was large. In PEI, for example, only people owning more than $325 worth of real estate could vote for "councillors," who comprised half the members of the legislature, and municipal voters in Charlottetown not only had a property qualification but also, as was common in the region, were required to pay a poll tax.[11] Even a generally sympathetic observer remarks upon the domination of Island politics by "farmers whose resistance to taxation was legendary."[12]

Provincial governments lacked the means to offset the Depression or to challenge the major regional interests. Cape Breton provides the extreme example of relative state weakness. Any provincial government presence in the coalfields was quite overshadowed by two huge organizations, the employer and the union, which were locked in class warfare. Over 12,000 men worked in the mines alone. Their earnings exceeded total provincial revenues, and they were tightly organized in the United Mine Workers (UMW) which, however divided locally by ideology and faction, was part of an entity powerful enough in 1939 to pull 300,000 men out of the American mines. The UMW was spearheading the Congress of Industrial Organizations' drive across the continent and in Cape Breton too, through men like Silby Barrett and D.W. Morrison, UMW District 26 president, member of the executive of the Trades and Labour Congress, and mayor of Glace Bay. Opposing the UMW was Dosco, a sprawling empire headquartered in Montreal, which spent $23 million on wages alone and made over $50 million in total disbursements, compared with the 1939 Nova Scotia budget of $12.3 million.[13] Dosco could secure tariff changes, subventions and contracts from Ottawa; it was Dosco executives who travelled to the UK to advise imperial war planners on Canada's manufacturing capacity; and only Dosco had the technical and financial information to justify its strategic mine closures and negotiating postures towards the enemy UMW. The company was powerful enough to hire top-rank Cabinet ministers to manage its lesser subsidiaries.[14] Premier Angus Macdonald was in no position to control either of these behemoths, or even to influence them very much.

More generally, the region's provincial governments simply could not confront major firms to extract investment or better treatment of workers, or take up all the slack in agriculture, the forest industries and the fishery, while still meeting obligations for education, transportation, health, and relief. Governments lacked not only the resources required to undertake such bold actions but also the will: they were directed by men from backgrounds and training which did not prepare them to shake up the existing order but to sustain it and advance it where possible.

By 1939, the long slump had induced a few limited initiatives to help industry. Macdonald had established an Economic Council, which discussed power development and surveyed the province's natural resources and manufacturing in order to attract capital to produce for export and for import-substitution.[15] New Brunswick, under the recent Aid to Industry Act, had extended loans and loan guarantees to several firms, mainly to process and store resource products, but also to sustain a near-bankrupt pulp and paper mill in Saint John. In 1939 Premier Dysart moved as well towards co-operation with local industry by creating the Advisory Board for Economic and Industrial Development, composed of businessmen who discussed industrial opportunities but turned, at the outbreak of hostilities, towards securing war-supply contracts from Ottawa.

Apart from these late initiatives to promote industry, the provincial governments had two responses to the Depression — relief and roads. *Per capita* relief payments in the region, like incomes, were less than those elsewhere in Canada, in part because some federal shared-cost programs were designed to meet conditions in more populous, urbanized, and richer provinces.[16] In addition, rural populations could more readily subsist with little cash, and voluntary organizations, dense in the Maritimes, may have played a greater charitable role than elsewhere, especially in the Roman Catholic communities. The provincial governments' general strategy was to push relief responsibility onto the municipalities (by making it possible for them to borrow, for example[17]), and to intensify their demands on Ottawa, while meeting acute needs with *ad hoc* measures.

Such measures were necessary in the winter of 1939, as the economy worsened. In Charlottetown, where 300 families were on relief, a mass protest meeting heard even leaders of the Canadian Legion denouncing as a "disgrace" a system which paid 2 cents per meal per person.[18] Nova Scotia's relief payments rose from $829,000 in 1937-38 to $1,109,000 in 1938-39, and yet total federal relief payments to the region dropped 44 percent from 1936-37 to 1938-39.[19] That winter, the Glace Bay sub-district convention of the UMW sent a chilling telegram to Angus Macdonald and to the prime minister, Mackenzie King: "situation here at present is desperate and we demand relief at once. If not we will take it. The men refuse to be responsible for action taken."[20]

The provincial governments were of course opposed ideologically to handouts, and were inclined to substitute what is now called "workfare" for the dole. Federal money, for example, was available to help cover the southern Nova Scotia fishermen's equipment losses (to be shared

75 percent – 25 percent with the province). But Macdonald insisted the fishermen do roadwork to earn it, despite the short time available before gear had to be bought, the difficulty of working efficiently on roads in winter, and the united opposition of the men, regional municipalities, and local Boards of Trade. "I have always understood," he stated in a press release, "that any right-thinking Canadian whether unemployed or not, whether he was in need of any government assistance or not, welcomed the opportunity of giving some return in the way of labour for any relief assistance that might be granted."[21] Premier Dysart, enunciating rather similar sentiments about stalwart independence and the hazard of demoralization, had ended the dole entirely in 1936, though the winter of 1938-39 was so hard that the government relented and sent cash into the cities.[22]

The major governmental initiative in the Maritimes, and the real system of relief, was massive spending on public works. This fell squarely within the parameters of acceptable state action and also was consistent with the political needs of Liberal incumbents. In the late 1930s, strict economy was exercised over normal expenditures on health and education, and in effect the human capital of the Maritimes was run down. But governments kept cash flowing, and people eating, through borrowing for public works. Hard-surfacing of roads began in Nova Scotia when A.S. MacMillan took over the highways portfolio in 1933. By 1940 he had built 1,000 miles of paved roads, and he similarly pushed rural electrification from 1937 on, as chairman of the Power Commission. The Dysart government borrowed very heavily for the same purposes. PEI started paving only in 1939, but road construction and maintenance absorbed a large part of its Depression budgets.

These expenditures were highly divisible, so supporters could be allocated work in appropriate measure, and they were congruent with the clientele networks — systems of hierarchical interdependence — which prevailed in stable, rural, primary-resource regions.[23] This was how Maritimes governments helped the deserving poor, and also aided the hard-hit businessman. It is important to recognize that in these decentralized systems, it was not only the politically-correct deserving poor who got help: partisanship could not justly run so deep in desperate times. Nevertheless, the flow of public works money, discerningly distributed, was both a substitute for relief and a cause of the incumbent parties' strength and success. If nothing else, "the sharing of the lower levels in the allocation of local patronage" required the "Liberal poll organizations to maintain a coherent existence."[24]

Apart from providing relief and roadwork, Maritimes governments could only encourage people to help themselves. Indeed, Maritimers had no choice during the Depression except to rely on themselves and on each other. By 1939, the main indigenous response to the economic and social crisis had crystallized in the ideology of co-operation, one suited particularly well to the culture and social structure of the region. Self-help took many forms. One was the colonization movement. In Nova Scotia and PEI, starting out on the land was an individual effort, as authorities offered on generous terms farms abandoned or seized for tax arrears. In New Brunswick, Crown lands were made available early in the 1930s. The response came mainly from Acadians, led by priests, who established many new settlements in the Northwest and the interior of the Gloucester peninsula. By 1939, over 11,000 people had settled in the bush, and although pulpwood sales brought in some cash, living conditions in many areas were abysmal.[25]

Better known is the mutual self-help movement which marched through the 1930s under the banner of Co-operation, led by Moses Coady, A.B. MacDonald, and others associated with the Extension Department of St. Francis Xavier University. In 1939, the Antigonish Movement was at its height, sponsoring 1,100 study groups, and having organized 29 consumer co-ops, 17 canneries, 5 fish plants, and other co-operative ventures, including a large number of credit unions.[26] In PEI, a parallel network operated from St. Dunstan's University. Beyond the local organizations were big regional producer co-ops, including Canadian Livestock Co-operatives (Maritimes) and the United Maritimes Fishermen, which helped in marketing and cannery construction. The strongest growth of co-operative institutions was among the Acadian people. Here, the ideology of the middle road between heartless capitalism and Godless communism was compatible not only with Church teaching after *Rerum Novarum* (1891) and *Quadragesimo Anno* (1931), but also with the desire of secular leaders to build collective capital through national unity. The mutual insurance society, *L'Assomption*, became in 1938 the "first Acadian millionaire."[27] Many young priests and future Acadian leaders served to spread its scope and build its assets: one of the most outstanding was père Clement Cormier, who headed the new École des sciences sociales et économiques at Moncton, founded in late 1939 with the help of Georges-Henri Lévesque of Laval University.

To facilitate collective organization, the New Brunswick government passed the Co-operative Associations Act in 1938. This expanded the range of permissible co-op activities, and within two years 21 new co-ops had formed, all but one in the francophone counties. More significant still was the growth of credit unions, allowed by 1936 legislation. Over 120 were created by 1940, mostly in the north of the province where, with the blessing of the Church, the organization was led by Martin Legère of Caraquet and M. abbé Livain Chiasson.[28] Acadian society at this time was proudly traditionalist: the motto of the collectivity's newspaper, *La Voix d'Evangéline*, was "Religion Langue Patrie." Yet Acadians were highly organized and dynamic, a fact illustrated both by their emerging economic institutions and by new social and political associations, including the Ordre des Commandeurs de Jacques-Cartier, which spread rapidly in the late 1930s, and the Association Acadienne d'Éducation, which expressed a powerful collective demand for better teacher training and francophone schools.[29] By 1939, l'*Evangéline* had a second motto on page one — "Instruire et Unir pour Agir."

Societies integrated around economic hierarchies are always vulnerable to class conflict when economic conditions worsen. In the Maritimes, much potential unrest was tempered by relief payments, absorbed by the co-op movement or enmeshed in established organizational structures. In three areas, however, self-help took the form of militant unionism. The first was the coal and steel industry where, in 1939, Dosco and the UMW continued their poisonous struggle, with the union becoming the first in Canada to ally itself with the new political party, the Co-operative Commonwealth Federation.[30] Second, despite huge obstacles, labourers had managed to organize in Charlottetown (the Labourers' Protective Union) and on the Miramichi (the Farmer-Labour Union of New Brunswick). The latter organization elected two sympathetic MLAs in 1939, but was in decline by 1940. Finally, where fishermen were squeezed by monopsonistic buyers and could form alliances with plant workers, unionization appeared a viable strategy. Much of this story has been told.[31] In 1939, the big struggle occurred in Lockeport, Nova Scotia, where fishermen and plant workers affiliated with the Canadian Seamen's Union struck for recognition. The Macdonald government did not hesitate to intervene in this very tense standoff, using both the RCMP and thinly-veiled allegations that the union was run by Communists.[32] Apart from these cases, the union movement in the region was moderate. Decimated at the onset of the Depression, it was growing rapidly by 1939, aided by modest extensions of collective bargaining rights in New Brunswick and Nova Scotia.[33]

A less visible manifestation of self-help, but one which was far more pervasive, could be found within the thick web of established organizations in the Maritimes. This old region had accumulated a wide and deep set of voluntary associations in the economic, social, cultural and religious realms. These formal organizations structured social life in the region: they were the tendons and tissue, if not the skeleton, of the community. Groups like the Oddfellows (IOOF), the Chevaliers de Colombe, the Baptist Church, the Women's Institutes, the sporting clubs, the Fish and Game Associations, the Rotary, the YMCA — all, along with the unions and co-ops and trade and professional associations, worked to order activity at the local level, while connecting Maritimers to national and international movements and events. These organizations were generally inclusive, and they permeated the regional society.

PEI provides an illustration. Throughout the glorious summer of 1939, the awful news from Europe and China accumulated each day. Yet Islanders maintained their orderly annual round. Rotarians gathered, then the Women's Institutes, the Baptists, the Scottish Clans, the IOOF, the Fox Farmers, the Catholic Women's League, and other groups. The usual Confederation celebrations were carefully organized, and Dominion Day was observed gaily and properly. In mid-August, the sixtieth provincial exhibition was held: there was "much interest in the horse racing."[34] Less than three weeks later, the P.E.I. Highlanders were assembled on the Exhibition grounds, awaiting orders to move to the mainland. But throughout the months before this, the atmosphere was one of willed normality.[35] In anglophone New Brunswick and Nova Scotia, the pattern was almost identical. Society continued to function in its established channels of regular meetings, ritual procedures and processes, and civilized discussion. And so it did in Acadie: *L'Assomption* held its 13th quadrennial Congress, and on August 15th the *Fête nationale* took place as usual, complete with its traditional historical tableaux.

Maritimers had held together during the Depression through this set of formal organizations. Though threadbare, these structures were largely intact in 1939. And in understanding Maritimers' response to the onset of war, their importance cannot be overestimated. For decades, the people of the region had invested much time, energy, money and commitment in sustaining a complex and fully-articulated set of social institutions. Through them, as well as through the newspapers and radio, Maritimers were linked to wider networks and currents of thought. But their own associations also structured opinion, through regular activities taking place in the local communities, according to indigenous custom. These organizations not only articulated, but also embodied, the common values of reason, due process, decency, and community involvement. With few exceptions, they operated on democratic principles, though the subtle hierarchies of offices, and the Victorian formality and measured rhythm of their activities, also instilled in those they embraced a sense of caution and deference to elites. It was these leaders, and not merely politicians, who took the people of the Maritimes into the Second World War. Through their very organizations, most Maritimers were informed, and they were sensible. Ultimately it was their own commitment to a shared and valued order, a reasonable and democratic order, that led the people of the region willingly to defend their communities, their country, and their commonwealth.

Throughout the winter and spring of 1939, European conflicts came closer to the Maritimes. As Spain fell to the Insurgents, some Mackenzie-Papineau veterans trickled back. A succession of submarine disasters testified to increasing preparedness, and in April there were reports of a submarine sighting off Halifax, which justified Ottawa's January allocation of $2 million to Atlantic defences and air installations.[36] The armament race ratcheted upward with the launching of the *Bismarck*. But there was no enthusiasm, much less jingoism, in the face of the Nazi pressure: "... peace- and freedom-loving peoples, for their own protection, have also to join in the mad armament race, turning their energies and money to the piling up of the engines of war. It is a bitter choice — but, frankly, what choice is there?"[37] The Acadians were less certain. On armaments, their organ echoed a Chicago *Tribune* line: "Rien ne sert de s'emballer. Quoi qu'il arrive en Europe ou en Asie, la froide raison nous dit que le Canada n'est pas sérieusement menacé."[38]

Isolationism became harder to sustain in the early summer, however, when Europe came to Canada. The King and Queen arrived on the Royal Tour, which would have been the event of the year, indeed of the decade, had war not followed so closely. This was the first visit to North America by a reigning British sovereign. It was designed to reaffirm the links of Britain with Canada (and with the U.S.A.), and to instil empathy with England's position. It succeeded brilliantly. The tour in the Maritimes was carefully planned to expose the royal couple to as much of the citizenry as possible. This required the fullest involvement by leaders of regional organizations, who were, for the most part, eager enough to associate themselves with monarchy that the biggest headache was restraining their enthusiasm and tendency to jockey for position. Their involvement was nevertheless crucial and quite revealing. Maritimers did not just encounter the royal couple *en masse*, as crowds; instead they appeared in their serried ranks, as Maritimes society literally was presented to the King and Queen.[39]

Prince Edward Island was visited on June 14th. Here the official emphasis was upon political and business leaders, and there was also a military cast to the events as the Boer War veterans attended the reception at Government House and 600 Great War vets marched.[40] But many other leaders were at lunch and tea, and ordinary Islanders packed Charlottetown, some of the estimated 35,000 having been brought in by five special trains which converged on the capital. Children stood several rows deep on Great George Street, and in times when a good pair of gray flannel pants cost $1.39, tickets to watch their Majesties' passage from bleachers in the fore-court of Tom Davies' Red Indian Service Station were worth $2.50. Even many of those whose imperial devotion and means were not so great could well have been attracted to town by the chance to see, that evening at the Sporting Club, Big George Leslie of Souris fight George Graham of Murray Harbour for the Island Heavyweight Championship.[41] Major sporting events, of course, are not scheduled haphazardly.

Nova Scotia society was more complex, but no less enthusiastic and well-primed for the visit. Among the crowds in New Glasgow, where the tour paused briefly, were six trainloads of veterans from Sydney, and the Dominion #6 Citizens' Band was one of several chosen to play for the King and Queen. In Halifax, the major stores all had big sales to greet the crowds. But the driveabout did not pass crowds; instead it moved through an orderly representation of society, "special guards" from various organizations having been assigned control over each portion of the route. Sections were handled by the Rotary Club, the IOOF, the Coalhandlers and many other associations.[42] The luncheon guest list featured provincial and municipal politicians (including D.W. Morrison from Glace Bay), the heads of major institutions, and leaders of the Salvation Army, the Jewish congregation, the United and Lutheran Churches, the Scouts and Girl Guides, the Women's Institute, and the Local Council of Women. By the time the Royals finally embarked on Sir Edmund Beatty's *Empress of Britain*, the city and the province had been systematically massaged and impressed.

New Brunswick was a different matter because of the Acadians' history and isolationist tendencies. At the time, the major event in Acadie was the start of work on the great Moncton cathedral, after extended fund-raising among people who strained to give even one or two dollars to honour Notre-Dame-de-l'Assomption and have their names honourably inscribed in the Livre d'Or.[43] *L'Evangéline* provided very little advance coverage of the tour, and an account of the Royal landing at Québec City competed with news of the preparations for the visit to Domrémy, France, of Québec's Cardinal Villeneuve, who missed the King and Queen because of his diplomatic assignment as a Papal legate to the dedication of Joan of Arc's basilica. In the event, the King made an exceedingly favourable impact among French Canadians. His bilingualism surprised many, and he and the Queen carefully enunciated respect for French-Canadians' traditions and language. When the tour reached Montreal to meet huge crowds, the success of this part of its mission was obvious.

In this atmosphere, Archbishop Melanson of Moncton decreed that his new cathedral's cornerstone would be blessed on 13 June, the day of the Royal visit. All in all, the Archbishop said, "On ne pourra trouver meilleure occasion pour apporter sa pierre au Monument de la Reconnaissance"; later he described the coincidence of celebrations as "un heureux hasard."[44] Priests were directed to encourage the faithful each to bring one dollar in an envelope bearing their name and parish: a big turnout might produce $40,000. Further instructions set in motion a parade to follow the benediction at 3 p.m. The Scouts, Cadets, bands, members of the Holy Name Society — indeed, all Acadians present — would proceed to the train station to help welcome their Majesties. And a great many did so. When the Royal train had stopped, children competed in chanting, "we want the King" and "Vive le Roi." When the Queen emerged, flowers were presented by two little girls named Lockhart and Doiron.

Much more seriously, the archbishop publicly advertised, on behalf of Catholics, "notre loyale soumission envers notre gracieux Souverain et envers notre digne et vénérée Souveraine."[45] Similarly, François-G.-J. Comeau presented an address to the King on behalf of La Société Nationale Acadienne, conveying the Acadians' "hommages" and their "assurance de leur loyauté indéfectible à la Couronne."[46] These remarkable commitments arose not merely from the necessity of co-existing with an anglophone population whose sympathies were now evident but also, as the archbishop stated in his advertisement, as a result of the social peace, justice and religious freedom enjoyed by subjects of the Crown. In affirming these values, and reinforcing loyalty to their symbolic defender, the Royal Tour was an unqualified triumph.

Peace and freedom were obviously eroding in Europe and China. Prince Edward Islanders could read in June that Germany was deporting some Polish Jews and sending others to concentration camps.[47] The Danzig crisis mounted. Britain sent its gold for safekeeping in the United States. Catholics watched Hitler's treatment of the German churches with increasing unease, and the Pope encouraged the Poles to resist Nazi pressure.[48] The Nazi-Soviet pact sealed matters, as it became clear that Hitler would stop at nothing. Reason, in the person of the British prime minister, Neville Chamberlain, failed. The public began to be mobilized, and they became ready to mobilize. Unusually large numbers of militiamen were trained over the summer. At the Nova Scotia Provincial Exhibition, a Military Preparedness Display included a simulated air raid, complete with "screaming hysterical women fleeing from the dreadful attack of sky raiders on their homes."[49] Militia volunteers were called to active service in late August, and army and air force units were opened for enlistment. Even before Britain declared war, the leaders of the Roman Catholic, Anglican and United churches of Nova Scotia issued statements supporting unity, empire and victory.[50] Coal miners decided against extending an especially serious wildcat strike to all the mines, and returned to work.[51] After Germany invaded Poland, full mobilization began, and Maritimers got set for war. The British Commonwealth, said the editors of the Charlottetown *Guardian*, was "one and indivisible, pledged unwaveringly to the support of the Mother Country in a cause which goes to the very root of all our cherished principles of justice, freedom and democracy. There will be no turning back."[52]

This mood prevailed as Ottawa weighed the situation. The class combatants of the coalfields turned partly toward the new enemy. Silby Barrett wired Ottawa on behalf of the steelworkers "to offer our co-operation in smashing Hitlerism," and the UMW forced all foreign-born workers out of the mines.[53] Dosco joined other large firms in a Labour Day message to announce that "In Crises Labour and Capital Stand Together," and to call on everyone to "consider *first* the welfare of the entire people of the Dominion and Empire."[54] (Dosco class B shares, trading on Friday, 2 September at $10.75, hit $14.25 on Monday.) Women's organizations across the region pledged their help. After Canada declared war, enlistment was brisk, and the officers commanding Military Districts 6 (NS and PEI) and 7 (NB) reported "very favourable" and "very loyal" public opinion, strong support from firms and local associations, and a surplus of recruits.[55] Dozens of men showed up each day in Halifax port seeking passage to England to enlist and fight sooner.[56]

The Acadian community, too, edged into the war. Having warned about the costs of war on 1 September, *l'Evangéline* was editorially silent the following week, reporting in detail on the War Measures Act and on demonstrations in Montreal against Canada's decision to enter Europe's war; it also, however, reprinted the Chamberlain-Hitler correspondence in full. On 14 September, the deed done in Ottawa, the paper's editorial noted that Canadians were at war "modérément," to defend their territory, without conscription. It saluted this compromise by "la majorité anglaise," which was showing "un désir très louable de ne pas heurter la population de langue française dont l'opposition à toute mesure de coercition est bien connue." Most significant to *l'Evangéline*, though, was the fact that Canada had declared war of its own free will: the country might have done otherwise; the community had made a free choice. The same could be said of Acadians and of Maritimers generally, whatever the global forces impinging on them, and however carefully their leaders had prepared the route to be taken if necessary. A reasonable people, they made a choice to fight a force which could not be stopped by reason.

Through the rest of 1939, the benefits of war to the region far outweighed the costs. There were blackouts, inconvenient shipping restrictions, higher prices, and some shortages. But produce markets were very strong, and governments now could help, as when Ottawa bought 69 percent of the Nova Scotia apple crop.[57] The steel industry worked flat out, and lumber, pulp and paper, and other manufacturing sectors picked up with wartime demand and war supply contracts. Stanfield's, for example, sold all its men's heavy wool socks to the forces. There was still no contract in the coal mines, but there were large new orders from Québec and, as an all-time production record was set in October, Dosco B shares reached $17.50.[58] At the end of September, led by the stellar performance of Clement Cormier, *L'Assomption* set a new weekly record for insurance sales.[59] Ottawa poured money into railway and airport improvements, and troop payrolls swirled throughout the region. By Christmas, people were spending, and, as one Halifax merchant said, "money is easy."[60] These words had not been heard in the region for years. Times were finally getting better. The sacrifices, Maritimers well knew, would follow.

NOTES

1. Canada, Dominion Bureau of Statistics, *National Accounts Income and Expenditure 1926-1956* (Ottawa, 1958), Tables 28 and 29. For valuable comments and suggestions while preparing this paper, the author thanks Peter Neary, E.R. Forbes and Norman Hillmer.

2. Canada, Royal Commission on Dominion-Provincial Relations, *Report* (Ottawa, 1940), reprint ed. (Ottawa, 1954), Book I, 146.

3. Canada, Dominion Bureau of Statistics, *Canada 1940* (Ottawa, 1940), "Cost of Living," 153.

4. Moncton, *La Voix d'Evangéline* [hereafter *l'Evangéline]*, 3 April 1939, 1. Hereafter all newspaper references are for 1939, unless otherwise indicated.

5. M.C. Urquhart and K.A.H. Buckley, eds., *Historical Statistics of Canada*, 2nd ed. (Ottawa, 1983), series N38-48.

6. *The Halifax Herald*, [hereafter *Herald*], 31 December 1938, 1; 31 January, 1.

7. *Herald*, 2 January, special section 3, 8; 4 May, 1.

8. For an account of the independent commission's report on Acadia Coal, see *Herald*, 1 March, 1, 7. On the contract negotiations, see Michael Earle, "'Down with Hitler and Silby Barrett': The Cape Breton Miners' Slowdown Strike of 1941," *Acadiensis*, XVIII (Autumn 1988), 56-90.

9. J.M. Beck, *Pendulum of Power* (Scarborough, 1968), 202-3, 220-1.

10. In New Brunswick, for example, payments for debt service in 1939 reached 52 percent of ordinary revenues, and a syndicate of banks refused to roll over imminent maturities unless taxes were raised. See R.A. Young, "'and the people will sink into despair': Reconstruction in New Brunswick, 1942-52," *Canadian Historical Review*, LXIX (June 1988), 127-166.

11. Frank MacKinnon, *The Government of Prince Edward Island* (Toronto, 1951), 215-18.

12. E.R. Forbes, "The 1930s, the Depression Decade," manuscript (1987), 4.

13. *Herald*, 14 March, 1; 15 February, 8; Nova Scotia, *Report of the Royal Commission on Provincial Development and Rehabilitation* (Halifax, 1944), Vol. I, "Minerals," 13: total 1942 disbursements were estimated at $97.1 million.

14. *Herald*, 26 January, 15; 29 July, 3; 20 January, 1.

15. *Herald*, 9 February, 8; 20 October, 14.

16. E.R. Forbes, "Cutting the Pie Into Smaller Pieces: Matching Grants and Relief in the Maritime Provinces during the 1930s," *Acadiensis*, XVII (Autumn 1987), 31-55.

17. Nova Scotia, *Statutes*, 3 George V [1938], c. 14 and c. 15.

18. *The Charlottetown Guardian*, [hereafter *Guardian*], 6 February, 1, 3.

19. Nova Scotia, *Annual Report of the Department of Labour for the Year Ended November 30 1939*, (Halifax, 1940), 7. (Figures include direct relief and Special Relief Work Projects.) E.R. Forbes, "Cutting the Pie," 53, note 80.

20. *Herald*, 30 January, 1.

21. *Herald*, 4 February, 3. See also 31 January, 1; 4 February, 2; 8 February, 1; 9 February, 1.

22. Forbes, "Cutting the Pie," 53-4.

23. R.A. Young, "Teaching and Research in Maritimes Politics: Old Stereotypes and New Directions," *Journal of Canadian Studies*, 21 (Summer 1986), 133-56.

24. J. Murray Beck, *The Government of Nova Scotia* (Toronto, 1957), 161.

25. A. Gosselin and G.P. Boucher, *Settlement Problems in Northern New Brunswick*, Department of Agriculture, Technical Bulletin No. 51 (Ottawa, 1944).

26. Ian MacPherson, *Each For All: A History of the Co-operative Movement in English Canada, 1900-1945* (Toronto, 1979), 168.

27. *l'Evangéline*, 22 December 1938, editorial, 3; 13 April, 2.

28. *l'Evangéline*, 17 November 1938, 1; Philippe Arsenault, "L'établissement des caisses populaires – offre un excellent moyen de relèvement économique à nos classes moyennes et pauvres," MA thesis, Université St. Joseph, 1939.

29. Alexandre-J. Savoie, *Un Siècle de Revendications Scolaires au Nouveau Brunswick 1871-1971*, vol. 2 (n.p., 1980); *l'Evangéline*, 25 August 1938, editorial, 3; 1 September 1938, 1; 6 July, 1.

30. *Herald*, 25 May, 2; 27 May, 2.

31. L. Gene Barrett, "Underdevelopment and Social Movements in the Nova Scotia Fishing Industry to 1938," in Robert J. Brym and R. James Sacouman, eds., *Underdevelopment and Social Movements in Atlantic Canada* (Toronto, 1979), 127-60.

32. *Herald*, 1 November, 3; 14 November, 9; 4 December, 3; 12 December, 1; 16 December, 1; 21 December, 9.

33. E. Larentson and E. Woolner, "Fifty Years of Labour Legislation in Canada," *The Labour Gazette*, L (September 1950), 1413-59.

34. *Guardian*, 14 August, 1.

35. Mackenzie King's heroic grayness helped allow this mood in Canada. In early August, speaking about European affairs to 4,000 guests in Toronto on the occasion of the 20th anniversary of his leadership of the Liberal party, he said, "One thing I will not do and cannot be persuaded to do is to say what Canada will do in regard to a situation that may arise at some future time and under circumstances of which we now know nothing." (*Herald*, 9 August, 1.)

36. *Herald*, 26 January, 1. See also 23 May, 9-14, special "Defence Edition."

37. *Herald*, 18 January, editorial, 6.

38. *l'Evangéline*, 12 January, editorial, 3.

39. See Bernard S. Cohn, "Representing Authority in Victorian India," in Eric Hobsbawm and Terence Ranger, eds., *The Invention of Tradition* (Cambridge, 1983), 165-209.

40. *Guardian*, 10 June, Section two; 15 June, 1.

41. I thank John Crossley for supplementary information about this event.

42. *Herald*, 10 June, map, 7.

43. *l'Evangéline*, 27 July 1938, 9; 11 August 1938, 6; 24 April, 1.

44. *l'Evangéline*, 25 May, 1, and editorial, 3; 15 June, 1.

45. *l'Evangéline*, 8 June, 10.

46. *l'Evangéline*, 22 June, 12; *Herald*, 22 June, 2.

47. *Guardian*, 9 June, 1.

48. *l'Evangéline*, 16 March, 1; 3 August, 2.

49. *Herald*, 25 August, 14.

50. *Herald*, 2 September, 2.

51. *Herald*, 31 August, 1; and 29 August, 1, 30 August, 1.

52. 4 September, 4.

53. *Herald*, 4 September, 3; 7 September, 3.

54. *Herald*, 4 September, 9.

55. National Defence Headquarters, Ottawa, Directorate of History, 113.302009 (D119). Roger Sarty kindly provided copies of these documents.

56. *Herald*, 30 September, 16.

57. *Herald*, 26 September, 1.

58. *Herald*, 2 November, 3.

59. *l'Evangéline*, 5 October, 8.

60. *Herald*, 23 December, 18.

"LIKE STEPPING BACK": NEWFOUNDLAND IN 1939

Peter Neary
University of Western Ontario

When the fateful year 1939 began, Newfoundlanders were approaching the end of their fifth year under a form of administration known as Commission of Government.[1] This was a constitutional arrangement that was unique in the history of the British Empire, having been forced on Newfoundland by the events of the Great Depression.

These events had dealt Newfoundland, which in 1935 (including Labrador) had a population of 289,588, a shattering blow. Constitutionally a self-governing British dominion when the Depression struck, Newfoundland was economically very vulnerable. Thus the country depended on the sale abroad of the products of three basic and to some extent interconnected industries: fishing, forestry, and mining. After 1929, as the Depression took hold, Newfoundland exporters soon found themselves facing declining prices and contracting markets. The result was large scale unemployment, widespread destitution and a sudden crisis in public finance. Since the income of the government of Newfoundland came mainly from customs receipts, public revenue fell off drastically as trade declined. In short order the authorities in St. John's were faced with a stark choice: to feed the poor and maintain at least minimal public services, or to continue to make the interest payments owed the country's bondholders, mainly abroad, based on fixed price contracts negotiated in better times. Initially, Newfoundland tried to keep going by borrowing more money from private lenders, but this source of funds soon dried up. The country then stumbled on from interest payment to interest payment with the assistance of the British and Canadian governments. The price of this assistance was high: Newfoundland had to enforce, at great cost in human misery, rigid economies in public expenditure and agree to the supervision of its accounts by a Treasury representative from London. In effect, the country passed into a form of receivership.

In June 1932, the conservative United Newfoundland Party came to power in the country, led by Frederick Alderdice, a Northern Ireland-born St. John's businessman and ardent imperialist. Alderdice personified orthodox business values. Nonetheless, so desperate was the financial and social situation facing him that he contemplated a rescheduling of Newfoundland's debt payments to lessen the burden of interest on the country. This notion, however, was categorically rejected in London. Newfoundland, it was argued, would have difficulty ever borrowing again and would disgrace the good name of the British Empire. Britain's dominions did not wriggle out of contracts. Alderdice conceded the point and at the end of 1932, in return for more Anglo-Canadian financial help, agreed to the appointment by London of a Royal Commission, to include British, Canadian and Newfoundland members, to look into Newfoundland's problems and to recommend a long-term solution to them.

In the summer of 1933, while this Commission was going about its business chaired by Lord Amulree, a Scottish Labour peer, Canada refused to help out with Newfoundland's mid-year interest payments and in effect abandoned its neighbour. This put the British in the position of having to go it alone in Newfoundland, and they gave careful consideration to what this would entail. The terms on which they would continue to prop up Newfoundland were ultimately specified in the report of the Amulree Royal Commission. This carefully composed document recommended that the United Kingdom guarantee Newfoundland's debt and provide the country with annual grants-in-aid to balance its budget. For its part, Newfoundland would temporarily give up parliamentary self-government in favour of Commission of Government. Under this arrangement, which was devised to take account of Newfoundland's dominion status, there would be a governor and six commissioners, three from Newfoundland and three from the United Kingdom; all would be appointed by the British. The Commission of Government would be responsible to the Parliament of the United Kingdom through a member of the British Cabinet, the secretary of state for dominion affairs.

After Newfoundland had requested that self-government be suspended on the terms offered and the British Parliament had passed the Newfoundland Act, 1933, the Commission of Government was inaugurated in St. John's on 16 February 1934. Under the terms of the legislation, self-government would be restored to Newfoundland when it was again self-supporting and upon the request of its people. This, to say the least, was a vague formulation. It was also one that would work very much to British advantage.

The thinking behind the report of the Amulree Royal Commission and the Commission of Government experiment typified one conservative response to the Great Depression. Newfoundland's troubles, it was argued, were essentially of her own making. Democratic party politics and fiscal irresponsibility had gone hand in hand in Newfoundland. Governments there had dissipated natural resources and invested foolishly in grandiose schemes. Party men had kept themselves in office by bribing the electorate with its own money. What was needed, therefore, was "a rest from politics," that is to say, an administration free from party and electoral constraints and conducted with only the public interest in mind.[2] At root, the Commission of Government signified a Tory vision of how the government of men might be replaced by the administration of things.

How did the change work out? The short answer is with decidedly mixed results. The Commission brought to Newfoundland the practices of the British civil service: the country had never had a government that moved paper so efficiently. The Commission also made some useful and ameliorative social and economic changes. It established the Newfoundland Ranger, a police force, to improve contact between the central administration and the rural population; reformed the magistracy; created a system of cottage hospitals and promoted health care generally; raised standards in education; assisted variously both individual fishermen and the fish trade; enquired into the hard conditions of life in the country's logging camps; started up land settlements and encouraged resettlement; and marginally improved the unfortunate lot of Newfoundland's thousands of relief recipients. Early on, however, the limits of Commission rule were indicated when the government retreated in the face of opposition from important vested interests. In education, for example, the Roman Catholic Church and the Church of England were able to confine the government to change that did not disturb the denominational principle underlying the school system of the country. The two foreign-owned pulp and paper companies operating on the island likewise demonstrated that they too had interests which could not be trampled on.

In its 1934 and 1935 published annual reports, the Commission highlighted its achievements and expressed cautious optimism that Newfoundland was on the road to economic recovery. But even though the world depression had reached its nadir in 1933, very bad times persisted in Newfoundland. Accordingly, towards the end of 1936, with relief and unemployment figures still at appalling heights, the Commission set a new course. At London's request, a long-term plan of reconstruction was devised which played down the relocation of people in land settlements in favour of rural revival based on known local economic possibilities, a nostrum that would be rediscovered in Newfoundland in the 1980s. The 1936 plan acknowledged that the task of bringing Newfoundland out of the economic doldrums would be long and difficult. Nevertheless, with the promise of reconstruction funding from London, the Commission made a fresh start. Unfortunately, it had hardly begun to carry out its plans when the country was dealt another body blow by the Roosevelt Recession of 1937-38. So great was the effect of this downturn in the North American economy that, with the threat of public disorder in Newfoundland never very far away, the Commissioners and their Dominions Office masters were forced into consideration of a more sweeping and therefore politically more dangerous programme of reform.

In the spring of 1938, J.H. Gorvin, an official of the British Ministry of Agriculture and Fisheries and an expert on rural rehabilitation, was sent to Newfoundland to advise the Commission on its development plans. Gorvin was clearly shocked by what he found and recommended the adoption of a complex scheme whereby relief funds would be administered regionally by new public bodies and used to put unemployed fishermen back to work. Gorvin believed that "the worst kind of contribution" a government could make towards reconstruction was "to pay out money without any parallel effort to impel the people to stand on their own feet." Doles caused "people to neglect the development of their resources," created "nothing permanent" and were "destructive of the greatest values in a nation" because of their tendency "to destroy moral fibre." Thus, while governments had a responsibility towards the unemployed, they must devise means to cultivate in them "the spirit of co-operative independence."[3] The long-term objective of the plan Gorvin advocated for Newfoundland was a fishing industry and rural society organized along cooperative and democratic lines. By definition, this was a goal sure to anger many vested interests within the existing framework of individualism and free enterprise. They could be expected to fight back hard. Gorvin's plans were unquestionably risky, but the dangers inherent in the *status quo* were also undeniable. By force of circumstance, the Commission had been brought at the beginning of 1939 to a fundamental choice about the future of Newfoundland.

In the first days of January, however, the most pressing immediate item of business on the agenda of the Commission involved an agreement it had signed with the Newfoundland subsidiary of the Bowater-Lloyd company of the United Kingdom on 29 November 1938.[4] The development of the timber resources of the Gander area had been a longstanding objective of

Newfoundland governments and the Commission, hungry for jobs, had also pursued it energetically. In 1937, the government had reached an agreement with Bowaters for the building of a pulp sulphite mill in the area, but this deal had fallen through when the company had bought out the operations based in Corner Brook, of the International Power and Paper Company of Newfoundland, Ltd. The deal signed in 1938 gave Bowaters sweeping rights over the timber of the Gander, but for expanded productive capacity at Corner Brook rather than the construction of a new mill. This arrangement touched off an angry protest by the Newfoundland Board of Trade, the voice of St. John's business. Too much, it was claimed, had been given away for too little. For short-term employment gains, the government had sabotaged the long-term best interest of the country. For its part, the Commission defended the agreement on the grounds that it was fair, that no other developer was available for the Gander limits, and that the pressing needs of the country's unemployed demanded immediate action. This argument prevailed.

The whole episode, however, left a bitter aftertaste and was indicative of an uneasy relationship that had developed by 1939 between the government and Water Street, the headquarters of St. John's business. The capital's business-men had been to the fore in pushing for Commission of Government, but in practice the new regime had been a great disappointment to many of them. It had kept organized business at arm's length and had failed to deliver prosperity. From its inception, the Commission kept a wary eye through the police on the unemployed for signs of disaffection, but as time passed it had also to worry about political attitudes within an increasingly resentful local establishment. In sum, by 1939 the government was walking a fine line between poverty and privilege and had reason to fear trouble at every turn.

While it was quelling the business uprising touched off by the Bowaters agreement, the Commission was also considering what to do about Gorvin's proposed root and branch programme of reform. His radical approach divided the commissioners, but they eventually decided to test a modified version of his scheme on an experimental basis in Placentia Bay. If things went well there, the changes envisaged would then be made in the rest of the country. In keeping with this decision, Gorvin was appointed to the Commission in May 1939, and in July was sworn in as Commissioner for Natural Resources. In July it was reported that organizers from the Co-operative Division of the Department of Rural Reconstruction were busy at work in Placentia Bay and that study clubs had been formed in a number of settlements. William Trucksis, "a co-operative expert from Ohio," was on the scene, and the organizing team was to be joined shortly by Jules Gottschalk, a handicraft expert from St. Louis.[5]

Gorvin's appointment and the energy with which he threw himself into his job brought new hope to Newfoundlanders. It was desperately needed. After ten years of economic adversity and deprivation, the country had developed a malaise which no public relations campaign could overcome. The mood of 1939 was indeed sombre, and there were many signs of a people and government close to the breaking point. Certainly that was the clear impression of Morley Richards, a staff reporter for the London *Daily Express*, who completed a seven week visit to the island in March 1939, and reported on its condition and affairs in a series of five articles. His language was harsh and his findings constituted a savage indictment of the British record in Newfoundland since 1934. Newfoundland, he wrote, was "sunk in misery with half its 300,000 people living on the starvation line." More than 70,000 people, 18,000 more than in the previous year, lived on a miserable dole which even the government admitted was "not enough alone to keep body and soul together." At the same time about 50,000 people were just above the dole level and malnutrition was "widespread and increasing." By contrast, two thousand civil servants were paid "nearly half as much again as the sum granted to the 70,000 people on the dole." To go to Newfoundland was "like stepping back into the Middle Ages."[6] The condition of the country was "a disgrace to the Empire" and a crash programme of action was needed to redeem the United Kingdom's good name.[7] Should Commission of Government fail, and this was a present possibility, the outcome would "bring discredit to British administration throughout the world."[8]

At the request of the Dominions Office, a detailed commentary on Richards' articles was prepared in St. John's. This work was undertaken by a committee of two commissioners, who produced a lengthy memorandum which disputed the reporter's charges one by one. Richards, it was asserted, had ignored a number of important matters: the extent to which existing conditions were "attributable to the present form of Government"; whether a responsible government "would have been more successful"; and whether the Commission had "contributed anything substantial to meet the conditions depicted." Richards had stated the true cash value of the dole, but the amount could not be raised without putting it "above the level of remuneration of a great number of the employed people, e.g., the fishermen." To do this would make "relief almost universal," remove "nearly all incentive to work" and precipitate "an economic and social disaster ... comparable with conditions in England immediately before the Poor Law Act of 1834." Richards' claims about the extent of malnutrition were likewise misleading. It was "no more widespread" than thirty years before and the "once prevalent" beri-beri had been "stamped out." By the same token, Richards'figure on the number of civil servants was incorrect and his comparison of the total of civil service salaries and the amount paid out in dole was "absurd."[9]

Similar ideas were expressed in a note written at the Dominions Office by P.A. Clutterbuck, who had been secretary of the Amulree Royal Commission and a key decision-maker on Newfoundland ever since. Clutterbuck's figures showed, as of May 1939, a relief population of 80,684 men, women and children, including the able-bodied, sick, aged and infirm. The figure for the same month in 1938 had been 57,100, while in 1934 the May total had been 72,691. Clutterbuck's figures also showed that the highest monthly relief total under the Commission had been registered in March 1934, when the government had 85,050 dependents. Yet the figure of 84,659 recorded in April 1939, was not far behind the record. This total, moreover, represented a considerable setback from the 1938 monthly high of 63,995, also recorded in April. Nevertheless, Clutterbuck disputed Morley Richards' inference from the cash value of relief payments, namely that "those in receipt of public relief" were "in a condition bordering on starvation." Relief in Newfoundland, Clutterbuck argued, was "intended primarily not as a full living allowance but as a supplementary allowance enabling recipients to provide themselves with such necessities of life" as they could not "grow or produce themselves." In failing to take account of this, Richards had exaggerated the plight of those on the dole:

> *With all these natural advantages there is no real comparison between unemployment conditions in Newfoundland and in England, and it is scarcely surprising that the scale on which relief is granted in Newfoundland should be lower than that at home. In Newfoundland the items on which the dole orders are mostly expended are flour, sugar, tea and salt-pork: these items added to home-grown produce and the resources available from the sea and the countryside, provide the man in receipt of relief with an adequate basis for subsistence. (It is indeed the view of the Commission that people can subsist without impairment to their health even on the dole rations alone; but the point is one which it would perhaps be as well not to make, since (a) it is qualified by the proviso that such people would*

not be able to undertake any hard work or expose themselves to severe winter conditions (b) it does not ... apply to the South West coast, the most depressed area in the Island) ... It cannot be denied that in certain individual cases, and sometimes in the whole of a small settlement where there is no local leadership and no initiative, the people have failed to take advantage of the natural resources available to them, with the result that their condition is altogether deplorable; but these are extreme cases and Mr. Morley Richards appears to have taken some of these and presented them as typical, thereby giving a distorted and misleading picture. His further allegation that those on relief are in many cases without sufficient clothing is also exaggerated. It is true that in the case of the able-bodied the dole orders provide food and household necessities only and not clothing; but nearly all able-bodied men receive opportunities for earning during the summer months and the clothing of themselves and their families is replenished from their earnings during those months. This applies both to those (the great majority) who go on relief only during the off season, as well as to the small minority who are in receipt of relief all the year round. Further, in cases of genuine distress, e.g. where children have not sufficiently warm clothing or suitable footwear to enable them to go to school in the winter, special issues are made by the Department of Public Health and Welfare. The allegation that shortage of clothing is shown by the number of cases in which sacking is worn is also misleading: flour sacking can be made into a very good coat or skirt for rough wear and is quite often worn in place of overalls (which with long rubber boots, are the common wear in Newfoundland).[10]

From this self-interested, chilling analysis, Clutterbuck next surveyed what had been achieved in Newfoundland since 1934. This in turn led him to the claim that the Commission had to be judged not only by what it had done but by what it had prevented:

Had trade conditions remained reasonably stable, the improvements made under the Commission in all these directions would have had a cumulative effect, the result of which would have been seen not only in a higher standard of living and improved social conditions but also in a steady decrease in the number of those seeking public relief. But, unfortunately, the tide of recovery started by the Commission was abruptly checked last year by the opposing tide of trade recession. Had Newfoundland been left to her own resources, this opposing tide would have engulfed the Island: as matters stood, a virtual deadlock resulted. To point out in these circumstances that the unemployment figures today are as high as they were five years ago is no proof that the Commission have failed. On the contrary, the true question is what would be the state of the Island now if the Commission had not been there to stand between it and disaster.[11]

Whatever the debating merits of this historical speculation, it is indicative of just how much by 1939 the British in Newfoundland had been thrown on the defensive.

Clutterbuck's detached logic is jarring when placed beside the anguished tone of contemporary documents emanating from rural Newfoundland. From the stiff collar world of Whitehall and the flour sack skirt world of the outport, very different messages were now being sent. In August, 1939, for example, resolutions were adopted at Harbour Grace, Conception Bay, and forwarded to the Commission of Government. These made the case that the working people of the country, having "suffered through ten years of near idleness" and with "their resources... worn threadbare," now had "nothing facing them but slow starvation." Conditions among the local unemployed had "become desperate," and with another winter approaching and promising still greater hardship, the time had come to take "a determined stand."[12] Specifically, the government was asked to increase the dole and to put people to work building roads and wharves in the area. Less politely, Harris Hill, the secretary of an Unemployed Ex-Servicemen's Association, had warned earlier in the year that out-of-work veterans were being "driven to desperation" and that "in any other country a solution would have been found, if not by those responsible, then by these outlawed men themselves."[13]

Unquestionably, J.H. Gorvin was a man of energy and imagination, but as he plunged into his labours there was good reason to believe that he must produce significant results quickly. Considering the scope of the transformation he was seeking to effect, this was a tall order.

Not even a cameo appearance in the country by the King and Queen at the end of their celebrated North American tour was enough to dispel the prevailing gloom. Newfoundlanders were told early in January that the royal couple would visit them on 17 June.[14] Much was subsequently made in the local press of this unprecedented event, and the triumphant progress of the King and Queen through Canada and the United States was followed closely and with great anticipation. When Newfoundland's turn finally came, a busy programme was efficiently carried out in the St. John's area.

But both privately and publicly a good many sour notes were sounded. The government feared demonstrations among the unemployed and worried over the security arrangements for their majesties. In a published letter, L.E. Emerson, the commissioner for justice, defended the employment of "permanent Special Constables" on the grounds that a reigning sovereign had never visited Newfoundland before and that those in charge of the forces of law and order had therefore to take account of "entirely new" contingencies. It was not enough to rely on the unquestioned "loyalty of Newfoundlanders." Indeed — and here is a statement perhaps best read between the lines — "to substitute loyalty for efficiency would be the height of absurdity." Accordingly, the government had rejected representations from the Newfoundland Board of Trade and the St. John's Municipal Council that the programme be revised to allow the King and Queen to pass through Bowring Park, a diversion that would have taken all of an extra ten minutes. There was "no portion of the route," Emerson ventured, "which would call for more professional units than this particular area. The trees, the shrubs, the winding paths, all of which go to make for its beauty, cause the most alarm in my mind, for reasons I do not need to elaborate."[15] By the same token and at royal request, the government a few days later passed legislation to prohibit the indiscriminate firing of guns, a customary Newfoundland form of greeting, by way of salute to the King and Queen.[16]

In the wake of the royal visit, one correspondent of the local press noted "the lack of cheering and of visible enthusiasm, the silence that was observed at times in the crowds that lined the route along which their Majesties passed."[17] The commentator attributed this to the fact that by nature the Newfoundlander did not "wear... his heart upon his sleeve."[18] But another observer blamed the apparently cool reception on the way the royal couple were transported from place to place — at high speed and in a car specially imported for the occasion that afforded only a glimpse of them as they were whisked by. This had led to "disappointment too deep to be understood by any who did not witness it."[19] Nor did Newfoundlanders hear much from the King himself, although it must be remembered that he stuttered and that public speaking was a great ordeal for him. In any event, the speech which he broadcast ran to only five brief paragraphs. He noted the "severe economic stress" of recent years, but forecast that their "qualities of courage and endurance" would enable Newfoundlanders "once more to surmount their difficulties."[20] With this attempt at inspirational words, his speechwriter had perhaps made the best of an awkward subject.

If there was a sign of hope in the Newfoundland of the first half of 1939, apart from Gorvin's appointment, it was to be found in advances in communication and transportation, which were drawing the country closer to the world family of nations. In January a radio telephone link was established between Newfoundland and Canada through the cooperation of the Canadian Marconi Company and the Avalon Telephone Company. This gave Newfoundlanders for the first time direct voice communication not only with the neighbouring dominion but through Canada with many other countries of the world. The new service was inaugurated with an elaborate ceremony broadcast by the Canadian Broadcasting Corporation and featuring an exchange of greetings between Sir Humphrey Walwyn, governor of Newfoundland, and Lord Tweedsmuir, the governor general of Canada.[21] Just over two months later radio station VONF (Voice of Newfoundland) of the Broadcasting Corporation of Newfoundland, itself a recent creation of the Commission of Government, came on the air in a ceremony carried not only on the Canadian Broadcasting Corporation but by the British Broadcasting Corporation as well.[22]

Then, in June, regularly scheduled transatlantic airmail service was inaugurated between New York and Southampton via a seaplane base at Botwood.[23] The Botwood base and a landing field at nearby Hattie's Camp on the plateau above Gander Lake had been opened up as a result of a 1935 agreement between the United Kingdom, Canada, the Irish Free State and Newfoundland to cooperate in a programme of experimental flights across the Atlantic to test the feasibility of regularly scheduled service. Subsequently, these countries and the United States had agreed to undertake this work jointly: the first flying boats passed through Botwood in July, 1937. Regularly-scheduled transatlantic service using wheeled aircraft posed greater difficulties, but in the summer of 1939 paving was completed on the runways at the Newfoundland Airport, as the facility being built near Hattie's Camp had been named.[24]

Yet another bright spot on the Newfoundland scene in the summer of 1939 was the iron ore mining operation at Bell Island, Conception Bay. This enterprise had slumped in the early 1930s, but after Hitler had come to power the Dominion Steel and Coal Corporation, owners of the mines, had found a big market for their product in Germany. They did not hesitate to sell. Nazi rearmament had revived Bell Island; Nazi war would revive Newfoundland.

When the British ultimatum to Germany ran out on Sunday, 3 September 1939, Newfoundland was at war along with the mother country. There was no parliament to decide in St. John's and, as in 1914, the British action automatically brought Newfoundland into the war. For its part, the Commission hurriedly brought into operation an apparatus of wartime administration under the terms of an act for the defence of Newfoundland that had become law on 1 September. Regulations issued under this act the same day dealt with the control of aliens; navigation by sea and air; the prevention of espionage, sabotage, signalling, etc.; the control of transportation and lighting; the prevention of enemy propaganda; censorship; the control of firearms, exports and imports, and foodstuffs and prices; and miscellaneous other matters. On 15 September, using its powers under the same act, the government also introduced foreign exchange control regulations.

In keeping with a defence plan adopted in 1936, the Commission had decided in the spring of 1939 to create a small home defence force. Captain Claude Fanning-Evans of the Durham Light Infantry was subsequently recruited to train it. In October, after he had arrived in the country, legislation was passed to create the new unit, to be known as the Newfoundland Militia. When the war began, responsibility for defence matters lay with the commissioner for home affairs and education, but this duty was quickly transferred to the commissioner for justice, L.E. Emerson, whose influence within the government now grew apace. The immediate financial consequences of the war were explained on 20 November by the commissioner for finance, J.H. Penson, in a broadcast speech before the Newfoundland Board of Trade. As part of its contribution to the war effort, Newfoundland would henceforth only look to the United Kingdom for grants-in-aid sufficient to cover its debt payments and other charges there. This decision would require both retrenchment and new taxes but the reconstruction programme the government had started would be maintained.

In truth, however, J.H. Gorvin's days in Newfoundland were numbered and his plans and dreams would go with him. By creating new employment opportunities and justifying new priorities in spending, the war would soon permit the government to abandon Gorvin's radical approach to reconstruction, which had been forced on it in the first place and which, as anticipated, encountered stiff business resistance. In social and economic policy, therefore, Newfoundland was fast turned in a quite new direction by the war.

Much happened in short order in Newfoundland after 3 September 1939, but the contrast with the unquestioning enthusiasm of 1914 is nonetheless striking. As in Canada, the government set out in 1939 to fight a war of limited liability. Newfoundland would be faithful and true, but its role must match its resources. In practice this meant no conscription, a small home defence force, and a recruitment policy for overseas service that directed most volunteers into the fighting forces of the United Kingdom, though Canada was also allowed to recruit in Newfoundland for her army, navy, and air force. In accordance with this approach, specially-designated Newfoundland units were in time created in the Royal Artillery and the Royal Air Force. The largest single contingent of Newfoundlanders to go overseas, however, belonged to the Newfoundland Forestry Unit. From the Commission's perspective this unit, which was based mainly in Scotland, had many advantages: it exemplified patriotism, soaked up unemployment and was paid for by London.

While facilitating enlistment for service abroad, the Commission pressed on London as early as 15 September the view that the defence of the Newfoundland Airport and the Botwood seaplane base was beyond its means. The Newfoundland government's answer to this serious problem was that the facilities in question should be turned over to the Royal Canadian Air Force for the duration of the war. This proposal was firmly rejected in London, but events would soon show the wisdom of the Commission's stand. In an age of air and submarine warfare, Newfoundland manifestly could not defend itself. The defence of Newfoundland was, on the other hand, integral to the defence of Canada and the United States, a situation those countries could not but acknowledge. Beset by difficulties of her own, Canada had abandoned Newfoundland financially in 1933 but on 8 September 1939, Mackenzie King told the House of Commons that the "integrity of Newfoundland and Labrador is essential to the security of Canada."[25] Henceforth, the relations of the two countries would hinge on that vital consideration. Newfoundland depended on Canada, but Canada now also depended on Newfoundland.

On 20 March 1940, while the "phoney war" was still in progress, L.E. Emerson gave the regular weekly Tuesday night recruiting broadcast over VONF. He chose as his subject "Newfoundland at War," and he used the occasion to review the history of the country during the previous six months. Newfoundland's record of service, he said, was "certainly not unworthy," considering the country's resources and population. Moreover, it compared well with what was being done "elsewhere in the Empire." Newfoundlanders were "fighting a crusade of Christianity against the forces of evil."[26] Perhaps they were, but what Emerson did not say was that in the process the war had given the government a new lease on life and had brought the country back from the edge of the economic abyss. That was fortunate for all concerned, but in truth Newfoundlanders had only just begun to pack up their troubles.

NOTES

1. I am grateful to the late A.P. Bates for his comments on this paper. For a detailed account of the background to and history of the Commission of Government, see my *Newfoundland in the North Atlantic World, 1929-1949* (Kingston and Montreal, 1988).
2. *Newfoundland Royal Commission 1933: Report*, Cmd. 4480 (London, 1933), 195.
3. *Evening Telegram*, St. John's, 15 July 1939, 7.
4. The agreement was embodied in legislation passed by the Commission on 31 December 1938. *Acts of the Honourable Commission of Government of Newfoundland 1938* (St. John's, 1938), 515-51.
5. *Evening Telegram*, St. John's, 27 July 1939, 6.
6. *Daily Express*, London, 27 March 1939, 10.
7. *Ibid.*, 29 March 1939, 8.
8. *Ibid.*, 3 March 1939, 9.
9. Public Record Office, Kew, England, Dominions Office Records (DO) 35/723/N2/41, "Commentary on 'Daily Express' Articles on Newfoundland Affairs of March 27th to April 1st," enclosed in Walwyn to Inskip, 11 May 1939. This and other transcripts of Crown-copyright records in the Public Record Office appear by permission of the Controller of H.M. Stationery Office.
10. DO 35/740/157/53.
11. *Ibid.*
12. *Evening Telegram*, St. John's, 14 August 1939, 6.
13. *Ibid.*, 8 May 1939, 6.
14. *Ibid.*, 4 January 1939, 5.

15. *Ibid.*, 6 June 1939, 5.

16. *Acts of the Honourable Commission of Government of Newfoundland 1939* (St. John's, 1939), 76.

17. *Evening Telegram*, 22 June 1939, 5.

18. *Ibid.*, 6.

19. *Ibid.*, 23 June 1939, 6.

20. *Ibid.*, 7.

21. *Ibid.*, 11 January 1939, 5.

22. *Ibid.*, 14 March 1939, 5.

23. *Ibid.*, 28 June 1939, 4.

24. *Ibid.*, 17 July 1939, 4. For a description of the Newfoundland Airport, see *ibid.*, 9 June 1939, 5.

25. Canada, House of Commons, *Debates*, 8 September 1939, 35.

26. *Evening Telegram*, St. John's, 20 March 1940, 9.

The Bureaucracy, Military and Foreign Policy

La politique étrangère, militaire et la bureaucratie

TWO WORLDS: THE CANADIAN CIVIL SERVICE IN 1939

Doug Owram
University of Alberta

A good deal has been written about Canadian civil servants. There have been studies of individual departments, of particular periods of reform, and of particular individuals.[1] This coverage is uneven, however. Certain periods, including the 1930s and the Second World War have received much more attention than others.[2] As one example, contrast the absence of studies of the civil service on the eve of the First World War with the work done before the Second World War. Classic studies like English's *Decline of Politics*, R.C. Brown and G.R. Cook's *Canada 1896-1921*, or the newer Bothwell, Drummond and English, *Canada 1900-1945*, manage to cover the era of the First World War barely mentioning even the name of a civil servant.

The reason for this is clear if one looks at the interpretations of national government put forward by Canadian historians. The historiographic image, with a few exceptions, of the nineteenth and early twentieth century civil service is one of patronage, and if not downright incompetence, certainly unimaginativeness and inefficiency. Bothwell, Drummond and English, for example, introduce the Post Office, Public Works and the Intercolonial Railway in the pre-1914 period only in passing, and do so to refer to them as "sinkholes of patronage."[3] Moreover, they are correct in their condemnation. Though certain technical functions like the Geological Survey were important, the general feeling is that politicians ran the country and made all the important policy. Civil servants operated at best as administrators. At worst, they were simply hacks. Such an interpretation, of course, mirrors criticisms at the time; significantly, these criticisms often came from those who succeeded this earlier generation and sought to reshape the civil service in their own image.

In contrast, the dominant interpretation of the civil service on the eve of the Second World War is inseparable both from the changes that took place within the civil service during the Depression and, more importantly, from the tremendous events of the war itself. The civil service is, according to this interpretation, on the verge of its finest hour by 1939.

Accordingly, the emphasis has been on those key elements of change and dynamism that existed within the immediate pre-war civil service. The personalities are familiar: Clifford Clark and Robert Bryce of Finance; O.D. Skelton, Lester B. Pearson, Norman Robertson, Hume Wrong, Hugh Keenlyside and some others from External Affairs. Throw in a clerk of the Privy Council or two, a few Trade and Commerce officers and the view that emerges of the civil service is promising. Indeed, the interpretation is somewhat whiggish, for, though we recognize the shortcomings of the 1939 civil service, we cannot resist tying it to the glorious feats soon to come.

This orientation points to the limitations of the studies thus far of the Canadian bureaucracy. For while there have been numerous studies of civil servants on the eve of the Second World War, there have been practically no studies of the civil service as a whole. R. Macgregor Dawson's 1929 study precedes this period, while J.E. Hodgett's 1971 work is very general in its focus, covering the entire civil service from Confederation to 1967. Only Taylor Cole's 1949 book, *The Canadian Bureaucracy*, focuses on this period while attempting to carry his work beyond the mandarin class.[4]

The reasons for the emphasis on the mandarin and the failure to look at the broader civil service are not hard to find. First, academics are interested in their own kind and academics have dominated interpretations of the pre-war civil service. Thus we have been especially interested in the careers and ideas of our generational predecessors, the erstwhile university professors or would-have-been professors whose names are mentioned in part above. Second, in undertaking our interpretation, we have been carrying on a traditional view that stretches back to the mandarins themselves. They were very conscious that they were a new breed and set themselves apart and above the lowly image of the reticent if incompetent patronage appointment of earlier years. J.A. Corry, himself a near-mandarin, developed this interpretation in an article written early in the Second World War. "Fortunately the Dominion Government is in a much better position to give sustained and intelligent direction and to apply comprehensive control in this war than in the last one. The Canadian civil service may still leave a good deal to be desired but it is far stronger than it was twenty five years ago."[5]

Corry's comment set the tone for the writings that followed. First, the civil servants themselves reminisced in eloquent terms about what was, they felt, a job well done. Then political scientists like Taylor Cole and journalists like the 1950s columnist Blair Fraser, and finally, historians picked up the tradition. It was reinforced by the Diefenbaker years and the apparent decline of the influence of the mandarin class. The era of Skelton, Clark, Wilgress, Pearson and the others assumed some of the aura of a golden age in which men were men and bureaucrats were policy makers of the highest order.

Such interpretations are not wrong. I would continue to maintain, as I have argued elsewhere, that the mandarins, the dollar-a-year men and others did do a successful job overall in the war.[6] I would also agree that these new intellectuals were a breed apart, as they themselves thought, from many of the more traditional types of civil servants. The problem is that the Wrongs, the Pearsons, the Skeltons or others can tell us little about the Canadian civil service as a whole. All the personnel of the Departments of Finance and External together accounted in terms of numbers for less than four percent of the total Canadian civil service. Even if one throws in departments like Labour, Trade and Commerce, the Privy Council and the headquarters personnel of the Department of Transport, the total percentage climbs to considerably less than ten percent of the Canadian civil service. And, of course, these totals include considerable numbers of individuals in routine jobs who are never mentioned in history books.

If we are to understand the civil service as it was in the years before the vast expansion brought on by the war, we must look not only at those parts which hinted at the future but at the entire body. If we examine what might be termed "the other civil service" at the end of the 1930s, it gives us a better perspective on just how drastic the changes were that took place in the years since. For by far the largest part of the bureaucracy was not peopled by a new breed of intellectuals but fit more closely into the stereotype of what Victor Thompson termed "bureaupathetic behaviour," including "attachment to routines and procedures, ... resistance to change; and ... a petty insistence upon rights of authority and status."[7] It was also comprised of an educational and social group quite distinct from the famous mandarin class.

In looking at the nature of the Canadian civil service in 1939, the first thing to note is that the vast majority of civil servants did not operate in the exciting areas of high policy. In 1939 the Canadian civil service consisted of approximately 46,000 employees. As Chart 1 indicates, the great majority of these worked in a few very large departments, with the rest scattered around many smaller ones. In terms of personnel, by far the largest of the departments was the Post Office, with more than 12,500

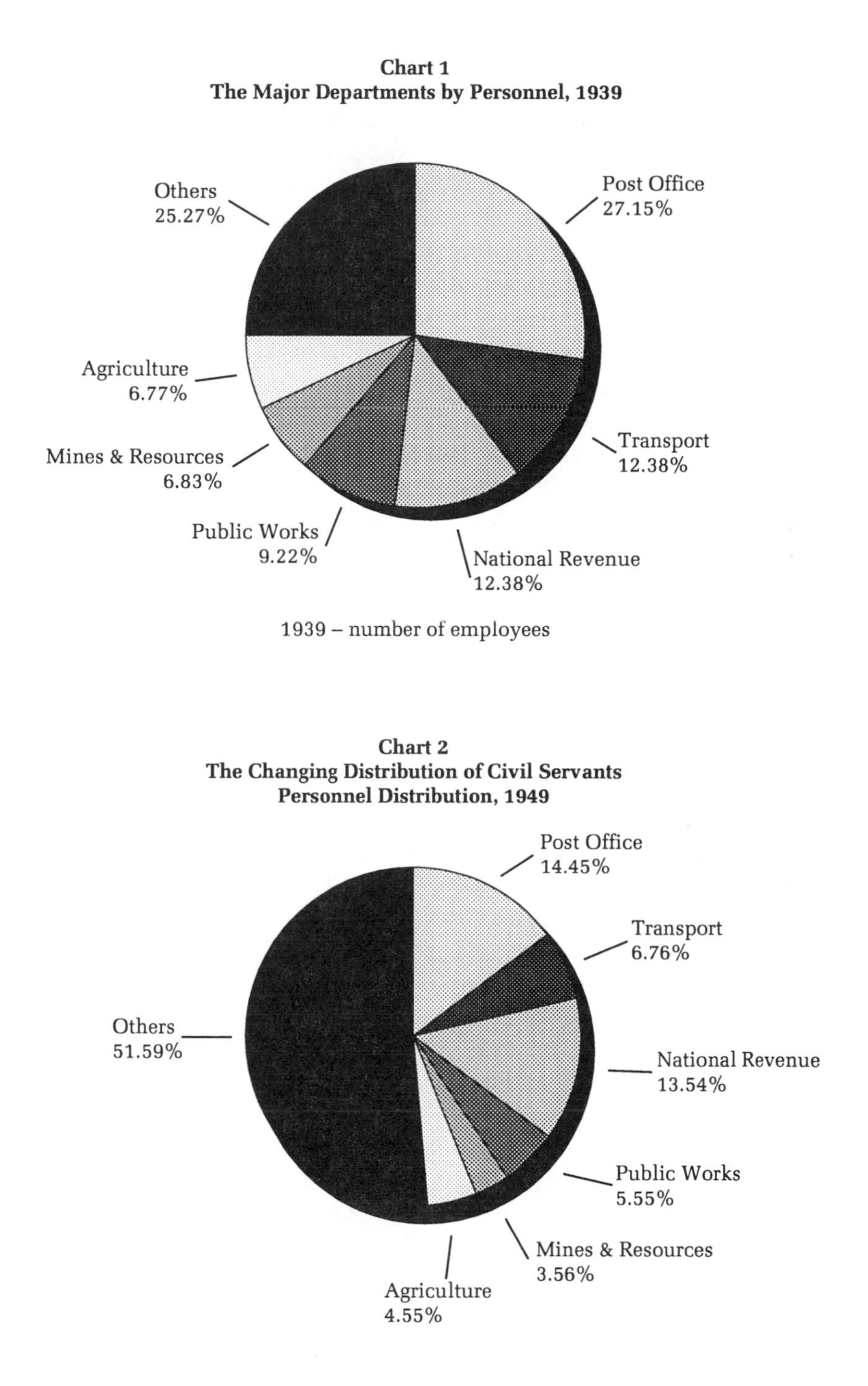

Chart 1
The Major Departments by Personnel, 1939

Chart 2
The Changing Distribution of Civil Servants
Personnel Distribution, 1949

employees. That department alone accounted for more than 27 percent of the Canadian civil service and it is tempting to argue that not one of them was a mandarin. After the Post Office, in order, the largest departments were Transport (5710), National Revenue (5706), Public Works (4250), Mines and Resources (3147) and Agriculture (3122). Together they accounted for nearly three quarters of the Canadian bureaucracy.

Personnel is only one measure of size. Another obvious alternative is expenditure, but here there are difficulties. If the numbers are to reflect much about a department's activity, they must distinguish between expenditures that simply flow through the department as part of an automatic statutory or other payment and those which involve some discretion on the part of the department. To give one example, the Department of Finance in 1939 expended more than $190 million, by far the largest of any government department. Yet the bulk of these funds were legislatively preordained and involved not real expenditure but public debt payments or transfers, usually to the provinces. Indeed, more than 95 percent of Finance's expenditures were in fact transfer or other statutory payments in 1939.

Table 1 attempts to make the necessary distinction between transfers and statutory flow-throughs on the one hand and operational or capital expenditures on the other, although there are certain gray areas that might move back and forth. Also excluded are expenditures within the Department of National Defence which cannot reasonably be included within the parameters of the term civil service. While recognizing that these figures provide only a rough guide, the interesting thing is the degree of correlation between personnel and expenditures. The Post Office is the most expensive as well as the largest department; the top six departments by personnel are also the biggest six departments by this measure of expenditure. Together they account for two thirds of the government's expenditures in 1939.

Thus if one is to look at the civil service as a whole, it is apparent that the departments mentioned above — the Post Office, Transport, National Revenue, Public Works, Mines and Resources, and Agriculture — must figure heavily in the account. An investigation of them reveals some interesting aspects of the civil service on the eve of war. First, these are for the most part hardly the glamour departments of government. Though parts of Transport and Mines and Resources had high profiles, the great majority of personnel and expenditures in these departments were concentrated on routine yet useful functions. Most obvious, of course, was the Post Office

Table 1[8]
Government Department by Discretionary Expenditures

	(thousands of dollars) $	*percent*
Total	153633	100
Post Office	35455	23.08
Transport	15486	10.08
Public Works	15484	10.08
Mines and Resources	13657	8.89
National Revenue	11899	7.75
Agriculture	9527	6.20
Health	9275	6.04
National Defence	8851	5.76
Trade and Commerce	8603	5.60
Finance	6910	4.50
RCMP	5823	3.79
Justice	5148	3.35
Legislation	2548	1.66
Fisheries	2036	1.33
External Affairs	1005	0.65
Labour	815	0.53
Secretary of State	730	0.48
Auditor General	473	0.31
Civil Service Commission	379	0.25

and its mandate to deliver the mail. In other departments, functions of an equally routine nature were the basic activity. In Agriculture and Fisheries, for example, food inspection was the largest single item in their budget. In National Revenue it was customs services across the country. In Public Works it was building maintenance and repair. And on it went.[9] That emphasizes what we often forget. The Civil Service in the years before 1939 was, as it had always been, primarily a body undertaking a large number of routine functions.

These routine functions reveal some of the other main characteristics of the civil service. The activities of these larger departments were such that their operations were spread around the country rather than centred in Ottawa. Thus well over a third of the Department of Agriculture's staff were on Experimental Farms located mainly in the West, while the majority of Mines and Resources people were either in the immigration ports or in the field working with Indians. All in all, it would appear that only about one in four civil servants worked at headquarters in Ottawa in 1939, a figure that had remained more or less constant through the interwar period.[10] The best example of this sort of decentralization comes, as might be expected, in the Post Office. There were some 12,000 post offices around the country in 1939. The fact that this amounts to one for every employee in the department only reflects the fact that a good many of the services in small centres were contracted out to general stores or other outlets. Even so, 92 percent of employees in this largest department worked outside Ottawa. Far more important to the department than operations in Ottawa were large postal operations like Toronto, Montreal or Winnipeg. Toronto, for example, accounted for a little less than a quarter of all Post Office revenue in 1939; the three centres between them accounted for well over 40 percent.[11] There were also hundreds of local centres with anywhere from a handful to a few dozen employees.

The story of the fluctuating personnel of the Post Office and their widely decentralized operations could be repeated with descriptions of bodies like Indian Affairs, Public Works and other groups. The civil service was in reality two worlds. At the top was a small elite of the highly-educated. They had access to the politicians, to the deputy ministers and to the social and intellectual elites of the nation and the capital. They are the ones that historians have naturally focused upon. They are also atypical.

The "average" civil servant was employed in one of two environments, neither of which was very glamorous. The first type of work was a blue collar activity of a routine or technical nature. Included among these were postal sorters riding the trains, canal workers ensuring that the locks worked, customs inspectors and immigration officers located either in major ports of entry or the small coastal towns and villages. Few were university educated. Many did not have high school education and only a small percentage worked in the sort of office setting that one associated with the bureaucracy. For these people, the civil service was not involved with international issues, economic planning or social policy but was a body that acted in basic ways to keep the national infrastructure functioning. The social ties, personal identifications and sense of community of these civil servants had nothing to do with Ottawa or the latest gossip on the political circuit.

The second type of ordinary bureaucrat was employed in an office and is thus more associated in the public mind with the civil service. These were positions for the most part of a clerical or low-level administrative nature. They included the huge majority of the almost one thousand employees of the Income Tax Division of National Revenue, and the processors of regulations, whether in Customs, Transport, Fisheries or, for that matter, in Finance. A higher percentage of them did work in Ottawa, though far from all, but once again few were connected to the world of policy or planning. Their days consisted of form filling, routine correspondence and the application of rules. Sitting, as contemporary photographs show, in large common offices behind rows of wooden desks, their work demanded a certain meticulousness and neatness but very rarely did it involve innovation.

This average civil servant operated in an atmosphere that was, by today's standards, rigid and intrusive, characteristics present right from the point of application for a position. Modern enthusiasms for freedom from discrimination on account of personal characteristics did not exist. Even when it worked as it was supposed to, the Civil Service Commission's system of competitive examinations based on merit were designed only to control patronage, not discrimination. Thus a manual of Civil Service Regulations from the 1930s reserved the right of the employer to specify such requirements as age, sex, health, habits, residence, and moral character "requisite to the performance of the duties of the position."[12]

There were also certain classes that faced formal discrimination. It was, for example, forbidden for a married women "whose husband is still living" to have a permanent position in the civil service. As a result of such rules, and the contemporary attitudes towards women in the workplace that these rules reflected, only one in five civil servants was a woman and most of these were concentrated in a few clerical and secretarial classifications. Equally striking is the degree to which restrictions existed which limited opportunities to a particular age range. Clerical and other lower grade examinations could be sat only by people between the ages of 18 and 35. Moreover, one of the most common reasons that deputy ministers gave when employing their prerogative of rejecting the first candidate of a Civil Service examination, was age.[13] It would have been very difficult in the late 1930s for anyone over the age of forty to have entered the Canadian civil service.

Once inside the system, the rigid hierarchy remained. By today's standards hours were long, though hardly harsh by contemporary standards; nine to five on weekdays and nine to one on Saturdays. More important was the attempt to provide a series of checks and controls over employees. All employees below the level of deputy, except for senior officials exempted at the deputy's request, were required either to punch a clock or to report to have attendance taken. For the great majority of employees, daily work was strictly monitored and repetitive. There was practically no contact with senior management. Rather, daily lives were controlled by lower-level officials whose interest was in maintaining the rules and whose management style was decidedly authoritarian. Fragmentary data from departments indicate a system that emphasized deportment, dress, orderly functioning and conformity.

For all of this orderliness, the civil servants were paid on a regular basis which, in the Depression years, was no small matter. To do a full-scale investigation of salary levels and their relationship to contemporary occupations goes far beyond the scope of this paper. Such data as is readily available, however, does give a fairly clear impression of salary levels. A low-level clerk made approximately $1400 a year, while office administrators such as a chief clerk had a base salary of $2400, a head clerk about $2500. By comparison, an Ottawa policeman made $1915 and a fireman $1751.[14] Such comparisons would indicate that at the lower- and low-management levels the civil service was relatively poorly recompensed. On the other hand, trade commissioners of the Department of Trade and Commerce seem to have been generally well paid. Dana Wilgress, the director of the Commercial Intelligence Service and one of those who does qualify as a mandarin, obtained a princely salary of $7800 when he was appointed to that position in 1933.[15] The relative high pay of senior officials and the low pay of middle management and clerical staff suggests that in these pre-union days there was a greater salary spread than is presently the case. Any firm conclusion here would require more systematic analysis.

Neither the working conditions nor the salaries should be taken to imply exploitation. The intrusive hiring and supervisory rules were not uncommon for the day. The job security was far better than average, at least for the permanent employee. Thus, however routine the job and however petty the supervisors could be, the Civil Service Commission found itself continually overwhelmed by applications. During 1937 alone it received more than 72,000 applications for employment.[16] It hired only a few hundred permanent employees. Rather, this image of dull, and rigid activity is important because of what it tells us about the nature of the civil service as a whole. It could appear that the civil service of 1939 was reflected more accurately in this routine and rigid system than in the more optimistic depiction that dominates if one concentrates on the university educated-mandarinite.

The civil service was a creature of years of austerity. The Depression, as will be discussed below, brought severe cuts to all government operations. The austerity of the civil service, however, preceded that. From the end of the First World War governments had, for reasons of belief or political appeal, found it desirable to try to cut back the civil service. Thus, the size of the civil service had hardly increased at all in the two decades since the beginning of the 1920s. However, there was considerable turbulence in the intervening period. The First World War had been followed by attrition in the early to mid-1920s, expansion in the more prosperous latter part of the decade and then sharp reductions in the Depression years. With the slow recovery of the economy in the later 1930s had come the slow recovery as well of the civil service. Still, the point to remember is that this was a body that was not used to expansion but at best a steady state. Promotions, opportunities or challenges came within a world with little in the way of new positions or organizations.

When the lack of overall growth is combined with the Depression the effects are significant. With national unemployment figures upwards of twenty percent, people did not readily leave secure jobs. Vacancies usually opened up only on retirement and, for at least a part of the decade, all vacant positions were frozen. This meant at least three things. First, for those employees in the system there was little room for advancement. Second, there was little new blood coming into the system. Once again the Departments of External and Finance saw more new people than most. This was partly because they were expanding at a relatively faster rate than the big departments and, because that expansion often took place at the higher levels, the impact of the new recruits was that much greater. Third, in a phenomenon familiar to academics who have worked through the last two decades, an absence of growth and hiring meant an aging civil service. In 1937 a census of civil service employees revealed that only four percent were under the age of 24. In contrast, nearly 13 percent were over 60. More than one in twenty was over the age of 65.[17]

The problems brought about by austerity can be demonstrated more specifically by looking at two quite different classes of employee. The first class involves that category of civil servant known as the temporary employee. Temporary employees had always been a part of the civil service. The very permanency associated with a civil service position created a lack of flexibility for managers in planning their personnel needs. Therefore, from the beginning they had resorted to temporary employees and through the years various parliamentary inquiries, royal commissions, and reports of the civil service commissioner had lamented their overuse.

In the early stages of the Depression, it appeared that temporary employees were an endangered species. As departments sought to cut costs, they dismissed large numbers of them. The result was a sharp decline in the percentage of temporary employees by the middle of the decade. This changed when the prime minister, R.B. Bennett, imposed a series of austerity measures on the civil service. The best known of these is the across-the-board ten percent pay cut. More important to the evolution of the civil service during the Depression, however, was the freezing of all permanent positions. Henceforth hiring could only be done on a temporary (maximum six-month term) basis. The result was to be expected. Temporaries found favour again. By 1939 the absolute freeze had been lifted and it was possible to be hired as a permanent employee by Treasury Board. As it liked to argue, however, the fear of being replaced provided "greater incentive to new employees" as well as greater flexibility for management.[18] Thus in 1939 the temporary employee was a significant and growing presence in the civil service, accounting for nearly one third of all civil servants. Of some 6400 appointments made the previous year, only 843 were permanent and 5563 were temporary.

Such a profusion of temporary employees created problems. Temporaries were not eligible for promotion, for transfer within the civil service or even for salary increments. They remained fixed in level and in pay, year after year. This was acceptable where the jobs were indeed temporary, as for example in the periodic census positions, but created an inefficient use of talent in other cases. As the Civil Service Commission complained year after year, there were numerous temporary employees doing what were in reality permanent jobs. The most dramatic of these were an estimated two to three hundred employees who at the end of the First World War had by oversight never been converted to permanent status. For nearly twenty years they had thus sat doing the same work and with the same pay! Even in less extreme cases the temporary employee had little incentive to be innovative or to aspire to more responsible positions. He or she had every incentive to stay out of trouble, to obey the rules and to hope that in six months their work would still be there.

The other example of the effects of long-term austerity comes at the opposite end of the scale — at the deputy ministerial level. In recent decades the top ranks of the Canadian civil service have been characterised by considerable movement. In part this was the result of the personal belief of Pierre Trudeau that managers could manage anywhere and thus it was possible to move senior officials around.[19] The advantages of a new insight into the position and the breaking up of entrenched fiefdoms were thought to outweigh any time required to learn the ropes.

Such was not the case in the years before the Second World War. The general lack of growth and change in the civil service was matched by a lack of change at the top. Deputy ministers rarely moved between departments and, most often, were appointed in the department where they had climbed through the ranks. Once in place a deputy could expect to stay where he was. There was thus quite a different managerial style in 1939 than has been the case in recent years. These were indeed fiefdoms to a large degree. Ministers would come and ministers would go but the deputies would remain. At the extreme were people like J.B. Hunter of the Department of Public Works. He had been appointed to the position in 1908 and thus by 1939 had been the permanent head of his department through eight governments and 31 years.[20] Others had served almost as long; R.H. Coats, the Dominion Statistician had been appointed in 1915. By comparison, the deputy minister of mines and resources, Charles Camsell, was a positive newcomer, having been appointed in 1920.

Not all appointments were long serving. The usual turn-over meant that in 1939 there were several deputies with only a few years' service in their present positions, though the average length of tenure for a deputy ministership in that year was approximately 12 years. Recent appointments, however, have to be kept in perspective. In many instances these were long-time public servants who had laboriously climbed up though the ranks. They might be new to the position, but were hardly fresh faces. Typical of this phenomenon was J.G. Parmalee, who had been deputy minister of trade and commerce since 1933. Parmalee had replaced C.T. O'Hara, who had been there since 1908. The replacement, however, did not imply a wind of change blowing freshly through departmental corridors. Parmalee had, except for his war service, been in the department since 1902 and had been assistant deputy minister since 1923. Indeed,

Parmalee comes as close as Canada ever got to the inheritance of offices. His father had been deputy minister of the same department. Something of his personality can be gained from the impression that Parmalee was appointed because he was known as someone who would not cause trouble and by the fact that he insisted everyone call him Major Parmalee.[21]

Parmalee is just one of many examples of deputy ministers who do not fit the image created by Clifford Clark or O.D. Skelton. Many of the senior officials showed a high degree of resistance to change. Change brought controversy. There were even some in the top ranks who proved that it was not only politicians who could feather their nests. As R.B. Bryce recounts, the Department of Finance had no effective leadership in the early years of the Depression when such leadership might have been thought so important. The deputy minister became ill early in 1930 and never returned. The assistant deputy minister was "in the process of being convicted of stealing bonds and money from the department."[22] Of course there were exceptions to this rule and it is often these exceptions that constitute the portion of the civil service that has received so much attention. Still, as a group the deputies were of an older rather than newer era of the civil service. The average age was nearly 60 years. At the time the war broke out, only one was under the age of 50, the undersecretary of state, E.H. Coleman, and he was 49.[23]

The top, therefore, mirrored the bottom. The senior managing rank of the civil service was old, not just in years but in service and therefore very often in approaches and ideas. When the war started in September 1939, many of them found it hard to cope. It was not only O.D. Skelton who found the pressure too much. In the first years of the war, three deputy ministers (Skelton, Hunter, and V.I. Smart of the Department of Transport) died in office and at least one other was forced to take sick leave (L.R. LaFlèche from National Defence), though his competence as much as his health was in question.

The lack of new senior personnel was reflected in the paucity of new activity. True, there had been some important changes, including the creation of a Department of Transport in 1936. For the most part, however, government departments had in the 1930s been faced with reduced expenditures, sometimes drastically reduced. This was, as we well know, not an era that believed in contra-cyclical budgeting. With government funds going into relief payments or into the debt of the Canadian National Railway system, there was practically no room for fiscal generosity to the bureaucracy. Annual government deficits had increased to the point where by 1939 nearly a quarter of all government revenue was needed just to cover debt charges.[24] Under such circumstances, operations became geared not towards major new projects or improved service but toward bureaucratic survival and retrenchment.

This is shown starkly in the case of the largest department, the Post Office. That department was burdened by the governmental assumption that it should be self-supporting and even turn a profit if possible. It had done very well in this regard until the Depression forced it into a deficit position by 1931. Over the next few years, the department fought to return to the black. Between 1931 and 1936, the budget was trimmed by close to 20 percent. Hundreds of small offices were closed or amalgamated and employees let go in large numbers. By 1934 the deficit had been eliminated and the Post Office was able to achieve a surplus in every year from 1934 to 1938 inclusive. In 1939 there was a small deficit but, as the deputy postmaster general pointedly reminded the government, only the free franking privileges accorded the politicians had prevented the institution from achieving a profitable position.[25] In such an atmosphere of retrenchment and fiscal austerity, however, there was little that could be attempted in the way of innovation or improvement.

The same pattern appeared in the case of Public Works, except that the department had never operated on a cost recovery basis. Still, as the landlord to the government and the maintainer of government property, it was a prime target for reductions when the Depression hit. New buildings could always await better times. Existing buildings could always go another year without a coat of paint. From a peak of $34 million in 1931, the Department of Public Works was able to slash its budget to that required for the skeletal maintenance of buildings. Given that by 1934 the amount dedicated to new construction was just over one-and-a-half million dollars, it would appear that the slashing had been severe indeed. It was the lowest figure for new construction since the early 1890s.[26] By 1939, as the figures in Table 1 indicate, the department's budget had recovered only marginally.

The examples could be multiplied, but they would generally tell the same story. To a greater or lesser degree, departments found their budgets reduced through the Depression years. Department after department could complain about over-worked staff, of an inability to undertake needed work, of a lack of resources. But little was done. With very few exceptions, programs stagnated, just as hiring did.

Setting aside the well known exceptions, therefore, the civil service on the eve of the Second World War was considerably less dynamic than that portrayed in those studies dealing only with the mandarin class. In fact, the combination of lack of growth, aging leadership, stagnating budgets, and demoralizing hiring and promotion procedures gives an image of a civil service beset by arteriosclerosis rather than a body about to manage a total war, the transition to the early welfare state, and the evolution of macro-economic management between fishing trips to the Five Lakes.

And this takes me back to the central point of the paper about the bifurcated civil service. In 1939, though few were aware of it, the civil service was about to undergo a major transition. It is striking how much the civil service of 1939 resembles that of 1929 or for that matter 1925. The Department of Transport had been created out of the old Department of Railways and Canals, and the Department of Interior had been abolished. Nevertheless, there is a remarkable continuity in the civil service as a whole in terms of size, personnel and function. That continuity was broken between 1939 and 1949. Not only was there the well-known growth, but internal allocation of money and power in the civil service shifted dramatically. The growth of the war and post-war years was not shared equally.

Many parts of the civil service were slower to recover from years of austerity and stagnation. For one thing, those not connected to national planning or to the war effort often found that they did not partake of the civil service growth which characterized the Second World War. Thus, for example, the Post Office saw both its total number of offices and its expenditures decrease between 1939 and 1946.[27] The Public Works budget did expand somewhat, largely to supply all those civil servants in other departments with buildings. Overall, however, those expenditures decreased. It also lost its high profile minister and its deputy minister early in the war. Many of its activities were removed to Munitions and Supply. Indeed, Transport and Public Works for a time shared one common minister. Many of the traditionally large departments would continue to be seen as inefficient, old-fashioned and unimaginative places well after the war. Blair Fraser, writing in the early 1950s, characterised Public Works as "the last surviving puddle of the Great Dismal Swamp of politics and patronage which once engulfed the whole government service."[28]

The absence of growth in formerly key departments had a profound effect. As Chart 2 indicated, those same departments which had accounted for some three quarters of civil service personnel in 1939 comprised less than half a decade later. Leadership had also changed. Of all the deputy ministers of 1939, only two were there by 1949, W.C. Clark of Finance and C.H. Bland, chairman of the Civil Service Commission. Thus a new departmental pecking order had been consolidated, and a new leadership had emerged within the civil service.

In the short interval between 1939 and 1949, the new, highly-educated, policy-oriented civil servant became the model for the future. The mandarinate, which had been small and exclusive in 1939, had begun to spread outward into the middle ranks of the civil service. Their high levels of education, degree of independence and belief in their own social mobility meant that older workplace traditions were displaced, department by department, by increasing numbers of managers and professionals. At the blue collar level, unionization in the 1960s ensured that the civil service of 1939 was recognizable in only a few nooks and crannies. At the same time, the new managers would find that they all could not be mandarins, however much they might feel they deserved to be.

NOTES

1. J.E. Hodgetts, *The Canadian Public Service 1867-1970* (Toronto, 1973); Cole Taylor, *The Canadian Bureaucracy: A Study of Canadian Public Servants and Other Government Employees* (Durham, North Carolina, 1949); R. McG. Dawson, *The Civil Service of Canada* (London, 1929); Mary Hill, *Canada's Salesman to the World: A History of the Department of Trade and Commerce* (Montreal, 1979); J.E. Hodgetts *et al.*, *Biography of an Institution: The Civil Service Commission of Canada* (Montreal, 1972).

2. See, for example, J.L. Granatstein, *The Ottawa Men: The Civil Service Mandarins 1935-1957* (Toronto, 1982) and my own *The Government Generation: Canadian Intellectuals and the State, 1900-1945* (Toronto, 1986).

3. See Robert Bothwell, Ian Drummond and John English, *Canada 1900-1945* (Toronto, 1987), 75.

4. J.E. Hodgetts, *The Canadian Public Service: A Physiology of Government 1867-1970* (Toronto, 1973); the full Taylor and Dawson references may be found in note 1 above.

5. J.A. Corry, "Some Aspects of Canada's War Effort," *Queen's Quarterly*, 47, 3 (Autumn 1940), 357.

6. Owram, chs. 10-11.

7. Cited from Fred Kramer, "Organization of Public Bureaucracies," in Kenneth Kernaghan, ed., *Public Administration in Canada: Selected Readings* (Toronto, 1985), 2.

8. Canada, Department of Finance, *National Accounts for the Year Ended March 31, 1939*. Note that this excludes routine transfer payments that largely pass through functions. It does include, however, any social program payments which might require a significant monitoring function. Thus, for example, the public debt which is funnelled through Finance is excluded. Old age pensions are included. Departments with discretionary expenditure below $300,000 are also not included.

9. *Ibid.*

10. *Canada Year Book, 1946* (Ottawa, 1947), 1142, has figures on temporary employees and permanent employees in Ottawa from 1925 on.

11. *Annual Report of the Postmaster General for the Year Ended March 31, 1939* (Ottawa, 1939).

12. Canada, *Civil Service Regulations* (Ottawa, 1936), 6.

13. *Annual Report of the Civil Service Commission for 1935* (Ottawa, 1935), 12.

14. M.C. Urquhart and K.A.H. Buckley, eds., *Historical Statistics of Canada*, 2nd edition (Ottawa, 1983), E100, on composite wage.

15. Hill, 408-9, 439. If one uses Buckley's figures, a 9.5 times increase would adjust these salaries to 1985 levels. Thus a Chief Clerk made about $22,800, Wilgress about $74,100.

16. *Annual Report of the Civil Service Commission for 1937* (Ottawa, 1937), 4.

17. Cole, 20.

18. Cited in J.E. Hodgetts *et al.*, *The Biography of an Institution*, 153. Note that for obvious reasons the war only accentuated the presence of temporary employees. By 1945, some 73 percent of civil servants were classified as temporary.

19. On the mobility of the deputy ministerial appointments in recent years, see Gordon F. Osbaldeston, *Keeping Deputy Ministers Accountable* (Toronto, 1989), 1.

20. See Doug Owram, *Building for Canadians: A History of the Department of Public Works 1840-1960* (Ottawa, 1979).

21. Hill, 437.

22. Robert Bryce, *Maturing in Hard Times: Canada's Department of Finance Through the Great Depression* (Montreal, 1986), 67.

23. A list of deputy ministers is available in the *Canadian Annual Review for 1939*. Their ages come from biographical details in such works as *Who's Who in Canada*.

24. Urquhart and Buckley, H168, H175.

25. *Annual Report of the Postmaster General for 1939*, 6.

26. Owram, *Building for Canadians*, 224.

27. *Canada Year Book, 1946*, 724.

28. Blair Fraser, "Backstage at Ottawa," *Maclean's Magazine*, (November 1, 1953).

THE COSTS OF NO COMMITMENTS: CANADIAN ECONOMIC PLANNING FOR WAR, 1939

Paul Marsden
National Archives of Canada

On 10 September 1939, the day Canada entered the Second World War, J.L. Ilsley, the acting minister of finance, informed the House of Commons that "the cost of a war effort by Canada does not lend itself to precise calculations in advance."[1] The truth was that the King government, as part of its long-standing policy of "no commitments" had refused to confront difficult economic decisions prior to the outbreak of war. Indeed, almost everything that Ilsley presented in his stand-in performance for the minister of finance was put together during the final days of August and the first week of September in a series of all night sessions. And when the government finally did come to terms with the need for wartime planning, it took a great deal for granted.[2]

The bureaucrats in the Department of Finance and the Bank of Canada only had the opportunity to discuss the general outline and not the specifics of economic planning for war. Their discussion revealed a consensus on how the war should be fought, drawing largely upon their experiences of the 25 years before. The Depression continued to cast an enormous shadow over these men, but the memory of the Great War provided a more powerful background to much of their thinking. The bureaucrats in both Ottawa and London built upon the economic lessons of that war. In the United Kingdom, a 1929 Treasury memorandum, "The Course of Prices in the Great War," concluded there had been two distinct phases to the war.[3] The first phase, from 1914 to 1916, was a chaotic and disorganized time in which the economy ran amok, spurred on by insatiable demand for equipment and food. The second phase, marked by the introduction of legislation and active controls, saw the productive capacity of the nation directed toward winning the war. The study blamed the mismanaged early years for the spiralling inflation of 1916 to 1920, concluding that these problems would have been worse had it not been for government intervention. All the combatant nations in the 1914-1918 struggle shared similar experiences: their economies were strained by wartime demand, resulting in violent jumps in the cost of living.[4] Inflation created inequities which, in turn, translated into social unrest. Many Canadians remembered the experience of the Great War in precisely this way, and in 1938 the studies prepared for the Royal Commission on Dominion-Provincial Relations (the Rowell-Sirois Commission) reinforced this view of the war's long-term impact.[5] Predictions of the future of modern warfare only strengthened these views. Military writers described a full scale mechanization of battle and the need for nations to mobilize all of their resources in order successfully to prosecute total war.[6]

It was these analyses of the Great War and predictions of the nature of future wars that provided the intellectual framework for wartime economic planning in Ottawa in 1939. Inflation was deemed the main enemy and active intervention in the economy was viewed as the means to combat it. The principle of "pay as you go," a phrase coined for the first war budget, stipulated that the war's costs would not be deferred to later generations. The government would not mobilize more resources than it could expect Canadians to pay for with their savings and taxes, nor would it allow increased demand for a diminishing supply of goods to fuel an inflationary spiral in the cost of living. For a number of reasons, some practical and others political, this was as far as planning advanced before the final week of August 1939. Canadian officials believed it sufficient to have this basic concept upon which to build. They were confident it would be a simple matter to create the bureaucratic structures with which to mobilize the nation's resources. Before looking at these structures, it is necessary to account for the principal characters in these events.

O.D. Skelton, the prime minister's most trusted adviser, was particularly influential in shaping King's policy of no commitments. Indeed, Skelton's personal convictions went some way beyond the prime minister's views: Canada should avoid participation in a future war at almost any cost. If, for reasons of allegiance to the crown, the country decided to fight, it must not be on the same open-ended terms as in 1914-1918. Rather than sending cannon fodder to the trenches of Europe, Skelton believed Canada should contribute with airmen and sailors, with her natural resources and her industries — not with her army.[7] He did not take into consideration that in 1939 the Canadian economy was not geared to even such limited contributions.[8]

King's Cabinet colleagues each had their own perspective on the policy of no commitments. Charles Dunning, the minister of finance, was innately conservative on financial matters, and as the country recovered from the

Depression he became even more so. In his role as keeper of the purse strings, he vigorously resisted expansionary budgets, whether the spending was on defence or relief.[9] Ernest Lapointe, minister of justice and King's faithful Québec lieutenant, was of the same cautious mind, a reflection *inter alia* of his constituency. T.A. Crerar, the minister of mines and resources, and C.D. Howe, minister of transport, were both pragmatists not inclined to spend their way out of a problem unless they could see no alternative. By contrast, the minister of national defence, Ian MacKenzie, and the minister of agriculture, James Gardiner, believed more money should be directed towards their respective departments, no matter what the costs. Like their colleagues, however, their interest was in current domestic issues, and even Mackenzie, despite pressure from the military staff, was not inclined to challenge the no commitments policy.

J.L. Ilsley, the Cabinet member who would play the leading role in Canada's wartime financial administration and economic planning, would have to wait until 1940 to get the finance portfolio, despite his capable performance in the summer of 1939 when he was acting for the ailing Dunning. Ilsley's substantive appointment, minister of national revenue, was not one of great standing, and he did not enjoy King's full confidence. Dunning's pleas to be released from public duty went unheeded as the prime minister continued to hold out the hope that the finance minister would recover from his illness and return. Ilsley, nevertheless, impressed finance officials, especially the deputy minister, Clifford Clark. Although passed over in September 1939 for the finance portfolio, Ilsely would make an important contribution to the first war budget and continue to develop effective relationships with the senior economic bureaucrats.

King's choice to replace Dunning was J.L. Ralston who had loyally served the prime minister in the past. A lawyer with a prodigious capacity for work, Ralston had been minister for national defence in King's 1926 administration, and then became finance critic when the Liberals formed the Opposition in 1930. He had left public life in 1935, but remained a staunch party supporter, and in August 1939 sent King an effusive note. The Prime Minister immediately offered him the finance job.[10] Ralston refused, but promised to serve if war broke out. Within weeks King was able to call in this promise. Ralston's glowing record as a front-line soldier during the First World War made him a particularly desirable addition to a wartime government, and King offered him the defence portfolio. Ralston, however, decided that real authority lay in the offices of the East Block and he insisted on the Department of Finance, to which the prime minister readily agreed. During the next nine months, Ralston's weakness as minister would be his inability to delegate to subordinates, no matter how trusted and experienced.

Clifford Clark and Graham Towers, the Governor of the Bank of Canada, were the two principal senior bureaucrats in the area of finance and banking.[11] They were realists, not inclined to push battles that could not be won in a Cabinet dominated by fiscal conservatives. However, on the issues of government debt, relief and dominion-provincial relations, both men favoured strong federal leadership and initiative, and, where necessary, intervention. Towers was trained as a banker and thought like a banker, with a strong faith in the self-correcting features of the market economy. Appearing before the Rowell-Sirois Commission in 1939, Towers had tried to temper the prevailing enthusiasm for John Maynard Keynes' General Theory and questioned its application in Canada.[12] In 1938, responding to a memorandum calling for exchange and capital restrictions in case of war, he correctly predicted that there would be no outflow of capital and that a depreciation of the dollar in the circumstances would not be a "disaster." He wrote:

> *It cannot be denied that substantial interference in the exchange or capital markets costs a great deal indirectly. Partial regulation is difficult to apply, and almost necessarily leads to a greater degree of regimentation. In such a case we would lose an extremely valuable asset, namely, the feeling that Canada is, a) a free market in which values are "real", and b) a feeling that our dollar is likely in due course to return to parity with the US dollar.*[13]

Clark was not so committed an exponent of economic orthodoxy. A strong supporter of the Rowell-Sirois Commission and the concept of centralization, Clark was convinced that the federal government should be better armed with constitutional powers to spend money on relief and unemployment. Yet at the same time he was aware of what was involved in raising money in conservative bond markets, such as London and New York, and he understood Canada's open economy better than most of his younger recruits, something they would only come to appreciate in the hot-house environment of wartime Ottawa.[14]

R.B. Bryce was one of these recruits. Clark had hired Bryce in late 1938 as a "financial investigator," an apt title considering the range of his later wartime duties. A student of Keynes at Cambridge, Bryce brought a powerful theoretical intellect to Ottawa. More important, he offered an understanding of the statistical background required before models such as the General Theory could be applied.[15] It was Bryce who was responsible for the only plans drawn up prior to September 1939, giving a rough outline of what Canada's wartime economic organization should look like. He envisioned a powerful, central coordinating body, a "War Economics Board," to coordinate policy and negotiate with other countries. Below it would fall a number of other boards dealing with specific fields of economic control: a Financial Control Board, a Defence Purchasing Board, a Transport Board, a Labour Board, and an Essential Industries Control Board.[16] This was roughly the structure that emerged at the outset of the war, with the exception of its centrepiece, the War Economics Board.

The lack of a central coordinating body would become the single overriding problem in Canada during the first two years of the war. In September, the Economic Advisory Committee (EAC) assumed the role of a central board, but it was a committee without real authority.[17] It could deal only with issues referred by Cabinet, and then could only make recommendations back to Cabinet. Still, in the first four months of the war, it became the body of first and last resort, and it would in this time period meet far more frequently than it did thereafter.

During the short special parliamentary session in September 1939, the King government introduced four major economic measures. They were the Excess Profits Tax, the Wartime Prices and Trade Board, the War Supply Board and revisions to the War Income Tax Act.[18] These four measures together represented the sum of government's economic policy and were an indication as to how Ottawa thought the war would unfold and how Canada would fight it.

The Excess Profits Tax was the only one of the four measures for which there had been some advance preparation. Indeed, its legacy could be traced directly to the Great War. One of the most enduring memories of that war was the "profiteer." During the war, a great deal of newsprint had been expended on the shell and bacon scandals, two infamous examples of government contractors making exorbitant profits from the selling of much-needed supplies to the Department of Militia and Defence.[19] The juxtaposition of two images — central Canadian businessmen getting fat and ordinary men rotting in cold, muddy trenches — was inescapable. Nor did the Business War Profits Tax of 1916, introduced to limit profits, have much impact.

During the interwar years, the issue of profiteering became inextricably linked with the manufacturers of arms, who were portrayed as the Great War's "Merchants of Death," and as public interest in disarmament increased, events like the Royal Commission on the Manufacture of Arms in the United Kingdom and the debate on neutrality legislation in the United States kept the question on the front pages. In 1935, O.D. Skelton was given the responsibility for looking into these questions in Canada, the result being the creation in January 1937 of the Interdepartmental Committee on the Control of Profits.[20] But the committee had few contracts with which to occupy itself. The limited amount of rearmament that took place in Canada from 1937 to 1939 hardly strained its resources.

Even so, the committee could not prevent scandal. The Bren gun affair created an embarrassing situation for the Liberal Government. The John Inglis Co. of Toronto had received a machine gun contract in March for which only it had tendered. The ten percent margin of profit was hardly excessive, but George Drew, a Conservative member of the Ontario legislature who thought himself a military expert, and George McCullagh, the publisher of *The Globe and Mail*, created a furor in September 1938, with accusations of patronage and profiteering.[21] This sorry little tale represented nothing more than a case of misjudgement, not wanton spending on guns, but the public was doubtless suspicious. Soon after the scandal broke, the prime minister resorted to the time-honoured solution of a Royal Commission, appointing Justice Henry Davis of the Supreme Court to investigate the contract. King, for obvious reasons, wanted the whole affair to end with as little damage to his government as possible. As a result, he was ready to agree to whatever Davis proposed. On 13 January 1939, the report was tabled. It really only contained one recommendation, and that was for the establishment of a board to monitor defence contracts.

At the centre of this recommendation was the principle that profits on armament contracts with the government should be tightly controlled. The members of the Inter-departmental Committee on the Control of Profits, who had this responsibility, had neither the opportunity nor the resources for this degree of supervision.[22] Davis had not actually recommended a limit to which profits should be held, but it was obvious to all concerned that something along these lines should be laid down. On 3 June 1939, the Defence Purchases and Finance Act created the Defence Purchasing Board (DPB) to monitor a profit limit of five percent of capital invested on any armament contract. All munitions contracts with private companies that were in excess of $5,000 would be subject to review by the board and the approval of, first the minister of finance, and then the governor in council. In King's desire to be done with the matter, he pushed the act through the House.

However, there was resistance from a number of quarters.[23] Davis's recommendation had been the most expedient response, particularly for public consumption. Yet there were those in the Department of Finance and outside of government who felt that creating such a bureaucracy to review contracts and to limit profits to five percent was not the answer. There was also some question as to whether an overworked and understaffed department could take the responsibility for reviewing the board's decisions. Nor was the manufacturing sector altogether pleased with what they saw as a deterrent to investment.[24] Even King's chosen appointee to head the DPB did not agree with the process. Why not tax profits rather then limit them beforehand?[25] The government went ahead and set up the DPB, and it functioned during the first two-and-a-half months of the war amid continued criticism.

Taxation, indeed the most readily accessible tool to control profits, did not receive detailed study before the outbreak of war, and there was then no time to give the issue the attention it deserved. In the aftermath of the Bren gun scandal, Clark and his officials were under extreme pressure to put together convincing measures against profiteering for presentation in the short session of Parliament in September 1939. They responded by taking the 1916 legislation, dusting it off, changing the V to a VI after King George, and putting it through Parliament.[26] This was an understandable response to a crisis situation, but fuller preparation would have prevented the eight months of confusion which followed for the business community. The Excess Profits Tax Act had hardly left the King's Printer when the complaints began flowing in to the minister of revenue. The act gave firms two ways to define profits. The first involved a calculation of average profits based on the previous four years' performance, the second required a calculation of capital employed. In each case there would be a graduated tax rate applied to the profits.[27] The government intended the second option for those companies that were still recovering from the Depression. Well-intentioned, the proposed tax did not foresee the number of companies that would be disadvantaged by the use of either option.[28] The biggest losers would be new companies, particularly in the mining and resources sector, where large capital outlays did not bring immediate returns. Nor was this the only problem. The commissioner of income tax, Fraser Elliot, was not pleased with the measure, fearing that excessive administration would be required. He told Clark that patching the legislation was not a solution, and that he could not be expected to bend and flex with each modification.[29]

The obsession of the government with restricting profits was primarily political, a reaction to the embarrassment of the Bren gun scandal. The tax would not contribute to winning the war nor further economic strategy. J.M. Keynes referred to such measures as "pseudo remedies," which raised to prominence "the least significant cause of rising prices."[30] True, it would bring some revenue into the federal coffers, but this could also be accomplished with the existing corporate income tax. The Excess Profits Tax only served notice that the government would not tolerate profiteers of any kind.

Control of profits was also irrelevant to the concept of "Pay as You Go." More important was holding down increases in costs and prices; these measures, if effective, would curb profits. At the Department of Finance, the question was defined even more narrowly. Officials felt that by controlling costs, they would be able to keep prices in line, and, with a progressive income tax structure, resources would be directed to fighting the war. If, on the other hand, labour costs were allowed to rise, there would be more purchasing power battling for a diminishing supply of resources. This could only result in an inflationary spiral. Thus, to guard against rising prices, the government created the Wartime Prices and Trade Board (WPTB). To emphasize the relationship between labour costs and consumer prices, it was to report to the minister of labour. Little beyond the basic outlines of this organization had been conceived before September.[31] And, as events unfolded in late 1939, the WPTB was not the forum in which price or cost questions were addressed. These matters were referred to the Economic Advisory Committee.

In the short term, the problem of prices was only one of supply. In October 1939, international supply difficulties, particularly with sugar and coffee, exerted upward pressure on prices. Yet the government's main concern was to be with declining prices for key agricultural products, including dairy and bacon. King had referred this matter to the EAC at agriculture minister Gardiner's behest when orders for dairy produce disappeared.[32] The crisis caused by the United Kingdom's action exposed an obvious weakness of the "no commitments" policy. The demand problems that occurred in the first three months of the war were all export-related. Ottawa had not communicated with London on the subject of markets in time of war. This lack of contact left the Canadians in the dark as to British intentions, and the High Commission in London had done nothing to advance the situation. Given the dramatic run on sterling which had taken place from mid-1938 onward, the loss of UK markets should have been anticipated. As it was, only the Bank of Canada seemed aware of the problem, and that institution had not communicated its concern to the Cabinet.[33] It was also no accident that agricultural markets for Canada were to be the first problem confronted. Throughout the war, even after the WPTB acquired real power, food prices and farm incomes would be a chronic difficulty, one that was never fully resolved. Farmers who had seen their incomes drop dramatically since 1928, understandably saw the high wartime demand as an opportunity for redress. Demands for floor prices came in the very first month of the war, and they were to continue until the summer of 1944.

The WPTB was also bypassed when the question of rising labour costs first arose. In September the government received a commitment from the major labour organizations to cooperate in the war effort. While this type of public announcement was good politics for both sides, it did not serve the purpose of some workers, particularly those whose wages still lagged well behind their 1929 level. Shipbuilders and coal miners were the first two unions to run up against the government's vague wage policy. Both represented sectors of the economy vital to the war effort, and in both wages were well below pre-Depression levels. The minister of labour, Norman McLarty, believed he could prevent a confrontation by introducing a cost of living bonus clause. He asked the EAC to consider this proposal and to include such a clause in government contracts to serve as an example to private industry.[34] It was natural that the Department of Labour would support such a step, and it was just as plain that the Department of Finance would oppose it.

A number of issues were in play. If the government was to guard against inflation, it would require accurate and up-to-date measures of the cost of living. The dominion statistician, Dr. Robert Coats, revealed to the members of the EAC that the existing cost of living measure had been arrived at between 1903 and 1906. "The weighting adopted at the time was based neither on family budgets nor on consumption figures, but was made up arbitrarily after an examination of the American practice and a few consultations with boarding house keepers," Coats told the committee.[35] They were working on a new measure, he stated. W.A. Mackintosh, who had just joined the public service and the EAC, warned that a broader measure of the cost of living would take in more of those things on which indirect taxes would land, complicating the war taxation program.[36]

The cost-of-living bonus question was not resolved at this time. Both Labour and Finance, however, recognized the merits of the other department's argument; they agreed that the labour market was still quite elastic, even after the unemployed were taken into consideration. The EAC recommendation was to delay the implementation of a cost of living bonus clause, with the caveat that if such a step was to be taken, it should only be done in conjunction with increased direct taxation.[37] Even so, the cost of living issue, like the farmer's demands for floor prices, would continue to haunt the government. The problem was a lack of hard statistics. If the government had had a better idea of the size and movement of the labour force, it would have been better equipped to make decisions on the allocation of manpower to both the military and industrial fields.[38]

The allocation of materials was the function of the Defence Purchasing Board. The difficulties with this board were not limited to the question of profits. The board had created a complicated procedure which had to be followed with each armament contract over $5,000. Contractors, forced to confront the bureaucracy for even rather small contracts, questioned the value of the exercise. This, they claimed, only served as an obstacle to rearmament: Canadian industry needed encouragement, not barriers. Some sectors, such as non-ferrous metals, had already been given a considerable boost by world rearmament. However, the manufacturing sector was still well behind its pre-Depression levels of output.[39]

The Defence Purchasing Board was, from the perspective of the Department of Finance, a disaster. Right from the outset of the war, with the whole department preoccupied with budget preparations and the drafting of legislation, the minister was required to bring each contract to Cabinet for approval. In addition, the inability of the Defence Purchasing Board to buy for the United Kingdom and other allied governments was an obvious weakness. Clark quickly became exasperated, and brought the matter to the attention of his new minister, Ralston, shortly after his arrival in the East Block.[40] Clark proposed that a War Supply Board (WSB) be established to fill the central role for the allocation of resources. They agreed that some organization similar to the UK Ministry of Supply was needed to coordinate supply policies and, if necessary, procure materials for the war effort.[41]

In the meantime, the Defence Purchasing Board continued its functions and was wound up only when the WSB was ready. King worried both about criticism that they were not doing enough for the war effort and that the public would believe contractors were getting away with exorbitant profits.[42] The WSB proved to be an inadequate response both politically and in terms of its powers and resources. The real need was for dramatic measures to take complete control of the procurement and allocation of defence resources. This would be fulfilled only with the creation of the Department of Munitions and Supply, under C.D. Howe's direction, in April 1940. Until then Ralston did his best to stay on top of all these questions, including the drafting of the regulations for the WSB, a process that went on well into October 1939. As in the case of the Excess Profits Tax, First World War legislation was the foundation upon which they built.[43] Watson Sellar and Gordon Scott, the two officials named to bring the board into existence, realized that this would not be enough. The regulations required a great deal of work. No one had considered, for example, how much power was being given to the WSB at the expense of National Defence.[44] In the illustrations provided to Ralston, it was clear that if National Defence undertook a major procurement of equipment, and the specifications changed, the contract would have to go back before the minister of finance, who would in turn have to take it to Cabinet. Ralston wished to control the entire war appropriation process.[45] Eventually, he was to realize that this placed too much of a burden on him and his department.

The WSB regulations did ease some of the conditions which the Defence Purchases and Finance Act had imposed. The board was only to be responsible for contracts over $15,000 and those under that figure in which tenders were not called or in which the lowest tender was not taken. Profits were now dealt with by the Excess Profits Tax. Still, the haste with which the WSB had been created was obvious. Just days before the War Supply Board was to take over from the DPB, Ralston's legal colleagues in Halifax warned him that some of the drafted regulations were *ultra vires*. When the departmental solicitor confirmed this, there had to be last minute rewriting.[46]

None of this took into account the real situation with respect to the ability of Canadian industry to meet war orders. There was an obvious need for some form of supervision or monitoring of the defence contracting process. Yet, at this time, the defence contracts were for mundane materials: boots, brooms, bedsteads and blankets.[47] Canadian manufacturers were not yet ready to mass produce the instruments of destruction required to equip modern fighting forces. Thus the Canadian minister in Washington had to go to the War Department in Washington to beg for 100-pound bombs for the tiny Royal Canadian Air Force. Mackenzie King, on the other hand, had so convinced himself of Skelton's argument that Canada's war effort could concentrate on resources that he never questioned what was involved in such a policy. In the absence of preparation, it fell to the Department of Finance to coordinate the allocation of resources in addition to its myriad other responsibilities.[48]

At the end of 1939, the strain of all this nearly erupted into the open. Wallace Campbell, the outspoken and disliked chairman of the War Supply Board, complained that the Department of Finance was standing in the way of the war effort. Campbell was president of Ford of Canada; his reputation was high, especially in Toronto, and he was not above enhancing it with frequent leaks to his cronies and the press. The leaks blamed Clark for the delay and obstruction of the WSB. King brought the matter before the Cabinet War Committee because he was well aware of the griping about Ottawa's direction of the war effort. Rogers, Ralston and Howe all sprang to Clark's defence.[49] All, presumably, began to draw the appropriate conclusions about Campbell. And members of Campbell's staff began to resign, a sure sign that something was wrong.

Fortunately for Ottawa, the War Supply Board was not really tested in 1939. When events in Europe overtook the continuing caution in Ottawa in the spring of 1940, the Department of Munitions and Supply was in a position to relieve the finance department of the heavy responsibility for allocation of resources. Even so, as a result of the lack of pre-war planning and hasty improvisation thereafter, C.D. Howe, as minister of munitions and supply, would have to fight for his position as the final authority on production and allocation. Only after he silenced his opponents in early 1941 was the question of control settled.[50]

The economic glue that was to hold the war effort together was taxation. There was a limit to the reach of institutional controls and organizations such as the WSB and later Munitions and Supply. A more pervasive and flexible device was required. Direct taxation, principally as implemented by the War Income Tax Act, was the government's main instrument. Ever fearful of the destructive forces of inflation, it employed such taxes to soak up excess purchasing power from the population. Personal income taxes, along with domestic borrowing and savings programmes, would allow the necessary management of the financial situation and produce the funds with which to fight the war.

The excess profits tax was in a different category. Although it did bring in some revenue, there was no direct effect on consumption. In addition, the indirect result of this tax was similar to that of the corporate income tax. It would reduce the capital available to firms for investment, and thereby diminish demand for the whole range of resources including labour. That might be helpful in an economy at full capacity, but Canada's was a far cry from this in September 1939. The solution was to make it applicable only for the fiscal years ending after March 1940. In the meantime, the government would use the corporate income tax to generate some additional revenue by increasing the rate from 15 to 18 percent.[51]

It was recognized that in the long run the real control over the economy would be exercised through the personal income tax. Finance officials, fearing soaring deficits, debated the ways to use this tax to bring revenue into the federal treasury immediately. A number of suggestions were canvassed. A two percent increase across the board would generate $8,000,000, or the the same amount could be collected by dropping the personal exemption by $200.[52] Although the revenues were attractive, Clark had already decided against these measures because they hit the lower tax brackets too hard. Instead, it was decided to impose a 20 percent surtax on federal income tax and consumption taxes on liquor and tobacco, the latter being an easy decision for the minister of finance to make, especially in times of fiscal strain. These taxes, aside from bringing immediate revenue, had the psychological effect of encouraging the sacrifice of luxuries in the service of the greater cause, which was politically useful in strengthening the government's image as a fit war administration.[53] These taxes would of course increase the cost of living, in direct opposition to the goal of limiting inflation, but the effects would not be important given the slack in the economy. It was harder to overlook the protests of the provinces, who complained about the lack of consultation and the infringement of their fiscal jurisdiction.[54]

The government, aware that the economy was in the earliest stages of recovery, deliberately avoided heavy new taxes in the first war budget. A short term loan would be negotiated in New York to provide additional funds immediately needed. Clark noted that this expansionary expedient was a one-time interim measure. Once the economy was stimulated, a heavy domestic borrowing programme would be instituted.[55]

Clark had laid out the general plans for these tax measures in a memorandum on 5 September 1939. This was the same day that the Cabinet Defence Committee sat down with the chiefs of staff to discuss expenditures on the armed forces. Clark told Ralston that it was not hard to estimate the revenues. It was, however, another matter to conjure up the rest of the picture.[56] As the acting finance minister was to say in the budget, the calculation of expenditures was far from precise. Many unanswered questions lay before them and officials were coping as best they could. Yet the principle of "Pay as You Go" obviously required a calculation of what costs were going to be incurred. It was not sufficient to have just one half of the equation covered; there would have to be hard and accurate measures of both revenues and expenditures. The lack of detailed advance planning, which was a consequence of the policy of "no commitments", prevented this. Of course, some of the cut-and-paste drafting of legislation has to be understood in context. Before the events of late August, King had been thinking in terms of a fall election, and it seems that he had only intended to have Parliament recalled to have the governor general issue the writ.[57] No attention had been given to drafting a parliamentary programme until the world was staring war in the face. Under these circumstances, the finance department's achievement was remarkable. In a matter of 19 days, a budget was drafted and written, and an entire bureaucratic apparatus was established to mobilize the nation's resources.

At the same time, the confidence of some bureaucrats that their understanding of developments in 1914-1918 provided a sound prescription for the coming conflict prevented them from grasping the scope of the task they faced.[58] Officials believed that the war would unfold much as the Great War had, with a prolonged deadlock on the fighting fronts. There would be ample opportunity to mobilize resources, methodically this time, under comprehensive state direction. The early onset of stasis during the "Phoney War" provided a false confirmation of these expectations. When Germany made its lightning offensives in the spring of 1940, time had already run out and demands on Canada became open-ended. Much of what was put in place in September 1939 would have to be abandoned or recast: the War Supply Board would be replaced in April 1940 by the Department of Munitions and Supply; the Excess Profits Tax Act would be totally rewritten; and in 1941 the Wartime Prices and Trade Board would be given real and dramatic power. Only the War Income Tax Act would remain, but as the instrument of much broader and deeper intervention than had been imagined. As pressures on the economy increased, the government would especially need more and more detailed information to produce realistic, well-targeted decisions. In 1939 that information did not exist, but the planners, in their enthusiasm, had not properly appreciated its critical importance. Well before 1945 the lesson would be learned.

In the end, all of the larger assumptions that officials made about the economy would be borne out, but in 1939 they did not have the means to refine those assumptions for effective action. A great deal of improvisation and adjustment would be needed to catch up to the swift-paced demands of world war in the age of mechanization.

NOTES

1. Canada, House of Commons, *Debates*, 10 September 1939.
2. National Archives of Canada (hereafter NA), W.L.M. King Papers, MG 26 J4, Reel C-4244, Committee on Emergency Legislation.
3. W.K. Hancock and M.M. Gowing, *The British War Economy* (London, 1949), 46-55.
4. Paul Kennedy, *The Rise and Fall of the Great Powers: Economic Change and Military Conflict from 1500 to 2000* (New York, 1987), 280-1.
5. Thomas White, *The Story of Canada's War Finance* (Montreal, 1921); *Report of the Royal Commission on Dominion-Provincial Relations* (Ottawa, 1940), Book One, ch. IV.
6. Of these authors, Liddell Hart was the most publicized in Canada. On 15 April 1939, *Maclean's* carried "Civilization in Danger," an excerpt from his Work, *Through the Fog of War.*
7. C.P. Stacey, *Arms, Men, and Governments: The War Policies of Canada, 1939-1945* (Ottawa, 1970), 9.
8. NA, Records of the Department of Finance, RG 19, vol. 512, file 124-0-181, R.B. Bryce to W.C. Clark, 16 November 1938. Also see Bank of Canada Archives, (hereafter BCA), Towers Memorandum No. 212, 20 December 1938.
9. H.B Neatby, *William Lyon Mackenzie King,* Vol. III, *1932-1939: The Prism of Unity* (Toronto, 1976), 187-89.
10. NA, MG 26 J1, vol. 276, Ralston to King, 9 August 1939.
11. J.L. Granatstein, *The Ottawa Men: The Civil Service Mandarins, 1935-1957* (Toronto, 1982), 29-52.
12. BCA, Towers Memorandum No. 236, Memorandum for Rowell Commission on Deficit Spending, 13 March 1939.
13. BCA, Towers Memorandum No. 181, Memorandum on Exchange and Capital Restrictions, 27 September 1938.

14. Robert B. Bryce, *Maturing in Hard Times* (Montreal, 1983), 121.

15. Granatstein, 256-9; Bryce's work on the national accounts can be found in NA, RG 19, vol. 3440, file N-7-1 and vol. 445, file 111-1R.

16. NA, RG 19, vol. 3449, Wartime Economic Organization, "Discussion of Wartime Organization and Control," August 1939.

17. NA, Records of the Privy Council Office, RG 2, P.C. 2698, 14 September 1939.

18. This overlooks the Foreign Exchange Control Act, but an arbitrary distinction between the domestic and the international is to be observed.

19. Michael Bliss, *A Canadian Millionaire: The Life and Business Times of Sir Joseph Flavelle, Bart.* (Toronto, 1978), 257-77, 336-62.

20. NA, MG 26 J4, vol. 159, file 1428, "Activities of the Department of National Defence since 1935."

21. Stacey, 101-2.

22. *Report of the Royal Commission on the Bren Machine Gun Contract* (Ottawa, 1939), 51-52. A copy of this report is in NA, RG 19, vol. 3983, file N-2-3.

23. NA, MG 26 J13, King Diary, 3 March 1939.

24. NA, MG 26 J1, vol. 275, Canadian Transport Association to King, 17 March 1939. Naturally, this organization did not say they were for armament profits. Instead, they claimed that they supported limits, but felt the government was rushing ahead without proper consideration.

25. NA, MG 26 J13, King Diary 7 July 1939.

26. NA, RG 19, vol. 451, file 111-14E. There is a marked up copy of the 1916 War Profits Tax Act in this file, dated 6 September 1939.

27. *Statutes of Canada*, 1939-40, 3 George VI C.4, Excess Profits Tax Act.

28. NA, RG 19, vol. 3427, "Budgets 1935-1939", Clark to Ralston, 30 September 1939.

29. NA, RG 19, vol. 3451, June 1940 Budget, Bryce to Clark, December 1939, "Memo re: Excess Profits Tax."

30. *The Times* (London), 14 November 1939, J.M. Keynes, "Paying for the War."

31. Christopher Waddell, "The Wartime Prices and Trade Board: Price Control in Canada in World War II," PhD thesis, York University, 1981, 18-28.

32. NA, RG 19, vol. 4660, file EAC-187-3, Minutes of EAC Meetings, 20 September 1939.

33. BCA, Towers Memoranda No. 190, 26 October 1938; No. 250, 18 April 1939.

34. NA, RG 19, vol. 4660, file EAC-187-3, Minutes of EAC Meetings, 11 December 1939, 13 December 1939.

35. NA, RG 19, vol. 4660, file EAC-187-3, Minutes of EAC Meetings, 11 December 1939.

36. NA, MG 26 J1, vol. 265, Report of EAC on Cost of Living Bonus, 15 December 1939.

37. *Ibid.*

38. The government made various attempts to make a coherent labour policy, one which combined inflation control and equity. Committees were struck and abandoned with great regularity. For the Department of Finance side of this story, see NA, RG 19, vol. 497, file 121-0-7, "Wage Policy" on the National Labour Supply Committee, the Labour Coordination Committee, the National Selective Service Manpower Committee, and the National War Labour Board in both its manifestations.

39. M.C. Urquhart and K.A.H. Buckley, eds., *Historical Statistics of Canada* (Ottawa, 1983). In terms of gross value of production, general manufacturing was 11 percent behind 1929 levels, and iron and steel was 27 percent lower.

40. NA, RG 19, vol. 3983, file N-2-3-1, Clark to Ralston, 5 September 1939.

41. NA, RG 19, vol. 3984, file N-2-5-1, Clark to Ralston, 9 September 1939.

42. NA, MG 26 J1, vol. 159, file 1426, Munitions and Supply. In this file are the notes Clark prepared for King's statement to the House on 13 September 1939.

43. NA, RG 19, vol. 553, file 145-S, Ralston to Johnson, 25 September 1939.

44. NA, RG 19, vol. 553, file 145-S, Watson Sellar and Gordon Scott to Ralston, 23 September 1939.

45. NA, RG 19, vol. 9, file 100-53-29, Sellar to Johnson, n.d. Sellar described a conversation with Ralston, who wanted all the war appropriation in one account for ease of control.

46. NA, RG 19, vol. 553, file 145-S, Parker *et al.* to Ralston, 25 October 1939, and Johnson to Ralston, 30 October 1939.

47. NA, RG 19, vol. 552, file 145, "Lists of Purchases," October 1939.

48. NA, RG 19, vol. 3983, file N-2-2-1, Committee on Defence Coordination, December 1939.

49. NA, RG 2, microfilm reel C-11, 789, Minutes of the Cabinet War Committee Meeting, 8 December 1939.

50. Robert Bothwell and William Kilbourn, *C.D. Howe: A Biography* (Toronto, 1979) 142-48. These pages relate the story of the Wartime Requirements Board, which tried to usurp Howe's role. Even after this, there were attempts at imposing another department over the structure of the war economy.

51. Canada, House of Commons, *Debates*, 12 September 1939.

52. NA, RG 19, vol. 3427, "Budgets 1935 to 1939," Elliot to Ilsley, 8 September 1939.

53. NA, RG 19, vol. 3427, "Budgets 1935-1939," Elliot to Ilsley, 8 September 1939.

54. NA, RG 19, vol. 212, file 164S-1940, R. Pearson to Clark, 13 September 1939. Pearson was the Deputy Provincial Treasurer of Manitoba.

55. NA, RG 19, vol. 3427, "Budgets 1935 to 1939," Clark to Ralston, 5 September 1939.

56. *Ibid.*

57. NA, MG 26 J13, King Diary, 27 June 1939.

58. Doug Owram, *The Government Generation: Canadian Intellectuals and the State, 1900-1945* (Toronto, 1986), 192-193. The title of this chapter, "The 'New Millennialists,'" is appropriate.

MR. KING AND THE ARMED FORCES

Roger Sarty
Department of National Defence

The prime minister took bold initiatives in military policy. Although he acted according to his own priorities, these reflected an understanding of defence requirements as well as domestic political considerations. It was also true that the politically-motivated restraints he placed on military expansion — and there are some striking examples from the early months of 1939 that have not previously come to light — flew in the face of his own military objectives. The service chiefs' profound awareness of this contradiction enabled them to reshape the military programme during the early months of war along lines they had long urged. They were able to do so, however, because the prime minister himself acknowledged the shortcomings of his pre-war policies. In important respects he proved a more committed proponent of military expansion than anyone had suspected.[1]

Canada's preparations during the last year of peace and her military effort during the first months of war were rooted in the rearmament programme that King had launched in early 1937. This initiative had been an act of political courage, for opposition was widespread and vociferous, and support tepid at best.[2] The prime minister had made the defence programme his own.

The services had asked in 1936 for $60 to 70 millions a year for five years to build up the navy from two to six modern destroyers, create a 23-squadron air force, and organize two army infantry divisions. This programme would provide modern coast defences against raids by enemy surface warships, submarines and aircraft and also create a force — the army divisions and a proportion of the air units — that would be available for despatch overseas to assist Britain in the main combat theatre.[3]

These requests derived not only from an assessment of needs, but from the services' past frustrations and their ambitions for the future. The land forces had made a large and successful contribution on the western front in 1915-1918. However, because of the prejudices and impulsiveness of Lieutenant-General Sir Sam Hughes, minister of militia from 1911-1916, the expeditionary corps of four divisions had been raised as a distinct special force. Although drawing heavily on the militia and its small cadre of regulars (the permanent force) for leadership, organization and recruitment, the overseas corps had no formal institutional links with the established service. In the end, most militia and permanent force units had been relegated to inglorious home defence duty. That fate had done nothing to elevate the generally low prestige and influence of the service in Canadian public life. Raising hundreds of special service units from scratch, moreover, had been as chaotic and wasteful a method for putting an army in the field as could have been devised. The militia general staff was therefore determined to keep effective control over the organization of a future overseas contingent.[4]

The navy, with 1083 regular and 1135 reserve personnel in March 1937, was endeavouring to overcome a much grimmer historical legacy.[5] Nearly scuttled by political controversy within months of its founding in 1910, the Royal Canadian Navy (RCN) had been limited during the First World War to a minimal coast defence role with small, weakly armed craft manned by ill-trained reservists. The failure of Britain to provide promised naval support had then left this inadequate force to counter German U-boats that hunted off Nova Scotia in 1918. Although the navy was successful in protecting major ships, it could not save the fishing fleet from heavy losses and failed to track down and attack the enemy submarines. Debilitating cuts in funding set back the service again in the early 1920s and still deeper cuts had been narrowly averted during the Depression.[6] The destroyer programme was a bid to create a big-ship, professionally-manned fleet that would at once provide effective coast defence and, as the embodiment of a long-term government commitment, secure the service's future against further destructive shifts in policy.

The air force, whose strength was 1107 regular personnel and half that number of reservists in March 1937,[7] was also struggling to establish itself as a national armed service. Over 20,000 Canadians had served in the British air forces of 1914-1918, but as individuals. The Royal Canadian Air Force (RCAF) had not been permanently organized until 1922 and until the mid-1930s was almost entirely committed to civil duties such as survey work and support for the Royal Canadian Mounted Police (RCMP). There was little time and equipment and only an embryo organization for military training. Administratively, the force was dependent upon and subordinate to the militia, the only one of the services that had a well-developed staff and a nation-wide system of bases and territorial commands.[8]

King was sensitive to the isolationist mood in the country, and had drawn his own lessons from the First World War. He never forgot that his power base in Québec rested largely on French Canada's reaction against the imposition of conscription by the Borden government in 1917-1918 to replace heavy casualties suffered by the Canadian Corps on the western front. He therefore gave priority to coast defence and to the air force and the navy, the services primarily concerned with that role, and set the ceiling for annual expenditure in fiscal years 1937-1938 and 1938-1939 at $35 million. That was half of what the military wanted, but still nearly double the level of the mid-1930s.

King publicly declared as early as February 1937 that rearmament was intended to strengthen the democracies against the dictators in Europe and the Far East,[9] but he and his colleagues emphasized that the programme was primarily for home defence. They particularly promised that the increased expenditure was not being used to make preparations for an expeditionary army. And the financial ceiling together with the priority for coast defences — harbour fortifications in the case of the militia — did in fact leave precious little for development of the field divisions. However, the General Staff persisted in making mobilization plans for the divisions with the justification that such mobile formations might be needed to support the coastal districts at home. Ian Mackenzie, minister of national defence, agreed that it was necessary to prepare for all eventualities. The militia, although last in line for increased appropriations, was much the largest of the services. By dint of requirements for basic infrastructure, it claimed the lion's share of the budget until 1939-1940 — $17.2 million in 1937-1938 and $15.7 million in 1938-1939. In the latter year, over 40,000 members of the non-permanent active militia (that is, reservists) trained, even if for only a few days and without modern equipment.[10]

Under the $35 million ceiling it was possible to improve the defences of one coast only. King and the military readily agreed that this must be the Pacific. Depleted as the strength of the Royal Navy (RN) was by the effects of arms limitations and the Depression, it still provided security to the Atlantic coast against the sea raiders of a European enemy. By contrast, in a Pacific war, the British fleet would be hard pressed to counter the formidable Japanese navy in the western reaches of the ocean, and would have no margin to safeguard British Columbia. Canada would be utterly dependent upon the strong US forces in the Pacific.

What was more, the sinuous, isolated coast of British Columbia offered the Japanese good staging points for interdiction of American supply lines to Alaska, or for raids on continental US ports. As the military had warned the government since the 1920s, if Canada was unable to secure the coast, American forces could be expected to occupy the area, a suspicion the president, Franklin Roosevelt, confirmed when he met with King in 1936 and after.[11] In that event, the ties to Great Britain that were an essential element of Canadian nationhood would be severed. Canada would be nothing more than an American protectorate. This was one reason why King, in the late 1920s, had supported development of the RCN through the acquisition of its first two modern destroyers.[12] In 1937-1938 his government moved quickly to complete the navy's expansion, immediately providing funds for the purchase of four destroyers offered by the RN; four of the navy's six destroyers were stationed on the Pacific.

The vulnerability of the west coast had also been the initial impetus for the air force programme. Warships alone could not hope to keep an effective watch over that vast littoral. The priority in US rearmament for the air services and coastal bases left no doubt about the Americans' readiness to do the job in default of Canadian action.[13] From 1934 the dominion government found itself resisting American pressure for development by the US services of an air route along the British Columbia coast to Alaska.[14]

What particularly commended aviation to the Canadian military was its mobility and flexibility. Air units could readily be redeployed from coast to coast, or overseas. King appears to have been impressed. Here was a service demonstrably essential for home defence that could also lend prompt assistance to Britain, without the danger — aircrews were small — of incurring so many casualties that conscription might be necessary. British leaders, moreover, intimated that air reinforcements would be the most urgently needed in the event of war, and Roosevelt, whose military and political judgment King respected, was convinced that air power was the best way the new world could help its friends in the old world.[15] Although King publicly pledged that Canada was bound by no military commitments to Britain and privately quashed most proposals for co-operative defence programmes, he did not entirely reject a British Air Ministry initiative in 1938 for Canadian assistance in air crew training and aircraft manufacture.[16] Indeed, aviation was one of the few industrial sectors that received significant government support.

In July 1938, after Hitler had moved into Austria and begun to press Czechoslovakia, the heads of the Canadian armed services warned the government that its programme bore no relation to reality, especially because there was almost no money for the Atlantic coast. The report called for acceleration of the army and air programmes and a new phase of naval expansion. Development of the German surface fleet with fast, powerful warships designed for distant operations, and the revival of the U-boat arm, had brought British warnings about the increased threat to the western Atlantic. Commodore Percy Nelles, chief of the naval staff, called for the purchase of a seventh destroyer and cruisers from the RN, early provision of fixed anti-submarine defences at eastern ports, and the placement of educational orders for two anti-submarine vessels with Canadian shipyards.[17]

Precautionary efforts during the war scare over the Czech crisis in late September proved the chiefs were not exaggerating about the state of unpreparedness. Fortuitously, the two new destroyers, *Ottawa* and *Restigouche*, had just arrived from the United Kingdom, giving a total of four destroyers on the east coast. (After the crisis, the two warships continued on to join their two sisters on the west coast, demonstrating the depth of the Canadian government's continued concern about the sovereignty and security of British Columbia even as Europe plunged towards war.) For the rest of it, there were only two recently completed minesweepers, and fewer than a dozen civil government ships; most of the latter were ill-suited for conversion into armed auxiliaries. Nelles decried a 'near tragic' state of affairs. As a result of the government's trimming of proposed estimates, the navy lacked over $2 million worth of basic equipment with which to complete the war outfits of the destroyers and auxiliary vessels and install even the most rudimentary fixed anti-submarine port defences. The important items were available only in the United Kingdom and could not be quickly acquired in an emergency. The air force was in much worse shape. Only six civil seaplanes were on station on the east coast, and only 28 other aircraft of any value — most lacking important items of armament and other service equipment — were to be found in the rest of eastern Canada. The sole operating base available was a seaplane facility at Dartmouth.[18]

One early result of the crisis was the RCAF's achievement of independence from the militia and status equal to that of the other services. Western Air Command had been established earlier in the year to control the expanding organization on the Pacific coast and, in the wake of the

Munich Crisis, Eastern Air Command was hurried into existence. This, together with a new Air Training Command in the central provinces, created a national command structure. In December 1938, Air Vice-Marshal G.M. Croil's appointment was changed from "senior air officer," a title that had signalled his subordination to the chief of the general staff, to "chief of the air staff."[19]

King's reaction to Munich had an important impact on the war preparations of all three services. Neville Chamberlain's unstinting efforts to seek a peaceful solution with Hitler removed the Canadian leader's reservations about British leadership. Clearly Britain would go to war only if absolutely necessary to defend freedom. That realization resolved King's agonies about the domestic political repercussions of Canada's entry into a major war. He called a Cabinet meeting on 27 September to issue a public statement in support of Chamberlain, informed his colleagues that if war broke out Canada would be at Britain's side, and slammed Senator Raoul Dandurand's support for North American isolation. There was a moral imperative for standing with Britain against the dictators, King declared, and he particularly emphasized that it was in Canada's clear self-interest to do so: "were Britain to be worsted in a world struggle, the only future left for Canada would be absorption by the U.S., if we were to be saved from an enemy aggressor."[20]

At the same meeting cabinet approved a governor-general's warrant for emergency defence expenditure of $7 million, most of it to purchase service aircraft in the US. The immediate outcome was embarrassing. After the US Army generously offered to make aircraft available immediately from its own orders, the Canadian government cancelled the warrant when Chamberlain's mission to Munich averted the immediate danger of war.[21] However, the long-term implications were important. Faced with slow deliveries from domestic and British sources, a Canadian service had turned to American types of major equipment for the first time. British officials interpreted the warrant as an encouraging sign that Canada would join in should war break out.[22]

The Canadian attitude during the crisis also eased nagging British concerns about essential naval co-operation. The small RN cruiser squadron based at Bermuda, headquarters of the America and West Indies station, depended upon free use of the strategic port of Halifax and upon the important reinforcement of the RCN destroyers. The Admiralty and Dominions Office had also worried that the King government might restrict communication between the Canadian and British naval staffs, as it had done in the case of the army and air staffs in 1937.[23] The exchange of naval information was much more voluminous and time-sensitive than for the land and air services because Naval Service Headquarters was the Admiralty's regional authority for the collection of shipping intelligence from Canadian and, through British consular offices, American ports. At the first inkling of a war-threatening crisis, the staffs at all ports were to be augmented to gather information about enemy movements, and to exercise control over allied shipping. These measures were vital for both economic mobilization and to direct friendly vessels away from areas where raiders might be operating. Speed was of the essence. Experience in the First World War had shown that the Germans would waste no time in deploying warships to distant waters for surprise attacks the moment war was declared. Canadian hesitation in mobilizing the North American intelligence organization into operation for a crisis might have grave results.

British officials had a bad moment when, during mobilization of the British fleet at the height of the Czech crisis, naval authorities despatched instructions directly to the naval staff in Ottawa without any prior notice that might have given the Canadian government a chance to determine its attitude. Yet the gaffe was scarcely noticed in Ottawa. Quite the contrary. King crowed: "It is quite evident that the mobilization of the British fleet had its effect" in bringing Hitler to accept Chamberlain's mediation.[24] An official at the British High Commission reported that even O.D. Skelton, the under-secretary of state for external affairs and one of the leading isolationists in the King administration, had allowed that "if this was the only mistake made ... we could well congratulate ourselves on having got round a difficult corner very successfully."[25]

In mid-October King, while vacationing in Bermuda, spent two afternoons with Admiral Sir Sidney Meyrick, the commander-in-chief, America and West Indies. According to Meyrick, King declared that the "readiness shown by the British Navy was a very big factor in the avoidance of war," and asked for details about deployments and plans for the America and West Indies station, thus allowing the admiral to expound on the importance of RCN co-operation. "I liked him very much, also his outlook," Meyrick wrote of King:

> *Amongst other things he told me that he hoped Canada would soon be able to put a stronger naval force into the field and agreed that the right place for Canadian ships was on the ocean and not in their*

home ports — which is the accepted belief of a great many Canadians that I have met, who comfort themselves with the idea that when they can see their destroyers they are being properly protected.[26]

It is also clear that Meyrick had made a hit with King: "I formed a high opinion of Merrick<sic> — a most delightful and I should think a most efficient man.'[27] Oddly, on this as on a later occasion, King did not record the substance of his discussions with the admiral, but his effusive letter of thanks leaves little doubt about the accuracy of Meyrick's account:

It will be a pleasure to me, when I return to Ottawa to let Nelles know of our conversations together.

I am glad to have so vividly in mind the relations of the two Naval services. In this particular, the visit has afforded a quite unexpected and helpful expansion of outlook upon defence matters of mutual interest and concern.[28]

This did not amount to a specific commitment. The admiral's report, however, contributed to an increasing confidence in London that any delay in Canada's entry into a war would be brief and might not interfere with early precautionary measures. In the following months the Canadian naval staff worked closely with the commander-in-chief's staff in perfecting preparations for mobilization.[29]

The three service chiefs presented draft estimates for 1939-1940 to the defence committee of Cabinet on 14 November 1938. These were based on the accelerated programme the chiefs had recommended in July, but they now called for still greater speed. The navy wanted $12.7 million, including funds for the immediate construction of four, rather than two, anti-submarine vessels, in addition to the purchase of the seventh destroyer from the Admiralty. The air force, which had laboured under the gravest deficiencies during the crisis, asked for $32.1 million, most of the increase to be used for the immediate acquisition of 99 aircraft from the US, together with provision of the necessary additional personnel and accommodation. Even with these American machines, the small existing stocks and the 78 aircraft ordered from British and Canadian sources in 1937 and 1938 (none of which had yet been delivered), the RCAF would still be 123 aircraft short of the 312 needed fully to equip the 11 permanent squadrons and partially equip the 12 auxiliary (reserve) squadrons. The militia asked for a more moderate increase to $26.4 million, among other things, to complete the west coast fortifications and make a start in building similar defences at east coast ports.

The total came to $71 million, but that figure was a minimum. Admiral Nelles advised that the government could no longer rely on the purchase of major ships at cheap prices from the RN, and should press forward with the construction of destroyers despite the high costs of building such sophisticated ships in Canada. Major-General E.C. Ashton, chief of the general staff, reminded the committee that the nearly $5 million worth of coast artillery equipment needed to complete the fortification programme had yet to be ordered from Britain, the only possible source of supply. Nor had the government done anything to address the much larger requirements for anti-aircraft and field artillery. As for the air force estimates, they had been drafted on the assumption that negotiations for training British pilots in Canada would result in Britain paying a considerable share of the costs of expanded training facilities.[30]

King was impressed by the service chiefs' warnings about the inadequacy of existing programmes to secure Canadian soil against the growing menace of the new German fleet and the Luftwaffe. When Cabinet met to consider the estimates in mid-December, he was pleased to find "[e]ven Québec members felt that considerable increases in estimates were necessary." Still, "after discussion," Cabinet sliced the total to $60 million: $8.8 million for the navy, $21.1 million for the militia, and $29.4 million for the air force. That was not all. From its reduced allocation, the air force had to find $6 million for training facilities that the air staff had hoped would be considered a British responsibility. In tortuous and extended negotiations, King had refused what the Air Ministry really wanted — the training of pilots recruited in Canada for the Royal Air Force (RAF) — on the grounds that it would be a binding military commitment. He offered only to allow British pilots to come to Canada to train in facilities wholly-owned and controlled by the dominion government.[31] Nevertheless, the estimates strikingly demonstrated King's commitment to air power. The RCAF received a shade less than half of the greatly-increased estimates, a sum that came close to the total provided for all three services during each of the first two years of rearmament.

The government's trimming of the proposed estimates dimmed the RCAF's hopes for a shopping spree in Washington, but snuffed out the big equipment programmes the navy and militia had urged for the coming year. Cabinet's initial interest in warship construction in Canada had quickly evaporated as the ministers worked the sums. The government approved only the purchase of the single British destroyer, which, like the destroyers acquired from the RN in 1937-1938, was available at a bargain basement price.[32] At this same time J.M. Stephens, president of Canadian Vickers shipbuilding, asked about the fate of an exploratory proposal by the British parent company and the Admiralty for a joint construction programme at Montreal that would deliver vessels to both navies. King merely repeated what he had said when the idea had been first raised in the summer: the Admiralty was free to place its own orders in Canada, but the government would in no way involve itself.[33] In the case of the militia, the Cabinet not only ignored the appeal for early new orders for large numbers of field and anti-aircraft guns, but so slashed the funding request that Major-General T.V. Anderson, Ashton's successor as chief of the general staff, declared that there would not be enough money to cover payments due for existing equipment orders.[34]

King promptly summoned the chiefs of staff to the defence committee of Cabinet again at the end of January 1939, when warnings arrived from Britain that war might break out within weeks. The chiefs, who appeared before the committee on 30 January, underscored how far the diminished estimates fell short of what was required. Capital costs alone to complete the 23-squadron air force ($27 million), the militia's coast defence, anti-aircraft and mobile forces ($79 million), and naval expansion ($68 million) amounted to nearly $175 million beyond what had been provided in the 1939-1940 estimates.[35]

The main new element in the chiefs' presentation to Cabinet was the large figure proposed for the navy. This put a price tag on the requirements for further fleet expansion and warship construction in Canada, about which Nelles had warned the government since mid-1938. However, his call for Canadian-built destroyers and the acquisition of much larger and more expensive cruisers to protect both coasts against powerful German and Japanese surface raiders had raised myriad technical and political difficulties. The uncertainties with which Nelles and his staff grappled had been resolved in a twinkling by the entry into RN service in late 1938 of the first new British "Tribal" class "super" destroyers. Surviving documentation is thin, but it leaves no doubt that these handsome ships created a thrill at Naval Service Headquarters in Ottawa. Half again as big as the RCN's existing destroyers, and mounting a gun armament fully twice as heavy, the new ships were virtually light cruisers that would stand a fighting chance against any but the heaviest Axis surface raiders. They also carried anti-submarine weapons, Canada's other main requirement, and yet were considerably smaller and cheaper than full-fledged cruisers. Unlike cruisers, moreover, there was a realistic possibility that construction of Tribals might be within the capacity of Canadian yards.

Nelles, in his report to Cabinet, now admitted that cruisers were not a practicable proposition for a service as small as the RCN, and he strongly urged Tribals as the alternative. Much of the $68 million estimated in capital costs for the naval programme was to build a sufficient number, at a rate of two per year beginning in 1939-1940, to expand the destroyer force to a full flotilla of nine ships on each coast. The chief of the naval staff also called for the restoration of the funds that had been cut from the draft estimates so that work could begin immediately constructing specialized anti-submarine craft.[36] Major-General Anderson, like Nelles, urged Cabinet to open the purse strings and dig deep. He asked that all of the projects lost from the draft estimates be reinstated, and repeated his predecessor's appeal for further large allotments for the supply of field and anti-aircraft artillery.[37]

The air force was in a rather different position than the other two services — cash-rich but searching for ways to spend its money effectively. The estimates contained as much money as apparently could be absorbed by Canada's infant aircraft industry, and more. However, neither the inexperienced Canadian firms nor overburdened British ones could produce at a rate that would be of any help in an early crisis. For example, delivery of 18 Canadian-built land-based maritime patrol bombers that had been ordered in 1937 would begin only in the summer of 1939 and not be complete until well into 1940.[38] These aircraft, moreover, were the earliest significant reinforcement that could be expected for Canada's "pitiably inadequate"[39] coastal air commands. By contrast, American firms could deliver 33 maritime patrol type aircraft by July 1939 through the special concessions the US Army was still willing to make for Canada. The necessary money, some $4 million, was available in the reduced estimates over and above funds for orders in Canada. The air staff therefore urged Cabinet to release the $4 million immediately, and supply a further $5 million to purchase any other suitable aircraft that might be had in Washington.[40]

The chiefs were wasting their breath in asking for more money. King did not disregard their appeals, however. The services needed funds from the upcoming fiscal year as soon as possible, but under normal procedures they would not be available until well into the spring, when Parliament voted the estimates. After the chiefs' presentation to the defence committee on 30 January, King immediately went to the leader of the opposition and secured his agreement to allow the services early access to the funds.[41]

Even so, political considerations precluded action on the most urgent requirement, aircraft from Washington. This was striking in light of the fact King had himself quickly raised the possibility of renewing the bid for US aircraft when, on 26 January, he received the British warnings about imminent war.[42] In Cabinet next day his colleagues poured cold water on the idea. It would be unwise to make such a large expenditure south of the border when the government was defending hikes in military spending with promises of benefits for Canadian industry.[43] Neither Croil's presentation to the defence committee, nor the air staff's subsequent appeals, succeeded in turning this argument. In early March, Cabinet shut the door on the purchases, with King leading the way:

> *I took the view which I think Council generally supported, that if war came, it would come probably this year. That we would not have the planes in time if ordered from the United States. If orders were given in the States and no war came, we would be confronted through a campaign with having given order of millions to American factories instead of our own. It was better, therefore, to give orders in Canada though they would be about a year later in being delivered.*[44]

Within a few weeks of this decision, the aircraft procurement situation brightened somewhat, or so the air staff believed at the time. The British Air Ministry intimated that it could now deliver 18 land- based maritime patrol bombers as quickly as US suppliers could meet this, the RCAF's top priority requirement. The Canadian air staff grasped the offer. It was only the promise of early deliveries that had commended American equipment. The RCAF was closely modelled on the RAF, had adopted British combat types of aircraft as the standard, and Canadian industry was tooling up to produce these machines. American equipment, and the doctrine that had influenced its design and intended employment, were entirely foreign, not least because US security regulations closely restricted information. Stringent American neutrality laws, moreover, raised profound doubts about continuing supply and technical support in the event of war. US prices were steep as well. With the decision to order the considerably cheaper British bombers, the air staff was able to expand procurement under the 1939-1940 estimates from 87 to 103 aircraft. The Canadian airmen were aware of the superiority of US maritime aircraft over the British equivalents, but only in general terms; the critical importance of the edge in performance possessed by the American machines would become fully apparent only under the unexpectedly extreme demands of maritime operations after the outbreak of war.[45]

However grave the problems of equipment were for the air force and navy, the purpose of the two services was self evident to the public and the government. The militia did not have that advantage. Alarm bells had started ringing at militia headquarters during the Czechoslovakian war scare, when there had been excited speculation in English Canada about raising an expeditionary force. This of course was welcome confirmation of senior officers' conviction that, at the moment of crisis, public sentiment for Britain would quickly over-ride the King government's promises that it was not preparing to send another Canadian army to Europe. Disturbingly, however, the calls for action were for a special force organized in the style of Sam Hughes, through the inspired voluntarism of leading citizens. There was scarcely a reference to the militia or to the general staff in Ottawa. According to Brigadier W.H.P. Elkins, commanding the Toronto military district, "it is the general opinion that ... troops would have been raised exactly as was done in 1914. If this idea is general it means that the Militia is looked upon only as a sort of internal security force ..."[46] In other words, the government's cautious emphasis on home defence and disavowal of an expeditionary force was threatening to undercut the militia exactly as Hughes's malevolent and unprofessional enthusiasm had done.

Senior officers, in their planning and internal discussions, now abandoned any pretext that the mobile divisions provided for in the mobilization scheme might be needed for home defence. "Under existing strategical conditions," one policy paper explained, "there is no risk of an armed invasion in strength. There is, therefore, no military need to mobilize this force for the defence of Canada in Canada." If the force were mobilized for home defence it would be merely to "re-assure public opinion."[47] Certainly, if the mobile divisions were to do nothing more than stand guard on the coasts against minor landing raids, there was no need for them to match the latest British organization, but during the last months of peace the general staff exerted an enormous effort in precisely such a reorganization. Headquarters also completed reorganization of the militia in the coastal districts so that specialized units entirely separate from the mobile divisions would be available for coast defence tasks. Complementary arrangements were concluded for the RCMP and provincial police forces to assume all but very limited responsibilities for internal security and the protection of vulnerable points.[48]

From the time of the Czechoslovakian crisis, the general staff had also been urging the defence minister to bring the mobilization scheme before the government for specific approval. There is no evidence that Ian Mackenzie did so. Indeed, the minister seems to have been deeply disturbed at the realization that the approval he had given in 1937 to plan for all contingencies had resulted in the raising of an expeditionary force as the centrepiece of the mobilization scheme.[49] When in January 1939, Colonel Kenneth Stuart, the militia's chief planner, put the staff's views before the minister in a long, closely argued paper, Mackenzie responded by scratching a question mark beside every reference to an expeditionary force.[50]

The sequel was both curious and important. Stuart's paper, with only the most blatant of the references to an overseas army excised, became the basis for a large section of the speech in which Mackenzie introduced the 1939-1940 estimates to the House of Commons on 26 April 1939. The prime minister had reviewed the draft in detail, and made only a "few changes and suggestions" before approving it.[51] Over two hours in length, Mackenzie's presentation was the government's major statement on defence during the session. Stuart's edited prose was still heady:

> *In regard to the larger issues ... no one can foretell the extent to which the resources of Canada might come to be committed in a world-wide struggle between ruthless aggressive forces of conquest and destruction, against which the combined democratic and liberty loving peoples would be compelled to unite for the defence of their freedom and their ideals. ... The extent of the effort required would be governed by the scope, intensity and length of the struggle.*

Mackenzie then listed the tasks the militia would have to perform in the event of war. The first five dealt with home defence, but the sixth and seventh went further.

> 6. *To have a reserve force available to meet the unexpected.*
>
> 7. *Should the eventualities of intensive conflict necessitate it, for the fundamental protection of Canadian institutions and Canadian ideals.*

The militia system of Canada to-day is capable of having ready, subject to public demand and parliamentary approval, a substantial force ready for active service within six months after mobilization. Our militia system of a large non-permanent force, with a small permanent establishment to provide highly trained staff and instruction, is precisely calculated for the necessities which have just been described.[52]

Nor was this the end of Mackenzie's candour. He also read the reports on the full capital costs for completion of the defence programme that the chiefs of staff had presented to the Cabinet defence committee in January, and presented detailed statistical information to show how far the government's programme fell short.[53]

It was a striking performance. The government had laid bare the service chiefs' criticisms of the rearmament programme and their dire warnings about the future. Here was stark notice that, should a major war break out, Canada could not escape a daunting, open-ended commitment. Here too was strong evidence that the general staff's campaign to bring the government to face the possibility that an expeditionary force might have to be despatched was having effect.

Immediate political advantage was no doubt a large part of King's reason for allowing Mackenzie to speak so frankly. The revelation of the true costs of adequate rearmament demonstrated the moderateness of the large increase in the estimates to $60 million; the government was admitting that it was probably erring on the side of caution. C.G. McNeil, the Co-operative Commonwealth Federation (CCF) defence critic, once again attacked the rearmament programme as ill-disguised preparation for the despatch of expeditionary forces blindly to repeat the horrors of 1914-1918,[54] while such Conservative speakers as Tommy Church, Howard Green and Denton Massey denounced the government for its mean-spirited failure to make more adequate provision for direct assistance to Britain.[55] But all agreed that a greater home defence effort was needed. Most importantly, from King's perspective, the small cadre of diehard Québec Liberal opponents of rearmament did not gain new adherents.

In bringing his caucus to accept the estimates, King had emphasized how vulnerable Canada was to attack: "I spoke of Germany demanding an air-base at Iceland, and how near that was ... I asked if it were not a fact, if London were shelled tomorrow, our own ships in all parts would not be shelled as well, with probability of immediate attacks on the St. Lawrence."[56]

Fortuitously, 12 days before Mackenzie presented the estimates in the Commons, there was a flurry of U-boat sighting reports by fishermen off Nova Scotia (on investigation, they proved to be imaginary) that caused a minor sensation, including a demand from Senator W.A. Griesbach for mobilization of the Halifax fortress.[57] Typically, King interpreted the incident as justifying his warnings to Québec that Canada could not stand safely aloof in a major war: "It [the appearance of U-boats in Canadian waters] is exactly what I would expect if war to be declared. The St. Lawrence would be closed almost immediately."[58] Certainly the naval staff took the scare dead seriously. The inability of the Admiralty accurately to track German submarines during the Munich Crisis, and Hitler's subsequent announcement of an expanded U-boat construction programme, had triggered alarm about the undersea threat in London and Ottawa. Nevertheless, King was unmoved by another appeal from Nelles for the anti-submarine vessel construction programme.[59]

Admiral Meyrick, during a visit to Ottawa at the end of June 1939, received renewed assurances from King that he "could rely on Canadian help in case of war."[60] So it proved. On 22 August, as the crisis over Poland deepened, the Admiralty despatched the first of the warning telegrams for precautionary mobilization. Mackenzie promptly authorized the naval staff to act,[61] and the next day the prime minister issued a press release that proclaimed the government's readiness to meet any emergency. Cabinet assembled on the 24th — King was relieved to find agreement that Canada must go to war if Britain did so — and authorized a governor-general's warrant for $8.9 million, most of it for the long-delayed procurement of American aircraft. On the 25th, the government instantly and warmly approved Meyrick's request that his northern division of two cruisers, HMS *Berwick* and *York*, should operate from Halifax.[62]

During the last days of August, Canada acted in concert with Britain in completing precautionary measures. Early on 26 August, non-permanent militia coast defence units were called out and had the fortresses at Halifax and Esquimalt ready for action by evening. That same day, permanent force RCAF squadrons began to move to the Atlantic coast, while the navy implemented control of shipping. On 31 August, two of the four west coast destroyers, HMCS *Fraser* and *St. Laurent*, departed on a high-speed two-week run to Halifax via the Panama Canal.[63]

When word reached Ottawa of Germany's invasion of Poland early on 1 September 1939, King acted quickly to demonstrate that Canada was preparing for war in her own right and not merely as a dutiful colony.[64] The general staff was authorized to mobilize the two infantry divisions for their nominal task of home defence, and the air force and naval reserves were called out. Thus, the Canadian forces had begun full mobilization two days before Britain declared war on 3 September, and nine days before the Canadian parliament endorsed the government's recommendation that Canada go to war.

The forces mobilized more swiftly than would have been possible at the time of the Munich Crisis, but were still modest by any standard. At Halifax, the only east coast port with anything like proper defences, the location of the old forts too close in to the harbour, and their obsolescent armament, meant that the guns could fire only about 10,000 yards seaward of the headlands; no funds had been available to start the new installations that would increase that range to 30,000 yards. Only the most basic fixed naval defence, an anti-submarine net, could be rigged during the fall of 1939.[65] The sole defence at other Atlantic ports was a few surplus guns that had been hastily installed on quick-set concrete pads. The most important of the modern fortifications on the west coast were complete, or nearly so, but were equipped with old armament because of the lateness of the orders for modern equipment from Britain.

Important projects had been carried out at the Esquimalt naval base, but little had been done to improve Halifax's cramped, outdated facilities. New naval bases needed to protect northern British Columbia and the Gulf of St. Lawrence had not been started. There had been good progress, however, in the construction of air stations on both coasts, and it was possible to rush the two most important aerodromes — at Dartmouth and at Patricia Bay, near Victoria — into use during the fall of 1939. The RCN would receive its seventh destroyer from Britain in the fall, but the availability and equipment of craft for local and anti-submarine defence were nearly as grim as at the time of the Munich Crisis. The RCAF now had 53 service aircraft more or less ready for operations but only 19 of these were modern types; the strength of the permanent force was 3142 all ranks and that of the auxiliary (reserves) 1111, just over half of the establishment for the planned 23-squadron organization.[66]

Nevertheless, Halifax was the British Empire's strongest position in the western Atlantic and preparations there were adequate to give the British commander-in-chief the support he most needed. The sinking of the British liner *Athenia* by a German U-boat in the north-east Atlantic on

3 September had led the Admiralty to conclude — incorrectly — that Hitler was launching an "unrestricted" submarine war against shipping without the "stop and search" procedure prescribed by international law. Winston Churchill, the First Lord, therefore immediately ordered the sailing of trans-Atlantic shipping in defended convoys. Thanks to the co-operative mobilization preparations since the Munich Crisis, the RCN was able quickly to organize the first of the famous HX series of convoys from Halifax; it sailed on 16 September. The RCN destroyers, HMCS *St. Laurent* and *Saguenay*, together with Canadian-built RCAF Supermarine Stranraer flying boats, reinforced the British cruiser escort during the critical first days of passage: a long-range U-boat was most likely to strike at a convoy as it left port.[67]

Action to secure Canada's coasts with some margin to relieve Britain's overextended forces in the western hemisphere was precisely the kind of limited effort King had in mind when formulating and selling his rearmament programme. In a paper on "Canadian War Policy" that Cabinet considered on 24 August, O.D. Skelton, a committed anti-participationist, recommended assistance to Admiral Meyrick throughout the North American area as a particularly suitable contribution. King and his colleagues heartily agreed. As for more direct aide to Britain, Skelton had framed his paper to head off the despatch of an army expeditionary force under the expected pressure of a groundswell of English Canadian opinion, as had happened in 1914. He explicitly urged a second element in King's rearmament programme that had hitherto been cloaked under the "no commitments" rubric: the hope that Canada could pitch in with air forces, thereby avoiding embroilment in the high-casualty land war and the necessity for conscription.

> *If any military action is to be taken overseas, it should, in the first instance, be in the air service rather than by military contingents. An announcement of an immediate and intensified programme of building planes and training men for air service in Canada and for a Canadian air force operating in France, would be effective from the standpoint both of military value and of consolidation of public opinion.*[68]

The military had anticipated this argument. Early in July, the chiefs of the air and naval staffs had endorsed the militia's view that, in the event of an early, major war, the only substantial assistance Canada could send to Great Britain would be an army expeditionary force.

It is often stated that the most effective contribution Canada could make would be an "air force contingent." That may apply in the subsequent stages of a war. But, in the initial stages of a war in 1939, when the demands of direct defence [of Canada] are taken into consideration, available resources, both of aircraft and personnel, will not admit of the despatch of an "air force contingent" [other than a few squadrons] ...[69]

When advising Cabinet on 29 August, the chiefs of staff honed this argument into a sustained brief for the despatch overseas of at least one of the two field divisions provided for under the militia mobilization scheme. The best early overseas effort that the air force could muster would be six squadrons — personnel only (say 200 or fewer per squadron) without aircraft or equipment.[70]

King reacted bitterly. "It is clear," he fumed, "that the Defence Department has been spending most of its time preparing for an expeditionary force, and that Mackenzie has been either conniving at this or not resisting it as he should, or knowing nothing about it." The recommendation, moreover, was entirely wrong. King was confident that the British request would be for air crew.[71]

In fact, the government learned on 6 September that Britain wanted both an army expeditionary force and large numbers of air crew.[72] King recorded his surprise at the strength of support in Cabinet for the despatch of an army formation. The upsurge of loyalty to the mother country that the general staff had long predicted was having its effect.[73] There were further unpleasant surprises for the prime minister. He was, in his own words, "incensed" at advice from Air Vice-Marshal Croil on 15 September that no formed RCAF units could be sent overseas at an early date. All of the limited number of qualified personnel available would have to be retained for training duties in Canada if air crew were to be turned out in anything like the number requested by the British.[74] King's anger left little doubt that he linked the air force's inability to provide a distinctly national contingent of formed units with what he now recognized as the necessity of sending army formations. As he saw it, the air force — the only alternative for effective assistance to Britain without the bloodshed and political trauma of 1914-1918 — had let the government down.

Cabinet considered the full armed forces programmes on 18 September, and the deliberations bore more than a passing resemblance to the pre-war estimates reduction exercises. The service recommendations came with a price tag of about $500 million for the first year of the war. Warnings by finance officials of national bankruptcy brought the government to lower the ceiling to approximately $300 million. The brunt of the chopping was, as usual, borne by the militia. Although the government confirmed the decision to send an infantry division overseas, it effectively rejected the general staff's plans for expansion of the expeditionary force.[75] Recruiting for the still incomplete second division was suspended in October and that formation remained in Canada. The total strength of the mobilized land forces, including the 16,000 men of the 1st Canadian Infantry Division who went overseas in December, was just over 60,000 personnel, as compared to perhaps 100,000 if the general staff's plans had been fully carried out.[76] Because of the government's refusal since 1937 to provide funds for artillery rearmament, the home forces were still equipped with slightly modernized First World War stocks, while the 1st Division units had to draw on British sources of supply.

Although cuts in the estimates compelled the air force to trim the number of squadrons planned for home defence,[77] the service was to undergo a much vaster, if somewhat different, expansion than that projected by the most ambitious of the pre-war plans. At the end of September, a proposal arrived from the United Kingdom for an air training scheme of breathtaking scope. As many as 20,000 pilots and 30,000 other aircrew were to be graduated in Canada each year.[78] King and his colleagues quickly accepted the idea in principle. The prime minister's main regret was that word had not arrived sooner, before he had made the commitment to send the 1st Division overseas.[79] One of King's demands in the protracted Anglo-Canadian negotiations that produced the British Commonwealth Air Training Plan agreement of December 1939, was that Britain should publicly declare that air training was the single most important contribution Canada could make, thus forestalling pressure for expansion of the expeditionary force. The British government willingly paid tribute to Canada's air undertakings but, under no illusions as to the mass of manpower that would be needed in the land war, refused to issue the statement King wanted.[80]

The main body of the air training negotiations centred on finance. After a great deal of haggling, Canada agreed to pay nearly half of the estimated total cost of $607 million for the whole of the three years projected for the scheme.[81] That was within the conservative financial limits that the government had placed on the war effort. However, officials believed that the bank would be broken if Canada had also to bear the very great additional cost of maintaining the Canadians who graduated from the scheme — 80 percent of the total — in equipped RCAF overseas squadrons. The service of Canadian airmen in nationally distinct units and formations, rather than scattered through the RAF, was important both to the air staff and the government, but not sufficiently so to overcome the economic concerns.

Hard Canadian bargaining ultimately resulted in an agreement that the British government would form a portion of the RCAF air crew sent overseas into RCAF squadrons at British expense. Air Ministry tardiness in establishing RCAF squadrons and channelling Canadian personnel into them became a major issue in Anglo-Canadian relations. Although in January 1943 the Canadian government undertook to pay the costs of RCAF overseas squadrons, more than half of the 70,000 Canadian aircrew trained under the plan served as individuals in British units.[82]

The one service whose programme was not significantly changed by the decisions of September 1939 was the navy. Senior officers saw their dreams come true.[83] Germany's apparent introduction of unrestricted submarine warfare aroused fears among the naval staff that, as in 1918, reinforcement of defences in European waters would force the U-boats to search for less well-protected shipping in Canadian waters.[84] The Admiralty, moreover, had already intimated that the RN would be dependent upon Canada for anti-submarine vessels in the western Atlantic.[85] Nelles's bid for a large escort construction programme was initially frustrated by the financial cuts, but King intervened to secure approval in February 1940 for the building of 92 ships, the greatest number industry could produce in an all-out two-year effort.[86] There were serious technical problems largely resulting from the government's pre-war failure to support naval shipbuilding. However, the Admiralty's development of the simple corvette design expressly for construction by non-naval, commercial yards meant that none of the difficulties proved insuperable.[87]

Rough-built anti-submarine craft did not fulfil the navy's requirements or ambitions. Nelles continued to press for Tribal destroyers to provide some independent Canadian defence against enemy surface raiders and — at least equally important in the navy's view — to establish the foundation for post-war development of a substantial seagoing service.[88] The difficulty, he soon discovered, no longer lay in the attitude of his political masters, but in the inability of Canadian firms to build these big warships under wartime conditions and the unwillingness of the Admiralty to accept orders for over-crowded British shipyards. Cabinet supported Nelles in his negotiations with the British and, when these finally bore fruit in the spring of 1940, approved orders in the United Kingdom for the construction of two Tribals for the RCN.[89]

Air forces soon proved to be at least as vital to maritime operations, even if in some different and more subtle ways, as imaginative pre-war prophets had predicted. Orders to the two Canadian firms that were building maritime patrol bombers were increased, but the unavailability of components from British manufacturers further delayed production.[90] In any case, the British aircraft types on order were obsolescent or inferior. The RAF itself was relying on American machines for its Coastal Command. Under pressure of war, the RCAF was finally able to adopt the same solution, beginning with the purchase of 20 maritime patrol bombers under the governor-general's warrant of 24 August and the diversion to the Maritime provinces of ten others from British orders in the US.[91] With American aircraft, many of them ultimately produced with assistance from the US by Canadian firms whose development had been stimulated by the pre-war rearmament programme, the RCAF's Eastern Air Command became one of the major Allied maritime air forces.[92]

It would be difficult to overstate the importance and scope of the contribution of Canadian ships and aircraft to the war at sea. Unheralded German success in mounting massed U-boat attacks on shipping across the whole breadth of the Atlantic, and the unpreparedness of Britain and the US for large-scale anti-submarine warfare, created a desperate demand for the types of ships and aircraft Canada had procured for coast defence. Canadian warships and aircraft were thus drawn into a major share of transatlantic escort of shipping, and a substantial role in European waters from the Mediterranean to the Arctic Circle. Because the Axis surface raider threat to Canadian waters that had so concerned the naval staff in Ottawa did not materialize, the fleet's larger warships were committed to a wide range of trade defence and surface warfare tasks in the European theatre and the Pacific.[93]

One of the most remarkable aspects of Canada's participation in the war was the nation's rapid emergence as a significant seapower. Although criticisms have rightly been made of failures in equipment supply, training and leadership that attended such hasty expansion,[94] the effort would have been impossible without the preparations made in 1937-1939, and the programmes that had been promptly mounted on the outbreak of war.[95] Much of the credit is King's, for he had consistently made maritime forces the top priority. His reasons for doing so went far beyond the politics of the conscription issue. He had long shared the worries of the military about Canadian security and sovereignty in the face of increasing danger of attack by aggressive overseas powers, the weakening of the strategic shield provided by Britain and rising American hegemony in the western hemisphere. He understood that imperial maritime defence was still an essential pillar of Canadian nationhood. Without strong British Empire sea forces, as he put it in January 1939, "there would be no independent Canada left; if Canada was left at all, it would be as one of the States of the American Republic."[96]

King never doubted, as well, that in a major war Canada would make a large commitment to assist Britain at the continental fighting front. Indeed, the prime minister embodied the deep English Canadian emotional attachment to Britain that the military had always counted upon in planning for the mobilization of overseas forces. The essential harmony between the prime minister and the service chiefs had been strikingly demonstrated by his willingness in April 1939 to allow them to speak directly to the public through Ian Mackenzie's defence estimates speech.

The only fundamental area in which minds did not meet was the issue of an army expeditionary force. Here too, in King's hopes before September 1939 that large-scale air assistance would provide the alternative to ground formations, lay the central contradiction in the government's limited rearmament programme. The prime minister's musings about dramatic air action were neither insincere nor impracticable, as was soon shown by the launching of the British Commonwealth Air Training Plan in 1939-1940. Nevertheless, his expectation in 1938-1939 that the RCAF, still in the throes of organization as a fighting service and hedged in its development by political constraints, could sustain an offer to Britain of early air support was utterly unrealistic.[97]

When King had a chance for reflection, however, he soon acknowledged that he had pursued pipe dreams at the expense of military effectiveness. On 28 September 1939, a date the prime minister thought significant because it was the anniversary of Chamberlain's mission to Munich, he brooded in his diary about the shortcomings of the pre-war programme. He came close to confessing that it was solely politics — his contest with the opposition Conservatives, who must not be seen to push him too close to the "imperialist" camp — that had brought him so severely to trim the British proposals of 1938 for air co-operation. He further admitted "regret" that "in seeking to avoid undue expenditure and criticism therefrom by Parliament," he had resisted the purchase of American aircraft.

The prime minister, not untypically, moved on from himself to shift blame onto others. British Air Ministry representatives had forced his hand by meddling in domestic politics through their appeal to ardent imperialists, while the chief of the air staff had made a "fatal mistake" in trying to grab money over and above his proper appropriations for purchases in the US (that, of course, was selective hindsight on King's part). The disappointments of the air programme, he concluded, "illustrate how much hangs on the tact, ability and understanding of human nature by individuals in strategic positions."

Astonishingly, in light of his charges of insubordination by the general staff a few weeks before, he then suggested that it was Major-General Anderson who had demonstrated those qualities. King mused that, given the strength of "popular demand," the general staff could well have pressed harder for an expeditionary army, and for one larger than the single division that was selected for overseas service. As he now saw it, the soldiers had loyally carried out the government's will by planning a home army whose organization would allow the despatch of a limited force if Cabinet so decided. That formulation was not far from the draft Colonel Stuart had supplied to Mackenzie, and the prime minister had approved for the defence estimates speech of April 1939.

The prime minister was certainly a friend of the navy and the air force, but he and the militia general staff were more closely in tune than either had realized.

NOTES

1. Existing accounts emphasize the gulf that existed between what the armed forces wanted and what the prime minister would sanction. E.g., James Eayrs, *In Defence of Canada: Appeasement and Rearmament* (Toronto, 1965), 134-53; C.P. Stacey, *Arms, Men and Governments: The War Policies of Canada 1939-1945* (Ottawa, 1970), 6-16, 107-9; *The Military Problems of Canada: A Survey of Defence Policies and Strategic Conditions Past and Present* (Toronto, 1940), 142-3; *Six Years of War: The Army in Canada, Britain and the Pacific* (Official

History of the Canadian Army in the Second World War, Vol. I)(Ottawa, 1955), 34-7, 47, 69-70.

2. Roger Flynn Sarty, "Silent Sentry: A Military and Political History of Canadian Coast Defence 1860-1945," PhD thesis, University of Toronto, 1982, 449-74; Norman Hillmer, "Defence and ideology: The Anglo-Canadian military "alliance" in the 1930s," *International Journal*, 33 (Summer 1978), 588-612, features important material from British archives on the background to and wider context of Canadian rearmament.

3. Joint Staff Committee, "An Appreciation of the defence problems confronting Canada with Recommendations for the Development of the Armed Force," 5 Sept. 1936, HQS 5199B, National Archives of Canada (hereafter NA), RG 24, vol. 2693; Mackenzie to Cabinet, 16 Nov. 1936, file X-4, NA, MG 27 IIIB5, vol. 24.

4. Stephen Harris, "Or There Would be Chaos: The Legacy of Sam Hughes and Military Planning in Canada, 1919-1939," *Military Affairs*, 46 (Oct. 1982), 120-6; see also, *Canadian Brass: The Making of a Professional Army, 1860-1939* (Toronto, 1988), 176-191.

5. Department of National Defence, *Report for the fiscal year ending March 31 1937*, 25-6.

6. Roger Sarty, "Hard Luck Flotilla: The RCN's Atlantic Coast Patrol, 1914-18," in W.A.B. Douglas, ed., *RCN in Transition 1910-1985* (Vancouver, 1988), 103-25.

7. Department of National Defence, *Report for year ending March 31 1937*, 73.

8. William J. McAndrew, "Canadian Defence Planning Between the Wars: The Royal Canadian Air Force Comes of Age," *Aerospace Historian*, 29 (June 1982), 81-9; W.A.B. Douglas, *The Creation of a National Air Force: The Official History of the Royal Canadian Air Force*, Vol. II (University of Toronto Press/Department of National Defence, 1986), pt 1.

9. E.g., Canada, House of Commons, *Debates*, 19 Feb. 1937, 1058.

10. Department of National Defence, *Report for the fiscal year ending March 31 1939*, 12-13, 40.

11. E.g., William Lyon Mackenzie King Diary, 31 July 1936, NA, MG 26 J13; see also House of Commons, *Debates*, 12 Nov. 1940, 55-6.

12. E.g., Hose to minister, 2 March 1925, file 302, NA, RG 25, reel T-1768; Hose, "Memorandum on Naval Policy," 30 July 1926, file 913, NA, MG 26 J4, vol. 124, 91015-34.

13. E.g., "Memorandum on the Present Air Force Requirements of Canadian Militia," circulated by director of military operations and intelligence to district officers commanding, 21 Feb. 1933, HQS 5902 pt. 1, NA, RG 24, vol. 2740; McNaughton to Ellington, "Canadian Air Liaison Letter No.1/1935," 30 Jan. 1935, file 'Air Minister,' NA, MG 30 E133, vol. 100.

14. Ns., "United States applications for privileges to fly aircraft over British Columbian land and coast," 21 July 1936, HQS 5199 pt. 2, NA, RG 24, vol. 2684; General Staff, "Unguarded Alaska?," 5 Feb. 1935, HQC 631-52-1 pt. 1, NA, RG 24,

vol. 2448; Department of State decimal file 811.2342, dockets 421, 424, 426, 432, 470 and 494, US, National Archives and Records Administration (hereafter USNA), RG 59.

15. E.g., King Diary, 5 Aug. 1936, 23 Oct. 1936, both typed and handwritten entries; see also entry for 17 Nov. 1938 and Douglas, 203.

16. *Ibid.*, 196-203; James Eayrs, 92-103.

17. Joint Staff Committee, 22 July 1938, "A Review of Canada's Position with Respect to Defence, July, 1938," HQS 5199-B, NA, RG 24, vol. 2693.

18. Joint Staff Committee, "Emergency Plan for the Defence of The Eastern Coast of Canada," 16 Sept. 1938, HQS 5199-0 pt. 1, NA, RG 24, vol. 2700; Nelles to deputy minister, 30 Sept. 1938, file X-51, NA, MG 27 IIIB5, vol. 32.

19. William J. McAndrew, "From Integration to Separation: The RCAF's Evolution to Independence," *Revue Internationale d'Histoire militaire*, 51 (1982), 131-158.

20. King Diary, 27 Sept. 1938; see also H. Blair Neatby, *William Lyon Mackenzie King*. Vol. III, *1932-1939: The Prism of Unity* (Toronto, 1976), 287-93.

21. Eayrs, 148-52.

22. Holmes to Dixon, 16 Oct. 1938, extract, Public Record Office, Kew, England (hereafter PRO), ADM 116/3802, ff. 79-83.

23. *Ibid.*, 83-4; Stacey, *Arms, Men and Governments*, 72-6; Troup, minute, 12 Jan. 1938, PRO, ADM 1/9488.

24. King Diary, 28 Sept. 1938.

25. Extracts from Holmes to Dixon, 16 Oct. 1938, PRO, ADM 116/3802, ff. 79-83.

26. Meyrick to "My dear Roger," 14 Oct. 1938, PRO, ADM 116/3802, f. 125.

27. King Diary, 16 Oct. 1938.

28. King to Meyrick, 17 Oct. 1938, PRO, ADM 116/3802, f. 126.

29. See PRO, ADM 1/9501, ADM 116/3802; NSS 1018-6-8 and NSS 1018-6-2, NA, RG 24, vol. 3852 and NSS 1048-48-1 pt. 4, *ibid.*, vol. 3971.

30. "Synopsis of Presentations made to the Defence Committee of Council, November 14, 1938," file 667, NA, RG 25 D-1, vol. 818; King Diary, 14 Nov. 1938.

31. King Diary, 7, 16, 21 Dec. 1938; Stacey, *Arms, Men and Governments*, 88-9; Douglas, 202-3.

32. King Diary, 7 and 12 Dec. 1938.

33. Stephens to Mackenzie, 3 Dec. 1938, King to Mackenzie, 22 Dec. 1938, file 165-38, NA, MG 27 IIIB5, vol. 29.

34. Anderson to minister, 19 Dec. 1938, file D-2000, Queen's University Archives, C.G. Power Papers, vol. 67.

35. King Diary, 26-7, 30 Jan. 1939; "Statement showing the ultimate objectives of the Canadian Naval, Military and Air Forces ...," 31 Jan. 1939, file 47, NA, RG 25 D-1, vol. 721.

36. "Objective of the Canadian Naval Service," 17 Jan. 1939, Naval Historical Section file (hereafter NHS) 1650-1 pt. 1, Directorate of History, National Defence Headquarters, Ottawa (hereafter DHist); "Statement Showing the Ultimate Objectives of the Canadian Naval, Military and Air Forces ...," 31 Jan. 1939, file 47, NA, RG 25, G-1, vol. 721; Nelles to minister, 3 Feb. 1939, file 189-31, NA, MG 27 IIIB5, vol. 29.

37. Anderson to minister, 30 Jan. 1939, file 47, NA, RG 25 D-1, vol. 621; Dewar to chief of the general staff, 12 Aug. 1939, DHist 112.1 (D81) is a useful review of action on most items of stores and equipment.

38. "Aircraft Order Situation - 28/2/39," Militia and RCAF estimates book, 1939-40, DHist 75/457.

39. Ns. [Croil?], nd. [Jan. 1939], "Canada's Present Defence Policy," DHist 181.002(D107). The quoted words described the state of the air defences at the time of the Munich Crisis, but the general thrust of the paper is that the aircraft situation had not significantly improved since then, and would not do so for some time to come.

40. Breadner to senior air officer, 17 Jan. 1939, DHist 76/198; Breadner to minister, 26 Jan. 1939, file X-52A, NA, MG 27 IIIB5, vol. 32; Air Council minutes, 31 Jan. 1939, S. 840-108 pt. 1, DHist; Mackenzie to King, 6 Feb. 1939, enclosing "Items of equipment for which authority might be requested...," file 187-3, NA, MG 27 IIIB5, vol. 29.

41. King Diary, 30 Jan. 1939.

42. King Diary, 26 Jan. 1939.

43. King Diary, 27 Jan. 1939.

44. King Diary, 2 March 1939.

45. Croil to minister, 2 Dec. 1938, DHist 74/628, folder A/4; Ns, [Croil?], nd., "Reply to article in Winnipeg Free Press of April 19th, 1939," S.096-105 pt. 1, DHist; Croil to minister, 12 May 1939, Militia and RCAF estimates book 1939-40, DHist 75/457; Air Council minutes, 14 and 21 March 1939, S. 840-108 pt. 1, DHist.

46. Elkins to chief of the general staff, 3 Oct. 1938, HQS 3498 pt. 10, NA, RG 24, vol. 2646.

47. General Staff, "Memorandum on preparation for War (General Staff Branch)," 10 Feb. 1939, HQS 3498 pt. 12, NA, RG 24, vol. 2647.

48. Sarty, "Silent Sentry," 556-63, 572-5.

49. Ashton to minister, 28 Sept. 1938, HQS 3498 pt. 10, NA, RG 24, vol. 2646.

50. Stuart, "The Problems and Requirements of Canadian Defence," 19 Jan. 1939, file B-30, NA, MG 27 IIIB5, vol. 34.

51. King Diary, 23 April 1939.

52. Canada, House of Commons, *Debates*, 26 April 1939, 3262-3, cf. Stuart, "Problems and Requirements," 21-8.

53. Canada, House of Commons, *Debates*, 16 May 1939, 4128-31, also 26 April 1939, 3250-1, 3256-8.

54. Canada, House of Commons, *Debates*, 13 May 1939, 4015-21, 4034-6, 16 May 1939, 4160-5, 18 May 1939, 4269-70.

55. Canada, House of Commons, *Debates*, 3 April 1939, 2554-6, 12 May 1939, 3999-4001, 16 May 1939, 4160-5, 18 May 1939, 4260-8.

56. King Diary, 23 March 1939.

57. Senate of Canada, *Debates*, 20 April 1939, 183; Canada, House of Commons, *Debates*, 20 April 1939, 2995.

58. King Diary, 14 April 1939.

59. Nelles to deputy minister, 16 May 1939, file 386, NA, RG 25 G-1, vol. 1904.

60. Unsigned, undated research note, "Liaison by Visit and Correspondence," which quotes Admiralty file M-00715/39, DHist, NHS 1700-193/96.

61. Rear-Admiral L.W. Murray interview, 1970, pp. 31-2, DHist biog file "L.W. Murray"; Captain E.S. Brand interview, 1967, pp. 15-16, DHist 81/145 pt. 7.

62. Neatby, 316; King Diary, 24-5 Aug. 1939; America and West Indies station war diary, 24 Aug. 1939, PRO, ADM 199/367.

63. On mobilization, see Stacey, *Six Years of War*, ch. 2; Gilbert Norman Tucker, *The Naval Service of Canada: Its Official History:* Vol. II: *Activities on Shore During the Second World War* (Ottawa, 1952), ch. 1; Douglas, 150-1, 373-80, 400-3.

64. King Diary, 1 Sept. 1939.

65. Roger Sarty, "A Structural and Narrative History of Fort McNab, 1888-1960"' (unpublished study, Halifax Defence Complex, Environment Canada, 1989).

66. "Notes for CAS," 12 Sept. 1939, DHist 77/543; "Statement showing the ultimate objectives of the Canadian Naval, Military and Air Forces ...," 31 Jan. 1939, file 47, NA, RG 25 D-1, vol. 721.

67. Admiralty to chief of naval staff Ottawa, commander-in-chief, America and West Indies, signal 2256/8 Sept. 1939, NS 1048-48-1 pt 4., NA, RG 24, vol. 3971; commanding officer HMS *Berwick* to commanding officer Atlantic Coast, 22 Sept. 1939, NSS 8280-HX 1, DHist mfm; Brand to director of naval intelligence, Admiralty, 25 Sept. 1939, NSS 1017-10-22 pt. 1, NA, RG 24, vol. 3841.

68. Skelton, 'Canadian War Policy,' 24 Aug. 1939, file 388 pt 2, NA, RG 25 D-1, vol. 780; see also King Diary, 25 Aug. 1939.

69. Chiefs of Staff Committee, "Canada's National Effort in a Major War," 4 July 1939, DHist 181.006(D276).

70. Printed in John A. Munro, ed., *Documents on Canadian External Relations* (hereafter *DCER*), vol. VI: *1939-1939* (Ottawa, 1972), 1268-75. The first draft, written by the general staff alone, had been submitted by Anderson to the minister, 28 Aug. 1939, and at the latter's request was reviewed by the other services and revised to take account of their roles, but the substance was unchanged (HQS 5199-S pt. 1, DHist). See also General Staff, "The Mobilization of the Mobile Force," 21 Aug. 1939, HQS 3498 pt 22, NA, RG 24, vol. 2648.

71. King Diary, 5 Sept. 1939.

72. *DCER*, 1301-5.

73. King Diary, 7 Sept. 1939.

74. King Diary, 15 Sept. 1939.

75. Chiefs of Staff Committee to minister, 17 Sept. 1939, HQS 5199 pt. 6, NA, RG 24, vol. 2685; Machlachlan and Desrosiers to minister, 18 Sept. 1939, file 53, NA, MG 26 J4, vol. 395, pp. C278350-3; King Diary, 18 Sept. 1939; Ralston to Rogers, 21 Sept. 1939, DHist, NHS 8200 (1939-45) pt. 3.

76. Stacey, *Six Years of War*, 55-72, 191.

77. Croil, "Policy respecting the distribution, war establishments and duties of RCAF Squadrons," 25 Sept. 1939, DHist 77/543.

78. Stacey, *Arms, Men and Governments*, 19.

79. J.L. Granatstein, *Canada's War: The Politics of the Mackenzie King Government 1939-1945* (Toronto, 1975), 46.

80. Stacey, *Arms, Men and Governments*, 24-5; Douglas, *Creation of a National Air Force*, 212-13; Eayrs, 109-112.

81. Douglas, 210.

82. Stacey, *Arms, Men and Governments*, 287, 301-303; F.J. Hatch, *Aerodrome of Democracy: Canada and the British Commonwealth Air Training Plan 1939-1945* (Department of National Defence, Directorate of History Monograph Series No. 1) (Ottawa, 1983), 206; D.J. Goodspeed, ed., *The Armed Forces of Canada 1867-1967: A Century of Achievement* (Ottawa, 1967), 179.

83. E.g., Nelles Diary, 6 Sept. 1939, DHist, Nelles biog file, folder A.

84. Nelles to minister, "Review of the Naval Requirements of Canada and the Existing Situation, 29th September, 1939," DHist, NHS 1650-1 (Policy) pt. 1.

85. *DCER*, 1301-5.

86. Cabinet War Committee minutes, 8 Dec. 1939, NA, MG 26 J4, vol. 423, pp. C302580-5; King Diary, 8 Dec. 1939, 29 Jan. 1940.

87. On warship acquisition, see Tucker, ch. 2.

88. Nelles to minister, "Review of the Naval Requirements ... 29th September 1939," DHist, NHS 1650-1 (Policy) pt. 1; Dreyer to secretary of the Admiralty, 31 Jan. 1940, PRO, ADM 1/10608.

89. Tucker, 33-4.

90. Stedman to chief of the air staff, "The Supply of Aircraft," 27 Sept. 1939, HQS 5199-S pt. 1, Federal Records Centre, Ottawa; K.M. Molson and H.A. Taylor, *Canadian Aircraft since 1909* (Stittsville, Ont., 1982), 124, 439.

91. Air Historical Branch, "The RAF in Maritime War. Vol. I. The Atlantic and Home Waters. The Prelude April 1918 to September 1939," DHist 79/599; Stedman to chief of the air staff, "Report on Air Mission to Washington, D.C.," 3 Sept. 1939, DHist 78/478; "Notes for CAS: Defence Measures Executed to Date," 12 Sept. 1939, DHist 77/543.

92. Molson and Taylor, 203-9; Douglas, chs. 12-16.

93. *Ibid.*; Joseph Schull, *The Far Distant Ships: An Official Account of Canadian Naval Operations in the Second World War* (Ottawa, 1961).

94. See, e.g., Marc Milner, *North Atlantic Run: The Royal Canadian Navy and the Battle for the Convoys* (Toronto, 1985) and , "The Royal Canadian Navy in World War II," in James J. Sadkovich, ed., *Reevaluating Major Naval Combatants of World War II* (New York, 1990), 41-60.

95. Michael L. Hadley and Roger Sarty, *Tin-Pots and Pirate Ships: Canadian Naval Forces and German Sea Raiders 1880-1918* (Montreal and Kingston, 1991); Roger Sarty et Donald M. Schurman, "La Marine Canadienne de 1867 à 1945," *Guerres Mondiales*, 157 (1990), 25-47; Michael J. Whitby, "In Defence of Home Waters: Doctrine and Training in the Canadian Navy during the 1930s," *Mariner's Mirror*, 77 (May 1991), 167-77.

96. King Diary, 19 Jan. 1939.

97. E.g., Croil to minister, 2 Dec. 1938, DHist 74/628, folder A/4; ns, nd, "Reply to article in Winnipeg Free Press of April 19th, 1939," Militia and RCAF estimates book 1939-40, DHist 75/457.

GOODWILL AND PROFIT: MACKENZIE KING AND CANADIAN APPEASEMENT

Angelika Sauer
University of Winnipeg

The growing number of studies on the Western democracies' response to the fascist threat in the 1930s has uncovered that appeasement, once believed to have been a universal and timeless label for a political phenomenon, in fact manifested itself in various shapes and forms. In its metaphysical dimension, appeasement was an attitude and aim common to all democracies. As the simultaneous collapse of the global economy and the international political order began to pose a profound challenge to their liberal-capitalist foundation, the Western democracies reacted by reaffirming the values that constituted their politico-social identity and shaped their perception of the international system. And yet, despite an obvious community of interests, they never managed to find a concerted solution to their problem. For appeasement also existed, as detailed studies of individual countries have shown, in a concrete dimension, as a host of different, nationally-oriented policies that would often override common concerns.

An examination of Canadian appeasement corroborates this pattern. Among Canadian decision-makers, appeasement was an "attitude of mind"[1] that reflected the traditions of liberalism, traditions which had shaped an entire political generation's thinking and perceptions. With the liberal's room to manoeuvre contracting in the 1930s, appeasement became a defensive strategy of external and domestic crisis avoidance in the face of revolutionary political, social and economic change. Translated into foreign policy measures, however, the Canadian response to the fascist challenge, just like its British and American counterparts, often closely resembled a projection of domestic social and economic demands onto the international stage. The Canadian policy of appeasement allowed the two elements, the idealism of the philosophy of goodwill and the pragmatism of the policy of profit, to coexist with a minimum of friction.[2] Yet when efforts to keep the peace in Europe failed, liberal ideology prevailed over narrow national self-interest, providing Canada's key decision-makers with the motivation necessary for the conduct of war. This study suggests, then, that there was an ideological continuity between Canadian appeasement and Canada's war.

The Philosophy of Goodwill

The historiography of Canadian appeasement, evolving from the early work of James Eayrs,[3] focuses alternately on Mackenzie King's support for British policy[4] and his attempts to promote and emulate the American approach to the preservation of peace.[5] The prime minister's direct "contribution" to solving the German problem, his exploits with fellow mystic Adolf Hitler, is quickly dismissed as "private and personal initiatives" of an eccentric individual.[6] Although providing telling insights into King's pivotal role in the conduct of Canadian foreign policy,[7] the version of events that emerges from these accounts fails to explore adequately the structural basis of his actions, ignoring King as the product, rather than the producer, of a certain political culture and its ideological underpinnings.

As a representative of the old, decaying world of lateVictorian liberalism, King reacted to the developments of the 1930s not in a unique or eccentric but in a very typical way. His belief in traditional liberal values and ideas, shared in the Anglo-Saxon democracies by many members of his generation, not only shaped his perception of reality, but also determined the manner in which it would be met. Faced with the combined challenge of economic dislocation, social transformation and totalitarian expansion, King's liberal mind almost automatically produced responses commonly associated with the term appeasement. To the proponent of liberalism, the champion of the philosophy of goodwill, appeasement was not necessarily a specific policy but a way of living.[8] The metaphysical element of Canadian appeasement should therefore be examined in its relationship to the traditions of liberalism.

The most obvious ideological link between Victorian liberalism and appeasement was the value attached to peace itself.[9] Liberals generally regarded a peaceful environment as the necessary condition for people to enjoy their freedom from externally-imposed restrictions. The experience of twentieth century warfare had, if anything, only added to this conviction. A modern war, after all, could not be fought without far-reaching government intervention in the economy and state encroachments on civil liberties.[10] For this reason alone, the preservation of peace constituted the foremost aim of any foreign policy inspired by liberal principles. Basically optimistic in outlook, the Victorian liberal believed that, despite numerous temporary setbacks, the path to peace and progress could ultimately not be blocked. "Just and right never fail to triumph," Mackenzie King wrote in early 1937. Having experienced the Great War as a political nightmare rather than a human tragedy, he managed to conserve a naive confidence, so characteristic of Gladstonian England. Frequent outbursts of hope and even complacency resulted.[11]

The approach to international problems generated by liberal optimism is easily identifiable with appeasement. In the face of a steadily deteriorating world situation, the liberal would not accept the doctrine of inevitable war, and scolded those who did for their "defeatism." Liberals liked to point out that there was no dispute between nations that could not be resolved by peaceful means.[12] This conviction was founded on two interrelated concepts: faith in the goodness and rationality of humanity, and trust in the idea of partnership and harmony in social and international relations. Rationality, the liberal argued, would ultimately subordinate narrow sectional interests to the broader good of the community. Central to this argument was a view of people as responsible individuals rather than members of a collective category, such as class, race, or nation. In fact, collectivist forces such as class consciousness were seen as dangerous enemies of liberalism.[13]

With this catalogue of beliefs, Victorian liberals were ill-equipped to confront the phenomena of twentieth century militarism, collectivism, and crass materialism. Nevertheless, they thought that they had something to offer a world slowly sinking into chaos. King reminded his party in early 1939 "that we were the one Liberal Government in the world today... That never in world's history was the necessity greater for Liberal principles being upheld than it is in the present."[14] He had, as one historian has described it, a genuine, liberal desire to be of service in the search for peace and even saw it as a divine mission to promote goodwill between persons and nations, between races and creeds and classes. In his mind, one peace mission and one friendly word might just be the "dust in the balance" that could save the world from another war.[15]

Goodwill, trust, and the assumption of common interests and rational behaviour strongly influenced the liberal perception of Nazi Germany and the resulting approach to the German problem. The absolute importance attached to the virtue of tolerance carried with it a fundamental willingness to change the status quo to accommodate the demands of revisionist forces within the global community, as grievances of the dissatisfied party were considered legitimate and concessions required. The core of British appeasement of Germany, this political strategy met with wholehearted approval in Canada, where the existing order in Europe was widely considered unjust and in dire need of "recasting."[16] The liberal way of thinking ruled out the possibility that Germany could be aiming at far more than revision of the international system, that the Hitler regime in fact meant to overturn it. The liberal appeaser assumed that, despite their aggressive posturing, Germans merely expressed a desire for justice and an improvement of the social conditions — precisely the goals that liberals themselves pursued in their world.

The liberal mind operated on the assumption that the Nazi dictatorship in Germany was a temporary phenomenon, the unfortunate "product of a society were masses have been neglected."[17] Yet even the masses consisted of inherently good and rational human beings who would strive to rid themselves of the totalitarian regime to establish a liberal democracy. The belief in the democratic instincts of "the good Germans," an integral part of the philosophy of the appeaser, survived even the outbreak of hostilities in Europe. The liberal considered the German people as natural allies of the Western-democratic powers. "Britain may be found fighting with the peoples of Germany who were seeking to destroy their dictators," King had written as early as November 1936. Three years later, Canada's declaration of war on Germany did not necessitate a corresponding change in attitude toward the Germans, as a King memorandum on possible war aims demonstrated. "The basis of all Liberal doctrines is trust in the people. Personally, I am prepared to trust the German people ... provided they are given the right and power freely to express their own wishes and desires.[18]

Much of the appeasement strategy of the Western democracies also rested on the assumption that there were so-called "moderates" in the Fuhrer's entourage, men who had the Gladstonian-liberal sense of responsibility that was said to guide all governing figures. In essence, the appeaser projected his own motivation not only on to the German people but also on to the German leaders.[19] Even Hitler was seen by King as a reformer and a man of peace — a belief the Canadian prime minister found hard to abandon as late as the summer of 1939.[20] By encouraging the alleged "moderates," bolstering their position in Germany with offers that would improve economic conditions in Germany, the appeaser hoped to inject his own ideas, values and options into the political debate in Germany, and to drive a wedge between the German people and the extremist elements of the regime.[21] "[Their] own people [will] come to deal with [the dictators]," Mackenzie King predicted. "Better let freedom assert itself from within as is the natural way."[22]

Appeasement, then, was also an indirect manifestation of the traditional liberal doctrine of non-intervention. The totalitarian nations could be entirely "left alone with their internal problems,"[23] or their people could be induced by fair play, friendly gestures, and positive examples from the outside to take matters into their own hands. The liberal appeaser would reject the argument that the demise of the Nazi regime could also be achieved by cutting Germany off her normal trade relations, thus forcing her by economic means to alter her political and economic system. Characteristically, King believed in the opposite approach of increasing commercial links with a totalitarian state, no matter how distasteful its particular regime or its ideology. In King's opinion, trade was an important message of goodwill, and an expression of "national friendliness."[24]

Enduring this strategy of economic appeasement, King adopted the typical "assumption of classic liberalism that the more extensive the contacts that [took] place between nations, the greater [were] the chances for peace." War, this theory suggested, was unlikely between nations which depended upon one another for vital commodities. Global economic integration, therefore, was regarded as a vital part of liberal international politics.[25] But Hitler's assault on all vestiges of "decadent" liberalism within Germany soon found its counterpart in similar attacks on liberal principles in international affairs. When Nazi doctrines of the sovereign nation state and its autarkic economy led to a successful reorganization of German trade on a strictly bilateral barter basis,[26] the liberal notion of multilateral interdependence no longer stood unchallenged.

Liberalism on the Defensive

The appeaser reacted to this new situation by clinging to the notion of Germany's reintegration into the political and economic system of the Western world.[27] At the same time, however, the proponents of appeasement felt a certain sense of uneasiness, lest liberal democracy and free enterprise capitalism, already weakened by the ravages of the Depression, might somehow not be equal to the political and economic challenge posed by the Third Reich. Most Western politicians observed Hitler's quick reduction of German unemployment and Schacht's ingenious trade offensive with considerable apprehension. Unable to ignore the widespread popular feeling, lingering in their own countries, that liberal capitalism had reached its limits, they suspected that "fascist ideas at least in economics would become irresistible." The appeal of state intervention in the economy had to be considerable to those who did not recognize the dangers of regimentation and control.[28]

To liberal believers in free enterprise, of course, a planned economy was an absolute anathema, but they already found themselves on the defensive. "The world situation has headed ... countries ... more and more in the direction of the extension of State authority and enterprise," King complained, "and I am afraid that Canada will not be able to resist the pressure of the tide." He also noted that popular dissatisfaction with the sluggish response of the traditional political apparatus to the economic crisis easily translated into criticism of the parliamentary democratic system itself. Discontented parties, King noted, increasingly emphasized strong leaders and fast solutions, a distinctly "European" way of handling problems.[29]

Traditional values and the traditional way of thinking were in danger of being swept away by a huge and uncontrollable wave of social, political, and economic change. Appeasement, both external and domestic, became the liberal's response to this danger, a response designed to preserve a place for liberal orthodoxy in a rapidly transforming world. The appeasers had to discredit revolutionary solutions to the crisis while, at the same time, creating enough breathing space for themselves to respond to the problems with reforms and compromise. "The most we can do," King observed with a dose of resignation, "is to hope to go only sufficiently far ... as to prevent the power of Government passing to those who would go much farther."[30]

The interrelationship between appeasement as a defensive strategy and the crisis of liberalism can be illustrated by the response to the economic problems of the 1930s. The liberal recipe to stimulate domestic economic recovery was a combination of federal retrenchment, reliance on private enterprise, and an expansion of international trade. The latter, to be achieved by removing artificial barriers such as protective tariffs from the established channels of trade, assumed a dual function in the second half of the decade. Lessening international tensions by forging links between nations, freer trade would also lead to an expansion of the global volume of trade, thereby triggering domestic recovery. This, in turn, would create room for domestic social and economic reforms.[31] The call for a more liberal trading system therefore was an expression of hope that the economic problems of the 1930s could be solved without fundamental and far-reaching structural adjustments of the national economy.

Finding constructive ways of dealing with domestic problems within the framework of traditional liberalism was not an easy task for any Western leader. In Canada, the King government, reluctant to admit the structural nature of the crisis and adamant in its insistence on moral rather than institutional change, refused to abandon its well-worn policy of balanced budgets, "honest money," and window-dressing emergency relief projects until 1938.[32] For the countless unemployed of Canada's cities and the impoverished grain farmer in the Prairies, however, the liberal work ethic with its emphasis on individual responsibility for employment, self-help, and voluntarism had lost its appeal. With Keynesian thinking infiltrating the higher ranks of the civil service, and even King's Cabinet, the liberal economic orthodoxy was under siege and eventually yielded, ever so slightly, to the pressures of change.[33] To Mackenzie King, whose motivation was fear of social unrest, the acceptance of cautious anti-cyclical fiscal measures was a typical liberal compromise, designed to accommodate as many social groups as possible. Yet, by combining his measures of social reform with a continued focus on private investment and international trade, he also managed to keep the scope narrow and the impact of his social appeasement strategy to a minimum.[34]

The preservation of peace was a vital precondition for the success of King's strategy of limited social reform for the sake of social appeasement. First of all, a peaceful global environment was necessary for the expansion of the volume of international trade. The second pillar of King's strategy, an increase in private investment to curb the need for public expenditure, required the restoration of confidence among business circles — an unlikely development unless global political tensions eased and the government managed to check inflationary tendencies at home. To the orthodox liberal, Mackenzie King, inflation was "a threat to the economic and social fabric ... [and] to national stability."[35]

His deeply-entrenched fear of the socially disruptive consequences of inflation has to be borne in mind to explain the absence of any real alternative to the policy of appeasement in the liberal's mode of thinking. Any other policy, especially one aiming at the containment of Germany by a preponderance of military power against her, would have required a drastic program of rearmament. Such a program, it was assumed, would fully absorb the weak economic recovery and trigger an inflationary spiral. A strict management of the country's limited resources would become necessary, and the dreaded elements of national planning would infiltrate the Canadian system on a wide scale. Most important, forced rearmament would impose serious financial constraints, rendering social spending impossible. Or, if social reforms and armament programs were implemented at the same time, Canada would face a skyrocketing federal deficit.[36]

For all these reasons, it was hoped to keep rearmament limited to a minimum acceptable to the majority of society. Combined with a traditional dislike of militarism, and reluctance to accept force as an extension of diplomacy, financial constraints circumscribed the liberal's response to Nazi expansionism.[37] Mackenzie King was painfully aware that any major increase in government spending on rearmament was likely to provoke "political and social unrest," an assumption well confirmed by the spirited debate surrounding the 1937 defence estimates. Although public acceptance of the necessity of higher spending gradually increased as the international situation deteriorated, King's reluctance to channel already sparse resources into the "unproductive" field of armaments did not diminish. Even on the day the Nazis occupied Prague, he openly deplored high expenditures on armaments, blaming the deficit in the 1939 federal budget on international tensions.[38]

In every respect, then, appeasement was the logical response that the liberal mind provided to the various challenges of the 1930s. External and domestic threats to the survival of liberalism merged into one, calling for a comprehensive strategy of crisis avoidance. A natural product of Canada's political culture and the beliefs of her decision-making elite,[39] appeasement seemed to offer liberal alternatives to revolutionary change. The broader philosophy surrounding this approach to world problems was shared in one form or another by most Western democratic leaders. Translated into concrete foreign policy, however, appeasement made its appearance in various distinctly national versions. A closer examination of the material foundation of the Canadian version may explain why this was the case.

The Policy of Profit

As a second set of factors in the analysis of appeasement, the concept of national self-interest addresses the issue of the social and economic bases of Canadian foreign policy. Indisputably valuable when applied to British and American policies, this approach has to be somewhat qualified in the Canadian context where the prevalence of traditional liberal values in governing circles worked against the emergence of a policy of self-interest. The prime minister frequently expressed his disapproval of what he alternately called the "materialistic," "scientific," or "academic" position, stubbornly insisting that Canadian foreign policy rested on a moral rather than a power political base.[40] The structure of the Canadian political system of the 1930s continued to be characterized by a relative separation of political and economic spheres. Economic interest groups, for example, had not yet gained the same strength and influence on government foreign policy as their counterparts in other countries.[41]

Nevertheless, advocates of a national foreign policy could be found not only among academics and critics on the left[42] but also among high-ranking civil servants, with O.D. Skelton of the Department of External Affairs as the most powerful among them. These advocates did not necessarily see their liberalism compromised by their regard for material conditions. Canada's situation in the world, they argued, was first and foremost defined by her status as a small power. Controlling only a fragment of the world's resources, the country could not afford great power luxuries, such as "prestige" or "knight errantry." Instead, Canada's foreign policy should be determined on the basis of her real power, her geographic position, and her national resources.[43] The government's task was to protect its people's vital concerns, even when those concerns appeared, if not trivial, certainly "less ubiquitous and mystical" than those of the great powers. Canada's foreign policy should always enable the country "to derive from its inter-national relations the maximum benefits."[44]

Mackenzie King could not dispute the logic of this argument. He was aware that, in the aftermath of the Great Depression, Canadians were preoccupied with the state of the national economy. Basically isolationist in their general attitude, their day-to-day interest in the outside world was restricted to questions of trade, tariffs and markets.[45] The government was expected to develop an approach to foreign affairs that would enhance the country's chances to grow and prosper. Canadian prosperity, it was believed, depended primarily on the preservation of existing markets and the opening up of new ones for Canadian exports. This formed part of the rationale for a Canadian policy of appeasement.

Peace and prosperity were inextricably linked not only in liberal ideology, as mentioned earlier, but also in very practical terms. As a contemporary study of Canadian foreign policy put it, "Despite the possibility of certain groups in Canada profiting from demands incident to war or the fear of war, there can be no doubt that in the long run Canada has a vested interest in the promotion of peace and the removal of fear from international society."[46] The economic lesson learned from the Great War suggested that an armed conflict could only produce short-term prosperity, a distorted boom that would be followed by another severe slump. The only group that could possibly benefit from war, the munitions industry, was kept under close public and political scrutiny. Nobody wanted the "merchants of death" to gain at the expense of the rest of the country.[47]

Agreement began and ended with this consensus on the vital importance of peace and international trade for Canada's national economy. To secure these ends, diverse regional and sectional interests demanded a host of often contradictory policies. The prime minister, normally remarkably insensitive to social and economic problems as such, was often forced to pay attention when these issues translated into a political problem, by threatening to split the Cabinet or the Liberal Party.[48] Identifying the survival of liberalism with keeping his party in power, King made the protection of the precarious balance of diverse interests his mission, his *raison d'être*. In the process, he allowed domestic economic problems to spill over into Canada's dealings with the world.

Most serious among the economic problems of the late 1930s was the rift that the Depression had caused between Eastern and Western Canada. Western Canada's potential for disrupting social peace became the prime minister's biggest ongoing worry, often eclipsing the political issue of Québec in importance. Solving the problems of a wheat-based economy was accepted as the core of Canada's foreign economic policy, but it seemed impossible to agree on the best way to go about it. In the Liberal caucus and in Cabinet, Western representatives and their demands for unilateral tariff reduction and price fixing for wheat were pitched against the interests of Central Canada.[49] This dichotomy found its way into a new and distinctly Canadian approach to what was commonly called "economic appeasement," or "economic disarmament."

Economic appeasement was an amorphous concept with widespread popular appeal all over the Western world. In the United States, Roosevelt's secretary of state, Cordell Hull, incessantly preached about the harmful effects of economic nationalism and the importance of trade liberalization, all under the heading of economic disarmament. The British government promoted closer bilateral trade with Nazi Germany, also claiming economic appeasement as its motive. The fundamental difference between the multilateral free trade perspective of the Americans and the bilateral "economic carrot" approach of the British remained unreconciled.[50] However, both approaches seemed to offer distinct advantages to different sections of Canada where the ideal of economic appeasement enjoyed non-partisan support.[51] The Canadian government's response was simply to fold the two elements, contradictory though they were, into the mix. The result, a distinctly national policy that sought the best possible international conditions for Canada's economy, worked remarkably well. It was here more than anywhere else that Canadian appeasement became a policy of profit.

The first element of Canadian economic appeasement stemmed from her direct trading relationship with Nazi Germany. Germany's value to Canada lay mainly in her function as an alternative market for wheat. In the 1920s, Britain, acting as the commodity capital and link between industrial Europe and the Empire-Commonwealth, had guaranteed a secure market and high prices for the Canadian staple, but the collapse of commodity prices and the emergence of European economic nationalism had badly damaged this trading pattern.[52] By the mid-1930s, Canadian trade experts agreed that there were two basic alternatives to solving the country's wheat marketing problem: the government would either have to find new markets for Canada's surplus wheat on the European Continent, or become involved with such far-reaching measures as price fixing and acreage restrictions. In this situation, Germany, once a leading customer of Canadian wheat and now anxious to bypass Britain in her dealings with the dominions, improved the odds of the first alternative.[53]

According to Canadian Wheat Board estimates, Germany provided a market for ten to twenty million bushels of Canadian wheat per annum.[54] W.D. Euler, minister of trade and commerce and Cabinet's most outspoken opponent of price fixing, thought this an important enough quantity to justify a special effort. Despite objections emanating from the Department of External Affairs, he vigorously pursued a special Trade and Payments Agreement with Germany, which was concluded in November 1936.[55] By balancing German-Canadian trade on a strictly bilateral basis as well as by agreeing in principle to value the Reichsmark at a fixed rate for customs purposes, the accord in effect represented not only Canadian acquiescence in, but also a positive sanctioning of, Nazi trading methods and currency manipulation. Not unlike its British counterpart, the Canadian-German trade agreement thus violated the doctrine of multilateral trade liberalization, the program of economic disarmament that the King government publicly supported. Yet it fulfilled its immediate purpose: sales of Canadian wheat to Germany increased substantially as did the general volume of trade between the two countries. Nazi Germany became Canada's fifth largest customer by the end of 1938; prairie wheat continued to feed Germans until the outbreak of the war.[56]

More substantial benefits accrued to Canada by jumping on the bandwagon of Cordell Hull's program of economic appeasement. The Canadian prime minister and the American secretary of state believed in the same broad principles, although both never lost sight of their respective country's needs. To King, who had to deal with Western Canadian calls for unilateral tariff reduction on manufactured goods as well as the demand of Central Canadian industries to be compensated for any loss of tariff protection with new markets, the extension of the 1935 trade agreement with the United States was urgent business. Yet the Americans firmly declined to reopen negotiations on the grounds that they first had to conclude a trade treaty with an industrial country, such as Great Britain.[57]

At this point Mackenzie King, delightfully aware of Canada's nuisance value in Anglo-American negotiations, began to campaign enthusiastically for a multilateral economic appeasement of the European situation.[58] Knowing full well that Hull's crusade aimed first and foremost at Anglo-American economic rapprochement, and that the British government could not negotiate unless released from some of its trading commitments to Canada, the King government secured the chance to reach a new and profitable agreement with the United States. The trade deal of November 1938 lowered tariffs on American imports, which delighted Western Canada; it also opened the American market further, thereby pleasing Central Canadian manufacturers. As in the case of the German-Canadian trade agreement, a successful Canadian policy of economic appeasement had grown out of the country's economic structure.[59]

In Defence of Liberalism

The country's socio-economic system, which could provide the basis for a national policy, also determined the allocation of resources to functions such as the conduct of external affairs or national defence. The limitations of the machinery for promoting the country's interest abroad hinted at certain institutional limitations which also made appeasement a rational choice of policy.[60] The Canadian foreign service was still in its infancy; to a large extent, the dominion depended on Britain for information about the world situation.[61] In Ottawa, a small number of highly qualified and highly intelligent but sadly overworked civil servants had to cope with a large array of both domestic and external matters. In Skelton's words, Canada had no "surplus brains" to spare to run the world — hence her natural preference for a low-key approach that focused on the essentials of peace and prosperity. The fact that the Department of Finance, for example, was so wrapped up in the domestic issues of the day that they could not and did not develop any contingency plans for war suggests that a country with Canada's limited bureaucratic machinery was best served by staying out of conflicts.[62]

This argument could be made even more convincingly when considering Canada's national defences. In this area, the King government had to deal with the consequences of years of financial stringency, during which the country's armed forces had slipped into a state of obsolescence and complete inadequacy.[63] With the international power constellation changing from mid-decade onwards, the field of national security was in urgent need of redefinition. Appeasement, with the necessary component of deterrence, was the natural choice for a country with limited resources. As the prime minister confided to his dairy: "It is going to be extremely difficult to do anything effective without a cost which this country cannot bear. We have been wise in placing our reliance on policies which make for peace."[64]

The King government based the planning of future national security provisions not only on political considerations but also on strategic realities. The political situation required that any increase in the country's spending on armaments was done gradually and with an emphasis on home defence.[65] This direction in Canadian military planning, however, also took into account that Britain herself had redefined her security policy in Europe, and had withdrawn into a position of limited liability, eliminating the option of defending her European interests by sending an expeditionary force to the Continent. Therefore Canadian strategists, although not entirely discarding the possibility of a "call for participation overseas by Canadian armed forces" in the event of a European conflict, emphasized coastal defence, the establishment of an aircraft industry, and the organization of Canada's overall industrial capacity as prime factors in the development of a national defence program.[66] In January 1937, the prime minister promised the Liberal caucus that Canada's rearmament program would not include preparations for an expeditionary force. Thus, limited resources would not be wasted on expensive equipment for a large army.

Thus, both financial constraints and strategic considerations supported the government's program of home defence. That it was also the safest course politically was, of course, an additional bonus. Mackenzie King was determined not to have the question of an expeditionary force, fraught with memories of social conflict and national disunity, rear its ugly head. Throughout 1937, he defended his position against comments made by some of Britain's incurable imperialists who still believed, in Skelton's words, that "Canadians were prepared ... to rush in tens of thousands to fight Europe's battles." Militia estimates were cut even further in early 1938 to find the money to purchase two destroyers. In Cabinet, the prime minister emphasized that destroyers had a stronger deterrent effect on aggressor nations. A similar argument had been used in the British Cabinet a few weeks earlier to justify the decision not to equip a large army for service on the Continent until Britain's most effective deterrents, air and sea defences,were firmly in place. In both cases, security policy, severely circumscribed by financial constraints, was defined not as preparation for a possible war but as a means to prevent it. Up until early 1939, then, Canadian and British rearmament policies were, paradoxically, an integral part of appeasement.[67]

For Canada, this particular form of "armament for peace" was also the only acceptable program. The government's tacit, and at times open, support for Neville Chamberlain's European policy rested on the firm assumption that any of his measures to settle the issues would stop short of sending an army to the Continent. Canadian politicians firmly believed that, even if the conflict with Germany came to a head, Britain would not dispatch an expeditionary force herself, and would not therefore expect the dominions to send troops either. The dominions would be asked to look after their own defences, and they would supply munitions and provide a few hundred pilots.[68] This reasoning still prevailed in late January 1939. Mackenzie King found his Cabinet entirely in agreement "that we would not countenance any expeditionary force." King then reassured his colleagues that Britain "won't want our people over there, only those who may volunteer for the air force."[69]

The situation changed dramatically in the spring of 1939 when British security policy underwent a revolutionary turnabout. Following a general shift in the public mood, the British government committed what was called a "field force" to the defence of France, the Low Countries, and Switzerland. This drastic reversal of strategy was followed by the introduction of conscription, and in late March by a unilateral guarantee of Poland's integrity and independence. While British preparation for a European war superseded appeasement and deterrence in a hasty and ill-conceived manner, the direction of the new policy, if not its implementation, could at least be justified on the grounds of British national interests. In Canada reasons for a policy reversal were harder to come by. The "sweeping... momentous... [and] sudden" change of British policy horrified the advocates of a Canadian foreign policy based on national interest.[70]

O.D. Skelton, King's top foreign policy advisor, predicted that the British commitment to sending a "field force" to the Continent was likely to increase pressure for a Canadian expeditionary force as well.[71] Highly critical of he British move, he was aghast that the guarantee to Poland, an area beyond the traditional British sphere of interest, had been given without securing the promise of Soviet cooperation. His External Affairs colleague, Loring Christie, added that the new policy of firmness was beyond Britain's actual capacity. "To challenge Germany in her strongest and in Britain's weakest point ... is another Charge of the Light Brigade ... The fact is that the advocates of the New Policy have overestimated the power and prestige of Britain in the present-day world ... They have consequently extended their forces and their diplomacy too thin." Both he and Skelton argued in favour of upholding the Canadian government's home defence program and protecting it from the consequences of Britain's blunders.[72]

As the proponent of liberalism, who was not even half converted to the notion of a realistic power political base for Canadian diplomacy, the prime minister had to wrestle with a different kind of problem. Critical of the British guarantee system, he "felt terribly sorry for the British Government in his situation." But he also realized that "the whole cause lacked the steadiness which it should have." A majority of Canadians, he told the British high commissioner, would not want to go to war on account of Poland or Roumania, countries not known for their liberal and democratic record. Moreover, he feared that Hitler would be tremendously antagonized and alienated by what must seem to him the "encirclement of Germany."[73] Above all, however, King worried about the broader moral foundations of the new course. He began to wonder how the values and concepts that had inspired his earlier support for appeasement and deterrence could survive in a conflict between Britain and Germany. The war had to be justified by a higher moral cause to win King's support.

In his appalling dilemma King sensed the limits of liberalism and his own philosophy of goodwill. In his work as industrial conciliator, he had learnt that liberal ends could not always be upheld by liberal means. Now Mackenzie King struggled to come to grips with the use of force in international relations. During the Czech crisis in September 1938, he had written: "We must remember that peace is an end; not a means to an end. The means to the end is upholding the right, making a moral order prevail in this world."[74] In the late days of the summer of 1939, the aging prime minister realized that the time had come to defend the higher moral order in the world, one based on the liberal principles of conciliation and reason, against the brutal attacks of an immoral power. Disputes would be solved, he explained to the German consul general, and there would ultimately be a just settlement; but, he added as an afterthought, a "just settlement" no longer meant a "peaceable settlement."[75]

Thus, the outbreak of the war witnessed the transformation of the liberal appeaser into the liberal warrior. Yet the prime minister knew that solving his personal dilemma was not enough. A great many Canadians would rush to war not for higher purposes but simply following the call of blood. After two decades of halting and often painful steps toward nationhood, this was no longer tolerable. At the other end of the spectrum, the advocates of national self-interest could not, and would not, provide a rationale for participation, as even the wildest propagandist was unable to produce a credible scenario of Nazi hordes threatening Canadian shores[76] The ideals of liberalism had to come to the rescue, where the *realpolitik* of self-interest could not provide a unifying cause. The Commonwealth was transformed in official Canadian terminology from an association of free and diverse nations into a higher agency for right, freedom, justice, and goodwill. With this romantic-liberal imagery, any notion of a separate course for Canada was nipped in the bud. Where appeasement had brought together liberal ideals and the concept of self-interest, and had allowed them to merge into a policy that was both rationally acceptable and emotionally appealing, the European conflict re-opened the schism.

What happened in the Canadian House of Commons in early September 1939, therefore, should be described as the last triumph not only of sentimental, colonial ties but also of Victorian liberalism over the modern notion of national interest. Skelton, in one of the most bitter and scathing memoranda of his career, deplored as the first casualty of the war "Canada's claim to independent control of her destinies." Britain had led the "stampede over the edge" and Canada would "trot behind, blindly and dumbly, to chaos."[77] To the scholar-civil servant, who based his thinking on tangible factors and rational logic, the sudden surge of emotions and old loyalties was as incomprehensible as it was inexcusable. To Mackenzie King, no matter how much he despised and dreaded war, it was salvation. Only a strong rush of feelings, an irresistible urge to defend liberty and democracy, could overcome his desire to tolerate the intolerable, and to reach a compromise with the uncompromisable. Facing the twentieth century challenge of fascist expansion, the young Canadian nation conjured up the past and ventured out in defence of liberalism.

NOTES

1. The term is Martin Gilbert's in *The Roots of Appeasement* (London, 1966), 3. The author is indebted to Greg Donaghy, John English, and H. Blair Neatby for their valuable comments on this paper. Special thanks to Norman Hillmer for his unflagging support and friendship.

2. Professors R.D. Cuff and J.L. Granatstein have identified this tension between ideals and pragmatic self-interest as a characteristic theme of Canadian foreign policy in the postwar era. See "Canada and the Marshall Plan, June - December 1947," Canadian Historical Association, *Historical Papers* (1977).

3. James Eayrs, *In Defence of Canada: Appeasement and Rearmament* (Toronto, 1965).

4. Reinhard Meyers, "Kanada und die britische Appeasement Politik," *Zeitschrift der Gesellschaft für Kanada Studien*, 2 (1982); and Rainer Tamchina, "In Search of Common Causes: The Imperial Conference of 1937," *Journal of Imperial and Commonwealth History*, I (October 1972).

5. Norman Hillmer, "The Pursuit of Peace: Mackenzie King and the 1937 Imperial Conference," in J.O. Stubbs and John English, eds., *Mackenzie King: Widening the Debate* (Toronto, 1978).

6. C.P. Stacey, "The Divine Mission: Mackenzie King and Hitler," *Canadian Historical Review*, LXI (December 1980), 503.

7. For example, J.L. Granatstein and Robert Bothwell, "'A Self-Evident National Duty': Canadian Foreign Policy, 1935-1939," *Journal of Imperial and Commonwealth History*, III (January 1975).

8. On the influence of a national political culture on foreign policy and the application of liberal principles to the governance of Canadian policy, see Denis Stairs, "The Political Culture of Canadian Foreign Policy," *Canadian Journal of Political Science*, XV (December 1982).

9. For a catalogue of Victorian liberal beliefs and convictions, see Ian Bradley, *The Optimists: Themes and Personalities in Victorian Liberalism* (London, 1980), and Michael Bentley, *The Liberal Mind 1914-1929* (Cambridge, 1977); for liberal principles in foreign policy, see George L. Bernstein, *Liberalism and Liberal Politics in Edwardian England* (London, 1986), esp. 173f.

10. See Frank Underhill, "The Outline of a National Foreign Policy," in Violet Anderson, ed., *World Currents and Canada's Course* (Toronto, 1937), 130-8. A self-professed American liberal, John Foster Dulles, told a gathering of Canadian and American experts that "[i]f we had a war, we would all become completely totalitarian." A. Corey, R. Trotter and W. McLaren, eds., *Proceedings of the Conference on Canadian-American Affairs*, [hereafter *Proceedings*], June 19 - June 22, 1939 at St. Lawrence University, N.Y., 98. The Canadian Prime Minister also associated war with the potential destruction of domestic liberties. See his memorandum on Canadian war aims, 2 November 1939, in Eayrs, 232-6.

11. National Archives of Canada (hereafter NA), William Lyon Mackenzie King Papers, MG 26 J13 [hereafter King Diary], 6 January 1937. Despite King's

personal fears and suspicions, which occasionally got the better of him, his combination of liberal and Christian beliefs allowed him to be optimistic about the prospects of global peace when the winds of war were already blowing. King Diary, 22 August, 29 August, 31 August, and 1 September 1939.

12. Canada, House of Commons, *Debates*, 30 March 1939; King Diary, 21 July 1939: "Without [conciliation], war would be inevitable; with [conciliation], it can be avoided."

13. H. Blair Neatby, "The Political Ideas of William Lyon Mackenzie King," in Marcel Hamelin, ed., *The Political Ideas of the Prime Ministers of Canada* (Ottawa, 1969); for King's attitude toward socialism and his idea of social partnership, see H. Blair Neatby, *William Lyon Mackenzie King, Vol. III, 1932-1939: The Prism of Unity* (Toronto, 1976), ch. 2.

14. King Diary, 18 January 1939. King conveniently ignored the difference between "Liberal" and "liberal."

15. Hillmer, "Pursuit of Peace," 151; King Diary, 31 December 1937, 20-21 May 1938.

16. King Diary, 2 January 1937.

17. *Ibid.*, 11 September 1938.

18. *Ibid.*, 3 November 1936; King memorandum on war aims, 2 November 1939, Eayrs, appendix, document 4, 232-6. Also, Robert Keyserlingk, "The Canadian Government's Attitude Towards Germans and German Canadians in World War II," *Canadian Ethnic Studies*, XVI (1984).

19. C.A. Macdonald, "Economic Appeasement and the German Moderates, 1937-1939," *Past and Present*, 56 (August 1972); for an example of this attitude in official circles in the United States, see Patrick J. Hearden, *Roosevelt Confronts Hitler: America's Entry into World War II* (DeKalb, Ill., 1987), 91, 96; for the characteristics of "governing men," see Bradley, 79 and Robert Kelley, *The Transatlantic Persuasion: The Liberal-Democratic Mind in the Age of Gladstone* (New York, 1969).

20. King Diary, 29 June to 1 July, 1937 and 21 August 1939. Robert Keyserlingk, "Mackenzie King's Spiritualism and his View of Hitler in 1939," *Journal of Canadian Studies*, XX (March 1986).

21. King Diary, 26 August 1939; for the same thinking in Britain, see Gustav Schmidt, "The Domestic Background to British Appeasement Policy," in W.J. Mommsen and L. Kettenacker, eds., *The Fascist Challenge and the Policy of Appeasement* (London, 1983).

22. King Diary, 11 March 1938.

23. *Ibid.*, 7 April 1939.

24. For the former approach to economic appeasement favoured by the United States, see Jesse Stiller, *George S. Messersmith: Diplomat of Democracy* (Chapel Hill, North Carolina, 1987) and Hans-Jurgen Schröder, "Economic Appeasement. Britische und amerikanische Deutschlandpolitik vor dem Zweiten Weltkrieg,"

Vierteljahresheft fur Zeitgeschichte, XXX (January 1982). For the latter, see King Diary, 1 September 1936, cited in Norman Hillmer, "Canada and the 'Godless Country,' 1930-1939," in David Davies, ed., *Canada and the Soviet Experience* (Toronto and Waterloo, n.d.), 65, and memorandum, "Re Ideological Crusading," (probably Loring Christie), 4 April 1938, NA, Records of the Department of External Affairs, RG25 D1, vol. 715, file 4, pt. 1-5: "So long as other states, whether called communist or fascist or what not, launch no attack on us we intend to preserve correct relations with them, and we do not intend to discourage between their people and ours the intercourse and trading which is the natural impulse of human beings."

25. John L. Gaddis, *The Long Peace: Inquiries into the History of the Cold War* (Oxford and New York, 1987), 224. Gaddis points out that this theory has been proven wrong by considerable historical evidence; it nevertheless continues to exist in liberal thinking which proves its tremendous psychological appeal.

26. See Detlef Junker, *Der unteilbare Weltmarkt: Das ökonomische Interesse in der Aussenpolitik der USA 1933-1941* (Stuttgart, 1975), esp. 94-5, and David Kaiser, *Economic Diplomacy and the Origins of the Second World War: Germany, Britain, France, and Eastern Europe, 1930-1939* (Princeton, 1980), chs. 3 and 4.

27. British Foreign Secretary Anthony Eden, for example, told delegates at the 1937 Imperial Conference that it was "of urgent importance to restore Germany to her normal place in the Western European system." Quoted in Bernd J. Wendt, "Economic Appeasement: Das Gewicht einer Krisenstrategie," in Karl Rohe, ed., *Die Westmächte und das Dritte Reich 1933-1939* (Paderborn, 1982), 70.

28. *Proceedings*, 44-55, 128. A similar concern was expressed by the American ambassador in London, Joseph Kennedy, who, considering ways to counter the German trade offensive in Latin America, wrote in March 1939: "To fight totalitarianism we would have to adopt totalitarian methods." See Junker, 210-13. For discontent in Canada, see Robert Bothwell, Ian Drummond and John English, *Canada 1900-1945* (Toronto, 1987), ch. 16.

29. King Diary, 1 April 1938, 8 March 1939.

30. *Ibid.*, 1 April 1938; the phrase 'crisis avoidance strategy' is used by German historian Gustav Schmidt in his works on British appeasement.

31. *Proceedings*, esp. 19-43. Also, Neatby, *Prism of Unity*, 126, 153.

32. James Struthers, *No Fault of Their Own: Unemployment and the Canadian Welfare State 1914-1941* (Toronto, 1983), 139-40.

33. Neatby, *Prism of Unity*, 249-57; see also Robert Bryce, *Maturing in Hard Times: Canada's Department of Finance Through the Great Depression* (Kingston and Montreal, 1986), 60, 116-9.

34. A.E. Safarian, *The Canadian Economy in the Great Depression* (Toronto, 1970), 229-41; for King's fear of social unrest, multiplied by such events as the occupation of the Vancouver Post Office in May 1938, see Struthers, 188-93.

35. Neatby, *Prism of Unity*, 31.

36. For similar considerations during the early phase of the Cold War, see C.P. Stacey, *Canada and the Age of Conflict, vol. 2: 1921- 1948: The Mackenzie King Era* (Toronto, 1981), 397. On the same type of discussion in Great Britain, see G.C. Peyden, "Keynes, the Economics of Rearmament and Appeasement," in Mommsen and Kettenacker, and Gustav Schmidt, *The Politics and Economics of Appeasement: British Foreign Policy in the 1930s* (New York, 1986). American liberals, as well, feared the adverse effect of military spending on social reforms and therefore often advocated a policy of isolationism. See Waldo Heinrichs, *Threshold of War: Franklin D. Roosevelt and American Entry Into World War II* (New York, 1988), 7.

37. For King's stereotypical view of militarism, see his misinterpretation of events in Germany in February 1938. King Diary, 6 February 1938. For his views on diplomacy and force, *ibid.*, 30 September 1936, 22 October 1937.

38. *Ibid.*, 15 March 1939 and King to Canon Heeney, 20 November 1936, quoted in Eayrs, 140. See also Neatby, *Prism of Unity*, 189-90.

39. William Christian and Colin Campbell, *Political Parties and Ideologies in Canada: Liberals, Conservatives, Socialists, Nationalists* (Toronto, 1983), 6. The authors argue that all three major parties shared their belief in liberal values. This assumption, however, has to be questioned in the case of the CCF. See Greg Donaghy, "The Rise and Fall of International Socialism in the Cooperative Commonwealth Federation, 1933-1949," M.A. research essay, Carleton University, 1989.

40. See, for example, King Diary, 26 December 1936, 12 September 1938, 27 January 1939. For the social and economic bases of British and American appeasement, consult the works of the German historians Wendt, Schmidt, and Schroder.

41. The influence of the Canadian Manufacturers Association as a tariff lobby group, for example, declined just when the Federation of British Industries experienced a powerful revival. S.D. Clark, "The Canadian Manufacturers' Association and the Tariff," *Canadian Journal of Economics and Political Science*, V (February 1939), and R.F. Holland, "The Federation of British Industries and the International Economy, 1929-1939," *Economic History Review*, XXIV (May 1981).

42. Underhill, "The Outline of a National Foreign Policy," and K.W. Taylor, "The Economic Bases of Canadian Policy," in Anderson, *World Currents*; A.R.M. Lower, *Proceedings*, 106-22; F.R. Scott, *Canada Today* (Toronto, 1938).

43. O.D. Skelton, "Central European Situation," 11 September 1938, Records of the Department of External Affairs, RG25 D1, vol. 724, file 66, and vol. 726, file 74; King Diary, 12 September 1938; Loring Christie, "Pending National Defence and External Affairs Debates," 28 March 1938, RG25 D1, vol. 715, file 4, pt. 1-5. The term "knight errantry," used by Mackenzie King in the House of Commons, clearly comes from Skelton.

44. O.D. Skelton to L. Christie, 5 April 1938, Records of the Department of External Affairs, RG25, D1, vol. 715, file 4, pt. 1-5; Skelton to Vincent Massey, 14 March 1939, in John A. Munro, ed., *Documents on Canadian External Relations* (hereafter *DCER*), vol. VI: *1936-1939*, no. 930, 1138-41.

45. Bothwell *et al.*, 295.

46. R.A. MacKay and E.B. Rogers, *Canada Looks Abroad* (Toronto, 1938), 37.

47. O.D. Skelton memorandum, 29 March 1937, quoted in Eayrs, 117; see also J.T. Shotwell, *Proceedings*, 231-32, and J.C. Kirkwood, "The War and Business," *Business Quarterly*, VII (Fall 1939).

48. For some examples, see Neatby, *Prism of Unity*, 256-7, 308.

49. King Diary, 16 March 1938, 22 June 1939. On the East-West split in the Cabinet, see *ibid.*, 20 March, 20 April, 25 April 1939; King watched with growing dismay how the argument of J. Gardiner on one side, and W.D. Euler and J.L. Ilsley on the other, got to the point where all three ministers threatened to resign.

50. On British economic appeasement, see Bernd J. Wendt, *Economic Appeasement: Handel und Finanz in der britischen DeutschlandPolitik 1933-1939* (Dusseldorf, 1971) and Schmidt, *Politics and Economics of Appeasement.* On American economic appeasement, see Hearden, ch. 2. On the differences, see H.J. Schroder, "The Ambiguities of Appeasement. Great Britain, the United States and Germany 1937-9," in Mommsen and Kettenacker.

51. CCF MP Grant MacNeil, for example, told the House of Commons: "As a trading nation we have economic importance, and I think on that basis we can make a definite contribution to economic appeasement and international cooperation." Canada, House of Commons, *Debates*, 25 March 1938, 1730-2. I am indebted to Greg Donaghy for this reference.

52. R.F. Holland, "The End of an Imperial Economy: Anglo-Canadian Disagreement in the 1930s," *Journal of Imperial and Commonwealth History*, XI (January 1983).

53. "German Trade With Canada in 1937," *Commercial Intelligence Journal*, 1782 (26 March 1938); S.A. Cudmore, "The Trade Agreements of 1938," undated memorandum, King Papers, MG 26 J4, vol. 281, file 2068.

54. J.R. Murray to W.D. Euler, 12 February 1936, enclosed in Euler to Skelton, 19 February 1936, Records of the Department of External Affairs, RG25 G1, vol. 1792, file 326, pt. 1.

55. On External Affairs' opposition, see memorandum by N.A. Robertson, 3 March 1936, King Papers, MG26 J4, vol. 219, file 2077; on Euler's special interest in the agreement, see Robertson to Wrong, 8 October 1936, NA, Norman A. Robertson Papers, MG30 E163, vol. 6, file 33.

56. "German Trade with Canada in 1938," *Commercial Intelligence Journal*, 1833 (18 March 1939). On the American reaction to the Canadian-German trade agreement, see Wrong to Robertson, 29 October 1936, Records of the Department of External Affairs, RG25 G1, vol. 1792, file 326, pt. 1; memorandum by Robertson, 3 November 1936, RG25 G1, vol. 1793, file 326, pt. 2; and Marler to King, 3 November 1936, King Papers, MG26 J1, vol. 222.

57. Ian Drummond and Norman Hillmer, *Negotiating Freer Trade: The United Kingdom, the United States, Canada and the Trade Agreements of 1938* (Waterloo, 1989).

58. King Diary, 16 April, 7 June 1937; see also Hillmer, "Pursuit of Peace."

59. For the continuing dual character of Canadian trade policy (combining bilateralism and multilateralism), see Robert Bothwell and John English, "Canadian Trade Policy in the Age of American Dominance and British Decline, 1943-1947," *Canadian Review of American Studies*, VIII (Spring 1977), esp. 63.

60. Hume Wrong called Canada's foreign service "pitifully inadequate." Wrong to Skelton, 8 December 1938, copy in NA, Lester B. Pearson Papers, MG26 N1, vol. 23; see also MacKay and Rogers, 216-20.

61. This "information" was filtered first by the Foreign Office and then by the Dominions Office: the sources on which it was based were seldom disclosed to the dominions. See Pearson to Skelton, 12 May 1939, *DCER*, VI, no. 960, 1179-81, and Pearson to Skelton, 23 February 1939, Pearson Papers, MG26 N1, vol. 30.

62. Undated handwritten memorandum of O.D. Skelton, Records of the Department of External Affairs, RG25 D1, vol. 715, pt. 1-5. On the functioning of the Department of External Affairs, see John Hilliker, *Canada's Department of External Affairs, Vol. I: The Early Years, 1909-1946* (Montreal and Kingston, 1990). On the Department of Finance's lack of planning, see Bryce, 228, and Paul Marsden's contribution in this volume.

63. Eayrs, 134-35.

64. King Diary, 26 August 1936.

65. King Diary, 20 January 1937, 10-11 February 1937, 14 March 1939. Martha Ann Hooker, "In Defence of Unity: Canada's Military Policies, 1935-1944," M.A. thesis, Carleton University, 1985.

66. Paper prepared by the Joint Committee, September 1936, printed in Eayrs, appendix, document 1. On British strategy, see Brian Bond, "The Continental Commitment in British Strategy in the 1930s," in Mommsen and Kettenacker, and Malcolm S. Smith, "Rearmament and Deterrence in Britain in the 1930s," *Journal of Strategic Studies*, I (December 1978).

67. King Diary, 11 January 1938; on the British debate, see G.C. Peden, *British Rearmament and the Treasury 1932-1939* (Edinburgh, 1979), 71-81.

68. King Diary, 31 August 1938, 24 September 1938.

69. *Ibid.*, 27 January 1939.

70. L. Christie, memorandum, "The New British Policy in Europe," 12 April 1939, *DCER*, VI, no. 946, 1155-64.

71. Skelton memorandum, "British Expeditionary Force," 10 March 1939, *ibid.*, no. 929, 1137-8. Skelton's suspicion that the Canadian military would secretly adapt to the shift in British strategy was well justified. To his utter dismay, the prime minister had to find out in early September that the chiefs of staff and the Defence Department had gone ahead with plans for a Canadian expeditionary force behind his and the minister's back. See King Diary, 1-5 September 1939, and Stephen J. Harris, *Canadian Brass: The Making of a Professional Army* (Toronto, 1988), esp. 186-89.

72. Skelton to Massey, 8 June 1939 and 26 July 1939, DCER, VI, no. 969 and no. 984; Christie memorandum, "The European Situation," 19 July 1939, *ibid.*, no. 981, 1205-21.

73. King Diary, 30 March, 16 April, 25 April 1939.

74. *Ibid.*, 11 September 1938.

75. *Ibid.*, 24 and 25 August 1939.

76. *Ibid.*, 24 August 1939.

77. Skelton memorandum, 25 August 1939, *DCER*, VI, no. 1005, 1247-52.

CANADA AND THE FAR EAST IN 1939

Gregory A. Johnson
University of Alberta

Mackenzie King grew apprehensive as he listened to the B.B.C. radio broadcast of Big Ben striking the midnight hour to announce the arrival of 1939. "I thought deeply of the significance of the strokes of that bell," he wrote in his diary,

> *of what had been saved to the world of anguish, this year, but even more of the possibilities of the New Year. The despatches I read this afternoon speak of Germany likely to force war because of an interior condition and of the possibility of Italy doing the same. It is all part of the madness of these dictatorships with their false doctrines and of the economic nationalism which has destroyed the friendly intercourse of nations, and helped to substitute international hate for international goodwill. One can only pray that in the Providence of God, war may be averted in the new Year.*[1]

The Canadian prime minister had good reason to feel pessimistic about the chances for peace in the coming year. Everywhere he looked the world seemed in turmoil, or close to it. The menacing situation in Europe remained uppermost in his mind, of course. But the Far East, too, concerned Mackenzie King. As he explained to a visitor in late January after being told that Japan had turned aside overtures from Italy and Germany to form a military alliance: "I don't trust Japan. I think there is some subterfuge here. I am sure all three have had an understanding from the beginning."[2] By early September he believed that Japan might even try to strike at Canada. "What may the Japanese not do in the Orient!" he exclaimed in his diary. "There are raiders and submarines on both the Atlantic and the Pacific coasts, and pocket cruisers. I have no doubt that we shall have some bombing of our coast and possibly some inland bombing as well."[3]

In many ways, Japan's pursuit of a "New Order" in the Far East forced a larger dilemma on Canada than the one created by European circumstances. On the one hand, policy makers in Ottawa were well aware that

Canada had limited interests in the Far East, and even more aware that these were not worth fighting over.[4] On the other hand, they realized that Far Eastern developments (and their response to them) could have a disastrous impact on Canada's position between Britain and the United States. For, unlike the situation in Europe, where Anglo-American relations generally harmonized, in the Far East relations between Britain and the United States were characterized by a growing rivalry.[5] The danger of becoming entangled in an Anglo-American rift was all too obvious to that small group of men in Ottawa mindful of the impact that diverging American and British interests had on Canadian foreign policy during the Far Eastern Crisis in 1932.[6] Worse still was the possibility of getting dragged into a war with Japan either through the United States or Britain and the potential threat that posed to national unity. This had been apparent at least since the mid-1930's.[7] It became something of a reality in 1939 because, while a crisis erupted over the Danzig Corridor in Poland during the summer, a crisis of equal magnitude raged over the British Concession at the Chinese treaty port of Tientsin. Canada came close to facing the prospect of entering a war against Japan instead of against Germany.

At the heart of Canada's Far Eastern dilemma lay the "undeclared" Sino-Japanese war, which had been escalating since its outbreak in July 1937. By the beginning of 1939 the Japanese occupied more than 1,500,000 square kilometres of Chinese territory and they had claimed some 800,000 Chinese lives. Through a series of earlier offensives, the Imperial Army had captured key strategic centres in China, notably Canton and Hankow, and had forced the National Government of Chiang Kai-shek to retreat to Chungking. Then, in November and December 1938, the Japanese government issued a number of statements calling for a "New Order" in East Asia. This was followed by a triple-pronged policy designed to destroy the Chinese war effort by wooing the Germans into converting the 1936 Anti-Comintern Pact into a military alliance against the Soviet Union (in the belief that by neutralizing a potential Soviet threat from the north, the Japanese war effort would somehow receive a boost); by exploiting the growing rift within the Kuomintang between Chiang and Wang Ching-wei; and by seeking to undermine Chinese currency. None of these measures worked. The Germans wanted a military alliance that was directed at all powers instead of merely against the Soviet Union. Wang defected and began negotiations with the Japanese for setting up a puppet government in the occupied territory, but they dragged on until 1940. The attempt to undermine Chinese currency was similarly thwarted by British and American stabilization loans to China.

Ultimately, the failure to achieve these objectives only hardened the Japanese determination to bring China to its knees. Throughout 1939 Japan sought to tighten its hold on the occupied areas and to make a more concerted attack on the ever-faltering Chinese currency. Initial moves in this direction were made with the seizure of Hainan Island off the South China Coast in February and the prohibition of North Chinese currency (fapi) in March. This was accompanied by new and more threatening gestures towards Britain, the one country that Japan began to view as the chief obstacle to its ambitions in the Far East. The aim was to drive a wedge between the United States and Britain and then to force the British into a Far Eastern "Munich" by exerting pressure on the International Settlements at Shanghai, Amoy, and the island of Kulangsu, and especially on the British Concession at Tientsin.[8]

These developments were closely watched in Canada, but Ottawa could do little to influence their outcome.[9] In early January, O.D. Skelton, the under-secretary of state for external affairs, and Mackenzie King's trusted advisor, pointed out that the "Japanese invasion of China has not yet been checked. Practically all the northern and eastern territories, and particularly the industrial and commercial centres, have been conquered." Although he believed that the likelihood of British or American military intervention remained small as long as Japan did not threaten their vital interests, he could perceive a hardening in the attitude of both London and Washington in the direction of a "definite possibility of an attempt to use economic weapons."[10] So far as Skelton was concerned, the imposition of economic sanctions against Japan would lead to war and there was no sign that the Americans or the British were willing to give each other a military commitment before applying sanctions.[11] He wanted the Canadian government to remain neutral and to avoid pursuing any policy that could provoke Japan. As was usually the case, Skelton expressed particular concern over British policy and the limited options left to Canada:

> *It is very illuminating as to the forces behind much of British foreign policy to note how aloof the British Government was when it was only a question of rescuing China from murder and loot, and how interested she is becoming when it is a question of saving the trade of British firms in Shanghai which hitherto have been very pro-Japanese and contemptuous of China. Meanwhile Canada is supposed never to think of her own interests in foreign policy.*[12]

The under-secretary may have been overestimating the political influence of British trading firms, but his observation regarding the threat to British interests was correct. In late January Hugh Keenleyside, the Department of External Affairs' resident expert on Far Eastern matters, reported that the Japanese prime minister, Baron Hiranuma, and his foreign minister, Arita Hachiro, had recently made statements which "constitute one of the most significant contributions to the history of Japanese foreign policy since Peary's [sic] 'Black Ships' ended Japanese seclusion in 1854." In part of his statement, Baron Hiranuma said: "As for those who fail to understand to the end and hereafter persist in the opposition to Japan, we have no other alternative than to exterminate them." When the Japanese Foreign Office was asked whether this threat applied only to the Chinese, an official replied that "the translation is correct as it stands."[13] Then, following the Japanese occupation of Hainan Island, Keenleyside warned that "[I]f the Japanese retain control of the Island and develop it as a Japanese naval base it will finally seal the doom of Hong Kong and it will be a direct threat to the usefulness of Singapore ... This action by the Japanese will completely alter the strategic situation in the Eastern and Southern Pacific." So far as Keenleyside was concerned, the threat to Britain was obvious and so, too, was the potential for war.[14] It is interesting to note that Britain's Dominions Office, perhaps fearing Ottawa would use the Far Eastern situation in order to escape European commitments, downplayed the Japanese seizure of Hainan. Within the Foreign Office and the Admiralty, however, officials expressed the view that Japan's actions were part of a long-range plan to absorb Borneo and Malaya and that the annexation of Hainan had been undertaken at the instigation of Germany and Italy.[15]

Mackenzie King, for his part, sought to remain aloof from Far Eastern affairs. His government had adopted an official policy of neutrality shortly after the outbreak of the Sino-Japanese war and he was determined to keep it that way. The prime minister's uppermost fear was that Canada would get dragged into an Anglo-Japanese war (or worse, into a simultaneous Anglo-German-Japanese war) without American support. But he was also concerned about the possible implications for Canada if the United States and Japan became involved in a conflict. He therefore did all that he could to prevent Canada from being placed in a situation where it could be held responsible for creating an "incident." For example, when the British Columbia members of the House of Commons tried to push through an act to exclude Japanese immigrants from Canada, he recorded in his diary that he warned them of "the position in Japan and the embarrassment which the passing of any exclusion measures would be to the British Government and the danger of the reaction to the parts of the Empire."[16] The exclusionist policy was subsequently blocked in the House, to the great relief of the prime minister and, indeed, the British.[17]

Mackenzie King's acute sensitivity over Canadian involvement in Far Eastern matters was further demonstrated by an episode involving Canada's chargé d'affaires at the Tokyo Legation, E. D'Arcy McGreer, and his wife, shortly after the Japanese seizure of Hainan Island in February. Lady Craigie, wife of British Ambassador Sir Robert Craigie, was gathering the wives of other diplomats together once a week to roll bandages for wounded Japanese soldiers. One Japanese newspaper quoted her as saying that she thought it was the duty of all women stationed in Tokyo to work hand-in-hand with the Japanese women because Japan was facing an emergency.[18] Recognizing the obvious attempt to mollify the Japanese and unwilling to compromise Canada's neutrality, McGreer objected to his wife taking any part in the operation. Offended by McGreer's attitude, Craigie stopped by the Canadian Legation to tell him that "when I decided that it was quite correct to hold these meetings, you also might have known that it was quite correct." McGreer explained that if the Canadian public caught wind of the situation, his government would be embarrassed. Skelton certainly approved of McGreer's stand and condemned Craigie for having "the gall to call at the Legation to voice his disapproval of the fact that Mrs. McGreer had not been attending these meetings." Mackenzie King was even more upset, and wrote a personal note explaining that he not only approved of McGreer's position "but would disapprove either he or his wife taking any action which in either *Canada* or Japan might give rise to misunderstanding as to Canada's complete neutrality ... in this Sino-Japanese war."[19]

Mackenzie King believed that he had some good reasons for pursuing a policy that would prevent Canada from being placed in a position where it could be held responsible for creating an international incident. International incidents could lead to war and he had no desire to see national unity upset by Canadian involvement in any Far Eastern crisis. Moreover, as he noted sourly in his diary, a war in Asia was "not worth the lives of white men for 'Business Interests'."[20] He also believed that Canada might be attacked if a war involving either Britain or the United States and Japan broke out in the Pacific. On more than one occasion he expressed the view that "Japan was very dangerous" and that Canada "might be faced with a world situation at any time" which necessitated better defences on the west coast.[21]

In fact, Canada military authorities had been expressing increasing concern over the defence of British Columbia since the termination of the Anglo-Japanese alliance in the early 1920s and especially since the Far Eastern crisis of 1931-33. By 1936 they were warning that "the liability of direct attack on Canada by Japanese forces has become a matter requiring urgent consideration and action in view of the menacing situation which continues to develop in the Far East."[22] The problem attracting particular attention was the maintenance of Canadian neutrality in the event of an American-Japanese war, a problem that was further complicated by Canadian obligations under the terms of the Anglo-American Treaty of 1871. The treaty gave Canada sovereignty over sections of the Straits of Juan de Fuca, but Japan might argue that these were international waters. If Canada failed to prevent the Japanese from entering or utilizing those areas, the United States could respond by using their armed forces to protect their interests.[23] The services argued that Canada's geographical proximity to and commercial relations with the United States would leave the country open to charges of non-neutrality by either the Americans or the Japanese, which could lead to a situation where the United States would move arms and men into Canada in order to protect American security, thereby violating Canadian sovereignty. "As Canada is, for practical purposes, incapable of resisting such a United States invasion there would be no course open except the humiliating one of accepting the violation of her sovereign rights," warned military officials.[24]

Mackenzie King agreed with his military advisors, especially after the American president, F.D. Roosevelt, informed him of "having [in] a number of leading Senators and asking them the question, what would the United States do if Japan attacked British Columbia. The agreement being instantly, why, of course, we would go in and help to prevent her getting a foothold."[25] His apprehension was further fuelled by Roosevelt's 1938 declaration at Kingston, Ontario, that "the United States will not stand idly by if the domination of Canadian soil is threatened by any other empire."[26] True, Mackenzie King publicly spoke of Canada's "obligations as good friendly neighbour," and said that "should the occasion ever arise, enemy forces should not be able to pursue their way either by land, sea or air, to the United States across Canadian territory"[27] Privately, however, the prime minister was perturbed by Roosevelt's "guarantee." "Roosevelt's assurance only added to our responsibilities," he recorded in his diary, "that we would have to see that our coasts were so defended that no enemy forces could operate from Canadian territory against the United States." Toward the end of January 1939 he wrote that he "pointed out to the

Cabinet that they must not mistake what the President said at the Thousand Islands Bridge; that it was not that the United States would not allow Canada to be dominated by any other Empire or country than the British. That if she had to come here and save us, the Empire being dominated, it would mean that Canada would become a part of America."[28]

The prime minister and his military officials were by no means the only ones expressing concern over the possibility of a Japanese attack on the West Coast. In early January 1938 Dr. Chang-Lok Chen, the Chinese consul general in Ottawa, delivered a widely reported speech to the Ottawa Gyro Club in which he said that "it was folly for Canada to take the view that she was secure from all attacks, that the Monroe Doctrine would protect her or that England would always be ready to come to her rescue." Canadians, he warned, "would 'rue the day' they neglected their western defences." Similar comments were made by Thomas Wu, associate editor of the *Shing Wha Daily News* and spokesman for the Ontario Chinese Patriotic League, who added: "If anyone with an unbiased mind looks at the situation in British Columbia they can see the Japanese menace." In addition, there were inflammatory press articles blasting the state of Canadian defence.[29]

Some allowance must be made for the fact that military authorities were seeking to use the Far Eastern situation in order to wring more money from the government for a larger defence budget and that Chinese representatives were attempting to raise more support in their fight against Japan.[30] Nevertheless, mounting concern over the Far East led to a secret meeting between high-ranking Canadian and American military officials in January 1938. Both sides agreed that if war broke out in the Pacific, the Japanese would conduct raids on the west coast from cruisers and aircraft carriers and the Americans believed that the Japanese would try to use the coast of British Columbia as a base for air or submarine operations.[31] Shortly after these meetings, the Canadian General Staff produced an interim plan of coast defence.[32]

By 1939 there was a genuinely held belief that a Japanese attack on Canada, however limited, was a possibility. In late January General T.V. Anderson, the chief of the General Staff, drew up a memorandum projecting "scales of attack" by Japan which ran as follows: "Occasional medium attacks, definite risk of torpedo, bomb or gas attack. Maximum of twelve aircraft from enemy cruisers, armed merchant vessels or improvised carriers."[33] Commodore P.W. Nelles, chief of the Naval Staff, and one of those who had attended the talks with the Americans in 1938, added to this at the end of January with the comment that, though the actions of Germany must be given first consideration, "the possible actions of Japan must be taken into account." He projected Japanese attacks by "up to 2 5" [two five-inch] Cruisers, 2 Submarines, 2 Minelayers, and 2 Armed Merchantmen to attack our West Coast ports and/or trade in British Columbian waters."[34]

As the Far Eastern situation continued to deteriorate, the probability of a war in that part of the world involving either Britain or the United States became almost as significant for the government as the European situation. Ottawa responded by giving priority status to the defence of the west coast of Canada until the summer of 1938 and by installing additional defences on the Pacific Coast, particularly in the form of artillery. Four of Canada's six destroyers were also stationed on the west coast. There was also a press campaign designed to demonstrate how well-defended British Columbia was.[35] These measures were rather meagre and designed to mollify public opinion more than to provide for a strong defence. For example, coastal artillery did not match the range of Japanese battleships. But throughout the 1930s the government struggled with financial exigency, and it was difficult to raise either public awareness or public support for substantive rearmament.

Increasingly frustrated by their failure to defeat China, the Japanese began exerting pressure on the international settlements and especially on the British Concession at Tientsin. After a series of minor incidents involving Chinese terrorists, a crisis broke when the Japanese blockaded the British Concession on 14 June 1939. Craigie later wrote that the crisis was like "a volcano whose sudden eruption threw into the political firmament all the pent-up feelings and animosities which had been simmering and boiling beneath the surface since Japan's invasion of China two years earlier."[36] The issues revolved around the circulation of North Chinese currency, the refusal of the British to hand over some fourteen million dollars of Chinese silver reserves sealed in Concession vaults, and the anti-Japanese activities carried out from the Concession by Chinese guerrillas.[37]

The crisis had alarming implications for other parts of the world. British policy had been based on the assumption that war would break out in Europe first and then perhaps spread to the Far East. Now, as the British prime minister, Neville Chamberlain, pointed out, "it looked as though it might be the other way round: for, if we sent our fleet to Singapore to deal with Japan, the temptation to the Axis Powers to take advantage of the situation would be almost irresistible."[38] From Washington, the British ambassador, Sir Ronald Lindsay, cautioned London against any action "that could be construed as a return to [a] policy of appeasement." He warned that concessions to Japan would be made at the risk of alienating the United States.[39] While expressing a desire to send a fleet to the Pacific, the Americans did not want to cooperate with Britain or give a guarantee of armed support in the event that Japan pushed the issue to war.

Though Ottawa remained aloof from the crisis, there was considerable concern over what could happen. In early June Lester B. Pearson, first secretary in the High Commission in Britain, had informed Ottawa of Craigie's analysis of developments in Japanese policy. The ambassador reported that Japan was attempting "to drive a wedge" between Britain and the United States. Pearson recognized that the Foreign Office did not agree with the ambassador, but he believed that there might be some truth to the allegation in view of recent Japanese approaches to the United States regarding the possibility of finding a solution to the tension in Europe.[40] Two days after the blockade of the Concession, Canada's high commissioner to London, Vincent Massey, passed on Craigie's warning that the "Japanese may have forced [the] issue at Tientsin, where United States interests are not so great, to drive a wedge between the two Governments."[41] Skelton agreed. He believed that from the Japanese "standpoint the time was well chosen, with German-Polish relations strained, and the Anglo-Russian negotiations up in the air. The place was equally well chosen, as the United States has no special interest in Tientsin, and it was easier therefore to drive a wedge between Great Britain and the United States." Though Skelton did not think that the British could retaliate without American support, he began to allow for the shadowy prospect of war. "It would be ironical," he wrote to Mackenzie King, "if, after declining to take any action against Japan to save the millions of Chinese from slaughter and starvation, we should find ourselves engaged in economic or military conflict in defence of concessions established after the Opium Wars." He went on to suggest that if Canada was asked to join in some form of economic retaliation, "we would desire to obtain some assurance from Washington as to support in the event of conflict."[42]

The type of assurance Skelton wanted from the Americans was not forthcoming. From the Washington Legation, Escott Reid reported that, although the Americans seemed to be adopting a stiffer policy, it was not working out that way in practice: non-interventionist sentiment in

Congress was growing, Congress turned down requests for funds to improve the harbour at Guam and the naval air base at Wake Island, and there was no sign that the American public would back a policy of economic sanctions with military force. Moreover, Merchant Mahoney, the chargé d'affaires at the Washington Legation, informed Ottawa that the chief of the Far Eastern Division of the State Department told him that "he did not foresee new developments in the Far Eastern policy of the United States."[43] In other words, the Americans would continue to sit back and await further developments. Without American support, London was forced to give Craigie a great deal of latitude to stage as graceful a withdrawal as possible. After several weeks of hard bargaining, the British had to accept the humiliating formula Craigie and the Japanese foreign minister, Arita, produced on 24 July as the basis for the negotiation of a settlement of the Tientsin crisis.[44]

The British retreat came as a great disappointment to the Americans. The secretary of state, Cordell Hull, later wrote that "[I]t was disturbing in that Japan had won a victory in her never-ending quest for recognition of 'special rights,' or 'special interests,' or 'special requirements' in China."[45] On 26 July, the American government gave Japan the necessary six months' notice for the termination of the 1911 American-Japanese commercial treaty. Washington's move surprised both Tokyo and London. The British were delighted at the rebuke delivered to Japan, but they were upset because the Americans had not notified them beforehand of the decision. Craigie rightly believed that Washington's decision was "just another flash in the American pan."[46]

Nevertheless, the American decision threw the British government into a quandary. The Cabinet discussed the Far Eastern situation at a series of meetings in early August and it decided to examine the possibility of abrogating the Anglo-Japanese Commercial Treaty of 1911, to which Canada was a party (it is also worth noting the foreign secretary's comment at one of these meetings that "the position in the Far East was now causing him more anxiety than the position in any other part of the world").[47] On 16 August London asked Ottawa for its views on the denunciation of the Commercial Treaty.[48]

Ottawa replied to the British request on 21 August. "It has not been found possible," the telegram began, "in the brief time thus available to secure definitive consideration of the question by the Canadian Government ... While we consider it is essential for full understanding of the situation ... we do not wish to imply that they would offset our desire to cooperate with the United Kingdom and the United States in any action which they might take, particularly so in view of the long-range interests involved." In the event, the government decided that it would stand by Britain.[49] But the question had been rather carefully considered even before the British made their request and the various discussions clearly demonstrated the limited parameters of Canadian policy. Pursuing his customary neutralist stance, Skelton wrote on 1 August: "It is not our business to offer any advice on the Tientsin negotiations at this eleventh hour, but if the negotiations break down and the British decide to follow the United States' example in denouncing the treaty, I do not suppose we could do otherwise." Nevertheless, he went on to warn that "[I]t must be borne in mind that if reprisals are made they will fall largely on Canada, and while I do not think there is any likelihood of reprisals taking a military form it is clear that if they did come in the Pacific the United Kingdom could not give any adequate support."[50]

A few days later, one of Skelton's officials, Norman Robertson, pointed out that under the Canadian tariff structure Japan would revert from a "most-favoured-nation" status to the general tariff, while American and British tariff structures would not necessarily alter their trading relationship with Japan. The danger here was that Canada could be left taking "directly punitive measures against Japanese trade at a time when neither the United Kingdom nor the United States were committed to taking similar measures."[51]

Although Skelton and Robertson believed that Canada should follow the British, they wanted a separate Canadian denunciation which would assert Canadian independence and avoid the appearance of taking the lead. Skelton, in particular, argued that Canada "should try not to get out in front."[52] Mackenzie King agreed, but he also feared that "with Japan, Italy and Germany together in secret conclave it is hard to believe that plans are not already made for simultaneous attacks in the Orient and Europe – a ghastly and appaling [sic] situation."[53] The fate of the world was in the hands of the great powers and Canadians could only hope that peace would prevail.

By the middle of August 1939, the negotiations that had been taking place between Craigie and Arita had broken down. The Foreign Office decided that it would no longer seek to conciliate Japan for fear of both alienating the United States and undermining the Chinese war effort. It was time to take a firm stand. Chamberlain agreed. Japan "had made things impossible," he wrote, "... and we must deal with the consequences as best we can."[54] The Japanese were equally adamant, and towards the end of August it seemed almost certain that Britain would go to war with Japan.[55] The situation was saved, most ironically, by the Germans. The announcement of the Nazi-Soviet non-aggression pact on 22 August threw Japan into a state of confusion. Japanese diplomacy had been governed by the 1936 Anti-Comintern Pact and Germany's betrayal of that agreement came as a great shock. The Japanese premier resigned on 25 August, on the grounds that the emperor had been given false advice, and the Cabinet fell a few days later.

The Nazi-Soviet pact made war in Europe a certainty; it also made certain there would be no immediate expansion of the war in the Far East. Germany invaded Poland on 1 September and Britain declared war on Germany on 3 September. Canada followed suit on 10 September. On 5 September, the new Japanese government informed Britain that it would remain neutral in the European war. Meanwhile, and to the surprise of none, the United States also declared its intention to remain neutral.

Despite the fact that after 22 August most Canadian policy makers knew that a war with Germany was imminent, the Far Eastern situation continued to be a source of concern. "The world position has changed since 1914, particularly in the Pacific," cautioned O.D. Skelton. "The defence of Canada," he stressed,

> *should be put in the foreground. Many statements have been made in the past year or two as to the impossibility in the event of war of Canada avoiding attack. If that is so, our first business is to avert that attack. Clearly any attack will be on a minor scale, but that minor scale may be greater than our shore and off-shore defences can meet. It should be emphasized, further, that we cannot in this war ignore the Pacific as we did in the last. (We have a potential enemy, not a friend, facing us there.) There is a big job in defending our coasts.*[56]

Allowance must be made for the fact that Skelton, who was basically opposed to Canadian participation in the war against Germany, was attempting to concoct an iron-clad argument so that Canada could keep its European commitment small. But his observation contained more than a grain of truth. As Hugh Keenleyside pointed out in early September:

The importance of Japan as the possessor of the third largest navy in the world, as the only major power in Asia and the Western Pacific, as the home of one of the greatest merchant fleets in existence, as a strong industrial nation, as the possessor of a highly efficient army, based on a healthy population of over seventy million, and as the inveterate opponent of the U.S.S.R., (which is now apparently prepared to cooperate with Germany) can hardly be exaggerated.[57]

Many Canadians believed that, as a small power with a population of barely 11 million and an almost non-existent Pacific defence system, their country presented Japan with a potentially inviting target through which it could strike at its enemies. This belief would grow over the next two years, and the eventual Japanese attack on Pearl Harbor in December 1941 would send British Columbia into a state of panic and confusion that would have costly repercussions.

That Canada demonstrated some concern over the Far Eastern situation in 1939 should come as no surprise. As early as 1935 Lester Pearson, then representing Canada at the League of Nations, wrote:

It is almost platitudinous now to state that Canada's position becomes impossible if Great Britain and the United States drift apart on any major [Far Eastern] issue. Like many other platitudes, however, this one involves a fundamental truth. Canada is a British Dominion. She is also an American State. She cannot permit herself to be put in a position where she has to choose between these two destinies. Either choice would be fatal to her unity; indeed to her very existence as a State.[58]

Fortunately, Canada was not placed in this position in 1939. Instead of supporting Japan's aggressive policies, Germany signed a non-aggression pact with the Soviet Union, thereby alleviating the tension in the Far East between Japan and Britain, and, at least for a time, between Britain and the United States. The Canadian government was thus spared the difficulty of having to decide whether to go to war with Japan at Britain's side and facing the problems that such a conflict would have raised in Anglo-American, Anglo-Canadian and Canadian-American relations. Nevertheless, the possibility was there in 1939, and it is well for historians to realize that Mackenzie King's government faced not one, but two, potential threats to Canadian unity during that fateful year. If anything, this makes King's aversion to overseas commitments all the more understandable and his accomplishment of taking a united Canada into the Second World War all the greater.

NOTES

1. National Archives of Canada [hereafter NA], W.L.M. Mackenzie King Papers, Diary, 31 December 1938.
2. *Ibid.*, 30 January 1939.
3. *Ibid.*, 6 September 1939.
4. *Ibid.*, see especially 26 and 30 August 1937; and NA, Department of External Affairs Records [hereafter DEA], vol. 723, file 64 (1-2), Loring Christie Memoranda, "Note on Departmental Conference," 20 October 1937 and "Consultations on Far Eastern Situation," 21 October 1937.
5. See especially Christopher Thorne, *Allies of a Kind: The United States, Britain, and the War against Japan, 1941-1945* (London, 1978), ch. 1; and S.W. Roskill, *Naval Policy Between the Wars*, Vol. 1 (London, 1968).
6. See Donald C. Story, "Canada, the League of Nations and the Far East, 1931-33: The Cahan Incident," *International History Review*, III (April 1981), 236-55.
7. If not in the 1920's. See especially Roger Sarty, "'There will be trouble in the North Pacific': The Defence of British Columbia in the Early Twentieth Century," *BC Studies*, 61 (Spring 1984), 3-29; *Documents on Canadian External Relations* (hereafter *DCER*), vol. V, no. 344, 336-9, McNaughton Memorandum for Bennett, "Sino-Japanese Dispute, Possible Canadian Commitments In Respect To ...," 24 February 1934; and Stephen J. Harris, *Canadian Brass: The Making of a Professional Army, 1860-1939* (Toronto, 1988), 179-83.
8. Bradford Lee, *Britain and the Sino-Japanese War, 1937-1939* (Stanford, 1973), 274ff; and Kyozo Sato, "Japan's Position before the Outbreak of the European War in September 1939," *Modern Asian Studies*, 14, 1 (1980), 129-43.
9. It is actually quite remarkable how much newspaper space was accorded to the Far East, especially in central Canadian newspapers. Ottawa, for its part, received regular reports on Far Eastern developments from the British government, and detailed, if somewhat dry, reports from E. D'Arcy McGreer, the chargé d'affaires at the Canadian Legation in Tokyo.
10. King Papers, vol. 211, file 2011, Skelton Memorandum, "Recent Developments in Sino-Japanese Conflict," 7 January 1939.
11. Skelton had developed this belief during the Far Eastern Crisis of 1931-1933. See James Eayrs, *In Defence of Canada: Appeasement and Rearmament* (Toronto, 1965), 7-8.

12. King Papers, vol. 211, file 2011, Skelton Memorandum, "Recent Developments in Sino-Japanese Conflict," 7 January 1939.

13. DEA Records, vol. 1754, file 804 (XIII), Keenleyside Memorandum, "Japanese Foreign Policy," 24 January 1939.

14. *Ibid.*, Keenleyside Memorandum, "Seizure of Hainan by the Japanese," 13 February 1939.

15. *Ibid.*, MacDonald to King, 25 February 1939; Lee, 176; and Public Record Office, Kew, England (hereafter PRO), Cabinet Records (hereafter CAB), CAB 24/284, C.P. 76(39), Halifax Memorandum, 30 March 1939.

16. King Diary, 10, 30 January 1939.

17. The British expressed more than a passing concern over this issue. See material in PRO, Foreign Office Records, FO 371/23560.

18. Tokyo *Nichi Nichi*, 16 February 1939.

19. DEA Records, vol. 794, file 467, McGreer to Skelton, 15 February 1939; McGreer to King, 11 March 1939; Skelton to King, with King's minute, 11 March 1939; King to McGreer, 16 March 1939; and McGreer to Skelton, 23 March 1939.

20. King Diary, 30 August 1937; and see also 26 August 1937.

21. *Ibid.*, see especially 11 January 1938; and 7, 22 July 1938.

22. Queen's University Archives, C.G. Powers Papers, vol. 67, file D-2000, Memorandum by the Joint Staff Committee, "An Appreciation of the Defence Problems Confronting Canada with Recommendations For the Development of the Armed Forces," 5 September 1936. This document is also reprinted in Eayrs, 213-22.

23. *DCER*, V, no. 344, 336-9, McNaughton Memorandum for Bennett, 24 February 1934; King Papers, vol. 124, file 913, Walter Hose, "Memorandum on Naval Policy," 30 July 1926; *ibid.*, vol. 75, ff.06411ff., Hose to King, "Memorandum on the Question of Canadian Naval Defence," n.d.

24. *DCER*, VI, no. 97, 88-99, "Appreciation of Canada's Obligations with Respect to the Maintenance of Neutrality in Event of a War between the United States of America and Japan," 14 October 1936; NA, Department of National Defence Records (hereafter DND), vol. 2505, file HQS 1066, Major B.D.C. Treatt Report, 1936; DEA Records, vol. 3429, file 1-1930/41, Hose Memorandum, "The Naval Defence of Canada," 26 August 1936.

25. King Diary, 31 July 1936.

26. It would now appear that Roosevelt was indeed troubled about the state of defence in British Columbia. The American Minister to Canada, Norman Armour, recorded in 1937 that Roosevelt said that "Canadian defenses were ... not only entirely inadequate, but almost nonexistent" and the President "felt that more should be done by the Canadian and American governments in developing a coordinated plan of defense for that important section of territory lying between northern Washington and the 'panhandle' of Alaska." (United States National Archives (hereafter

USNA), Washington, D.C., Records of the Foreign Service Posts of the Department of State, RG 84, vol. 284, box 1486, Armour Memorandum, 9 November 1937. I am indebted to Alan Mason for providing me with this reference.)

27. Quoted in Eayrs, 183-4; and King Diary, 20 August 1938. Roosevelt's speech was aimed at Japan as much as it was at Germany.

28. King Diary, 20 August 1938 and 27 January 1939. Note also the entry for 19 January 1939: "If we ever cease to depend upon the British fleet on the Pacific coast and the Atlantic, and place our whole reliance in the U.S., there would be no independent Canada left; if Canada was left at all, it would be one of the States of the American Republic." (19 January 1939).

29. Records of the Foreign Service Posts of the Department of State, vol. 4, box 1490, Armour to Hull, 11 January 1938; Ottawa *Citizen*, 6 January 1938, which also contained an article titled "Canadian Defence Weakness 'Menace' to U.S. Security"; Toronto *Star*, 8 January 1938.

30. Though it should be noted that there is no evidence to suggest that the military was deliberately seeking to exaggerate the military threat. It is also worth pointing out that in December 1941 the research section of the Japanese Ministry of War in collaboration with the Imperial Army and Navy General staffs prepared secret blueprints that had Alaska, the Yukon, British Columbia, Alberta, Washington state and Central America coming under the jurisdiction of Japanese Governments-General. Imperial War Museum, London, International Military Tribunal for the Far East, exhibit 1334, transcript 11969-73, Ministry of War, Research Section, "Land Disposal Plan in the Greater East Asia Co-Prosperity Sphere," December 1941.

31. King Papers, vol. 157, file 1411, Ashton Memorandum, "Conversations on Defence Questions," 25 January 1938; Nelles Memorandum, "Conversations held in Washington, D.C., on the 19th and 20th January 1938." See also FO 371/22107, Pirie Memorandum, 22 January 1938. The meetings were attended by General E.C. Ashton, chief of the general staff and Commodore P.W. Nelles, chief of the naval staff, and Major-General Malin Craig, chief of staff of the United States Army and Admiral William Leahy, chief of naval operations.

32. NA, Ian Mackenzie Papers, vol. 30, file X-27, General Staff Memorandum, "The Interim Plan of Coast Defence," 31 January 1938.

33. DEA Records, vol. 721, file 47, Anderson Memorandum, "Statement of Military Precautionary Measures in Canada," 28 January 1939.

34. NA, Mackenzie Papers, vol. 32, file X-52A, "Appreciation of the Situation," 30 January 1939.

35. See, for example, *The Globe and Mail* (Toronto), 3 December 1938, front page article bearing the title "Canada's Pacific Forts Among World's Finest"; and the Toronto *Daily Star*, 15 July 1939, which carried a piece titled "B.C. Defences To Rank With Best In World." These were considerable overstatements, to say the least. See also T. Murray Hunter, "Coast Defence in British Columbia, 1939-1941: Attitudes and Realities," *BC Studies*, 28 (Winter 1975-76), 3-28.

36. Robert L. Craigie, *Behind the Japanese Mask* (London, 1946), 72.

37. See Peter Lowe, *Great Britain and the Origins of the Pacific War* (London, 1977), 72-102; Lee, 174-204; and *Documents on British Foreign Policy* (hereafter DBFP), third series, vol. IX.

38. Quoted in R. John Pritchard, "The Far East as an Influence on the Chamberlain Government's Pre-war European Policies," *Millennium*, 2 (Winter 1973-74), 17-18; and see Lee, 189.

39. *DBFP*, third series, vol. IX, no. 264, 227-8, Lindsay to Halifax, 26 June 1939.

40. King Papers, vol. 211, file 1678, Pearson to King, 9 June 1939.

41. DEA Records, vol. 723, file 64(1-2), Massey to King, 16 June 1939. In all probability, this telegram was drafted by Pearson.

42. King Papers, vol. 211, file 1678, Skelton Memorandum for King, 19 June 1939.

43. NA, Escott Reid Papers, vol. 5, file 2, Draft Telegram of 20 July 1939; DEA Records, vol. 1754, file 804 (XIII), Mahoney to King, 20 July 1939 (drafted by Reid); Mahoney to King, 26 July 1939.

44. *DBFP*, third series, vol. IX, no. 365, 313, Craigie to Halifax, 23 July 1939; DEA Records, vol. 1754, file 804 (XIII), McGreer to King, 24, 27 July 1939.

45. Cordell Hull, *The Memoirs of Cordell Hull*, vol. 1 (New York, 1948), 635.

46. *DBFP*, third series, IX, no. 444, 382-3, Craigie to Halifax, 1 August 1939. Lee, 196, attempts to argue that the Americans were seeking to stiffen Britain's hand. There is little evidence to support this claim. Hull himself later admitted that the idea of abrogating the treaty had been discussed for some time. See Hull, *Memoirs*, I, 636; and see also Jonathan Utley, *Going to War with Japan, 1937-1941* (Knoxville, Tenn., 1985), 62-3. Utley demonstrates that rather than seeking to bolster Britain's attitude, Hull and Roosevelt were seeking to preempt domestic legislation which would have damaged Hull's Asian policy.

47. Quoted in Lee, 198.

48. FO 371/23567, Circular B., no. 273, London to Ottawa, 16 August 1939.

49. *Ibid.*, no. 46, Ottawa to London, 21 August 1939.

50. King Papers, vol. 211, file 2011, Skelton to King, 1 August 1939.

51. *Ibid.*, Robertson Memorandum, 5 August 1939.

52. DEA Records, vol. 723, file 64(1-2), Skelton Memorandum for King, 19 August 1939.

53. King Diary, 21 August 1939.

54. Quoted in Lee, 201.

55. Craigie, in his *Behind the Japanese Mask*, 73-4, wrote that the younger Japanese officers (who often wielded more power than their superiors) "were determined to exploit the affair to the point of war." He added that Whitehall had information "showing that the Japanese General Staff had their plans fully laid for a single-handed war with Great Britain."

56. King Papers, vol. 395, file 52, Skelton Memorandum, "Canadian War Policy," 24 August 1939.

57. DEA Records, vol. 776, file 365(1), Keenleyside "Memorandum For Dr. Skelton," 3 September 1939.

58. NA, H.D.G. Crerar Papers, vol. 13, file D.M.C. & I9A, L.B. Pearson, "Canada and the Far East," April 1935. This was reprinted under the pseudonym "T," "Canada and the Far East," *Foreign Affairs*, 13 (1934-35), 388ff.

COMMENTARY

J.L. Granatstein
York University

"If you were to ask any Canadian, 'Do you have to go to war if England does?' he'd answer at once, 'Oh, no.' If you then said, '*Would* you go to war if England does?' he'd answer 'Oh, yes.' And if you asked, 'Why?' he would say, reflectively, 'Well, you see, we'd *have* to.'"

Thus Stephen Leacock, writing in the *Atlantic Monthly* in June 1939 for an American audience, had summed up Canadian opinion as the world hovered on the brink of war. He was precisely right, too, and his brilliant formulation a half century later still rings true, certainly to most historians of the period.

Perhaps that near unanimity exists because the process of revisionism of the history of the pre-war and wartime eras has been so slow in Canada. The professional historians have tended to accept the party line, laid out by Charles Stacey and his disciples (of whom I would be one). This has largely left the revisionist field to the Bacques and Brydens and, much less appetizingly, to the Zundels and Keegstras. That is why Brian Villa's book on Dieppe and, in this book, Terry Copp's attempt at a revision of the usual view of public opinion in Ontario are so important. At last, a major re-thinking of Canada's role in the war may be in the making.

What themes emerged from the papers presented in this book? First, and most obvious, was that ordinary life went on in Canada in 1939. The Depression and the approaching war took second place in our politics to Dominion-Provincial relations and to the Royal Visit of 1939. They ought not to have, of course, for the nation was in a bleak state in 1939, its Gross National Product being only a small percentage of the current one. There was scarcely any preparation for war, financial, industrial or military. And yet what seems strikingly apparent in all these papers is that the coming of war, even the limited liability war policies with which Canada started the conflict, was relatively good for the country. There were steel orders for the Maritimes, air bases for the Prairies, and increased lumber sales in British Columbia. The bureaucracy expanded, the soldiers got promotions on this side of the ocean, industry received start-up orders for everything from battledress to rifles to shells and trucks, and the farmers began to harvest their 1939 crops with the expectation they could sell them for good prices. The astonishing economic progress Canada made during the Second World War was foreshadowed by the first four months of the conflict. Clearly war, or at least war without fighting and casualties, was profitable for the nation.

Another theme is equally evident. Canadians were remarkably Eurocentric in 1939. The events in Asia, as Greg Johnson's paper shows, took place in a vacuum insofar as the public was concerned. It can still startle us that there was almost war over Tientsin or that Britain feared a fight with Japan in August 1939. What would King and Canada have done if that had come to pass? Moreover, the Canadian Eurocentrism could blank out our nearest neighbour. Where is the United States in these accounts of 1939? If papers had been presented on 1945 or 1956 or 1995, the United States would have figured prominently, as so it should. But in 1939, Canada was still a British dominion with all that implied.

We must also remember that the government of Mackenzie King had at least one advantage that Sir Robert Borden had not had a quarter century before: the lessons of the Great War were burned into the national and governmental consciousness. That meant that the bureaucracy had some ideas how to organize to fight a war. It meant that there was an explicit promise against conscription, delivered by King to Québec in March 1939, and significantly Conservative leader Robert Manion had said the same. In 1939, the message on manpower was "never again."

Canadians had said "never again" about going to war too. The neutralists, isolationists and League supporters, as well as the vast majority of Québécois, through the 1930s had been desperate to keep Canada out of any European war. There was scarcely any enthusiasm for war to be found. Of course, after Hitler's invasion of Poland, substantial support for participation in the limited liability war favoured by the government, as many of the papers here demonstrate, was evident. In Newfoundland, Ontario, the West, and even in Québec, if Canada had to fight, so be it, but the less the better. Undoubtedly, it is fair to suggest that the 1940 general election, when examined in context with the Québec provincial election, was a fair assessment of the mood. French Canada supported the limited liability war offered to them by Adélard Godbout, prompted by Ernest Lapointe, Chubby Power and P.J.A. Cardin, rather than the isolation sought by

Maurice Duplessis. And the national campaign of February and March 1940 demonstrated that Mackenzie King, who had accomplished the almost impossible feat of bringing the country into the war without rioting and bloodshed, was more in tune with the national mood than the cocky provincial Napoleon who ruled the Ontario roost. Even after the Fall of France, Dunkirk, and a succession of additional British military disasters, it took a hard sell to make Canadians enthusiastic about a total war to support Britain.

All this suggests that opinion was more than a bit wobbly in 1939. The English Canadian elite accepted the justice of Britain's cause and was on side on the war, but there was the Co-operative Commonwealth Federation (CCF), the Communists, the ethnics, many Québécois and intellectuals and a host of university students who were cool or opposed to participation. Even many of the brightest and best federal bureaucrats, such as O.D. Skelton, Loring Christie, Lester Pearson and Escott Reid, were recent converts to belligerency or lukewarm at best. The media in English Canada and many of the papers in Québec were spouting the official war time line at full blast, but I am not certain that this demonstrated the full range of public opinion. How could the critics speak up in the face of the War Measures Act or when the full force of elite power could be directed against such benign comments as those that repeatedly put Professor Frank Underhill of the University of Toronto History Department in fear for his livelihood in the late 1930s and in 1940? To use a more recent example, it is as if the fact that all the parties in the House of Commons, eight of the nine legislatures of English Canada, and most of the media supported the Meech Lake Accord meant that it was popular; it wasn't. Neither was the war, despite the newspaper evidence to the contrary.

Nor was the decision for war in September 1939 an informed and independent one either, despite Terry Copp's vigorous argument to this end. Copp has become the country's leading military historian through applying his fresh and iconoclastic mind to misunderstood or ignored events. Here he takes on a harder subject. He does not help his argument with the space he gives H.S. Hamilton, the Liberal M.P. from Algoma West, who moved the Address in Reply to the Speech from the Throne in the special war session of Parliament in September. Hamilton's ringing words about democracy and liberty and about the war being truly Canada's read well, but they do not solidly support the line that Ontario and Canada made its own enthusiastic decision to go to war. Hamilton was a Great War veteran, a member of the very large group of Canadians who had fought against Germany before and who were almost by definition predisposed to support the idea of putting the former enemy to rights once more. Then, he was a backbench Liberal of no particular distinction singled out to make an important address at the very outset of a war. Was he to pronounce this second war a struggle for Britain? How would that sell with the doubters? There could have been no doubt in Hamilton's mind that this war (like the last in the minds of veterans) was going to be Canada's war.

At the Prime Minister's request, Hamilton showed his speech to J.W. Pickersgill in the Prime Minister's Office, and Pickersgill has told Terry Copp, who kindly gave me a copy of his letter, that he was "very sparing" in his revisions. Both the mover and seconder of the Address in Reply were veterans, and their attitudes, Pickersgill thought, should be heard. But he added that "Hamilton I felt was expressing a Tory attitude in Ontario which incidentally I did not share." "A Tory attitude in Ontario" — that is a revealing phrase, and one to which Copp gives no weight at all. He should. Ontario was in the war, to be sure, but enthusiastic support at the outset was limited to those Liberals and Conservatives who, by class and attitude, harked back to an older Canada, to an allegiance that was already starting to fade. The independence, the enthusiasm, the sense of national interest that Professor Copp discerns by reading the press and Hansard were simply not there. The divisions of opinion that had exacerbated the debate in the 1930s remained unhealed in Ontario, in Québec, and across the land.

Why did we go to war, then? Did we have to go to war just because Britain did, as Stephen Leacock asked? Legally, the answer was no (though some doubted that). Did we fight in our own national interests? I suspect that in 1939 the only fair answer was in the negative once more. Why then? Because, as Leacock put it so shrewdly, we had to. And why did we have to fight? The answer, I continue to believe, is all too clear: because Britain went to war. In September 1939 Canadians still felt a sense of obligation, however misplaced, to the Mother Country. It would take another generation before that feeling finally disappeared.

COMMENTAIRE

Serge Bernier
Ministère de la Défense nationale

En 1939, la population canadienne a-t-elle été plus marquée par les effets encore présents de la dépression qui se terminait ou par le début de la guerre? Il apparaît, de ce qui précède, que les préoccupations économiques étaient bien plus importantes que les subtilités diplomatiques qui, d'étape en étape, allaient mener à la guerre. Les textes sur Terre-Neuve [pas encore une partie du Canada, en 1939], les Maritimes, les Prairies et la Colombie-Britannique nous en disent beaucoup plus sur la misère dont on commençait à peine à sortir, en 1939, que sur les hostilités qui débutèrent à la fin de l'été.

Lorsque les Terre-Neuviens et les Canadiens marchent au combat, ils ont derrière eux la douloureuse expérience des années 1914-1918, d'où leur volonté résignée laissant peu de place à l'enthousiasme. D'ailleurs, avant la fin de 1939, les premières pertes canadiennes dans les zones de combat seront signalées. Mais, ce souvenir de la Première Guerre mondiale leur dit que la nouvelle situation permettra une relance de l'économie et que les territoires canadien et terre-neuvien risqueront peu de recevoir des coups directs. Ce que sera la réalité de la guerre pour chacun des Canadiens n'est pas encore bien définie: au moins a-t-on déjà certaines quasi-certitudes fortifiantes en sus des inévitables calamités prévisibles.

En 1939, on vit dans une reprise très lente qui est déjà vieille de plusieurs années. La protectionnisme a joué un rôle, aussi bien dans les performances commerciales et économiques mondiales, des années 1930, que dans le déclenchement de la guerre. En effet, pour pallier la crise, les pays ont eu tendance à fermer leurs frontières et l'autarcie que certains avaient voulu créer avait engendré des ressentiments aussi bien que des pressions psychologiques et économiques qui pouvaient trouver un aboutissement initial dans la feu et la sang : bien sûr, à moyen et long terme, la solution aux problèmes d'ordre économique ne pouvait se trouver dans la guerre. La population canadienne n'ignorait pas les rôles positifs et négatifs des tarifs douaniers, même si toutes les implications des seconds n'étaient peut-être pas entièrement comprises. Chose certaine, les hautes sphères du monde dit civilisé se préparaient à tirer les conséquences de cet aspect de la situation générale existant en 1939. Aussitôt que la guerre serait terminée, en faveur des 'bons', bien entendu, des solutions seraient imposées aux vaincus comme aux vainqueurs.

Si un petit nombre de mandarins (au Canada comme ailleurs dans les pays en guerre contre l'Allemagne nazie) se permettaient, dès 1939, de réfléchir à l'après guerre, on peut douter que les pensées des dizaines de milliers de fonctionnaires canadiens, cadres intermédiaires et exécutants, aient été fixées ailleurs que sur l'immédiat. Comme le montre Doug Owram, la dépression avait fait subir à la Fonction publique des coupures sévères qui avaient résulté en une stagnation et une insécurité qui ne sont pas loin de rappeler la situation qui est actuellement vécue par cette institution. La guerre allait relancer le fonctionnariat, le faire croître aussi bien en nombre que par les nouvelles responsabilités qui lui reviendraient, surtout à compter de 1940. Cela dit, l'expérience et la loyauté qui s'étaient développées au sein du service public, durant les années 1920 et 1930, seront prêtes à offrir leurs fruits dès septembre 1939.

À l'époque, ce qui se déroulait dans le monde était rapporté et commenté par les nombreux médias d'information presque aussi rapidement qu'aujourd'hui. En ce sens, les variables entourant le pacte germano-soviétique d'août 1939, telles que présentées par George Urbaniak, sont des plus intéressantes. Cette entente fut, à la fois, une révolution à l'Est et le dernier des nombreux éléments annonciateurs de ce qui allait suivre neuf jours plus tard.

L'article de Wesley K. Wark nous dit beaucoup sur les intérêts premiers de organisateurs du colloque. Voilà que le Canada entre dans une guerre *mondiale* en 1939. Or, on a choisi de nous présenter une communication au titre ambitieux ("Diplomatic Revolution in the West: 1939, The End of Appeasement and the Origins of the Second World War") mais au contenu très restreint se limitant, en fait, à la diplomatie allemande de la Grande-Bretagne. Or, même en cela, les déficiences restent nombreuses. Ainsi, Wark ne souligne pas assez le fait que les Britanniques ont agi durant des années comme s'ils ne comprenaient pas ce qui se déroulait sous leurs yeux. Même si l'on percevait très bien ce qui se préparait, on se refusait à réagir et ce, en raison d'intérêts à court terme. Tout cela allait mal tourner. L'auteur ne mentionne que brièvement les liens qui existent en 1939 entre la Grande-Bretagne et la France. À mon avis, le refus britannique d'endosser d'un peu plus près les vues politiques françaises concernant le centre de l'Europe est une des causes premières de la catastrophe. En se concentrant sur la diplomatie allemande de la Grande-Bretagne, et en écartant sa composante française, on ne fait pas entièrement justice aux possibilités avancées par quelques protagonistes du *Foreign Office* dont les idées ont été écartées pour le plus grand malheur de tous. La perception qu'adoptent les décideurs, après avoir consulté leurs conseillers, est d'une importance primordiale : on n'a pas assez parlé, dans ce colloque (qui ne pouvait naturellement tout couvrir) du rôle central que jouent les grands chefs. Les orientations qu'ils ont choisi d'appuyer en telle ou telle circonstance ont eu des incidences importantes sur le déroulement du scénario qui a conduit à l'hécatombe.

La présentation d'Angelika Sauer a le mérite de nous laisser voir jusqu'à quel point le commerce a joué un rôle non négligeable en ce qui concerne l'application du principe de l'apaisement par le Canada. Peut-on se surprendre qu'une époque qui laisse les principes moraux être ballottés au gré d'intérêts terre à terre à court terme finisse par aboutir à l'affrontement dont septembre 1939 ne marque que le début? Une fois le conflit enclenché, de nobles idéaux qui avaient déjà été très amochés avant la guerre ne purent que descendre encore plus bas dans notre ordre des priorités. Il n'y a aucun doute que les Canadiens en général ont envisagé cette conséquence dès 1939 et que les Québécois, en particulier, savaient ce que les hostilités signifieraient pour eux. La guerre n'avait pas encore commencé qu'on parlait déjà de conscription. De fait, le discours anti-conscriptioniste des libéraux, dans l'entre-deux-guerres, avait vécu quelques modulations à l'approche de l'échéance. Les pressions psychologiques et politiques allaient peser sur le petit peuple du Québec qui, même avant 1939, n'était pas ignorant du fait que la guerre approchait. De quelle façon l'affecterait-elle restait une question ouverte?

Au nord-est de Québec se trouvait Terre-neuve, un 'pays-colonie' qui, en 1939, entra en guerre aussi automatiquement que le Canada l'avait fait en 1914. Vingt-cinq ans après 1914, le Canada avait 'énormément' fait progresser son statut par rapport au terre-neuvien : il mit quelques jours à rendre officielle une décision dont les militaires n'avaient jamais douté, eux qui avaient commencé à lancer leurs préavis de mobilisation plusieurs semaines avant le grand saut. Le signe avant-coureur que la démocratie canadienne allait devenir autoritaire en temps de guerre, comme cela ne manque pas d'arriver dans ce genre de situation, était donc donné. Les idéaux des années 1920 étaient en berne depuis longtemps, au Canada comme ailleurs. Restait à savoir, en 1939, si notre pays allait se chercher un rôle de première importance sur la scène internationale, par le revers de l'événement majeur qu'il vivait déjà depuis quatre longs mois au moment où l'année 1940 naissait. Combien de Canadiens, au fond d'eux mêmes, enviaient leurs voisins américains restés pacifiques tout en mettant en marche une industrie de guerre pro-alliée prospère?

Mackenzie King pouvait bien dire que le Canada entrait en guerre pour toutes sortes de raisons (démocratie, justice, liberté, etc.) autres que le seul appel du sang qui avait encore une immense résonance sur une grande partie de la population anglophone du pays. Peu importe ses efforts, la participation au conflit allait rouvrir une grade blessure nationale. Que Mackenzie King ait décidé d'impliquer le Canada dès l'ouverture de la Deuxième Guerre mondiale, nous fait conclure qu'en 1939, le Premier ministre ne contrôlait pas la destinée du pays. Ou serait-ce qu'il ne voulait pas la contrôler? Toujours est-il que sa guerre 'personnelle' se limitera à sauver les meubles, situation qu'il avait envisagée bien avant 1939.